SIMON BLAXLAND-DE LANGE has for many years worked as an educator for people with special needs as well as a writer and translator. A keen amateur musician and gardener, he is a co-founder of Pericles Translations and Research, Pericles Training and Work for adults with special needs and the Pericles Theatre Company. Together with Dr Vivien Law, he co-founded the Humanities Research Group and the British group of the Humanities Section of the School of Spiritual Science, and has been a member of the Council of the Anthroposophical Society in Great Britain since 2013. He participated in the Foundation Year course at Emerson College beginning in the autumn of 1972, which was the last year of Cecil Harwood's teaching activity at the College. He is the author of *Owen Barfield, Romanticism Comes of Age, A Biography* (Temple Lodge Publishing, 2006)

A. C. Harwood

SUN KING'S COUNSELLOR
CECIL HARWOOD

A Documentary Biography

Simon Blaxland-de Lange

TEMPLE LODGE

Temple Lodge Publishing Ltd.
Hillside House, The Square
Forest Row, RH18 5ES

www.templelodge.com

Published by Temple Lodge Publishing 2021

A CIP catalogue record for this book is available from the British Library

ISBN 978 1 912230 71 6

Cover by Morgan Creative featuring image of Cecil Harwood in Switzerland by Christine Hebert
Typeset by Symbiosys Technologies, Visakhapatnam, India
Printed and bound by 4Edge Ltd., Essex

White waves of Arthur's castle wall
And Sun-gold in the spray,
And knights like stars in Arthur's Hall
And he like Sun of Day
   (refrain from Cecil Harwood's poem 'A Song of King Arthur')

There may be times when what is most needed is, not so much a new discovery or a new idea as a different 'slant'; I mean a comparatively slight adjustment in our *way* of looking at the things and ideas on which attention is already fixed.

   (Owen Barfield, the first words of the Introduction to his book
Saving the Appearances)

Contents

Introduction   1

PART ONE   5

1. Ralph Vaughan Williams, Rudolf Steiner, and a
   Meeting in Cornwall   7
2. Family Backgrounds: Lord Olivier and Minister Harwood   18
3. Personal and Professional Engagement   22
4. Marriage and the Founding Years of Michael Hall   33
5. Early Writings   52
6. Waldorf Translator, Editor, Playwright and Author   66
7. Prelude to Chairmanship of the Anthroposophical
   Society in Great Britain   79

PART TWO   97

1. The Minehead Years   99
2. The Anthroposophical Society in Great Britain in a Time of War   155
3. Family Man, Advocate and Adviser   175

PART THREE   185

1. The Destiny of Britain within Europe and the
   Wider World and the Individual Human Spirit   187
2. The Anthroposophical Society and the Healing of Divisions   221
3. Anthroposophia, New Friendships and the Role of Eurythmy   245

Conclusion   271
Notes   272
Index   284

Introduction

Eric Hobsbawm entitled his magisterial account of what he referred to as 'the Short Twentieth Century, 1914–1991' *The Age of Extremes*[1]; and the picture that he paints of at any rate a substantial part of that time is one of destructiveness and savagery on a scale which has no parallel in the history of humanity. His book, like countless other histories of the twentieth century, is a record of what actually happened and why events took the course that they did. But whereas there can be no questioning of the accuracy and appropriateness of such a historical analysis (although of course interpretations will and should differ), it can also be possible to consider strands of that historical tapestry—including particular figures and what they thought and did—which have not hitherto appeared at the visible surface of historical scrutiny, even though they were no less present than those that form the basis of accounts such as that of Hobsbawm. Human life, as is also the case with the natural world, engenders countless seeds and germinal possibilities, some of which may remain hidden or dormant for a while until such time as those rampant growths (or, in human terms, those ideas, assumptions and attitudes) that have for a time dominated the landscape wither and die off, thus revealing and giving space to what had previously been stifled and hidden.

It is abundantly clear from the later chapters of Hobsbawm's book—and also from the writings of any reasonably perceptive modern historian, journalist or novelist—that things cannot simply continue along the tram-lines laid down at the height of the age of materialism in the nineteenth century and inherited by the twentieth century and into our own time. There is, arguably, nowhere in the world where this is more patently obvious than that land which the founder of anthroposophy, Rudolf Steiner, associated in a very particular way with the development of the consciousness or 'spiritual' soul,[2] namely Britain (I deliberately use this name rather than 'England' firstly because this is how I experience the situation and secondly because I believe that this is what Steiner meant—many people in his time used these names interchangeably); and recent political events such as the referendum of 2016 and its sequel have merely heightened the need for some new thinking. The conventional, prevailing view is that the inherited ideas, assumptions and attitudes about human existence should not be questioned and that the future is in the hands of science (whatever that may be) and technology and—some would say—ultimately has little place for the continuing existence of humanity. But this is where the study of the

Humanities, which of course includes the study of history and philosophy, has so crucial a part to play, in that the notion of a further evolution of humanity can then be explored as an alternative possibility. In this respect I need additionally to refer in this introductory section to the work of Cecil Harwood's close friend Owen Barfield, who highlighted the importance of grasping not merely the idea but also the reality of the evolution of human consciousness. Moreover—and this is to be understood in the context of what has been said earlier about the tragic wars that brutalized the twentieth century—he gave a remarkable lecture about the respective cultural gifts and impulses of Britain and Germany and the German-speaking world of Central Europe, or the English-speaking and German-speaking cultural worlds, at a World Conference on Spiritual Science held in 1928 in London, graphically summarizing his insights at the end of the printed version of the lecture[3] in a highly imaginative passage describing a dance in which 'two divinely tall spiritual forms' are engaged, one representing the Spirit of the German nation and the other the British Folk Spirit (or, in a certain sense, respectively Faust and Hamlet). Barfield's essential point here is that these two cultures urgently need to collaborate with one another at the deepest possible level (for reasons that Barfield gives in the essays based on his lecture).[4]

These are the thoughts out of which the present book has its origin. Is it possible to find in the history of the twentieth century a representative figure who, in his thoughts but most especially in his deeds, embodied inspirational qualities which can speak now to those willing to embrace and develop—in Owen Barfield's words—a new 'way of looking at the things and ideas on which attention is already fixed'? No doubt one could identify many such figures and also events with which they were associated; and another person would doubtless seek to explore different occluded paths of social and cultural memory. However, with all that I have already said in mind, I have chosen to go back in historical memory to an event that took place—far from the centres of academic life and political sovereignty—in Cornwall in 1922 and to one representative figure in particular. This was a time when the folk song and dance revival that could be said to have been prompted in 1903 when Cecil Sharp heard the—appropriately named—gardener John England singing 'The Seeds of Love' in the vicarage garden of Hambridge, Somerset[5] was still a potent force, and therefore when the work of the Folk Spirit whose activity impregnates this land and the language and culture of the people who dwell here was still very much in evidence.[6] This could put us in touch in a more conscious way with those powerfully creative forces that even today, when it has become unfashionable to think about such things except as a means of fuelling narrowly reactive behaviour, are *also in our own time* working invisibly in the background of human affairs. The event in question was one of a series of similar gatherings organized in conjunction with the English Folk Dance Society to which Owen Barfield referred in his reminiscences[7]; and it was hosted by Maisie and Evelyn Radford at St. Anthony in Roseland, near Portscatho in Cornwall. The representative figure whom I have chosen as the principal subject of this book is Alfred Cecil Harwood (it was, according to his son Laurence, apparently his own choice to use his second name of 'Cecil' rather than 'Alfred', with its meaning of 'elfin' or 'wise counsellor' and its deep associations with early English history), who, together with Owen Barfield, encountered Daphne Olivier (as she was then) and, through her, became acquainted for the first time with the work of Rudolf Steiner. The purpose of what follows is to become more conscious—with the benefit of hindsight—of the human connections, cultural movements and spiritual beings that were contributing to what came together in September 1922 in Cornwall and then led to Cecil Harwood's life's work in pioneering and developing the New School in Streatham (now Michael Hall Steiner-Waldorf School in Sussex) and the Anthroposophical Society in Great Britain.

Lastly by way of introduction, I should like to add a few words about the book's structure. After some thought, I have decided to retain a conventionally chronological approach to this biography of Cecil Harwood. However, interwoven within it is a kind of inner structure, whereby four aspects of his life can be discerned: the 'Nativity' of his early years and his and Daphne's antecedents; the 'Baptism' of his meeting with anthroposophy and Rudolf Steiner and his bold plunge into teaching and administration; the 'Three Years'—as it were—of his dedicated work with the Anthroposophical Society under the banner of words from his 'Song of King Arthur', 'or sorest quarrel healed'; and the 'Resurrection' or harvest in the form of his many lectures and writings, which combined his deep study of anthroposophy with a profound awareness of the relevance of Steiner's ideas to the contemporary context. Running through the whole of his life as a kind of life-theme was a commitment to truth, to the spiritual quality in the individual and in the cosmos, to being in service to a renewed Christianity as represented by the grandiose figure of Michael.

I am indebted to Henry Howlett, a current teacher at Michael Hall, for these and other suggestions which I have gladly incorporated into this biographical study. It is also due to him and to Christine Hebert, who made a number of Harwood's letters available to me and spoke out of her many years' friendship and association with him, that I have sought to emphasize the truly Michaelic (or Christianized Arthurian) quality that lived in him. Nothing, however, would have been even remotely possible without the utter devotion and whole-hearted support of Harwood's son Laurence, through whom I have also benefitted from the support and good will of his sister Lois Olivier and her daughter Fiona Athanassaki. Most of the letters from which I have quoted—in particular those from Daphne Olivier and Marguerite Lundgren—come from his lovingly garnered archive. I have also greatly appreciated the help and efficiency of Ian Botting, the Librarian at Rudolf Steiner House. And I gratefully acknowledge the many supportive conversations locally in Forest Row with Stephen and Libby Sheen, who have helped to keep this project alive over the many years of its making. Laurence Harwood, Fiona Athanassaki and Stephen Sheen have also generously contributed the photographs included with this book, although two of the photographs have been kindly made available by Owen A. Barfield, trustee of the Owen Barfield Literary Estate. I also extend my gratitude to those members of the community in and around Michael Hall who, in addition to Henry Howlett and Stephen and Libby Sheen, have supported this book's publication: William Forward, Mark Fielding, Christine and Oliver Fynes-Clinton, Maria Finnemore, Daniele Gaillemin, St Clair Leveaux, Beth Honeyman, Vanessa King, Mara Lane, Ingrid Lidberg and Nino Radojcin; and also to Bob Wills for his generous gift. Finally, my thanks are due to my wife, Paulamaria, for her supportive and enthusiastic companionship throughout this lengthy period of the book's gestation and for her meticulous attention to verbal detail and semantic coherence over certain passages which I have shared with her.

Simon Blaxland-de Lange
August 2020

PART ONE

1. Ralph Vaughan Williams, Rudolf Steiner, and a Meeting in Cornwall

It was, I believe, not fortuitous that Owen Barfield and Cecil Harwood should have encountered anthroposophy not in the academic citadel of Oxford University but at a Cornish festival of English folk song and dance. I shall therefore begin with a summary of certain relevant aspects of the English folk song and dance revival (especially its Cornish manifestation carried by the Radford sisters) together with a consideration of some composers whose work was associated with it (and specifically Ralph Vaughan Williams, who was well-known to the Olivier family, gave Daphne singing lessons and included her as a violin player in his Dorking concerts).

As already indicated (see note 5), the English Folk Dance Society had been founded by Cecil Sharp in 1911; and by 1923 this Society had branches in 36 provincial English towns, one in Edinburgh and two in America.[8] Among these branches was a Cornwall Folk Dance Society, which organized its first annual folk dancing festival in 1920 (the year that Owen Barfield made his first visit to the county in a folk dancing capacity[9]) at Penzance, when on Saturday 28 June three thousand people gathered to watch hundreds of dancers (with as many as 650 performing at any one time) grouped into 42 teams (although the emphasis in Cornwall was always on enjoyment rather than competition) dancing to an orchestra of a dozen violins, clarinet, drums and two pianos.[10] The festival of 1921, the report of which especially singled out the 'tremendous impetus' of Lady Mary Trefusis, took place in June at St. Austell, where an even larger number of dancers gathered: 'The spectacle of a thousand dancers performing together in those quaint, simple but extremely graceful old English dances, to the strains of exquisite music played by an orchestra which formed the hub around which the company danced, with the hundreds of spectators watching the scene and forming the rim of this huge wheel, was one that was very pleasing to those who can appreciate art in action.'[11] By 1922— and the pattern was repeated in 1923—there were at least two folk dance festivals in Cornwall during June (or sometimes May), on a comparable scale to those in 1920 and 1921. Something of the magnitude of these events is captured in a photograph that appeared in the *Western Morning News* dated 29 June 1920, where an extensive plot of land the size of a playing field (and they generally were playing fields of one kind or another) is covered by dancers in white dresses. And then it must be remembered that something of a similar kind was happening all over the country, although not necessarily on the same level.

Now that this background context has been briefly delineated, there are two figures whose representative gifts and impulses on behalf of, respectively, the British and Central European cultural realms need to be briefly characterized before the individuals who first encountered one another at St. Anthony in Roseland in September 1922 can be brought to the centre of the stage. The first of these to be considered is the composer Ralph Vaughan Williams (1872–1958).

The point here is not to present a biography of Vaughan Williams or to offer an analysis of his compositions but simply to describe three especially pertinent themes in his life and work, themes which are in each case also fully manifested in Cecil Harwood's life and being.[12]

The first of these themes is his love of English folk songs and, more broadly, his dedication to the Folk Soul of Britain, in all its various aspects. As chronicled in detail in an article by Tony Kendall entitled 'Through Bushes and Briars: Vaughan Williams's earliest folk-song collecting'[13], Vaughan Williams was familiar with John Broadwood's *Sussex Songs* (1889) and with Lucy Broadwood and J.A. Fuller Maitland's *English County Songs*, originally published in 1893; and his musical enthusiasm was stirred especially by the melody in this latter volume to the song 'Dives and Lazarus', on the basis of which he composed his orchestral work *Five Variants of Dives and Lazarus*, a piece which, as Kendall describes, 'permeated his whole life and was performed at his funeral service in Westminster Abbey in 1958'. In Kendall's account, the story began with an invitation to lecture on the subject of 'The Characteristics of National Songs' in Brentwood, Essex in the early spring of 1903. In the December of that year he returned to the area and accepted an invitation to tea from the vicar of Ingrave, which is a few miles to the south-east of Brentwood; and it was probably on the following day, 4 December, that he collected the first of his collection of around 140 songs from this area of Essex, 'Bushes and Briars', from a land-worker called Charles Potiphar. He went on to collect over 800 songs between 1903 and 1913, many of them from the area around his childhood home on the slopes of Leith Hill, Surrey.

Vaughan Williams was, however, a 'double man'—this odd but very helpful epithet was coined by Wilfrid Mellers in his book *Vaughan Williams and the Vision of Albion*[14] to refer to Vaughan Williams's capacity to encompass potential opposites or dichotomies in his being. Thus although he was fundamentally English both in his origins and upbringing and in his interest in folk songs, there was a distinct Welsh component in his ancestry (his paternal great-grandfather, John Williams, was born at Job's Well, Carmarthen, in 1757); and this Celtic strain may have contributed to his breadth of vision, his 'awareness of the numinous' (Mellers) and his devotion to the totality of the islands which had together given rise to the British Empire. Thus Rob Young could say, for example, that he was 'a patriot to the extent that he loved the land and poetry of Britain'.[15] Similarly, he has been described as a Christian agnostic or even—in Sir Steuart Wilson's phrase—a 'disillusioned theist'; and just as he was a rural countryman by birth and a Londoner by adoption he also combined the scientific and industrial expertise of his Darwinian and Wedgwoodian maternal ancestry with a refined artistic sensibility.

This first theme was musically distilled in a quite particular way in his *Fantasia on a Theme of Thomas Tallis*, which, when first performed at the Three Choirs Festival in Gloucester Cathedral on 6 September 1910, brought his music into the public domain; and it can of course be discerned in a large number of especially the works composed in the first half of his life. But it is in the slow movement of his second (London) symphony where this theme in Vaughan Williams's life and musical sensibility becomes a quality of mystical insight, through which a deep suffering is transformed into joyful affirmation. The London symphony was written during the years immediately preceding the First World War and was, indeed, prompted into being by George Butterworth in 1911, when he said 'in his characteristically abrupt way: "You know, you ought to write a symphony"'[16], and was given its first performance in London on 27 March 1914. Wilfrid Mellers puts his finger on the spiritual essence of this symphony when he writes: 'The juxtaposition of London and Nature is the point, a harbinger of what is to be the central theme of Vaughan Williams's life's work.' And then immediately afterwards he asks: 'Is London the biblical City of Destruction or the New Jerusalem or both?'[17] There is in this symphony something that spiritually goes far beyond the brash, confident imperialism and anti-cultural materialism which bore a major responsibility for the First World War (and, as already indicated, continues to exert a dominant influence on modern life), although these qualities are also reflected in Vaughan Williams's symphony; and at the beginning of the slow movement (where, as Mellers indicates, we feel a relationship with the mood of *The Lark Ascending*, likewise written just prior to the 1914–1918 war) the listener is gently ushered by the beautiful cor anglais melody into a mood of quiet reflectiveness newly emerging from the bustle of the city, out of which mood an inner exultant joy—the source of which is that same celestial region to which the lark aspires—suddenly fills this tranquil space and opens up boundless new possibilities for an inner, spiritual transformation.

At the climax of this passage the mood of the music evokes an echo of the *Fantasia on a Theme of Thomas Tallis*, now interwoven with the reflections emanating from the tranquil heart of the great city; and so it is as though the spiritual impulses which brought about the great cultural awakening that this land experienced in the sixteenth century are again available to serve a new task inspired not by Mars the bringer of war but by the winged messenger of the Gods, Mercury, the bearer of healing forces for the future. That this is no chimera of the musical imagination is confirmed by Vaughan Williams's third—or 'Pastoral'—symphony, which was conceived in 1916 in the Flanders battlefields (where the peace-loving composer was serving in the Field Ambulance Corps, having volunteered for military service despite being too old for conscription), where horror and intense suffering are transformed into an angelic innocence and a potential for new birth epitomized by the pentatonic tones of the wordless soprano solo with which the symphony ends.[18]

The second theme arises out of a particular aspect of Vaughan Williams's 'double nature'; for although he belonged to the upper middle class and, hence, to the more privileged echelons of society, he had strong egalitarian leanings and, according to Rob Young, 'was a socialist in all but name to the end of his life'.[19] In his book *Electric Eden*, Young firmly includes Vaughan Williams among those who took part in the gatherings of illustrious artists and radical thinkers at Kelmscott House, Hammersmith, in the last year or so of William Morris's life (Morris died in 1896), even though he was, it would appear, less fully involved than his intimate friend and fellow composer Gustav Holst (who was two years younger than Vaughan Williams).[20] Similarly, he was the total opposite of an aloof aesthete and firmly believed that every effort should be made to include everyone in music-making and to fully engage with the life of one's locality.[21] The Leith Hill Musical Festival, which was inaugurated in Dorking in 1905 as a means of encouraging amateur choirs and choral societies and continues to this day, is a prime example of Vaughan Williams's dedication to these ideals.[22]

Similarly, the great energies that he expended on editing *The English Hymnal* were prompted by motives of this nature rather than by devotion to the Anglican Church. He was also joint music editor—with Martin Shaw—of *The Oxford Book of Carols*, first published in 1928. (Martin Shaw also collaborated with Vaughan Williams in editing the music for *Songs of Praise*, published in 1925.)

If there is one of Vaughan Williams's works that illustrates this theme in his life it is probably his early ballad opera *Hugh the Drover* (1910–1914); for not only is it expressed through his original conception of the work but also in the way that he responded to the differing notions of his librettist,

Harold Child. (See his letters to Child reproduced in Appendix 1 of Ursula Vaughan Williams's biography.) Wilfrid Mellers concludes his chapter on *Hugh the Drover* with a characteristic insight: 'In the years of the First World War, Vaughan Williams's Drover was a John the Baptist to Bob Dylan's magical Tambourine Man in the crucial late 'sixties: the drugs Hugh pedalled being the wind, the stars, and the open road. Such dreams were needful; and they still are.'[23]

The third theme under consideration here is that of the Quest: the search for something beyond the familiar world, for the numinous, the world of spirit, but in a way that is not abstracted from life but involves a journey that engages the whole of one's humanity. Vaughan Williams's favourite image in this connection was that of the Pilgrim who, like John Bunyan's Christian, sets out on his inner journey of the soul towards the celestial city. Indeed, Bunyan's *The Pilgrim's Progress* was for Vaughan Williams 'literally the labour of a life-time' (Mellers), culminating in the completion in 1951 of his opera based on Bunyan's allegory. Moreover, during the 30 or so years when he was preoccupied at one time or other with *The Pilgrim's Progress*, the music associated with it found its way into other works, for example his radiant and deeply contemplative fifth symphony (first performed amidst war-time turbulence in 1943). In Wilfrid Mellers's view, 'its religious, social and political implications colour most of the works of Vaughan Williams's maturity, whether they carry a literary text or function by way of symphonic argument' (op. cit., p. 205). Other compositions which can be directly associated with this theme of the inner quest of the soul include his early settings of Walt Whitman's poetry, 'Toward the Unknown Region' (1906) and 'A Sea Symphony' (1909), and his setting of texts from the Book of Revelation, *Sancta Civitas* (1925). It is very difficult to assess the specific nature of Vaughan Williams's religious or philosophical views or, say, his attitude to death (as it happened, his own death—in his sleep from a coronary thrombosis—was largely unheralded by illness and, hence, by a period of gradual preparation). However, there is the inescapable fact that, quite without any outward prompting and at a time when these works were to a far lesser extent the standard fare of choral societies, he championed annual performances in Dorking Halls of Bach's *St. Matthew Passion* from 1931 onwards and also latterly his *St. John Passion*, which came to be regularly performed in St. Martin's Church, Dorking.

To conclude this section on Ralph Vaughan Williams we now need to form a picture of his compositional activity and the public awareness of it in the summer and early autumn of 1922. His much-loved romance for violin and orchestra *The Lark Ascending* (composed in 1914 and revised in 1920), had been first performed at Shirehampton, Gloucestershire, on

15 December 1920, while its first London performance was on 14 June 1921. His Pastoral symphony had—as already noted—had its first performance in London on 26 January 1922, while the first performance of the pastoral episode 'The Shepherds of the Delectable Mountains'—the first portion of his *Pilgrim's Progress* music to be written—was at the Royal College of Music in July 1922. The celebrated *Mass in G Minor*, composed in 1920–1921, was first performed in Birmingham on 6 December 1922. The *English Folk Songs* suite for military band had its first performance in Twickenham on 4 July 1923, while *Hugh the Drover* was first performed in London in July 1924. Both *Sancta Civitas* and his deeply passionate suite for solo viola, wordless mixed chorus and small orchestra *Flos Campi* were composed between 1923 and 1925, the latter first performed in London on 10 October 1925 and the former in Oxford on 7 May 1926.[24] This was therefore a particularly fecund period in the composer's life when, moreover, all three of the themes identified were prominently featured.

The figure representing Central Europe in the context of Daphne Olivier's first encounter with her future husband, Cecil Harwood, and his friend, Owen Barfield in Cornwall in 1922 is Rudolf Steiner. Daphne, who had been invited to join the concert party in Cornwall by the Radford sisters—who were friends from Cambridge University—because of their need for someone with her skills on the violin, had in the previous month been attending the conference where Steiner spoke on 'Spiritual Values in Education and Social Life' at Manchester College, Oxford (15–29 August 1922), of which she had heard when staying with her parents at Ramsden Hall near Witney. She had evidently been deeply impressed by the cultural and social impulse that Rudolf Steiner had brought to this holiday conference, which had been organized by Dr. Millicent Mackenzie, Professor of Education at Cardiff, and had been attended by around two hundred people, including a number of individuals prominent in the fields of education and social and political life. This was a period during which, after two distinct seven-year periods devoted to developing and communicating his research into spiritual science, or anthroposophy, through his books and numerous lectures, both to members of the Anthroposophical Society and—as was the case in Oxford—to the wider public, Rudolf Steiner had been focussing on transforming his ideas into instruments of dynamic practical change within the wider world, including—by the time of his death in 1925—the fields of agriculture, medicine and psychiatry, curative education, economics, architecture together with the visual and performing arts in addition to education and social life in general. He also gave detailed indications during this time to a group of priests seeking a renewal of the Christian services and liturgy. An important gateway to this period of practical implementation had been a book where he had for the first time delineated the way in which the threefold nature of man's inner, soul-disposition of thinking, feeling and will manifests itself in the physical nature of the bodily organism in the form of head (nerves and senses), the heart and lungs, and the limbs.[25] Closely associated with this were his immense endeavours to influence the way in which the negotiations were being conducted at the end of the First World War towards formulating a viable foundation for a future for a Europe that had been torn apart by years of conflict, the basis of which endeavours was the ready connection that could be made with the three respective realms of the social organism. Following the failure of these efforts to gain a proper hearing, he had from 1919 onwards been focussing more upon the realm of education, the transformation of which he had come to view as an essential prerequisite if any fruitful change was to come about in the socio-political realm.

However, the conference at Oxford that Daphne Olivier attended, which represented the introduction of Waldorf—or Rudolf Steiner—education to Britain[26] and, in George Adams's words, led to 'the beginnings of the Rudolf Steiner school movement in this country, some of whose ablest representatives found their way to us during the preparations or as an outcome of the Conference'[27] was—as its title suggests—an ardent endeavour on the part of all concerned (thus not only Rudolf Steiner but the organizers, the hosts at Manchester College and the numerous educationalists and other dignitaries who attended) to imbue not only education but the social and political life of Britain as a whole with a renewing spiritual impulse.

The original intention had been that Rudolf Steiner would give six lectures on education and six on social life and 'other questions of the day'. What actually happened was that the weight of his contribution lay more on the side of education, in that he gave nine seminal lectures outlining the full scope of Waldorf education (*The Spiritual Ground of Education*, Anthroposophic Press 2004) and three more aphoristic and directly accessible—but deeply thought-provoking—lectures on the past, present and potential future of human social life (see *Rudolf Steiner Speaks to the British*, Rudolf Steiner Press 1988); and when he spoke on 28 August 1922 in connection with the founding of 'An Association for Further Work along the Lines of these Lectures', what he said pertained mainly to education.

The Conference was, moreover, fully and generally enthusiastically reported by the local and national Press. The following extracts from an article entitled 'The Soul and the Teacher' published by *The Nation* give something of a flavour—albeit expressed in somewhat provocative terms—of the profound interest that Rudolf Steiner's lectures must have stimulated in a context of profound social and cultural malaise:

> Education was once a plank in reconstruction; teachers were to be better paid, for discontented teachers were a public danger. Besides, they held the future in their hands; they were the pillars of society. Today economy is all the rage; appointments are not being made, and classes grow larger and larger. Yet many teachers are also artists, until discontent and overcrowding prove fatal to inspiration and technique. Experience, too, is at a discount. The young are cheaper, and so (since salaries are graded by age) the higher posts go to the less experienced, and a few more pounds are saved... Yet teachers still go on, weary and not a little disillusioned, in some deep corner of themselves cherishing a battered ideal, dreaming at times of an experimental school where they may become artists again. And when they can they crowd to hear of such a place, as now they crowd to Oxford to hear what Dr. Steiner thinks of spiritual values in education and social life... Whoever heard of applicants for a teaching post being asked first of all of their opinion of the soul? Yet this is just the question Dr. Steiner seems to put to his hearers. An uninterested visitor may well mistake details of his meaning, and convey a wrong impression; yet even at the risk of misapprehension or doubt, its value to education should not be passed over in silence... You may not believe in reincarnation. You may dispute the existence of the spiritual body, scoff at the connection between metabolism and the will, or mistake the new art of 'visible speech', eurythmy, for dancing. You may, of course, deny the immortal element in man; in that case you will care for none of these things. But if you admit it, you must face the consequences as Dr. Steiner faces them, honestly. Call him dreamer, occultist, clairvoyant, even crank, but do not doubt his consistency and ability. You know how worried you have been lately about the state of Europe. If you cannot go to Oxford or to Dornach in Switzerland, you might perhaps call at the Board of Education or any other government office, and ask what provision they are making for the souls of the people.[28]

Among these young potential teachers whose quest for a radically different and more spiritual educational impulse had led them to attend these lectures was Daphne Olivier. George Adams continues his reflections on the Conference by singling out this particular participant:

> I think especially of Daphne Olivier (later Harwood), who died in 1950. She came from the tradition of the Fabian Society, whose founders included her father, a leading colonial official, as well as Bernard Shaw. With her sensitive

artistic nature, her candid enthusiasm and singleness of heart and mind she became Rudolf Steiner's devoted pupil. Several very talented young men, who in subsequent work have understood how genuine Oxonian tradition may be united with anthroposophical spirituality, and have since become the bearers of the Anthroposophical Movement in this country [as the editor notes, this refers especially to Cecil Harwood and Owen Barfield], became acquainted with it in the first place through her.[29]

As will be described in greater detail in Chapter 3, Daphne Olivier also participated in the further lecture courses that Rudolf Steiner gave in Britain in August 1923, the education course in Ilkley (5–17 August) and the International Summer School in Penmaenmawr (19–31 August). Steiner's last visit to Britain was in August 1924, when, in addition to giving lectures in Torquay on both education and general anthroposophy together with lectures to members of the Society in London, he was able to visit Tintagel, a visit that inspired the following passage from a lecture that he gave in London on 27 August 1924. This is a passage which, it seems to me, offers a wholly appropriate backcloth to the life of the person whose life and achievements will be chronicled in the pages that follow.

> Today I can speak of this earlier form of Christianity [Steiner had introduced the lecture by referring to a form of Christianity that existed before the Mystery of Golgotha, citing words from St. Augustine to the effect that 'Christianity did not begin with Christ; there were Christians before Christ, only they were not so called'] by starting from impressions which came in a place not far distant from Torquay (where our Summer Course has been held), in Tintagel, whence proceeded the spiritual stream connected with King Arthur. It was possible to receive the impressions which can still come today at the spot where King Arthur's castle with its Round Table stood—impressions which come above all from the magnificent natural surroundings of this castle.
>
> At this place where nothing but ruins remain of the old citadel of King Arthur, where we look back as if in memory across the centuries that have elapsed since the Arthur stream went out from thence, we realise how stone after stone has so crumbled away that there is hardly anything to be recognised of the old castles which once were inhabited by King Arthur and those around him. But when with the eye of spirit we look out from the place where the castle once stood, over the sea with its iridescent colours and breaking waves, the impression we get is that we are able at this place to penetrate deeply into the elemental secrets of nature and of the cosmos. And if we look back with occult sight, if we can visualise the point of time which lies a few thousand years ago, when the Arthur stream had its beginning, then

we see that those who lived on Arthur's Mount had, as is the case with all such occult centres, chosen this spot because the impulses necessary for the tasks they had set themselves, for their mission in the world, needed the play of those forces which nature there displayed before them.

I cannot say whether it is always so, but when I saw the view there was a most wonderful play of waves surging and rippling up from the depths—in itself one of the most beautiful sights in all nature. These waves hurl themselves against the walls of rock and as they fall back again in seething foam the elemental spirits are able to rise up from below and come to living expression. From above, the sunlight is reflected in manifold forms in the waves of the air. This interplay of elemental nature from above and from below reveals the full power of the Sun and displays it in such a way that man is able to receive it into his being. Those who can imbibe what is given by this interplay of the beings born of the light above and the beings born in the depths below, receive the power of the Sun, the impulse of the Sun...

Those who lived around King Arthur absorbed this play of weaving, working nature into their very being. And most significant of all was what they were able to receive in the first centuries after the Mystery of Golgotha... Before the Mystery of Golgotha had come to pass, the knights of King Arthur's Round Table stood on these rocks, gazed at the play between the Sun-born spirits and the Earth-born spirits, and felt that the forces living in this play of nature spirits poured into their hearts and above all through their etheric bodies. Therewith they received into themselves the Christ impulse which was then streaming away from the Sun and was living in everything that is brought into being by the Sun forces. And so, before the Mystery of Golgotha, the knights of King Arthur received into themselves the Sun Spirit, that is to say, the Christ as He was in pre-Christian times. And they sent their messengers out into all Europe to subdue the wild savagery of the astral bodies of the peoples of Europe, to purify and to civilise, for such was their mission. We see such men as these knights of King Arthur's Round Table starting from this point in the West of England to bear to the peoples of Europe as they were at that time what they had received from the Sun, purifying the astral forces of the then barbarous European population—barbarous at all events in Central and Northern Europe...

If in the first centuries of our era people looked out over the sea, and had been prepared by the exercises practised by the twelve who were around King Arthur and who were concerned above all with the mysteries of the zodiac, if they looked out over the sea they could see not merely the play of nature but they could begin to read a meaning in it—just as one reads a book instead of merely staring at it. And as they looked and saw, here a gleam, there a curling wave, here the Sun mirrored on a rocky cliff, there the sea dashing against the rocks, it all became a flowing, weaving picture—a truth whose meaning could be deciphered. And when they deciphered it they knew of the spiritual fact of the Mystery of Golgotha. The Mystery of Golgotha was revealed to them because the picture was all irradiated by the Life-spirit of Christ [Steiner explains in a portion of the lecture which has been omitted here what he means by this] presented to them by nature...

And so on the one hand we have the story of the Mystery of Golgotha, legible in the book of nature for those who were able to read it, working from West to East. It represented, as it were, the science of the higher graduates of King Arthur's Round Table. And on the other hand we have a stream flowing from East to West, not in wind and wave, not over hills or in the rays of the Sun, but flowing through the blood, laying hold of human hearts on its course from Palestine through Greece into Italy and Spain... Two streams come to meet one another—the pre-Christian Christ stream, etherealised as it were, and the Christian Christ stream. The one is known, subsequently, as the Arthur stream; the other as the Grail stream. Later on they came together; they came together in Europe, above all in the spiritual world...

When we consider this significant Arthur stream from West to East, it appears to us as the stream which brings the impulse of the Sun into earthly civilisation. In this Arthur stream is working and weaving the Michael stream as we may call it in Christian terminology, the stream in the spiritual life of humanity in which we have been living since the end of the 1870s.[30]

I do not know if Daphne Olivier or Cecil Harwood attended this lecture and heard these and the other words that Rudolf Steiner spoke on that occasion; but Cecil in particular had something of the quality of a true Arthurian knight (or, in modern parlance, he was a valiant representative of the Michael stream). It is also maybe significant that in his later years he loved to visit Tintagel.[31]

2. Family Backgrounds: Lord Olivier and
Minister Harwood

Daphne Olivier was born on 18 October 1889 in Maida Vale, London. She had two older sisters, Margery (1886–1974) and Brynhild (1887–1935), while a fourth sister, Noel, was born on Christmas Day 1892 and lived until 1969. The sisters were the daughters of Sydney Olivier (1859–1943) and his wife Margaret, née Cox. Olivier was such a notable, original and larger-than-life figure in his time that it is important to sketch a few details about his biography, interests and approach to life.[32] He was, according to his wife's memorandum, the fourth of the eight children of the Rev. Arnold Olivier (descended from a French Huguenot family) and his wife Ann Elizabeth. On leaving Tonbridge School in 1878 he went to Corpus Christi College, Oxford, where he formed a friendship with one of his future colleagues in the Fabian movement, Graham Wallas. Mainly because he couldn't think of a better way of providing himself and his future wife (they married in May 1885) with an income, he applied for a clerkship in the Treasury and Colonial Office, and in the spring of 1882 he joined the Colonial Office in this capacity. He shared an office with one Sidney Webb, who was his age and had been born and schooled in relatively impoverished circumstances near Leicester Square and had already become friendly with George Bernard Shaw, who was three years older than he was; and in January 1884 the Fabian Society was formed. These reformatory ideas amidst a London full of squalor and poverty were an on-going passion for him, and in addition to the fortnightly meetings of the Fabians there were regular visits to William Morris at Kelmscott House, Hammersmith. Both Sydney and Meg (as Margaret was generally known) also went on excursions to cultural centres such as Weimar, Dresden and Bayreuth in the early years of their marriage.

Because of his Fabian interests, Olivier would in the normal course of events have had little hope of promotion in the Colonial Service or of being sent anywhere as a diplomatic representative of the country. However, it turned out that Olivier had outstanding gifts as a financial administrator, and in the autumn of 1890 he was sent to Belize as acting Colonial Secretary because the finances of the British Honduras were in a mess. Thanks perhaps to his ability to teach himself double-entry bookkeeping on the voyage out, he made an outstanding success of this task and returned to England in the spring of 1891.

On his return, the family moved from London to a pair of cottages called 'The Champions' on the Surrey-Kent border near Limpsfield. Margaret Olivier recalls that many fellow Fabians came to visit them there, and their other friends included Edward and Constance Garnett, Henry Salt (founder of the Humanitarian League) and Octavia Hill, the social reformer and future founder of the National Trust. George Bernard Shaw would also visit and, later on, H.G. Wells, who taught the Olivier girls croquet. The girls were free to roam wherever they liked through the woodlands with the children of their parents' friends.[33]

Although Olivier had other postings and colonial duties in between, his next major appointment was as Colonial Secretary of Jamaica from 1899 until 1904. (He returned to fetch Meg and the girls in December 1900, and they remained with him for three years.) He loved the island, and—apart from his formal duties as acting Governor—he threw himself with heart and soul into the task of establishing a firm practical foundation for the lives of the people, devoting particular attention to agricultural questions and to the viability of the cane sugar industry, and also endeavouring to ensure that all the inhabitants of the island—whatever their race or colour—had an equitable livelihood. In this respect he was fully applying the principles of his Fabian ideals.[34]

After his family had returned to England in the autumn of 1903 he came back to Jamaica to help with mitigating the destructive effects of a hurricane on the island. It was clearly apparent from numerous testimonies that when he eventually left in September 1904 people were very reluctant to see him go; and when on 14 January 1907 there was a catastrophic earthquake which virtually destroyed the capital, Kingston, the only available option in their minds was to 'send Mr. Olivier!' He duly returned to Jamaica this time fully as Governor, and remained there until the end of his term in 1913. These six years as Governor were 'probably the most interesting and the happiest of his life, certainly of his official life' (Margaret Olivier). In the autumn of 1907 Meg and the children arrived; and the following spring Brynhild and Daphne returned to England in order to study at Cambridge, while Noel would board at Bedales.

Olivier's last diplomatic tenure was in 1924, when Ramsey MacDonald—forming the first Labour Government—made him Secretary of State for India and elevated him to the peerage (some Labour members of the House of Lords were needed, and he was the most suitable candidate even to the extent of thoroughly looking the part).

By this time, he had already—as he thought—retired from public life, a decision that was marked by leaving London, thus relinquishing the houses in St. John's Wood and Highgate where he and Margaret lived until the end of the war. They had retained the lease on the Limpsfield house, but as the owner refused to sell it they looked elsewhere for a retirement home in the country. In 1920 Sydney eventually found a small Elizabethan house called 'Old Hall' in the village of Ramsden, North Oxfordshire; and he and Margaret finally moved there in the autumn of 1921. They remained there until 1937, although for health reasons Olivier needed to spend the winters on the south coast after his severe bout of pneumonia while holidaying in Switzerland in August 1931. They had built themselves a house in Bognor Regis, where they lived until Lord Olivier's death in February 1943.

★

By the time of Daphne's meeting with her future husband, she had become well-established as a teacher. After being largely home-schooled by her parents and governesses, she had attended Newnham College, Cambridge, where she took her BA in Medieval and Modern Languages in 1913. In her quest for a philosophy of life and for new teaching methods, she attended the Coué Institute in Nancy, France, and in December 1922 was granted a certificate to teach the Coué Method, 'having proved her knowledge of physiology and psychology to be sufficient' for the purpose. She would stay with her parents from time to time, and it was during one of these visits that she chanced to pick up a leaflet announcing Rudolf Steiner's lectures in Oxford in August 1922 from a friend's house nearby.

There is comparatively less detail available about Cecil's background and upbringing. What we do have, however, is a fine, professionally-taken family photograph, where his parents, William Henry Harwood and Mary Elizabeth née Wells, are posing with their six children, Arnold, Hilda, Maurice, Gwen, Eric and Cecil. Cecil, the youngest, is sitting like a kind of angelic waif on his father's lap. This photograph must date from around 1900, when Cecil was two years old. His father had been born at Eckington, Derbyshire in 1856, as the second of three children of Jabez Harwood (1823–1862), a surgeon, and his wife Emma Hardy. He trained for the Ministry at Headingly College and in 1882 became the Minister of Union Church, Sunderland, where he not only built up a great reputation for himself as a preacher but also became one of the town's leading citizens.[35] In 1892 he accepted the co-pastorate of Union Chapel, Islington (London), together with Dr. Henry Allon, who—having served there 48 years—died shortly after a few months leaving Mr. Harwood as the sole pastor. During his 22 years as a Congregationalist Minister at Islington (1892–1914), he became one of the leading figures of Nonconformity in London. Finally, he responded to a call to become the Minister of the recently formed Church in Mill Hill, which at the time was still a country village (there was a link between Union Chapel and Mill Hill in that Dr. John McClure, Headmaster of Mill Hill School, was a member of Union Chapel congregation until he transferred his membership to Mill Hill in 1917). In March 1918 the name of the Mill Hill Church was changed to Union Church, to reflect the inter-denominational outlook of the congregation. Harwood's ministry at Mill Hill continued until his death on 18 July 1924, by which time membership of the Church had increased three-fold. A couple of months before his death, he had written some words of cordial greeting to his son Cecil on a postcard sent from Brussels: 'I hope that some light will soon shine on the future.'

3. Personal and Professional Engagement

Alfred Cecil Harwood was born on 5 January 1898 at 25 Aberdeen Park, Islington. I have not come across any testimonies about his early childhood, and he first features in Owen Barfield's recollections of his youth[36] through the fact that both men attended Highgate School as day boys both living in the North London suburbs. Originally, Highgate would have been somewhere between Harwood's home in Islington and Barfield's in Whetstone, and Barfield describes their first meeting on the first day of the autumn term 1910 (they remained in the same class and usually at adjoining desks throughout the whole of their school careers). Later on, when Harwood's family had moved to Mill Hill, they would have shared part of their train journey to Highgate, as Barfield describes in the following evocative passage:

> Morning after morning, it is the same. My (steam-driven) train from Totteridge reaches Finchley Church End, which is the junction for Mill Hill. The carriage-door opens to admit more passengers and among them is Harwood's round, almost girlishly smooth face, usually with a smile on it, though there is probably none on mine. Perhaps it is half-impudently *challenging* the fact that there is none on mine; but perhaps not, since smiling much was one of his recognised characteristics—even amid the severities of the classroom. Within my memory it is the kind of smile it is difficult to describe; possibly because its effect depended a good deal on how you were feeling yourself; bland, if you happened to be feeling disgruntled, blithe when you were gruntled... I have dwelt on it because, for some reason (whether from memory or from continued observation I am really not sure), it is a kind of keynote in my mental picture of the whole man. If, on the one hand, it betrayed a certain surface tendency to feel frankly quite pleased with himself, or at all events with what he was just now saying, on the other it signalled a deep-rooted serenity of spirit which was to stand him in good stead throughout his life...

There is a reference to this same quality of Harwood's in C.S. Lewis's *Surprised by Joy*:

> ... He [Harwood] was different from either of us [i.e. Lewis and Barfield], a wholly imperturbable man. Though poor (like most of us) and wholly without 'prospects', he wore the expression of a nineteenth-century gentleman with something in the Funds. On a walking tour [of which these Oxford friends undertook a great number], when the last light of a wet evening had just revealed some ghastly error in map-reading

(probably his own) and the best hope was 'Five miles to Mudham (if we could find it) and we *might* get beds there', he still wore that expression. In the heat of argument he wore it still. You would think that he, if anyone, would have been told to 'take that look off his face'. But I don't believe he ever was. It was no mask and came from no stupidity. He has been tried by all the usual sorrows and anxieties. He is the sole Horatio known to me in this age of Hamlets, no 'stop for Fortune's finger'.[37]

Harwood and Barfield would also occasionally visit one another at home, and Barfield came to be acquainted with the 'cultured, mildly majestic Nonconformist Minister', while Harwood became accustomed to the challenging questions of Barfield's highly rationalist, agnostic father. Harwood's school-career was crowned with the award of several prizes for proficiency in the Classics, and he was—according to his daughter Lois—awarded a classical scholarship (as was Barfield).[38] Meanwhile, Barfield noted his friend's precocious delight in words as such and in the way that they come to mean what they do—thus one reads a book not only for what it says but for the way in which it is said. This love of language would be a quality that remained central throughout Harwood's life.

Instead of going directly to Oxford, Harwood was obliged to enlist for active military service in 1916. He recalled to his daughter Lois that he had once been asked to lead his platoon to a village held by the Germans, 'only to find, to their huge relief, that the Germans had already left. He maintained that it was thanks to appendicitis that he was invalided out of France and escaped an almost certain death in the trench warfare' (from his daughter Lois's memoir).

In 1918 Harwood was finally able to take up his classical scholarship at Christ Church College, Oxford; and some six months later he was joined at Oxford by Barfield (although Barfield was at Wadham). During their second year Harwood initiated an arrangement whereby they shared with two other men a house in Pembroke Street, to which they would invite all their undergraduate friends and thereby had a first taste of adult social life. One prominent member of this group of undergraduates was C.S. Lewis, who was born in the same year as Harwood and Barfield (1898). This academic-cum-social life continued after Harwood and Barfield had taken their degrees in 1921. The two friends lived alone together while they commenced their post-graduate studies, initially in rooms in Grove Street and, for the remaining terms of that academic year (1921–2), in a furnished cottage called 'Bee Cottage' in the village of Beckley. They both not only fulfilled the requirements of their studies but also—copiously— wrote poetry and articles and welcomed many visitors, not only Lewis but also his many acquaintances; and Capt. W.O. Field (1893–1957), who had been an intelligence officer in Harwood's platoon, also participated in these meetings. (In a certain sense, this was the initial nucleus of what came to be known as the Inklings.) Nor should the significance of their walking tours in Oxfordshire and sometimes further afield be omitted. As Lois Olivier notes:

> ... the route was carefully planned to allow for a pub lunch and overnight stays in acceptable inns. Father revelled in the countryside, and always [in later years] retained his enthusiasm for a walk, stick in hand, pipe in mouth, with the 'rucker' on his back (or a child on his 'soldiers'). In later days, I recall sundry differences of opinion with my mother as to the virtues of certain debated short cuts: father fearing that mother's choice would lead to a bog (which was often the case).

Once this period at Bee Cottage had come to an end, Harwood took up what Barfield describes as 'a rather unsatisfactory publishing job in London, living for a time in rooms in Pimlico with a friend from Barfield's former college (Eric Becket). 'He was,' Barfield reports, 'at that time making a rather half-hearted attempt to turn himself into what used to be called a "young man about town", and even the Bloomsbury set were not wholly outside his orbit. I don't think the experiment could ever have succeeded. But there was another reason why it did not last long.'

As detailed in my book on Owen Barfield[39], Barfield had—as a mark of his membership of the English Folk Dance Society—in the past two years joined an amateur concert party that toured some Cornish towns and villages for a week or two in September with a programme of music and including historical dances in costume. In 1921 Harwood—who, according to his daughter Lois, 'was a competent pianist and organist' and had in the meantime also joined the English Folk Dance Society—accompanied Barfield for his visit to St. Anthony in Roseland. Both men were to meet their future wives through these festive gatherings, and Harwood's bride-to-be was—like Barfield's—several years older than her future bridegroom. Daphne, the 'dark and dreamy' Olivier sister (the characterizing words come from *A Socialist in the West Indies*, p. 7), had been invited for the first time to join the party in order to sing and play the fiddle. As far as I am aware, we have no direct account from any source of this seminal event in September 1922. All that is therefore possible at this stage is to try to bring to our minds an imaginative picture of these two individuals (Barfield is also present, but he is a kind of mediator in the personal destiny of the other two) in the light of the more substantial information hitherto presented about their backgrounds: Daphne, the deeply thoughtful daughter of a charismatic, highly esteemed and free-thinking English grandee who cannot have been an easy person to disagree with, fresh from hearing in Oxford about principles of education and social life to which she wanted to devote all her future energies; and Cecil, a younger man by over eight years who was still hoping to carve for himself a career as a poet and writer[40] and who was not—so far as I am aware—actively seeking a new philosophy of life but whose innate Christianity must have been implanted within his youthful soul—even if only indirectly—by the fervent preaching of his father.

It is clear that Daphne maintained and intensified the connection that she had formed with the educational ideas of Rudolf Steiner, and the people associated with them in England, once she had returned from Cornwall to her London base at 14 Oakley Crescent, Chelsea. It is also clear that she and Cecil had made an impression upon one another, although no intense feelings became evident in their letters for over a further year. Cecil and Owen, for their part, reverted to their respective tasks and locations: Owen to Oxford and his post-graduate Litt.D thesis on *Poetic Diction* and to further developing his relationship with Maud Douie (they married on 11 April 1923); and Cecil to London and his literary career. Rudolf Steiner's ideas must also have made an impression on them. At some point subsequent to their initial meeting with Daphne Olivier in September 1922, they both began, 'rather sceptically' (according to Barfield), attending some weekly lecture-readings which George Adams (then George Kaufmann) was conducting at 46 Gloucester Place, London. This apparently went on 'for some time'.

The next development was initiated through a letter that Daphne wrote to Cecil on 24 August 1923 from Penmaenmawr, North Wales. Prior to travelling to North Wales, she had attended the public course of lectures given by Rudolf Steiner in Ilkley between 5 and 17 August 1923 *(A Modern Art of Education)*. Two crucial events took place at this conference, the essential purpose of which was to describe in a very practical way the principles of Waldorf education. These events were summarized in a report by Helen Fox:

> At Ilkley we teachers came nearer to the resolve to try to start a school, and decided to confer with George Kaufmann who was acting as interpreter and a kind of young courier to Rudolf Steiner... George Kaufmann arranged a meeting for us with Dr. Steiner, Frau Dr. Steiner and I think one or two other friends. We told them of our resolve and asked him if he would approve of such a step. Rudolf Steiner looked very thoughtful for a moment, and then said 'Ja!'. And when Dr. Steiner said 'Ja!' in that full, rich voice of his, this was no mere acceptance; one experienced it as a deed. After this he spoke to us very quietly and seriously, saying how vital it was that if we did start a school it should be 'a good school', able to take its place beside other educational establishments in England, not just an interesting little

experiment somewhere in a corner. We then asked Dr. Steiner to choose the
teachers, to which he replied 'Who would like to undertake this work?' We
indicated the four of us who were there, Miss Effie Wilson, Miss Dorothy
Martin, Miss Daphne Olivier and myself. 'But you should also have a man',
said Rudolf Steiner. So the first step was taken, but only the very first. We
had no prospect of children, no house, no money. Then a miracle happened.
Our decision was public at the Ilkley Conference, and immediately three
anthroposophists, with incredible trust, came forward, each offering £ 1000
to buy a school house. These were Mr. Christopher Gill, a solicitor from
Bath, who gave us valuable advice on business matters, Mr. Edward Melland
and Miss Elizabeth Stuttaford, a wealthy lady who had been studying Dr.
Steiner's work for many years.[41]

The day after the end of this educational conference, Daphne accompanied the group—including of course Rudolf Steiner himself—making
the train journey from Ilkley to Penmaenmawr, where Daniel Dunlop
had organized a first International Summer School (although the weather
that particular August bore little relationship to summer) on the theme of
The Evolution of Consciousness as revealed through Initiation Knowledge (19–31
August 1923). And it was from Penmaenmawr that she wrote to Cecil on
24 August:

> I wonder how you are liking your work? Is there any chance that you
> would ever now feel moved to join us in an educational enterprise—if
> we got it launched—the foundations of an English Waldorf School? We
> are keener than ever to try. There is a nucleus of six women teachers—
> and the backing of a committee of ways and means—and Dr. Steiner
> would give us a Special Training of six weeks next August, if everything
> else can be got under way. But of course we want *children* as well as
> money—and as yet we don't know where. Will you tell Owen about it?
> I don't know his address. Some of the [German] Waldorf teachers have
> been over here. They make one feel it is the most skilled and fascinat-
> ing profession there is. You are an artist and a poet and a musician and a
> scientist all in one. I'm sure the 'edition de luxe' business won't give you
> nearly such scope. But in any case we have up till Christmas to find the
> funds—and teachers would not be called upon to decide before about
> March. Do think about it.

Harwood evidently declined this initial invitation. But George Adams
(Kaufmann) had asked him if he would like to meet Rudolf Steiner in
person after the Ilkley and Penmaenmawr Conferences, when he would
be departing for the Continent by way of Liverpool Street Station. (This

would have been in early September 1923, thus shortly after the founding of the Anthroposophical Society in Great Britain in his presence in London—at 46 Gloucester Place—on 2 September.) To this, Harwood agreed. 'It had been only a brief encounter, from which Cecil Harwood had carried away an impression of kindliness, straightness and tallness, perhaps emphasised by the long coat that was worn, and of an unusual formation of the face.'[42]

Both from the source of the above suggestion and from Daphne's next extant letter (18 January 1924), it is apparent that the weekly anthroposophical study sessions embarked upon by Cecil and Owen referred to above must have been continuing in quite a serious vein. Moreover, despite Cecil's initial refusal to commit himself to the new Waldorf School project, Daphne indicated—clearly in response to an interest that he had expressed—that 'I should be very glad to talk about the school with you some time. I shall get in touch with the latest developments of it as soon as I get back [she was at her parents' home recovering from bronchitis]. One realises, of course, the further one goes, that it's a pretty serious undertaking. But we aren't daunted so far.'

By the time that she wrote to Cecil on 5 May, it is evident that these two young people were also beginning to want to meet up socially for its own sake. Daphne was, in addition, trying to use her numerous social contacts to support his possible career in publishing. When she wrote to Cecil in July 1924 he was convalescing from a nasty attack of mumps; and after expressing her sympathy she adds: 'I do hope you and Field will come to the camp. I think it may be rather nice. Though the camping ground from what I hear is rather exposed to the blaze of the sun and the ravages of horses and cows—water to be fetched in pails etc. and the sea the far side of a line of villas. However, there are walks up behind—and the sea is the sea...' By the 'camp' Daphne is referring to the second International Summer School, which was to be held in Torquay in August 1924. Rudolf Steiner was to be giving a course of lectures on *True and False Paths in Spiritual Investigation* (11–22 August); and he had also undertaken to give some lectures (there were seven of these, held between 12 and 19 August) specifically for the little group of people who had committed themselves to form the nucleus of the new school. As it turned out, recuperating from mumps tipped the balance in favour of Cecil's attending a conference that he had not otherwise planned to participate in—this is, at any rate, the view expressed by Joy Mansfield, who adds: 'He... spent a week there [in Torquay] attending the last three days of the Conference, and during that time decided, with Steiner's approval, to become a teacher' (Joy Mansfield, op. cit., p. 17). Crispian Villeneuve fills in a little of the background to this—seemingly somewhat drastic—change of personal destiny on Harwood's part:

> Unlike the previous educational courses at Oxford and Ilkley, which had been fully public, attendance at this [educational] course was in principle restricted to intending teachers, though a few other interested people were also admitted. Among these latter was Daphne Olivier's friend Cecil Harwood, who with other younger participants at the Summer School was camping in a field just outside the town.
>
> Now at Ilkley in the previous year, Steiner had told the four ladies intending to start a school they must also have a man. But though a whole year had passed by, no such man had yet been found.
>
> Helen Fox related that at Torquay these same ladies 'had some talks with Rudolf Steiner on practical and educational matters'. During one of these talks Steiner pointed towards Harwood, who happened to be in sight, and simply asked the ladies: 'What about him?'[43]

Villeneuve then expresses in his own words the concluding part of this great Torquay drama:

> Steiner's own departure took place on the... day [after the end of the whole Conference], 23rd August. He was travelling to London by rail. In the meantime Cecil Harwood had been persuaded to join the teachers' group. Wishing to tell Steiner of his decision, he turned up at the last moment in Torquay railway station. They had a brief talk in the waiting room, just before Steiner boarded the train [op. cit., p. 1065].

On 28 August a telegram was sent to Harwood (who was at the time staying at the Radfords near Portscatho) on Rudolf Steiner's behalf—he remained in London lecturing until the end of the month—with the message: 'Doctor Steiner wishes you to join school January next, please call'; and according to Daphne Olivier's letter to him sent at that same time, Harwood was allocated by Steiner the task of teaching the 5th Class—'probably the hardest job of the lot!', she added. But most significant for their future relationship were the words with which she began this letter: 'Dear Cecil, Thank you for your letter. I like it that you tell me you are happy—the thanks I should be embarrassed by—except that I feel it's part of your "Gratias Tibi Agimus" echoing to human beings.' Harwood additionally telephoned Barfield to inform him of his decision, while expressing his view that Rudolf Steiner was 'a simply astounding man'. Barfield added his own thoughts to what his friend had told him: 'He did not say so, but it was clear, even through the microphone, that he had become a dedicated man.'[44]

What precisely occurred between Daphne and Cecil over the course of the next couple of months can only be surmised from a lengthy letter written to Cecil by Owen Barfield on 9 November 1924. Cecil may well have proposed marriage and felt that he had been rejected. His friend's letter is not only of biographical interest with respect to all three parties concerned but a fine example of a literary form in its own right:

My dear Cecil,

It makes one feel a little queerish to think of the number of things that were a-brewing when Maud Douie got into conversation in the Three Arts Club with a stranger called Constance Prescott, who happened to be looking for rooms. Your news—that is to say the first part of it—was not an absolute stunning surprise to me, though I had no actual conviction that your feelings ran that way. Thank you for telling me.

Among the many thoughts which have passed through my cerebral sieve since receiving your letter, I would like to tell you the one that has left the most pronounced deposit, though in doing so I run the risk of making an ass of myself and jarring on your nerves. It is merely this, that from the *information* in your letter—as apart from its depressed tone—I should be compelled to form the opinion that you have had the kind of response which is practically equivalent to an acceptance. I do not feel much confidence in my opinions on the feminine enigma, or rather I should say that I simply have not got any opinions—but I do feel pretty sure of this—that nine tenths of the ultimately successful proposals that are made by and to serious and sensitive people start off in the way yours has done. My father's did and forty years ago, and my brother's did about two years ago. Whereas in my own case the refusal jolly well *was* irreversible, and I had the sensation of rebounding from a stone wall to nurse my bruises as well I might.

Have you (a) put yourself in the lady's place and realised that, unlike you, she has probably not allowed herself to dwell on the question beforehand and to think it out in all its bearings? They daren't. And have you tried to imagine what it would be like to have a life-time proposition like that sprung on you suddenly? In all human probability she is now working out the sort of questions which you worked out before you took the step.

Have you (b) considered the heavy responsibility which a woman takes on herself by merely admitting that her decision is not irrevocable—or even by allowing a man a loophole of behaviour by which to kid himself into believing it possible? I know that this is a thing which even ordinary women feel very deeply about indeed—and I leave you to complete the syllogism.

For which and other reasons, though you have my sympathy and I am far from seeking to make light of the kind of tortures you must be enduring, until I hear more of the matter or more time elapses, you are not going to have my condolences. And I take it you will not think it is tempting providence for me to tell you how much I like Daphne, and, what is more important, that

I have liked her more the more I have seen of her. She is a charming soul in a charming body.

There is one thing more I would like to say, if it can be said without an odious presumption of intimacy. I was a good deal younger than you are, when I went through a something similar experience, and I had not got certain resources which I believe you now have. Moreover, we are really very differently made. But I remember so very keenly that I felt as though I should pass away altogether if I had not my father and Marion Radford to write to, and you to live with. Not knowing how you are situated in that respect, or how you feel, I nevertheless do not want to close this letter without an attempt to make you understand that—no, I can't say it. It sounds like the most bloody kind of invitation, and it is really an attempt at a mere bald state-ment of fact. How absolutely in the dark one is about the way another fellow is feeling! It was Marion, wasn't it, who said that her deepest regrets in life were for the things she had not said, and I remember that you were impressed by this when you told it to me. Births, deaths, and marriages and rumours of marriages are the Saturnalia of the spirit—they give a kind of temporary license to its unbridled lusts after its fellow-beings. What I have tried to con-vey in this paragraph is as you take it, kind Sir, an anything, an everything, a nothing, a kickshaw, a bubble, an echo of eternity or a *faux-pas*—with a heigh-ho the wind and the rain.

I do want you to be happy and, if you are miserable, to make you a little less so in any way that should be in my power.

Good night, Owen! [with a mournful face inscribed within the 'O']

Owen was proved right in his judgement of the romantic situation in ques-tion; and Daphne's next letter, postmarked 28 November, enclosed a ticket for a dance 'if you would like to come', and was—for the first time—signed 'Love from Daphne'. And as a kind of postscript: 'It *is* true and not a dream, isn't it?' There was a flurry of fond letters around this time, including one dated 1 December referring to an invitation from Adelyne Vaughan Williams asking both Daphne and Cecil to supper. And then Daphne adds: 'You know there is a real thing that can come right across space and make us together even when we are apart, but I believe that is of the spirit, not the soul. That is why we have to go right through the looking glass to see into wonderland. My love to you Darling. I've been praying that I will be able to make you happy. Yours, Daphne.' These messages were accompanied by the excitement of informing their parents (Cecil's father had died in July that year).

On 28 November Eric Beckett—whose London home of 2 Lupus Street Cecil Harwood shared—sent the following jolly letter to Mill Hill, where Harwood was often staying with his widowed mother during this time:

Caro Cecilio mio,

Yes—confound me—I saw the truth at a glance. My efforts to appear calm and unobservant were no doubt transparent but you see one must wait to be told! But I did feel an ass. However, I jogged across the Park, humming a mild echo of your own bliss and in a state of otherwhereness produced by this event, went out to a smart dinner with coloured socks! A thousand congratulations. You will be splendidly happy and I rejoice with you. (Oh, I will be secret: but it was nice of you to tell me.) May all the butterflies and fairies attend you. Ever yours, W.E.B.

Cecil also received congratulatory letters from the three Radford sisters. These are also included here, since otherwise these ladies, who were—without setting out to be such—the midwives of everything chronicled in this volume and much else besides, tend to remain such shadowy figures. Thus Marion Radford wrote as follows from Bath on 5 December:

My dear Cecil,

In the first place, let me infuriate you by saying I have known it since the summer! And then if that doesn't finish off an eternal friendship, accept my love, my very warmest sympathy (which it seems to me as much needed in happiness as in grief!) and give the same to Daphne, whom honestly I scarcely know but remember as perfectly charming. Have reason to know too how utterly good she is in the real sense of that very ill-used word. Yours ever, Marion.

The same day, Evelyn and Maisie Radford wrote to Cecil in a similar vein from St. Anthony in Roseland. This is Evelyn's letter:

My dear Cecil,

If I am pleased, but only if—I think it's lovely, bless you. Did I tell you once long ago before you had occasion to know it, that Daphne was a darling? As to yourself, it would be more proper for me to tell Daphne what I think about you than to tell you—though as someone once said events, anniversaries and the like are really designed to give people a chance of saying the things they don't say every day, let me tell you that you are a dear and blessed person and that your happiness matters a mighty lot to your friends, of whom… well, you know all that. One always gasps at any real news (Owen told us the night before in a taxi, and we said in the words of one of the operas 'What further to surprise us?' and then did gasp), but really it seemed very unsurprising and just natural. I think almost sub-consciously one had felt you very understanding and near to each other ever since that Devon time, when by the way you were each of you very comforting in a chaos of mixed emotions and queer circumstances. Anyway, your letter next day made it seem wholly natural and made me very happy for you both… You are not allowed to speak of Roseland as a matrimonial agency—but I will admit that we have some rather nice friends, and if they go and marry one another, dash it that's their affair, and if we are glad, well that's ours. Dear Kets [this sobriquet was also used in several letters by Daphne], I *am*—very glad. Yours always, Evelyn.

And Maisie also wrote a heart-felt letter, evidently having been in the same taxi as Evelyn:

Dear Cecil,

Owen made a dramatic announcement of your news in the taxi-cab as we trundled home after the operas in a kind of wild dream: it was good to hear next day from yourself and make sure we had not dreamt it along with Prince Jerelon and the ballet and everything else! I love Daphne and I am so glad she will be happy. I know she will be. Give her my love and tell her how glad I am. I have wanted so much to see her again ever since the Devon tour when I saw her a good deal and which she kept very happy for me in spite of a good deal of worry—I nearly asked her to come on with you from Torquay... and only didn't because I was afraid of having too many visitors for Mother. You will both come before long, won't you? This is an inadequate kind of ramble... but it brings you much love—and I am *really* glad for you both—ever so glad... I wish you could have seen our operas—they really were lovely in spite of the hair-raising episodes, as when the cornet insisted on doubling the clarinet and the only flute was sent to Newquay to measure a lady for a fur-coat and only returned by motor five minutes before he had to play. Owen was dancing wonderfully. It was jolly having them... Do come up on the 15 Dec. or thereabouts. Till then, much love. Yours always, Maisie Radford.

4. Marriage and the Founding Years of Michael Hall

Since the decision to start a Waldorf school was taken during the Ilkley Conference in August 1923, a group of determined individuals—including Irene Groves—had successfully identified a suitable building in Leigham Court Road, Streatham and there was a resolution to purchase it. The original hope had been to start the school in the autumn of 1924, but there was too much that still needed doing to the building. Besides, even though a small group of teachers was ready to begin (although none can have been happier to have more time to study Steiner's educational courses than Daphne Olivier and Cecil Harwood), the search for children had by no means reached Rudolf Steiner's suggested minimum for making a start (one hundred). The school—called simply 'The New School'—formally opened on 20 January 1925 with five teachers and seven children. As Joy Mansfield describes in her history of the school, 'Cecil Harwood had the leading class with two girls of about eleven; Daphne Olivier the class below; Dorothy Martin, the Nursery. Music, art and languages were shared out between them. The housekeeping fell to Helen Fox and special care of the boarders; Daphne Olivier coped with the secretarial work; Effie Wilson took eurythmy, of prime importance in any Waldorf school' (op. cit., p. 20). At first the school grew slowly, with twelve pupils in the second term and about thirty in the third, then a more substantial jump to a hundred in autumn 1926. By 1932 numbers had crept up to about a hundred and fifty. More teachers joined, and in 1930 the property next door became vacant and was purchased, with the result that it was possible for a school Hall (suitable for the plays that Cecil Harwood was writing by then to be performed) to be built between the two properties. When after a fundraising campaign the new Hall was opened on 23 November 1935, the school was renamed 'Michael Hall' at the same time. A reader who wants more details about the school's early years will find a more than adequate account in Joy Mansfield's book, *A Good School*. The intention here is to focus largely—albeit to a great extent indirectly through Daphne's letters and from other sources—upon Cecil Harwood's role at the school (Daphne increasingly withdrew once she started to have children). However, it is first necessary to revert to the sequence of letters that they wrote to one another over the next period of their lives. Finally, we shall draw again upon the memoir that Lois Olivier wrote about her father, because of the unique insight that it affords about the Harwoods' early family life.

The first thing that one is reminded of as the sequence of Daphne's letters (hardly any of Cecil's appear to have survived) resumes in March 1925 is the extent to which both she and Cecil lived for a much wider cultural landscape than Leigham Court Road, Streatham could alone offer them. Daphne was still actively engaged at the Royal College of Music, and Cecil must have given a lecture that meant much to her: 'Do you know when you look—not "funny looking"—but beautiful? When you talk about truth, like you did this afternoon. And then I'm all melted and humble. Love from Daphne' (letter dated 9 March 1925). Her next letter would seem to be expressing condolences over a family member's death: 'I do hope you will have had a peaceful night and be feeling better about it all. I do wish I could comfort you—only it seems idle to say anything. I will only be thinking of all that beauty which is in the spirit and which must be all round her healing her. Sometimes I feel one has to keep drinking in courage and patience from God as one must breathe in the air if one would keep alive. Goodnight, Bless you, Your Daphne.' And shortly afterwards— on 25 March—she writes once more about their busy cultural lives (Cecil is most likely lecturing to a group of members of the Anthroposophical Society): 'Darling, I'm thinking of you so bravely taking on this lecture tomorrow—after all your other work. Bless you for it. I am most torn. I hate leaving you all in the lurch. I thought for a while this evening could I do both and hire a motor from Wigmore Hall at 9: I could get in half an hour. Would 9.30 be any good?... Goodnight Darling—you seem to get more and more good—I wish I could. Love from your Daphne.'

Daphne continued writing deeply affectionate letters—and no doubt Cecil did too—over the next few months, during which time they continued to live at their respective London addresses in Chelsea and Pimlico. They were married in August 1925. It was clearly a festive occasion ('Why is Daphne having all this pomp?', queried one of her friends), and in church. Eric Beckett was best man. Shortly before the day (it was a Friday, and from the evidence of the letters probably the 21st), both Daphne and Cecil exchanged several letters; and one from Cecil has survived:

> My darling,
>
> It was so sad not to see you, but I comforted myself with various things I did towards next Friday. I think of you for whole days at different times I have been with you. Today it has been all in this run on the rocks at Torquay, and the time when you came and bathed with me alone in the middle of the day, and then left me to think of the tide—and I wonder what else? I do reproach myself for many things when I think how sweet and gracious you have been to me ever since I have known you. You gave me light and love and faith—and now yourself too! Good-night—Darling. Your Cecil (lots of kisses).

On the Thursday of the week before the wedding, Daphne wrote the following from her sister Noel's home, 33 Elm Tree Road, St. John's Wood:

> My dearest Darling,
>
> I've found your nice, delicious letter waiting here—and I'm writing now just after we've finished dinner and the others are on the rampage in case later on I should miss the post. It's an awful thing that about not being called by the same name—'cos after all *your* name will be just the same! Well, well... I wonder what words he will say over us then? I wish it could have been Steiner's[45]—it's splendid of you to have remembered to write to him about it. Fancy kissing the wee ring—all abshurd [sic.]. I've been being so tremendously practical and matter-of-fact all day—it's still going on in me like clockwork—and so I'll just say that The *Burbery* is *here*. So I hope you won't be worried not finding it at O[akley] Crescent. On the other hand my wedding dress has not arrived—so if you see me without 'pomp' after all it'll be a test, won't it? But I don't think it'll come to that. Darling—this rumbling of the world will wear off tonight. I am sleeping in little Benedict's room—beside him. That ought to be like a blessing and a striving, oughtn't it? I wish I could have a communion service early in the morning. I will think the meditations which will help me to that; and then that will lead on to thinking of you all in holy, grateful loving thoughts. God bless you my own Dearest. Good night, love from Daphne Olivier.

And on what must be the evening before the great day, she writes:

> Darling—
>
> Just to say goodnight (kiss). Bless you, sleep well. I went up to see the Church just now all by myself. It is rather wonderful that it should be *that* church.[46] I'll tell you why *tomorrow*! My love to you once more. I'll shall [sic] see you then really standing by Becket in the gloom at the end of the aisle? Isn't it extraordinary? LOVE from Daphne Olivier (kiss).

★

In the meantime, Cecil was proving his worth as an essential member of the New School's founding group. Jesse Darrell, who joined the teaching body in September 1928, gives a clear picture of this in his appreciation of Cecil Harwood's contribution to the school:

> It as essential that, from the start, the School should be run as efficiently as possible, as an enterprise that was seriously intended to stand its ground firmly in the modern world; it must inspire confidence as an earthly institution. In the achievement of this, Harwood was altogether indispensable. If he had

everything to learn as a teacher, he seemed to have everything needed to ensure that the School should go on being there to teach in. His thinking was clear and respectful of facts—wooliness of mind in others was a real trial to him. How often, to the relief of us all, sometimes of those who didn't agree with his opinion, he would clarify a problem and bring it into shape. And if it was perhaps to be expected that the arrangements he planned for the School left little unregarded and were practicable and consistent, it was impressive, to say the least, to see how at home he also was in the world of action. He was fully-fledged as a man of deeds, as well as of thought, so that he could turn his will without difficulty to what needed to be done at a given moment. When children's reports were to be written, he could make use of any spare interim minutes to get on with one, and without their quality suffering at all. It upset him at meetings if discussion rambled too far and pushed the decision (yet again perhaps!) to the following Thursday. With him as chairman or treasurer—he held the record for the tenure of both—we knew that no unnecessary grass was growing under his feet.

Invaluable though these capacities of his were for the good running of the School, it was owing to others again that he could do so much to ensure that the running was in the right direction and the runner in good heart. His thinking was not only lucid; it was also creatively imaginative. It could spread wings and, Pegasus-like, carry him and his readers or listeners towards the heights where the truth is more living and more truly seen. Testimony is borne to this not only by his plays and poems, his books and articles, his lectures to which one looked forward and back with equal delight, but also by the vision..., the intimation in him of how the future of the School would best be served. A sleep after his first sight of Kidbrooke [the eventual home of Michael Hall in Sussex] left him sure that here should be its new home.

Cecil Harwood did take a class through the Lower School, but his teaching was mostly of the older children, where his clear, imaginative approach to knowledge, in conjunction with his active, creative life in practical affairs, could give reality to what he taught them. The anthroposophical picture of man, which inspired him as a striving individual in both these spheres, and which he did so much to bring to life in the School he loved, gave a glow, an artistic form and coherence to all that he brought forward, so that his lessons became an enriching experience for life.

Cecil Harwood threw in his lot with the education when the Uriel phase of the year [i.e. the height of summer] was moving towards that of Michael[mas], when the awakener of the historic conscience in man was to be succeeded by him who summons man to courageous self-knowledge and self-renewal. There was something of all these elements in Cecil Harwood and something therefore of them in all that he gave to the education and to much else.[47]

It was not possible for Daphne to maintain her initial full commitment to the school after she and Cecil started to have children, although she continued her involvement in other ways, such as by translating many of Rudolf Steiner's lecture courses, especially those on education. As Lois Olivier reports in her memorandum about her father referred to above (see note 38), John, the eldest, was born on 31 May 1926.[48] Her own birth followed in January 1929, that of Laurence on 12 June 1933, Mark in October 1934 and Sylvia in May 1937. During the latter stages of her first pregnancy, Daphne must have spent quite a lot of time at her parents' home in Ramsden (between Witney and Charlbury), both for her own sake and to support them in their old age. Five of her letters from the last month or so before John's birth have survived. The last two of these are dominated by her anxieties arising from the General Strike (understandable enough for a woman about to give birth to her first child)—will there be any coal, milk, trains or post? But those from (probably) April 1926 are full of insights into her preoccupations and interests, and some excerpts will be given here:

> Darling, I got your two letters written on Wednesday and Thursday this morning [Saturday—she generally gives the day but not the date]. It was lovely to get them. I'm writing this in case you may get it on Monday morning [Daphne wrote all these letters to 40 Leigham Court Road, Streatham Hill, where Cecil would have been wholly involved in teaching and his other numerous school commitments]. I expect Father and I will manage the journey quite simply together. I came by train from Oxford yesterday to Charlbury—and it was quite alright—only of course stopped everywhere. I'll phone to you from Noel's. I want if possible to get to Gloucester Place on Monday to give Miss [Dorothy] Osmond her lectures—but the chances of getting them published now seem, alas, rather small... The concert was exquisite. The chorus though not quite mature enough for the 'Sancta Civitas' [by Vaughan Williams]—but very lovely and ethereal in the piano and pianissimo parts.—It was strange that beautiful youthful gathering in the Sheldonian—a sort of oasis in this chaos—rather too frail in such a world, like an iridescent raindrop in a thunderstorm. Mother and I hurried away before the end to catch *the* train and were brought up to the 'Waterloo Arms' by Warner in a charabanc. I'm a little tired today—but it was lovely getting out and seeing 'life' after being such a mouse for weeks. I'm glad you're all so serene still. Will I see you I wonder on Tuesday? My love to you, Darling—thank you for nice letters. Your Daphne (kisses).

In her next letter, sent towards the end of April, she expresses her wish that Cecil could come and:

> be here in the evenings—and see all the fresh green and sniff the scents. It's been rather murk and wet these last days, but when once one is out and

walking along one feels it *is* spring all the same—and can't go backwards alto-gether... I've sent off Miss Osmond's first lecture heavily corrected [Dorothy Osmond translated a large number of Rudolf Steiner's lectures from German, and the implication of what Daphne writes is that she was editing the transla-tions]. I hope she won't mind. It took me three mornings' rather concentrated work.—I'm posting your wash by this post, also the lecture for Dorothy... The article on Medicine in *Anthroposophy* is interesting—because written from the point of view of an ordinary scientist. It is refreshingly precise. But he gets up against it rather when he tries to state the whole matter from *within* the scientific outlook—regarding Dr. Steiner's 'mystical philosophy' as *outside* the scope of his article. It can't really be done. However, I think it would be quite a useful article to give to Peggy or Noel to read. In fact the whole magazine could be sent to a good many of one's friends... Wouldn't it also perhaps suit Becket?... I had a letter from Miss [Mabel] Cotterell, very gushy about the school. You don't say whether there are to be any new children this term? Does that mean, no?...

There's very little for me to tell you that I do. It's much the same every day, a kind of routine—varied by occasional indisposition of various kinds—head-aches or tummy aches—but not much! They seem, however, just to check one's activity and reduce it to a very small amount. Father has got Graham Wallas' new book *The Art of Thought*. I almost tremble to read it, because I feel I shall disagree so. But one oughtn't to get like that ought one?—I can't get very good at those songs just now, because I can't breathe as vigorously as one ought. At least it seems to me it's bound to oppress the nymph if I do. But I can at all events learn the airs...

Her next letter followed a few days later (identifying when the letters were written is dependent on trying to decipher postmarks on the envelopes in which Cecil kept these treasured epistles):

Darling, Your lovely long letter has just come. Thank you very much for it. It is good to hear you're so far ahead with fixing up the extra teaching—and about Dorothy and Sheen [Arthur Sheen, who had joined The New School in November 1925 as a science teacher] speaking at the general meeting [pre-sumably of the Anthroposophical Society in Great Britain]. I'm so pleased. And about the effect of Stuttgart on Sheen.

I thought I might have written again to you yesterday to catch the morn-ing post—but I got a bit weary as the evening wore on because I had been [for] quite a strenuous walk with Tristram in the rain along the Leafield [a village a little to the west of Ramsden] road and into the forest. It was rather lovely in the forest glade, all dripping and silent—the rabbits seemed to feel they would have it all to themselves and were playing on the turf—and a great tawny-red cock pheasant was strutting with long tail sweeping the wet grass. When birds did sing it was startlingly clear and sweet. Tristram got all hushed and happy with quite a different light in his face...

The lecture I'm revising for Miss Osmond is a splendid one. It will be very good to have them as a book. Thank you very much for sending me *Anthroposophy*. It seems to me most promising. I liked Mr. Wheeler's article and Mr. Dunlop's editorial is quite good, isn't it? I haven't read Owen's yet.

I'm glad the wretched accounts are finished. Mother said 'I'm glad he doesn't like these niggling details'. She doesn't consider it necessary to a proper appreciation of mathematics. It's rather in the nature of 'chores' which somebody has to do. But it's a shame it should always be you.

I've nearly finished Steiner's *Lebensgang* [his autobiography, *The Story of My Life*, which was at the time untranslated]. It's wonderful for giving one a grasp of the order in which his thoughts developed, and consequently in which his books were written. And it makes a great difference to have those pictures of his life in Vienna, and then in Weimar for nearly ten years, and then at Berlin—instead of the merely abstract information that he did live in those places at various times. It is all written so that you can see his destiny working through from period to period—from within and from without...

Goodbye for now, Darling. Little one sends greeting—if I can judge by his sometimes tremendous upheavals! Sometimes I wonder whether he really will stay put for another five weeks! My love and kisses, Your Daphne.

By the time she wrote again on 1 July, she reports of the Old Hall, Ramsden's newest arrival:

Darling,

I found your letter as I brought little John down the slippery curly stair—because I fed him later. Thank you very much indeed. I love your description of the Ballet—and of the two Clares—that is just what they are like. But I find one acquiesces in their attitude very readily—especially in the case of Clare Balfour. There is something very strong and virtuous behind that quiet confidence. She is a sculptor—and putting her will into her hands she develops herself (her ego) and gains that real power which is beyond caprice and personality. I'm glad you liked the beech woods. They were the only temples we worshipped in as children.

Little John is beautifully asleep now in the shade of the lilac. I gave him water last night instead of milk—it was as if I had offered him a stone instead of bread. He lamented loudly—and I walked about—and nearly gave in—and then as I had him cuddled against me I began speaking to him—then I sang a little and behold he was asleep. So I laid him down in my bed where we were—and for fear of rolling on him went and got into yours! I shall be awake with John still by the time you get from Witney because I've pushed everything on later to see how it does. You'll not be answering this letter but coming instead. My poor Tenge I hope you won't be too tired with that long walk to the hooting of the owls. It will be lovely to have you here. Goodbye till then, Yours Daphne (kisses, also from John).

This letter was immediately followed by another one, as Daphne hoped that Cecil could bring a small thermos flask with him so that she could start giving John water at night (it had struck her that this was the simplest way of keeping it warm). Her attentions are clearly divided between 'Little John' and her anthroposophical work:

Also—will you bring the rest of that lecture for me to copy out? The East-West translation I mean.

I went up the field where you played golf with Tony this evening. My first walk. The hay is cut in the meadow beside it. It is perfect up there. It was very soothing as I've had rather a restless day with Little John. He's peaceful at last. God bless him.

I've finished the lecture about Hermann Bahr [she might be referring to a lecture that Rudolf Steiner gave in Berlin on 1 May 1917]. It's most entertaining. I suppose Bernard Shaw with his *Joan of Arc* is another example of a contemporary who has struggled through to a certain conception of spiritual truths.

Father is away all this week—so Mother and I are alone. She helps me all the time—the only trouble is that we differ slightly about how much one should 'take him up' from his cradle. But she soothes him so well it seems very ungracious to remonstrate. Much love to you Darling and goodnight. It will be lovely to see you on Friday. Your loving Daphne (lots of kisses).

A letter written about a week later, mostly concerned with John and with visits from elderly aunts, reveals a couple of interesting points about their living situation. Cecil, it would appear, no longer has his 'room' (this is presumably his place with Eric Beckett in Pimlico). And Daphne concludes her letter with a question: 'Shall we make up our minds whether we will stay in Streatham till beginning of Sept. in any case—or is it contingent on not getting lodgings? What about finance? If I have time I'll write a word or two when your letter has come... My love to you, Darling, your Daphne.'

This letter was followed by another, written the day after the visit of Aunt Evy and Aunt Maud, apologizing for the 'mouldy' nature of the previous one and including glimmerings of insights into what was going on around the young couple:

My Darling,

Thank you for your dear letter. Thank you also for your information about the 'staff'. It sounds excellent... I'm so sorry there are many 'troubles' [from the context, these probably pertain more to the Anthroposophical Society than to the school]. I wish I could help... I think one of us really must try and go down and lecture on Anthroposophy to the Heretics soon—if they still exist. [The aunts were accompanied by a Mrs. Lloyd] who proved to be the mother of a young man for whom I had—or who had for me—between whom and myself (is that right?) there existed a certain penchant—one summer holidays that we spent in a party in the Lake District. I remember he got on a white horse in a field—and I jumped on behind from off a fence and felt very happy as we trotted along. Also there was a rock pool that we bathed in - and we played hide and seek in the waterfall. But he married a very good girl who did splendid war work in the Ministry of Food. 'She makes him an excellent wife', his mother said. And they have three children. The mother is a charming old lady full of kindliness and wisdom... Edith has sent me the book she was making about her sister Mildred. A collection of writings—and the one by the maid Foyle. Mildred does live in these descriptions. (I mean the Edith of Wilton—who gave us the big box which I haven't tidied.)

After emphasizing the importance of registering John's birth within six weeks, Daphne goes on to write about a proposed holiday in Bridport.

About Bridport. I wish I knew how nice it was. I hope it isn't too towny. Our holiday would cost £ 18 at that rate. Can we afford it? Or would you be just as happy with a ten days' walk with Owen? I shd. be quite happy in the little house—I'd get a friend to stay.—Will they take a baby?—If you don't think it too much, will you write and say we'll come and there's a baby. So then they can object if they like. Must stop for Miss Beams to catch the post with this. Much love to you my Darling. I do hope the troubles will right themselves. Your loving wife, Daphne (lots of kisses).

This letter was in turn immediately followed by a postcard with this message:

On second thoughts about lodgings and talking with Mother—it *does* seem rather extravagant when one can take so little advantage of them—as I shall be able to this year. So it all depends on how much you would prefer to be there than anywhere else. So sorry to leave it to you in this way again. But I'm anxious for you to have a proper holiday as you've been at Streatham all the term—so mind you tell me frankly what you wd. like...

Cecil had been working to prepare the 'little house' (they were renting 51 Angles Road, near to Leigham Court Road) for his growing family; and after two further letters from him, Daphne wrote again on 27 July:

> How lovely of you to have done so much in that little house. I'm glad you like doing it and were happy there [throughout his life Cecil was keen to engage in practical tasks, including building work].
>
> Now about this holiday—certainly let's cancel it if we're hard up. I shall be quite happy to stay on in the little house and, as you say, it will probably be better for John. For instance, I can begin training him to have his feeds at the times which will fit with the teaching—it won't get upset again by an extra move. As you say, we can have all sorts of fun. As long as you get a good walk with Owen and blow away the cobwebs and nightmares of this term. Poor Darling, you must have got terribly overstrained to be getting bad dreams. I wish I had been there to kiss them away. Don't be worried about the finance. I've got that £ 50 in Lever's that I can sell out if need be. I saved it when I was teaching in the L.C.C. and we may as well use it when we have most need. Or better still if we could get the hostel money back—because that was meant for furniture and things for the house—and it is not invested so well as Lever's.
>
> I think linoleum all across the stairs will be cleanest and simplest—yes, blue is nice. Mother says you can get a cheap grey one for the bathroom like Noel did—she got it in Kilburn somewhere. The downstair passage and stairs will have to be strong linoleum—yes yellow will be nice and light for the passage... If you have time for any others—I think the *kitchen* and whichever bedroom we are going to use. Do you think yellow? Or pale bluey grey? The west bedroom has an appalling paper remember—but that's rather a big one to do. It's difficult to think out the colours without seeing them—anyhow: *not* green or red or brown—but you wouldn't!... Goodbye for now - and much love and sweet dreams and kisses from Daphne (big kisses) and John (little kisses).

The above letter was sent with another one written the following day:

> Darling,
>
> Thank you for your tiny wee letter. It was nice to get it. But I wish you didn't get so tired. How splendid for the children to have a party, though.— Well, by now your teaching work will be over and school broken up. I wonder if you are pleased with the term? It's been a very difficult one.
>
> I didn't have time to answer your point about Helen [Fox] yesterday. Yes—it certainly does seem an easier undertaking to have her, than Wof [W.O. (Walter) Field, who had joined the staff shortly after the school was founded]—because she is so wonderfully careful not to give trouble—and as you say I dare say she wouldn't mind watching that John doesn't wake sometimes if I want to get out. Also, as you say, there is Ruth [Melland] about—who is her great friend.

[Helen Fox was responsible for housekeeping and boarding at the school and Ruth Melland was, among other things, the school secretary.] That's our point of view. From hers—I think it would be much better if she didn't have to go back into lodgings by herself—I'm sure she's done enough of that. Of course, it would have to be clear that it was only for a year, say—and then we might be wanting the room. So will you be writing to her? And what about the rent? Can she afford what we estimated? Otherwise that is a drawback. She's got her own furniture and may want to bring it. But as we haven't any too much that might be an advantage. [The letter continued with further queries about colours for rooms, with preferences expressed for pink and peach blossom especially for the baby.]

The following day, a Wednesday, a further brief letter was added:

Darling,

Thank you so much for your letter. I'm glad you've been getting more sleep! About the holiday, if you're really happy to give it up, the only question is whether the people will be very much upset. I'm quite glad to stay in the little house, as I said—and shall find a hundred things to do. When it was settled we should go I was quite agog for *myself*, to brush away the froustyness of so much coddling—but I did have a few misgivings about little John. So that my mind will on the whole be more at ease to stay in one place—and I'll try and get some longer (two-hour) walks here instead. I don't know about staying the extra week, and I believe Mother has asked Bryn here. But I could stay till the 17ᵗʰ [August] I expect—and then I could get a friend to stay with me till you come back.

I wonder if you could enquire about a charwoman, or maid, who could help with John's washing when we get back? Otherwise that will take me about an hour and a half a day.

I'm so glad the financial prospects are a little brighter.

Don't feel you ought to stay on and do things to the house now if you are feeling tired and stale. You will have fresh zest later on. Is it insured? Or what about its being looked after while we are away?—The reports sound most formidable!

Little John took up the time I'd hoped to be writing to you—so I'm again rushed for the post. Goodbye, Darling. It will be lovely to see you. Your loving Daphne (usual kisses).

The next day Daphne wrote a further letter:

My Darling,

Thank you for a lovely letter—it's noble of you to stay up and do more things—but I'm glad you'll be coming with Father. Are you really coming quite soon after you get this?

I'm getting quite excited about that little house. It's fun that we didn't have it all at once with being married, because now it's an adventure by itself...

Soon you will be here—and then you can rest. My love to you, Darling. Kisses from little John and me. Your Daphne.

Cecil must indeed have come soon after this letter was sent, but—judging from where Daphne sent a further couple of letters sometime in August—must thereafter have gone to spend time with his mother at 12 Winterstoke Gardens, Mill Hill. At some point he must have experienced a problem or disappointment of some kind, not associated with the school (which was on holiday) but with what in her next letter Daphne refers to as 'the Museum' ('it is a shame and a horrid waste', she comments); and she adds: 'I hope your time with Owen will be some compensation.' Apart from some descriptions of the supreme beauty—'all mellow and golden'—of the harvest mood at that time, with 'a blessing in the air tonight' because 'the harvest is in the barns and ricks and the warmth and sweetness seems like the relief coming from those men's hearts', Daphne is preoccupied with a query from H.G. Wells, the subject and nature of which are not stated, except that Wells was also seeking the opinion of Noel and a certain Miss Dunsmuir about the matter concerned.

Shortly after this Daphne and Cecil had a rendezvous at Paddington; and from there the family must have settled into the house on Angles Road, Streatham, in close proximity to the New School. It was pointed out earlier that there was a substantial increase in pupil numbers in the autumn term of 1926 (hence the slight relaxing of financial concerns), but this would also have meant that Cecil's energies needed to be devoted in that academic year quite substantially to the school (although he doubtless also continued to carry responsibilities within the Anthroposophical Society). One can only guess what the background was to Daphne's next extant letter, clearly (on this occasion) postmarked 1 July 1927. It was addressed from 51 Angles Road to 'Cecil Harwood Esq., *at* Glyn Garth, Menai Bridge, Anglesey'.

Friday

I wasn't thinking unkindly of you, Darling—only wondering a little about fate—and how much it is our destiny to be weaned by one thing and another from having a personal life at all. I suppose it is the learning of the hard lesson of the second commandment. But it goes slowly—as also does the controlling of the impulse 'to be a suicide if one can't be a murderer' as Weininger put it.

Effie [Grace Wilson, eurythmy teacher at the school and—when it was founded—the teacher with the greatest knowledge of anthroposophy and Waldorf education] has given me her eurythmy ticket for tonight and will look to John. She is a dear.

God help you with your lecture, Darling. *Love* from Daphne.

Life must have continued at 51 Angles Road for Cecil, Daphne and their little child for a further year or without changes or upheavals. However, 1928 was a year marked for both Cecil and Daphne by a significant strengthening of their links with the wider anthroposophical movement. In Cecil's case both of the most important manifestations of this were a reflection of his work with the New School. Thus on 6 June he wrote a letter to the Secretary of the Anthroposophical Society in Great Britain (George Kaufmann) which was published in *Anthroposophical Movement* (a weekly newsletter for English-speaking members of the Anthroposophical Society) on 10 June 1928 requesting books on a whole range of subjects for 'a really full and comprehensive [teachers'] library' encompassing 'every branch of human knowledge with which, at one time or another, the children have to be brought in contact' and also books for the children themselves. He signed this with his own name (Cecil, not A.C.) on behalf of the College of Teachers of The New School. A little over a month later, the children of The New School were presenting a demonstration of educational eurythmy (together with pupils from Kings Langley Priory) at Rudolf Steiner Hall, 33 Park Road, on 23 July; and Cecil himself gave a major presentation on the theme of 'Imagination in Education and Social Life' in the course of a day specifically devoted to Rudolf Steiner's educational ideas (28 July).[49] Both of these latter contributions formed part of a large-scale World Conference on Spiritual Science and its Practical Applications which was based at Friends' House, Euston Road between 20 July and 1 August 1928; this event, organized mainly by Daniel Dunlop, was wholly in the public domain and attracted considerable interest among the wider public and newspapers.

Then in the autumn of 1928 Cecil must have made it possible for Daphne to attend the Opening Conference of the (Second) Goetheanum that was held in Dornach from 29 September until 7 October. From the way that she begins her letter, dated Wednesday afternoon (this must be 3 October), which was written facing the setting sun on the Goetheanum Terrace, it is clear that Cecil had attended the first part of the Conference, as did his colleague William Mann:

Darling,

Now you are in the middle of all the work again—and perhaps it is like a dream that you ever were here? Unless the journey still leaves you weary—I think round you, coming home after tea to our blessed little one—now perhaps (5 o'clock)—and then you will work in the blue room—or go back to the school? No it's Wednesday—I hope that something of Dornach still is with you like a blessing. Bless you both [big kiss, little kiss]. These are wonderful days—unbelievable—if not so simply actual. That coming home to the

Swiss house in the valley takes me gently back into the every-day world; yet in a way, the very naturalness of that walk through the quiet sleeping village is more remarkable than the magic of an enchanter's wand.

If this letter seems light-headed you will forgive it—if you remember that I am sitting right beneath those great curved walls—that the valley is filled with a transparent warm blue haze, and the air with the sound of cow-bells—and the sun is sinking very gently and softly into opal-coloured mists above the hills.

The people are in the lectures. We had a magnificent—stupendous—lecture from Rittelmeyer last night[50] - enough to nourish a life-time. And this morning a most beautiful and moving lecture on the animals by Poppelbaum[51], who has real greatness and combines the modesty of a scientist with the warmth of a poet.

The waves of it all seem to lap one round with happiness. Or rather, it seems to get into one's breath.

It *is* really true... And then the urgent thing is that the rest of the world should know. That responsibility for the others getting it is the real task in our English society—and what I hope will be emphasised at the quarterly meeting.

As for the deeper trouble—one must work with one's thoughts to heal that—and have faith that Michael can really make us all into his 'pupils'—and give us understanding of what is wanted of us.

There will obviously be grievous folly—and mistakes made here, but we must not *fear*—as I think sometimes one does too easily—that the intrigues and pettiness which give Ahriman and Lucifer their opportunity will really overthrow the purpose of the Spirit of the Age.[52]

The mystery plays are a great revelation to me. One finds the answer to one's half-obscure questions—almost startlingly. For instance, I had been feeling—how would it be with our love—if, as it seemed here, as far as your own inner spiritual advancement is concerned I am completely unnecessary to you—and neither have you, apparently, any deep concern or interest in mine. But I realised that it was a kind of egoism to wish it were otherwise—to be sad if one can't be directly instrumental in spiritual help, instead of blessing the Gods when *they* give you their gifts—and being content to give what you would gladly have in our life together and companionship—'O Mensch, erkenne dich'.

Much love to you my Darling—the sky is all pink now. Kiss our little one for me. I will start back on Monday. Your Daphne.

A further letter from Dornach to Cecil followed on Saturday 6 October:

Darling,

It was lovely to find your second letter propped up against the flower vase when I came in last night. I am glad John is well and you are at all events getting fed—I expect you are beginning to feel your lecture hanging over you. I hope you will get some peace this week and to think about it.

I kissed all the kisses and snuffed [sniffed] the paper where Tenge's firm and emphatic hand had passed [kiss]... bless it.

I am just going to hear Frau Kolisko[53]. Yes, the eurythmy was magnificent. I've never seen anything like it. We have had none since [Wednesday]—but shall have some after tea today. And then in the evening [Albert] Steffen reads his new play. So it is a lovely day. Yesterday I felt rather oppressed, and I think the reason was that we started off with Boos' lecture which was full of sound and fury.[54]

Today we have had Beckh[55], who was great—and Fräulein Röschl on Ovid[56], also very beautiful. So I feel refreshed instead of exhausted.

I gave your message to Miss Stuttaford [one of the benefactors of The New School referred to earlier], and had a nice talk for a few minutes with her. She is very glad she has been here, as it has made her much happier about the outlook in the Society. And she herself volunteered that a large part of the misunderstandings came about because some had come in 'from above', through the esoteric, and some from 'below' through the practical, and we have found a meeting place. We were interrupted by someone. But I hope you'll have an opportunity for a real talk with her when she gets back (she travels Tuesday evening). She is really a great dear.

I have been hearing of an American group who are carrying out the Three-fold state ideas—starting from their own daily needs—restaurants, laundry, farm products. Owen is going to try and get one of them (Courtney) to write an account of it for our News Sheet... I'm sure that is the right way to set about solving our financial difficulties. It needs someone with the initiative to start. Capital could be got for a thing like a laundry by getting potential customers to stump up £ 10 each. For instance at Streatham one could raise £ 100 like that straight away—because our laundry *costs* us £ 12 a year. I know this isn't worked out in detail. But Newnham College, for instance, found it paid to run their own laundry—and one could enquire the details of organisation from them.

Saturday evening. I've just come out of the eurythmy and must send this now—or it won't go tonight. There will be no time after Steffen.

The eurythmy was beautiful. A lot from Steffen's *Wegzehrung*[57] which I should have appreciated more if I had read beforehand. On the whole a much lighter programme than Sunday—nothing so stupendous as the Apocalypse—but very lovely. But it still remains almost as great an experience to come out onto the terrace and look up at *it*, shimmering and towering up into the sky where the stars are coming out.—And this valley all round—it changes every hour, as do the cloud shapes over it—it seems to love the Goetheanum too, and to be caressing it with its beauties. Much love to you, my Darling—and to our blessed one [lots of kisses]. Kiss him for me and this for you [big kiss] my so dearest. Your Daphne.

After these vivid glimpses into the aspirations and preoccupations of these two people who were evidently so deeply in love with one another, the written records become largely silent and one can only imagine the many-sided life that they shared in Streatham with their growing family. One last letter has been preserved from this time shortly after their second child Lois's birth in January 1929 which, while adding little of substance to the picture that has been evoked, nevertheless contains some touching and beautifully descriptive passages. It was written from her parents' home in Ramsden on Wednesday, 17 April and posted the following day to Cecil's mother's home in Mill Hill. (Mrs. Harwood, who was to die three years later, must have appreciated her son's care.)

> Darling,
>
> ...I didn't write yesterday after getting your letter as I still didn't know where to write. It was lovely hearing from you—it must have been a wonderful time. And now this morning I got your letter from the hill by the sea. It's been a great joy to think of your having all these lovely days. But I was touched that you wanted me to be having it too, thank you for telling me that... It gets queer without you—the first day goes on fairly normally till the evening, when I miss you most, having more time to turn round. Then as the days go on I get a sort of sinking feeling from time to time—it does seem that it is the *heart* that feels heavy—that isn't a mere phrase... But I have had happy peaceful times with John... and this morning we came up to the pond round about by way of that long line of larches—and suddenly up rose *two* wild ducks, the humble brown one and a most dazzling mate with bright green neck flashing in the sun. Their beauty and wildness gave me a thrill of joy which was on the edge of pain—as the beauty of spring so often is. They were young love in the spring sunlight—as the Kyriotetes had made it. One of the clumps of rushes was hollowed out and wound about in the hollow with dry rush. I do hope they will come back and put the beautiful eggs here.
>
> Perhaps you will decide to sleep tomorrow night at Mill Hill—and meet us on your way back. I must chance it and send this there... Your loving Daphne [big kiss].

★

Lois Olivier's memoir of her father is a valuable addition to the perspectives offered by *A Good School* (the history of Michael Hall which supplies an outline picture of its Streatham days) and by Daphne's letters. I shall quote here from her description of the period of the family's life at Angles Road:

That unprepossessing house leased by my parents in Angles Road saw the arrival of four more of us... Luckily, there was a long garden into which we could overflow. On summer days we would have our meals—even break-fast—outside at the garden table. Father used to keep the top lawn neatly mowed, and if it was particularly hot we would have fun dashing in and out of the spray while he held up the hose pipe. The lower garden was less kempt. There were several tall trees, one of which supported the swing. Even C.S. L[ewis] took turns at pushing the inexperienced swingers on his visits. The older ones would soon 'work up' to an almost horizontal and precarious position. There was a fine lime tree which we used to climb, and from which a good view could be had of neighbours' gardens and passing trains. It was thought rather daring to venture over the interven-ing fence and put a half-penny on the line in the expectation of it being flattened into a penny coin. Father had made us a hut to play in on rainy days. It was here that John and I and the neighbour's boy Dennis enacted our plays. My mother's wardrobe would be raided for costumes. She had a green velvet dress (made by her dress-maker) which served very well for the Frog Prince.

In the 1930s, my mother had the assistance of various young women, some of them 'au pair', others lodging while involved with the school in some capacity. They were usually allocated the small bedroom over the scullery, entry to which could only be gained through the bathroom. One of these helpers recalled how she was once trapped there while my grandfather was taking a day-time bath prior to attending the House of Lords. She was privy to a rehearsal of his speech, his voice booming out above the splashing.

I remember one pan-cake day when, the supply having been greedily guzzled, father gave instructions to whoever was in the kitchen to continue making them until further notice... Just before the War, we had an Irish girl—she used to take us for walks to Streatham Common, and sang 'Red Sails in the Sunset' and 'Tipperary'. We were sorry when she hurried back to Ireland.

Our parents yearned for the countryside. At weekends we had sallies—after father had learnt to drive—into Surrey or Kent: to Box Hill or Limps-field. Sometimes we called on Vaughan Williams, who was a good friend of my mother's, at his home in Dorking. My mother was particularly glad to escape from Streatham, and school holidays were enjoyed either in Oxford-shire with the grandparents [where, as John Harwood recalls[58], the family learnt to swim in the Windrush and Evenlode rivers], or, after taxing journeys, in 'our' small (rented) cottage in South Cornwall, near the Dodman point. On one occasion when we set out with the car loaded with 5 children, 3 adults, bedding, food, nappies etc., we broke down about half-way. Father managed to get a lift and returned with a garage mechanic. After some investigation and consultation it was decided to part-exchange our vehicle for another second-hand one. The transfer of belongings then proceeded at the roadside and it was fairly late by the time we reached Boswinger.[59] If it was a spring visit, we would find that Mrs. Mitchel, the farmer's wife, had lit the range, our mattresses would be steaming in front of it. The blue and white striped jug would be full of rich milk with a bowl of cream also in readiness. The next day we lost no time in getting down to the beach, with my mother following later in the morning with the younger ones and a picnic. Besides the enticements of the sea-shore in the summer there was the excitement of riding on horse-drawn farm carts, perched high on the straw when returning to the ricks. But the modus vivendi was not plain sailing at the cottage. Cooking was carried out on a double-burner oil stove, with the kettle boiled on the range. Water had to be fetched in twin metal cans, and there was, of course, no bath. (Probably, having been accustomed to this sort of life, the transition to conditions during the War years was made easier.) There were candles and oil lamps for lighting and sometimes an oil stove would be lit upstairs to warm the somewhat dank bedrooms. On one occasion, a fire was caused when a mattress was being aired too near the oil stove. We were all sent off for a long walk with Joan[60], the current helper. When we returned, mother was sewing up a distinctly smaller mattress, while father had cut down the bed to a single one. Father put his practical skills to work to improve the cottage. For instance, he re-built the outside loo, using drift wood we had hauled up the hill after 'wrecking' expeditions, when we often also found prized green or pale blue glass balls wedged among the rocks.

In the mid 1930s the school had acquired a neighbouring property. It was on the completion of a new school hall in the intervening space in 1935 that the school had a second baptism with the name 'Michael Hall'. But the school was only to remain there for further four years.

It had become clear even before the Second World War began at the beginning of September 1939 that the school would need to move from its cramped existing site in Streatham, both because of the London County Council's demands for extensive alterations to the buildings and because of the need for more land for playing fields, gardening and overall expansion. When the war began and immediate evacuation became a necessity, the recently opened Wynstones School in Gloucestershire made an offer to accommodate Michael Hall; but it was apparent that there wasn't really adequate space there for both schools. As Arthur Sheen's wife's family had strong links with Minehead in Somerset (her father was a councillor in the town), it was decided to evacuate the school to there from London; and Cecil Harwood bore the principal responsibility for enacting this decision and communicating it to the parents.[61] Lois Olivier describes the circumstances: 'War broke out while we were again enjoying a sojourn in Cornwall. Father had to return to London to see to the arrangements for the great exodus of school—and teachers' households—to the safe haven of Minehead'. Of the around three hundred children who had been pupils by the end of the academic year 1938–9, a much smaller number took part in the evacuation: 'On September 1st 1939, early on a fine summer morning, the evacuation took place, a hundred and thirty children taking part. They drove through towns where other evacuees had already arrived by train and were being escorted through the streets. A sense of unreality hung over everything.'[62] But this is to anticipate the consideration of the second half of Cecil Harwood's life which will follow in the ensuing part of this book.

In a certain sense it is appropriate to mark the time when the first half of his life merged into its second half in 1937, which happens to be more or less its chronological mid-point; for it was in 1937 that he was appointed Chairman of the Anthroposophical Society, a post which he held until the year before his death, 1974. Although Harwood continued to be involved with Michael Hall until the end of his life, this appointment represented a significant change of emphasis in his life. But before we begin to consider this later period of his life in greater detail, it is important to let Harwood's own voice—hitherto muted because of the marked absence of surviving letters or autobiographical writings from his own hand—to sound forth through the many articles, poems, stories, plays, translations and other writings deriving from the first half of his life. I shall consider—and where possible feature—these under two broad headings: literary productions emanating from his own creative muse and writings engendered by his teaching work and his work for the Anthroposophical Society.

5. Early Writings

In 1979 a volume entitled *The Voice of Cecil Harwood* was published by Rudolf Steiner Press under the editorship of his life-long friend Owen Barfield. This volume contains a representative sample of Harwood's writings over the course of his life but largely excludes his numerous contributions to anthroposophical literature as such, on the grounds that it had been Barfield's hope—which did not in the end find fulfilment—that a selection from the many essays and articles (and three books) that he wrote mainly for anthroposophical periodicals or for the journal *Child and Man* would appear in the form of a companion volume. The present intention is to offer a balanced survey of Harwood's output (and, in this section of the book, focussing on the first half of his life), while bearing in mind that—as Barfield indicates in his Introduction—Harwood's contribution lay predominantly in the form of spoken lectures, of which there are for the most part no written records other than his barely decipherable notes. Nevertheless, his particular genius was as a writer of the English language, even though much of what he wrote after his initial thoughts of making writing (or publishing) his career was—as Barfield points out in his Introduction to the book referred to above—prompted by outward needs.

By and large I do not propose to reproduce the content of this previously published miscellany of Harwood's writings, and the interested reader is referred to the many gems that it contains. However, I shall include two short poems from that collection, the first of which is an early poem addressed to Owen Barfield at the end of a happy period of two years when they had been living together in or near the vicinity of Oxford.

> Nous n'irons plus au bois, no more O friend! O friend!
> Our laurels are cut down, our glory sets behind;
> And is it hard, when Heaven blows, for the reeds to bend?
> O we were oaks, and laughed alike at reeds and wind!
>
> We shouted, and the Morning Stars together sang,
> For we were sons of God and could there be an end?
> O Eden! And the Gate that murders with its clang!
> And shuts us from the wood for evermore O friend!

The second poem was probably written shortly after Harwood had heard Rudolf Steiner speaking in Torquay in August 1924 and had become convinced that the anthroposophical path of knowledge was one to which he wished to dedicate his life:

> Return, O stars. Countless as you, they wait
> Your coming on the cliffs of earth, and stare
> Unresting, in part hope and part despair.
> Return. The wind sets homeward. He that late
> Fixed with his sovereign eye your bounds of state,
> Pale princes in the empty courts of air,
> Has hailed the watcher who sets free his care,
> Whose master-key unlocks at last heaven's gate.
>   O my sweet lost ones! O my soft, my own!
> Heard you the trumpet, dreaming in your towers,
> And with the dew-drops fallen, come you down
> To dwell among us in the homely flowers?
> Even to those levels that no thought may span
> Thus eloquently streams the breath of man?

To these two tender, visionary poems I append a third of a very different kind. Indeed, it is not really a poem but a bit of humorous doggerel which demonstrates Harwood's all-too-human mirthful side. It was written in pencil on a scrap of paper in Barfield's handwriting as a quizzical record of both men's early attempts to master the German language following their initial explorations of Rudolf Steiner's anthroposophy. I have left some quaint inaccuracies in Germanic usage unaltered (and it is, of course, largely nonsense anyway):

Wie kann Mann eigentlich aus der Anthroposophie heraus eine wirkliche Geistes-lebens-rätsels-lösung finden? [i.e. How can one find a solution to the riddle of life's mysteries out of anthroposophy?]

Rein menschlich	Klipp and Klar and Ganz and Gar
[the purely human	They went a walk together;
dimension]	Said Klipp and Klar to Ganz and Gar
	'We're having splendid weather'.
Wechselwirkung	So they began to spriess and spross,
zwischen Natur und Mensch	Zu wirken und zu weben,
[interaction between nature	Cried Ganz and Gar to Klipp and Klar:
and man]	'Wie herrlich ist das Leben'.

Eintritt des Esoterischen   Said Klipp to Klar: 'Since here we are
[an esoteric dimension   Zusammen mit einander,
enters into the situation]   Ich Sage, 'Gar ist ganz ein goose,
                                           And Ganz ist gar ein gander'.

Die Freiheit wird von den   Cried Ganz und Gar: 'You go too far,
verschiedensten gesichtspunkten   Es handelt sich um Freiheit,
besprochen [Freedom is discussed   Ein Geistes Mensch ist frei, nicht wahr';
from the most diverse points of view]   Und so enstand die Zweiheit.

Lösung [solution]   So all began to spit and spar,
(the purely spiritual dimension)   Und auseinander streben.
                                           Das Goetheanum vördert ja
                                           Nur freies Geistesleben.

In addition to composing poems, Harwood made several early incursions into the domain of the short story. One delightful example, 'Mr. Bowlby and the Silver Stater', is included in *The Voice of Cecil Harwood*. This had been published in the Christmas 1924 issue of a periodical called *Truth*, which also published some of Barfield's early compositions. However, there are two further examples which Barfield did not include in his collection of Harwood's writings and which deserve to be reproduced here. The first of these appeared in *The New Age* (8 May 1924) and well illustrates Harwood's sense of empathy with someone who has got himself into a bit of a pickle and doesn't quite know how best to extricate himself from his predicament:

Mr. Garnsea

'What's the good of thinking about it now?'

Mr. Garnsea repeated the words aloud to himself as he got up, in the hope that the sound of his own voice would startle him into the effort of opening the glass door and climbing the stairs to the bedroom where his wife would lie awake until he came. But although he could form a perfectly clear picture in his mind of himself turning the handle of the door, himself kicking his feet well into the narrow slippery stairs, and himself in the mirror wrenching the collar from his shirt and telling Mrs. Garnsea she ought to have been asleep long ago—yet, tonight, none of these things appeared to be any more a part of his daily life than the paintings of the goddesses dancing in the woods, and ladies at their toilet tables, which he had seen in the picture-galleries. For even as pictures, now he looked at them again, these visions of himself were misty and obscured, fading from the walls like the picture of the King when the lights were turned up in the cinema at the end of the performance.

As he sank back into the wicker chair by the almost cold fire he fancied himself sitting again on the hard bench in … Street Police-court, waiting to answer the charge in the warrant that he folded and unfolded in his hands. But all the time he pretended to be studying the warrant he was saying over to himself the speech he had carefully prepared for the time when the magistrate should ask—no doubt rather severely: but he would not be frightened of that—what he had to say. 'In the first place, your Worship...' Why hadn't he stuck to it instead of taking the policeman up when he said it had all happened at half past nine? He might have known he would only get muddled once he started arguing instead of sticking to what he had to say. But half past nine! 'It wasn't half past nine, your Worship; it wasn't barely quarter past, and I heard the church clock strike it while the policeman was still in the shop... You can't always be listening for the time, your Worship. ...It was only a packet of Players, and my watch must suddenly have stopped gaining because it said quarter past, too... Yes, but it had been gaining all the week before and I've got a witness here to prove I told him that very morning I must take it to the watchmaker because it didn't seem to make any difference where you put the regulator... But it's just the same when you expect it to go wrong when it goes right as when it goes wrong when you expect it to go right... But your Worship!—'

Thirty shillings! Well, that meant you were supposed to know the time by instinct. If they didn't want you to sell cigarettes after it was nine they should let you know when it was nine; buy you a decent watch, or come round and tell you, or ring a bell like the Doomsday Book. Why wouldn't they let him call a witness to prove his watch was wrong? Because it was really just the same as being wrong. Why didn't he simply say it was wrong and be done with it? He might have known they would never understand it was no good a watch being right when you expected it to be twenty minutes fast. Anyhow, it didn't pay to tell the truth. The policeman lied and the magistrate believed him; and he lied and got thirty shillings. Thirty shillings meant as much to him as a thousand pounds to some people. Why couldn't they take as much trouble to find out the truth in his case as they did when there was a lot of money in it?

But did they always find out the truth when there was a lot of money in it? Mr. Garnsea had never doubted before that when you went to law you got at the truth in the end, though, no doubt, it cost a bit. But suppose you knew as much about the cases in the papers as he knew about his own, would they all appear just as much of a muddle, and just as unjust as his being fined thirty shillings because of his watch? It was easy enough to get muddled however innocent you were; perhaps people had been hung before now because they didn't say the right thing in the witness box; and all the time they could no more help it than he could his watch. What a world it was! No justice anywhere that you could be certain of, and yet everyone pretended that they were so careful to find out the truth. Why wouldn't they let him call his witness? All he wanted was to prove that his watch had been gaining all the week, and to ask how he could be expected to know it had suddenly started going right? If he hadn't had a witness he could have understood them convicting him, because then it would only have been his word against the policeman's, and anyone might have thought he was telling a lie to save himself. But of course it didn't make any difference to his being innocent whether he had a witness or not. There must have been plenty of innocent people who hadn't had a witness, and what could you do when it was simply one man's word against another? Why wasn't there a way of going back into the past and having a good look round for yourself and seeing exactly what had happened when things went wrong?

For by this time Mr. Garnsea felt he was no longer concerned with the one particular thing that had gone wrong with him. He could still see a magistrate turning papers over in the middle of a long table, and other people on each side of him doing the same. And there was still a policeman saying one thing, and a man leaning on a rail saying another, and arguing about a watch which had gone wrong (or rather it had gone right, but it was the same thing when you expected it to be fast and it wasn't). But it wasn't his policemen, or his magistrate, or his watch, or, indeed, his Mr. Garnsea arguing about the watch. It was everybody's watch, and everybody was in the witness box, and everybody was on the bench, and everybody was leaning on the rail and trying to say that it was all due to the watch, that nobody was to blame at all. The real Mr. Garnsea was somewhere up in the roof of the court looking down on all this going on below him; and as he looked he saw that they were all disagreeing with each other, and that there wasn't the faintest kind of hope that all those people would ever really understand what the other person meant. Everyone quarrelling about nothing, and no-one really knowing the rights of the case, and no justice anywhere. Why couldn't people—?

'Aren't you coming to bed?' Mrs. Garnsea called from the top of the stair—'sitting there worrying about that wretched fine?' 'Worrying about the fine?' thought Mr. Garnsea angrily. 'Me worrying about thirty shillings?' But he remembered in time how much there was wrong with the world, and softened his voice.

'All right, I'm coming.'

In the other story, originally published in *Truth* some time in the early 1920s, the sublime and the every-day are interwoven in the author's wry but sympathetic portrayal of the way that ordinary human beings try to manage their lives:

Jordan Water

It was the Penwillys' first child, and it was to be called Albert George.

'Fine old English names, too', said the Vicar, who, being a bachelor, had heard of its arrival a week later than most of his parishioners. He had now stepped into Mr. Penwilly's shop to offer his congratulations. 'When will you be bringing it to be baptised?'

'That's for the Missus to say' replied the owner of the shop, leaning reflectively against an enormous Victorian wardrobe, which towered like a mountain in the middle of a miscellaneous crowd of smaller furniture, china, and general household effects. 'Not this week, nor the week after. But maybe the week after that—if Mrs. Penwilly is about again by then.'

'Any time you like', replied the Vicar, looking about him to discover the best passage through the wilderness of wood and crockery to the door. He had selected a route and taken the first careful step, when his glance fell on a small Jacobean press, which stood by itself with proper superiority, in a comparatively clear corner. His face kindled with the light of a lover. 'Ah, I see you still have that little press. How much are you asking for it now?'

'I can still let you have it for ten pounds', replied Penwilly, at once becoming professional. 'It's small, but it's as pretty a piece as you'll find.' He threaded his way towards it, and started to pull out the drawers. 'Just you try them, sir—they run in and out like a dog's tongue.'

'They certainly work very smoothly', the Vicar admitted. 'But your price is a little high, Mr. Penwilly. I see the corner has been repaired.' The Vicar had tried the drawers and called attention to the mended corner a dozen times before, but Penwilly was indefatigable in matters of business. 'You can't expect an old piece to look like new', he objected, and stepped back to admire it the better.

'The Vicar called this morning', Mr. Penwilly told his wife when he had closed the shop for the dinner-hour. 'He's still after that little press; I think he'll have it in the end too.'

'Did he come on purpose to see it?' enquired the good lady.

'Well, not exactly—he really looked in to enquire after you, my dear. And he wanted to know when we should be having the boy baptised.'

'There's time enough to think about that', replied his wife. 'But of course you told him we should want it done with Jordan water?'

'Jordan water!' echoed Penwilly. 'What good will that do the boy, I'd like to know?'

'The Parkers had their boy done with Jordan water', was the indignant reply, 'but you can't think of anything but your silly furniture'.

Penwilly scented a storm in the distance, and the doctor had told him that of all things his wife must not be agitated. 'I'll mention it next time I see him', he conceded, and was rewarded with the privilege of being permitted to hold his baby.

Apart from a brief love affair in which he had engaged when a young and inexperienced curate, and which, somewhat to his relief, had terminated unhappily, the Vicar had been immune from all the passions of life except two; and his not too richly endowed purse gave him no great encouragement to pursue either of these. He had a passion for collecting old furniture and bric-a-brac, which the Rector of the neighbouring parish of Shipley had been known, no doubt from jealousy, to describe as more powerful than discriminating; and a longing, equally strong, for foreign travel.

The great event of his life occurred when a distant female relation—of whom he had hardly heard, and whose sole reason for approving him in this way was that he had taken holy orders—had bequeathed him the sum of two hundred pounds in her will. He had wired for a locum tenens that same day, and started on his travels the next morning. He had begun with the south of France, and then taken an extensive tour over Italy. He had crossed to Athens, ascended to Constantinople, and descended again to Egypt. From Palestine he had brought back a peculiar treasure—a large wine bottle, which he had filled with his own hands in the muddy, though sacred waters of the River Jordan.

Of course, as he had explained to those parishioners whom he favoured— in itself a distinction—with the sight of the bottle, he had no belief in any peculiar efficacy of the water. It was a matter of sentiment, that was all. The parishioners entirely approved of this rationalistic manner of looking at the water, and congratulated themselves that they had a Vicar who was so delight-fully free from the superstitions of the new High Church movement.

But at the same time the bottle came to be regarded with remarkable ven-eration. The yellow colour of the water, and the sediment at the bottom, were treated as something quite extraordinary. And when it was recollected that the Queen and her family (though not of course the Prince Consort) had all been baptised with water specially brought from that very river, it began to be invested with the sanctity of a relic.

Parents from the neighbouring parishes brought their children to be bap-tised in water so pregnant with sentiment, and the Rector of Shipley—no doubt once more from jealousy—had hinted in public that his brother of Dangerley made handsome profits out of the sale of this unwholesome indulgence. Whether this was so or not, it was certain that in view of the Vicar's strong aristocratic prejudices, in which his travels had only served to confirm him, and of the limited nature of the contents of the bottle, the favour could only be granted to the privileged few. To be baptised with it was not only an omen of future success for the child, but a visible testimony to the position of its parents. Shopkeepers were, of course, rigorously excluded from its benefits.

But a month before Albert George Penwilly cut his first tearful caper on the stage of the world, the first child of John Parker—who kept one of the three butcher's shops in Dangerley, even if he had married a distant connection of the Vicar—had received his baptism from the coveted water. There could be no doubt as to the fact, because on these occasions the Vicar would appear, carrying a diminutive bowl, into which he had himself poured the few drops necessary for the ceremony. But the certainty of the fact was no bar to the discussion of its rights and consequences; and at all the gatherings and tea-fights which Mrs. Penwilly had had time to attend, before she was compelled to keep her house, the subject had been dissected in a disinterested and scientific spirit which would have done credit to the Royal Society.

The Vicar meanwhile was also worrying. Out of his scanty revenue, he had contrived during the year to save the sum of twenty five pounds, with which he had projected, for that spring, a holiday in the Black Forest, a district he had never before visited. But the vision of the Jacobean press danced like a temptation before his eyes. If only he could get it for five pounds, he might—by travelling third and staying in none but the cheapest hotels—manage the holiday on the other twenty. But on fifteen, no; it simply could not be done!

He remained sitting in a high-back chair in his study—he had no furniture as recent as the age of comfort—revolving the problem of life, and putting the black oak, which he knew, against the Black Forest, which he could almost as clearly imagine.

The following day the Vicar was stung all over his body by the desire of possession, while Penwilly's wife incessantly reminded her husband of his promise to speak about the Jordan water.

It happened that the two men met, as the furniture-dealer was returning from a sale at a farm a few miles away. They stopped, as they both had something very special in their minds; they conversed for some time about the weather, the crops, and the arrangements for the annual fair which was shortly to take place. As soon as they had exhausted these topics they stared at each other with some awkwardness, and said nothing. But the patience of the church outlasted that of the laity, whose representative came at last abruptly to the point.

'Mrs. Penwilly says that of course it will be Jordan water', he remarked, in a tone between statement and enquiry. It was the first the Vicar had heard of the subject, and it took him a few minutes to adjust his mind.

'Oh yes, the baby', he said at last. There was a further pause, the Vicar apparently making no attempt to supply an answer to the question. He was, perhaps, a little outraged at so blunt an approach to a matter which was one to be handled with delicacy; but he had his reasons for wishing to remain on good terms with the furniture-dealer. All the same Mr. Penwilly was compelled to reinforce his question.

'We both want it to be Jordan water', he remarked with a questionable concession to his wife's opinions. The Vicar saw that he must make some sort of reply.

'Really, Mr. Penwilly, I find it hard to know what to say. I am afraid—only too much afraid—that the water is almost exhausted by now. And I know they will want it for the new baby at the Hall—that is, I am told that there is to be a new baby at the Hall', he added, somewhat confused. Mr. Penwilly stuck to the point.

'It only takes a few drops', he protested.

'Yes, I know', replied the Vicar, 'but really there are only a few drops left, and I have promised several people...' Suddenly an idea struck him; his face lightened and his voice hardened. 'No, Mr. Penwilly, I am sorry, but it is quite out of the question.'

The furniture-dealer said nothing, and the Vicar hastened to open another subject.

'About that little press—I suppose you've not changed your mind yet?'

'I always stick to my word, Sir. Ten pounds or nothing.'

The Vicar found less difficulty in concealing his disappointment than he would have imagined.

'You'll meet me yet, Mr. Penwilly. Good afternoon.'

Both men walked away, disappointed but meditative.

No doubt it was with the Englishman's love of treating serious lightly, that Penwilly mentioned casually on his return home:

'I met the Vicar, and he says the Jordan water's almost used up, so we can't have it. What there is he wants for the new baby at the Hall.'

'So it's come, has it?' asked his wife, allowing herself to be side-tracked by the interest of the subject.

'Not yet,' replied her husband. 'But when it does.'

Mrs. Penwilly had lost the proper moment for an explosion, without even obtaining any fresh information. But she decided to ignore her own digression.

'And you let it go at that?' she asked sarcastically.

'Well, what could I do?' replied the unfortunate man, with conciliatory meekness. 'After all, it won't matter to the boy what water he's baptised with. I doubt if he'll ever be able to tell the difference,' he added, with an attempt at light-heartedness. But Mrs. Penwilly was not going to be put off again.

'So you don't even want the boy to be properly baptised,' she remarked, with an ominous absence of heat.

'It's not that at all, Maggie. But I can't see what difference a few drops of water out of a bottle are going to make.'

'The Parkers' boy was done with Jordan water', was the only answer he received. 'Do you think your son's not as good as a butcher's?'

Penwilly disregarded what he considered an unfair question, and replied also with a statement of fact.

'The Vicar says there's not enough water to do it.'

'The Vicar can find the water all right if he likes,' replied Mrs. Penwilly, more from a knowledge of human nature than of the contents of the bottle. Then she came crudely to the point. 'You let him have that little press cheap, and he'll do it all right.'

Penwilly was as pained as the Vicar had been at this blunt interference with the proper reticence of his business, and answered for the first time with some temper in his voice.

'I can't bargain with the Vicar about a thing like that, and I'm not going to.'

'Oh aren't you. Well, I'm not going to have my boy baptised at all, unless it's done properly.'

The shop bell rang, and Penwilly escaped from his family with some temporary relief, but with a heavy sense of life's abiding complications.

Neither of them mentioned the subject of the baptism during the rest of the day, nor even for the following three. But there sprang up between them that constraint which always appears, when two people are continually avoiding a pitfall in their conversation.

Penwilly also found that the domestic arrangements were not so entirely to his satisfaction as they had been during the first years of his married life, and he could not attribute the difference entirely to Albert George. If he happened to be a few minutes late for breakfast, his bacon was not kept hot in the kitchen, but placed unrelentingly on the table at the appointed hour; then after breakfast he would find that his boots had not been cleaned, the servant pleading that she had received special instructions to leave the boots until she had done the bedrooms, in case the doctor called. In the evening, his slippers were not to be found at all, and the mustard pot—Penwilly liked plenty of mustard—held nothing between the dried brown on the rim and the negligible sediment of yellow at the bottom.

Albert George, of whom custom was making Mr. Penwilly more timid and less proud, was too closely connected with the subject of the quarrel to exercise a healing influence. The poor man continued to stand in front of the cradle, gazing with an almost religious awe, but he chose as far as possible the rare moments when his wife was out of the room. Secretly also he was tormented by a conscience, which would insist on informing him that he himself had had the idea in his mind—before his wife had suggested it—that it would be the easiest thing in the world for him and the Vicar to come to terms. On the whole it was the most unpleasant three days he could remember.

On the fourth day the Vicar again entered the shop—to enquire about the progress of the child. Mrs. Penwilly herself brought Albert George down for him to see, but she had too much feminine wisdom to interfere in a battle which she knew was better left to her husband. After the baby had been duly flattered, magnified, and compared with both the lines which had joined in his production, she withdrew and left the field clear for a preliminary skirmish, or a full engagement, as circumstances might determine. The two men came to business pleasantly, though with some misgivings on both sides.

'Ah! I see my little press,' exclaimed the Vicar, in a tone of surprise, which would certainly not have suggested that he had kept one eye on it even while he was admiring the baby. 'What are you asking for it now?'

'Well, I don't know, Sir,' replied the furniture-dealer, clearing his throat for the great effort which was to follow. 'If you were to offer me eight pounds, I might be open to consider it. But I should have to think it over.'

The Vicar repressed a furious impulse to make the offer on the spot. He shook his head and smiled.

'Let me know when you've taken off the other three.'

It was only to be a skirmish, and after the two parties had hardly done more than look at each other, the Vicar withdrew. Penwilly saw him out of the door.

'Oh, before you go, Sir,' he said at last, as the Vicar held out his hand, 'what about having the boy baptised? Mrs. Penwilly has fairly set her heart on having it done with Jordan water. It will be a great favour if you can manage it.'

'I shall have to think it over, Mr. Penwilly,' replied the Vicar, with perfect understanding. 'I fear it can't be done—but I'll think it over.'

'Thank you, Sir. Good afternoon.'

'You say that Mrs. Penwilly particularly wishes it?' enquired the Vicar, as an afterthought. But the shop door had already shut, and he got no reply.

Penwilly went up to his wife, who looked at him with enquiring eyes. But he said nothing, so she complained that he had banged the door when he came in—which he had not. It was still to be war!

When his housekeeper brought him his tea, the Vicar remarked: 'I've just seen Mrs. Penwilly's little boy, Mrs. Tay. A fine little fellow!'

Mrs. Tay put the tea-pot down on the Chippendale table, and the cosy over the Bristol tea-pot.

'They say he's the image of his mother, Sir.'

'Exactly,' replied the Vicar, trying to remember which parent he had said that Albert George most resembled.

'She's fine woman, Sir,' volunteered Mrs. Tay, hanging conversationally on the door-handle.

'Ah, you know her?' enquired the Vicar, becoming suddenly interested.

'Well, I can't exactly say that, Sir, but I know a good deal about her.'

'Would you call her a—determined woman?'

'Oh, most so, Sir. They say there's no doubt who's mistress in that house.'

She waited a few moments longer at the door, but the Vicar showed no signs of carrying on the conversation.

As soon as she had gone, he went to his writing desk and wrote a letter. It was not a long one, but he composed it with considerable care, and read it over a number of times before he finally shut it up in its envelope. His tea was lukewarm when he finally poured it out.

For the rest of the week Penwilly found that matters became worse rather than better. If he went out for half-an-hour to see a friend in the evening, he was accused on his return of deserting his house and leaving his family unprotected. On the other hand if he remained at home and tried to take a helpful interest in the management of his baby, he was certain to be reproved for interfering. Either he woke the boy up just when Mrs. Penwilly had contrived to get him off to sleep, or he allowed him to fall asleep at the precise moment when his mother most required him to be awake.

On Saturday evening he returned from a brief visit to the Three Hammers—his wife had limited him to a quarter of an hour's absence—to discover Mrs. Penwilly occupied with the baby, and the parlour deserted. The fire had been allowed to go out, and an indefinable air of desolation had spread itself over the room. He sat down in an arm-chair by the cold grate and took out a letter which he had carried about in his pocket for several days. It showed signs of having been thumbed and pored over, but this did not prevent Penwilly from reading it again, with as much attention as if he had received it by that night's post. It ran as follows.

The Vicarage,
Dangerley.

Dear Mr. Penwilly,

I hear that the Hall baby is to be baptised in the town, where its god-parents live, so there is some possibility that I might be able to oblige Mrs. Penwilly in the matter of which you spoke to me. But of course it will depend on the circumstances.

Yours very truly,
Anthony Wood.

P.S. I am prepared to offer you six pounds for the press. Please let me know whether you accept my offer.

Penwilly read and re-read the letter. He had undertaken far too many subtle negotiations in the course of his business not to appreciate the offer which it contained. From the next room he could hear the sound of his boy crying, and his wife trying to quiet him, and he had to restrain an impulse to go and offer his help. With a sudden movement he thrust the letter into his pocket, took a piece of notepaper out of a cupboard, and sat down at the table.

'Dear Sir', he wrote in reply,

I am very glad to hear you will be able to oblige us and I accept your offer of six pounds ($£6$) for the press. We would like the boy to be baptised before you go away which we hear you are doing shortly.

Yours faithfully,
Thos. Penwilly.

His wife came down as he was putting on his overcoat in the passage.

'Where are you off to now?' she demanded sharply.

'Just to take a note to the Vicarage.'

The good lady smiled at him. 'Come upstairs first and see baby—he's sleeping like an angel.'

Thomas went.

Albert George was baptised on the following Sunday week, at three o'clock in the afternoon. There was a large gathering of interested persons from the town, and all Mrs. Penwilly's relations drove over in a wagonette from Shipley, where the Rector—who was not impervious to rumour and had seen the party start—included in his evening sermon, preached on the text of 'Love one another', a special caution against superstitious practices.

The Vicar arrived in the church with a bottle tucked under his arm, and in the expectant silence which preceded his re-appearance, hooded and surpliced, from the vestry, a slight hollow report was heard, not unlike that which accompanies the drawing of a cork on more secular occasions. A murmur went round the church, in which those who, like Mrs. Penwilly, were prepared to hear them, could easily distinguish the first broad syllable and gentle termination of the word 'Jordan'.

After the ceremony, the congregation crowded round the fortunate baby, and the Vicar, who had already had an opportunity of a close inspection, withdrew to the vestry carrying the little bowl with its precious drops of water. There, with the relief of a man who has had to handle some disagreeable object, he proceeded to wash his hands in a small zinc basin, fed by a tap from a cistern which collected the rain off the church roof. He dried them on a small towel, put on his coat, and was on the point of opening the door to go out, when he turned, as though he had suddenly remembered something, and emptied the little bowl down the zinc basin. Next with the air of a man performing an action so familiar that it hardly costs him a thought, he took up the almost empty bottle, thrust its neck under the tap—and turned the water on. As soon as it was about quarter full, he turned the tap off again, thrust the bottle under his arm, walked out through the church-yard, where he nodded to the departing congregation, and disappeared into the Vicarage.

That evening Penwilly tidied up a few bills and letters, with a view of putting them on the proper files. One of the papers, on which he lingered with exceptional interest, was headed: 'Mr. T. Penwilly, Dr. [Direct] to Henry Hobbs, Furniture Manufacturer'. The only item which appeared on it was: 'Press, Jacobean Style, £4 0 0d.' It had been paid the previous week.

Both Penwilly and the Vicar slept well that night, and waking refreshed and invigorated, busied themselves cheerfully with their duties. After all, every profession has its mysteries.

6. Waldorf Translator, Editor, Playwright and Author

By the time that Cecil Harwood attended the first part of the Opening Conference of the Goetheanum from 29 September 1928 (of which Daphne attended the latter part), his reputation as a master of the English language was such that he was—together with William Mann[63]—entrusted with the task of translating the religious services that Rudolf Steiner had created for the first Waldorf School in Stuttgart into English.[64] According to Joy Mansfield, the services were dictated to them in Dornach by Herbert Hahn, and they translated them on their return journey to England (see op. cit., p. 27). Possibly on the strength of this achievement, Harwood was asked the following year (1929) to take on a key role in the task—shared with Rev. Alfred Heidenreich and others—of translating the services and rituals that Rudolf Steiner had given to the Christian Community into English.[65]

Harwood had in his youth been strongly drawn to the world of publishing, and in 1930 he embarked upon the task of editing 'a magazine for the education founded by Rudolf Steiner' which he named *Child and Man*. The first issue appeared in the latter part of 1930 (the early issues were not dated) and included a review of the performance of *A Midsummer Night's Dream* which was given on 21 June that year 'in the beautiful garden of the house recently acquired by The New School'. This review helpfully includes the words of an appeal for funds for the building of a stage and Hall in the area between the new house and the original building, words which—we may be sure—were written by Cecil Harwood, who would also be responsible for the pageant 'King's Forest' or 'The Shepherd of New Gifts' performed in Streatham on 27 June 1931 and again in 1932[66]:

> Wonder not, Gentiles, you that late descried
> An Ass-head, silent led to fairyland,
> To see Nick Bottom now, with tongues untied
> And ass's-head unloosed, before you stand;
> Titania's self commands me back to say
> (Herself dispersed in the whispering air)
> If we have pleased you with our half-done play
> Set in the Summer of this garden fair,
> Then sadly think how soon this leafy spot,
> Our stage, shall be laid waste by Autumn's gale,
> How then to please you with another plot,

Midsummer's Dream being turned to Winter's Tale?
Yet grieve not; there's a plan to make all good—
Could we between these houses build a Hall—
As well, with your most courteous aid, we could—
That were a place to act the Seasons all!
So, Masters, Bottom pleads to generous ears,
In Summer's height remember Winter's need,
Be prodigal to my fairy messengers—
Peaseblossom, Cobweb, Moth and Mustard Seed!

Apart from writing the Editorial of this first issue of the magazine, which, he says, 'is directed to articles describing the method of approach to the teaching of a few characteristic subjects in a school founded on the principles of Rudolf Steiner', Harwood also himself wrote an article entitled 'Nine Years Old', where he tries to explain to his adult readership (the magazine was not intended for children) what is actually going on at this crucial time of child development. There was also a short editorial contribution entitled 'Are Fairy Stories True?', where Harwood unerringly portrays fairy stories as possessed of a truth that is discernible only by an imaginative faculty. After the first year or so his contributions became less frequent and the editorial introductions briefer or even altogether absent. He must have been grateful that there were capable teachers such as Arthur Sheen and Francis Edmunds (who joined the school in 1932 to take the new Class One) who were well able to write out of their respective areas of expertise, leaving him the task of discerning and describing the general principles of child development in the wider context of human evolution as a whole. In a certain sense, the publication of his book *The Way of a Child* in 1940 can be considered as a kind of fulfilment of this task in so far as it pertained to the first half of his life and to the time before the school's evacuation to Minehead (for it would, of course, have been written before then) at the beginning of the Second World War. And yet some of the contributions that Harwood made to these early issues of *Child and Man* contain the essence of what would later appear in the form of a book for the wider public. I shall therefore include, by way of examples, two of these magazine articles here.

The first is an article on the theme of 'Children's Questions', which appeared in vol. 1 no. 3 of the journal:

Children's Questions

From about the age of three children begin to be full of questions, and it is sometimes a matter of great difficulty for their parents to find the right answers to them. Every question demands its own individual answer, but it can be of great value in deciding what answer to give to have a clear idea of the kind of answer which is required. For it is altogether wrong to imagine that a little child should be given the same kind of answer as would be suitable for a child of eleven or twelve, but in a simpler form.

The range of questions which even young children will ask is truly astonishing. Indeed, in many respects the youngest children will often ask the most fundamental questions—on life and death, and life after death, and many subjects on which their parents have often resigned all hope of definite knowledge. A child of four (to quote an actual example) has asked these questions in the space of a few minutes:

Do men die? Will you die? Shall I die? What do the angels say to you? Are angels shy? Who made God? Do you like God? When you die do you come alive again?

It must come as something of a shock to little children if parents declare themselves unable to answer questions fundamental to a knowledge of human life, and the questions of children must be a challenge to many parents to carry their thinking to the point of becoming clear and certain on many things which they are often content to leave unsettled.

There are two things, however, to be noticed about the questions of little children: they will often ask question after question in rapid succession, as though it were not so much information they were seeking, as the satisfaction of hearing the answering voice; and they will listen with more pleasure to an imperfect answer which is spoken with love and warmth in the voice, than to a complete and final reply given in a matter-of-fact tone. It is, indeed, to a large extent true that when little children pour out their endless questions they are seeking something much deeper than the mere satisfaction of curiosity; they are seeking to bring around them the living tones of the human voice. For the voices which they hear do not remain arrested in their consciousness, as is the case with adults, but penetrate even to those deep unconscious processes which take place in the building up of the physical body. Indeed Rudolf Steiner has shown the exact connections of the sounds of the alphabet with the formation of the different organs of the body; and hence it is that Eurythmy, which expresses the various sounds of language and music in movements of the limbs, is not only an art, but can also be used as a means of healing.

It is, therefore, just as much a matter of *how* you answer little children's questions as of *what* you answer. Pure full tones of speech (and modern voices, especially those of intellectual people, are often terribly clipped and dry) not only give a child a feeling of blessing, but help him to form his bodily strength for later life. A child is first nourished by his mother-milk, and then by his mother-tongue.

But as a guide to what kind of answers little children need, it is often to be noticed that a child will supply the answer to his own questions, and not infrequently reject the answer given by the adult for another of his own invention. Such answers which children give to themselves as a rule are much more full of fantasy than those which an adult would supply. A child asks: Why does the sun take the water up into the sky? and then adds: Is it for the angels to drink? Or seeing a piece of wire-netting over the funnel of a steam-roller, he asks: Why do they put that netting on it? but immediately adds: It must be to keep the birds from building their nests there.

It is not easy for an adult to copy this wonderful power of fantasy, and a certain sense of intellectual truth may often stand in the way. But it is always good to remember that what little children need is a certain living fantasy in the answers they receive. To offer them logical explanations (however true to a scientific mind) is to give them a stone when they ask for bread.

Sometimes little children's questions arise plainly from their desire to unite themselves with words to the objects around them. A child sees a caterpillar for the first time, and asks: 'What is that?' 'A caterpillar.' 'What is a caterpillar?' But what he wants from the second question is not a definition of a caterpillar in ideas, but the joyous affirmation of the reality before him: '*that* is a caterpillar.' 'A Spae-woman lives by telling people their fortunes and interpreting their dreams', says the *King of Ireland's Son*, 'that is why she is called a Spae-woman.'

When the children have passed the age of six or seven they naturally need much more connected answers to their questions than when they were younger. They wait more consciously for the reply, instead of living in the speech which is the answer. It is at this age, for instance, that children will ask many questions about the heavenly bodies, the nature of the sun and stars, the creation of the world, etc. And ready to supply the answer are numerous Children's Encyclopaedias, Newspapers, Science books, and what not, with beautiful diagrams of the Sun, a flaming ball on a black page, many times the size of the earth, or a man cut in half showing the heart like a pump, the lungs like a pair of bellows, the nervous system like a set of telegraph wires, etc. Whether or no these things are in any sense representations of the truth is not for the moment the question: though it is worth noticing that by the time scientific theories reach popular children's books they are often quite out of date even judged by their own standards.

There will be plenty of time for children to investigate scientific theories at a later age, when they can really understand some of the conceptions on which they are based. For these scientific conceptions arose only at a very definite point in human history, and the mind of a child is not to be compared to the wave of intellectual thinking which historically brought them to birth.

A child between seven and twelve or so has in him much more of the piety and luxuriant imagination of the Middle Ages. To him the stars are not vast spheres incredible millions of miles distant in space; he feels their clear shining beauty as something very close to him. The sun is not a huge stationary mass of burning gasses; its rising each day fills him with a wonderful feeling of joy and thankfulness. The pictures of the heavenly bodies in mythologies are far truer to children than the distances and dimensions of modern astronomy. The Norse people said that wolves swallowed up the sun at the time of an eclipse, and to a child, who has a fine sense of the *devouring* quality of darkness, the nature of an eclipse is much better expressed by such an image than by a diagram of revolving shadows. For in an eclipse it is truly *as though* the wolves devoured the sun, and that 'as though' is, after all, the furthest claim made by the true scientist. Newton did not say that the planets are attracted to the earth by gravity; but that they move *as though* they were so attracted, and it is not his fault that men have made a dogma of a hypothesis.

It is, in fact, of real importance not to give a child scientific conceptions on these subjects too soon. They tend to destroy the vivid feeling and imagination proper to this age; and, because they are received before the child has developed the power of following the thoughts on which they are based, they become matters of faith instead of matters of knowledge. Very few people in their adult years have even the will to investigate the mathematics on which is based the Newtonian planetary system or modern atomic theories. In a sense a scientific age is the most credulous of all ages. A thousand years ago a man could at least say: 'I see the sun move with my own eyes'; but today many a man has to say: 'Somebody proved a long time ago that the sun stands still. I forget exactly who it was, and I don't know how he proved it, but it's a fact all the same.'

When children begin at this age to ask, How a thing is made? It is worth while considering how much of the true explanation has real meaning for them. There are children's books to describe how everything is made, but from such books children often get a very superficial, it may almost be said glib, impression of the work men have to do in the world. Such works are generally illustrated with photographs which give children a very easy picture of various processes, but very little feeling for the real conditions under which the work is done. A few flashlight pictures of miners hacking at a seam, together with a section of a mine with the cage descending, and a child will soon think he knows all about a coal-mine, and turn to the next page to discover how a gramophone works, or what the Great Wall of China looks like. But there is something extraordinarily superficial, muddled, and uncreative about such a way of acquiring information; it is really far better for children to make their own pictures in their mind's eye from living in descriptions they hear of the intense silence under the ground, of men walking to their work for miles in galleries where they cannot go upright, of the dripping of water, etc., etc. In short, they should have some such picture of the inwards of the earth as George Macdonald gives of the interior of a mountain at the beginning of *The Princess and Curdie*. And, above all, the mine should not be an isolated fact, but a knowledge of mining should come as part of the children's general thoughts at the time, in some connection with chemistry, perhaps, or history or geology.

One of the worst results of children's books of the 'How it Works' type is that a child will often collect an extraordinary amount of theoretical information and forget to observe things which come within his own ken. Many children can describe the solar system, but they do not know where the full moon rises, or what planets are in the sky. They know a lot about the assembling of a motor-car, but are very vague as to how butter or cheese or soap is made. It is always best to try to keep younger children's questions as to how things are made to those objects which they can really understand and observe, perhaps by themselves making them. Generally speaking, it is much easier to impart information to children too early than tactfully withhold it until a better season.

But a certain reticence in answering children's questions is of great help in keeping the questioning faculty alive. For it is a sad fact that the power of asking questions only too often fades away as children grow older. It is perhaps a test of whether children's questions have been answered rightly in their younger years to see how profound are the questions they ask when they are older, and if they are readily satisfied with the answers. For by the time they reach a more intellectual understanding towards the age of fourteen they should have a strong desire to probe every question in life to the bottom, and not be lightly satisfied by theory without knowledge. For children of this age there is a deep meaning in that part of the story of Parsifal where, as a young man, he first sees the wounded Knight, but does not ask of him the question he should. Many of the questions which children should have in their hearts at this age will indeed only be answered by life itself. They stand in the threshold of life, and life will answer them; but only if they put to life the right questions.

My second example is taken from vol. 2 no. 3. Again, the same theme of child development sounds forth, now placed within a somewhat different context; but Harwood is now taking the opportunity to deepen the substance of what he is saying so that it becomes apparent that the—more playful—theme of child development relates intimately to the whole drama of human evolution, the mystery of man's creation and the origin of language:

On Words and Phrases

Everyone who has to do with young children will have noticed the extraordinary delight they take in repeating names. To point to an object and repeat its name again and again, often in a tone far purer and more exact than that of the adults from whom the word was first learnt, is one of the great joys of early childhood. Then as soon as he can ask questions, the child's constant 'What is this?' must be satisfied with the name of the thing he has seen—a name which, once heard, he will remember for the rest of his life.

It is a mistake, however, to imagine that this delight in words is merely the delight of recognising objects through the senses. On the contrary, as the very purity and musical quality of the sound would indicate, the little child's experience of words is essentially a poetic one; which means that, like the poet, the child feels an inner, as well as an outer, relation between the sound and the thing. To the poet the words, Moon, flower, rain, are not arbitrary symbols, but the quality of their sound is related in some way to the quality of the things they express. If it be asked in what way the only answer can be that the same formative or creative power produced the thing works also in the moulding of the word. There is ideally a harmony between the word of human speech and the great creative word of God made manifest in the world of nature.

This harmony can be experienced in that fine inner ear with which one listens to music and poetry (for the physical ear hears only the sound), but it can be felt in a more comprehensive way in the movements of Eurythmy. Anyone who practises the movements underlying the different sounds of speech indicated by Rudolf Steiner will feel deeply the relation between the simple sound and its appropriate movement, and will begin to look upon nature with fresh eyes, not as the product of physical forces alone, but as the manifestation in its diverse forms of the creative power of the Word.

The name, then, in its original purity expresses the essence of the thing, and though in the course of time words have become degraded from their original high state, poetry in the different languages can only exist because some element of this creative force is still to be found in them. The languages of earlier peoples are not only more poetical than modern speech, but they are also more associated with power—like a creative power—exercised by means of the word. The charm and the spell, the uttering of the right word to make the occasion auspicious, were an essential and important part of daily life in earlier civilisations. Children still feel this old magic that lies in words. It is wonderful, for instance, to see how they are fascinated by the story of the giving of the first names by Adam in the Garden of Eden. The Lord God brings before Adam in turn all the fowls of the air and the beasts of the field. 'And whatsoever Adam called each creature, that was the name thereof.' But Adam not only knows the names of the creatures, he has also dominion over them—because he knows their names. Young children savour such a story of the first giving of names in a way unknown to adults—unless they understand and appreciate the creative origin of speech.

Folk tales and myths are also full of stories of power acquired through knowledge of the name. Everyone will remember the story in *Grimm* of the dwarf who lent his aid to the miller's daughter by spinning the straw into gold on condition that when she was married to the King she should give him the child that should be born to her. When he claims the child, she must surrender it unless within a certain time she can discover his name. At last one of the Queen's servants hears him singing in the forest 'Rumpelstiltskin is my name'; and when his name is known he is at once in the power of the Queen.

Hearing such a story, young children do not ask why the dwarf loses his power on his name being known; they still feel intimately the primeval power of the word. At a somewhat later age, too, when the children come to learn something of Egyptian history, it makes a profound impression to learn how a man of Egypt distinguished between his names. For at birth he was given two names—a public name by which he was to be known during his earthly life, and a secret name which was to be revealed to the priesthood alone, and by which he was to be called again only when at the moment of death he passed through the gates of the spiritual world. Such a custom signifies much for the knowledge of human evolution. For the secret name was the name of his true ego which at that stage of history could not be incarnated on the earth. It was the time also when the Jewish people could not pronounce the 'unspeakable name of God' because that name contained in it the name of the ego which only descended to the earth with the coming of Christ. Thereafter the 'secret name' of the Egyptians became for the followers of Christ the 'Christian name' which could be openly used. In words also the secret places were made plain and the rough places smooth.

The three stages of childhood described by Rudolf Steiner, and often outlined in this magazine, may be considered from this point of view of words and names. The child in the first six or seven years of his life takes the chief delight in the simple names of the objects around him. It is astonishing with how simple a story such a child will be satisfied. You can tell him of the farmer walking down the lane and seeing the horses drinking out of their trough, the cows lying in the meadows, the pigs in the pig-sty, etc., and then returning home again; and he will be completely satisfied with the almost bare list of names. And you will not be surprised that he is so satisfied if you remember what the experience of the name meant to the earlier peoples of the earth; and that when you see a child sitting on the grass and saying 'Flower, Flower,

Flower' again and again to himself—or rather to the Universe—he is enjoying the flower in an immediate way which is lost to modern adult consciousness. For in the little child, as Rudolf Steiner has said, Body, Soul and Spirit are one, and he experiences the creative spiritual and soul force in the objects of nature around him. The repeating of the name is the affirmation of the spiritual principle which he recognises and enjoys.

But after the seventh year a change comes over the lives of children. They will no longer be content with such simple stories, naming this and that object in which they delight. They begin to look for qualities of the soul in the stories to which they listen. They themselves must feel from the story hope, joy, sorrow, pity (which they readily give), triumph when the bad king comes to a bad end—all the feelings of the human soul presented to their eyes in the pictures of the story they hear. They like it also when the story reveals the soul quality of the kingdoms of nature, the tenderness of the flower, the anger of the sea, the majesty of the lion. For they still feel the physical world around them as the image of deeper powers, not as the ultimate fact of existence. But in passing to the stage when they appreciate the world as pictures they are descending one step further on their descent into matter, following in their small lives the path which the human race has trod in the long ages of history. For in the beginning man lived immediately with the spiritual forces of the world, with the gods; and finally he denied the existence of the Divine, and explained the world by means of abstract laws reasoned out of physical appearances by abstract thinking.

It is this third stage which is reached by children about their fourteenth year; though, of course, it will come earlier if they are encouraged in critical thinking. From this time on children begin to take pleasure in those words in which no picture is inherent, distinctions such as 'cause' and 'effect', 'quality' and 'quantity' begin to engross their minds. At the same time the natural artistic or poetic power which a child may have shown will often become barren. For Body, Soul and Spirit have now become separated in his nature, and the physical world on which the child looks is the physical world and nothing more. He has reached the age when he must begin to learn to 'give back to Nature what we owe' if he is to see the world in its entirety and not merely as the field of purely physical forces.

Whether the adult human being will be able to recover the natural vision and inspiration of childhood will depend on many things. But the greatest help he can have is to have been nourished in the right way as a child; and the thoughts and words of the adults around him are nourishment to the child no less than his physical food. For example, Rudolf Steiner has pointed out how bad it is for a child if his father or mother or nurse use baby language to him; the child cannot himself yet pronounce the names of the objects around him, but it is a true satisfaction to his Spirit to hear them pronounced by those who can. To speak clearly, beautifully, and truthfully, is one of the first things which parents owe their children. Or when the children are older and begin to ask their innumerable questions a wise adult will always try to give his answer in the form of a picture, avoiding abstract words which deny a living process behind what the child sees. A child of seven or eight will perhaps ask, What is a rainbow? And his parent may endeavour to explain to him the process of refraction of light. But it is not 'refraction' which awaked in the child the sudden joy which he felt on seeing the great shining arch, nor which made earlier peoples look upon the rainbow as the bridge between earth and heaven. The colours which arise between darkness and light, earthly darkness and heavenly light, are indeed a bridge between two worlds, and it is a right instinct which makes the child's soul feel something like a revelation of heaven in the shining colours. So it will perhaps be better to answer such a question by means of a story, even though it can, perhaps, only be promised at the time when the question is asked. But the child will cherish it all the more eagerly because of the interval of time. And if you give the child at this time a picture in words of what the rainbow is he will the more easily overcome the stage through which he will almost inevitably pass when the rainbow, like the colours in the spray of the garden hose, is 'only' refracted light.

During all his childhood, when the child's relation to words and names alters so profoundly, there is one word he uses which is of special significance, the one word which for all human beings possesses a different meaning. At about the third year the child for the first time calls himself 'I', a word which has climbed into the high places of language only since the advent of the ego principle in Christian times. Today we say 'I think', 'Je pense', because we feel thinking is a personal activity of our own; but to the ancient Greeks and Romans thinking was something superpersonal, and just as we say '*It* rains', '*it* thunders', so they said 'It thinks in me', δοκεῖ μοι, mihi videtur. Today, however, even as early as the third year a child feels the force of his individuality and calls himself 'I'.

But before he calls himself 'I', he calls himself by the name his parents gave him, and to a child his name—his Christian name—is of great interest and importance. In older times the giving of the name to a newborn child was an event of great importance, and in many stories the name is revealed to the parents in a dream, or by the appearance of an angel. Some parents still have a kind of secret intuition as to what their child should be called, but not infrequently nowadays a name is chosen at random, like the drawing of a lottery ticket. Rudolf Steiner himself often suggested double names for children, and in combination old names often spring into new life. How different, for instance, is the force of the name Michael when associated with the second name Angelo. But the important thing is that the name should be chosen seriously, for a reason which has some deep foundation in the parents' lives and thoughts. For just as the child finds his first relation to the world through the names he calls the things around him, so he finds the first relation to his own being through the name by which he is called. The names of the woods, the trees, the stars and the sun are wonderful gifts given to him by his Mother-tongue, and his mother and father can give him a no less wonderful gift if they can find the right name by which he should be called.

In *The Way of a Child*, which has been continuously in print ever since it was first published, Harwood presented his considered thoughts on the education of children garnered over his years of experience at Michael Hall. The book begins with a striking paragraph which makes it clear how meaningless it is to engage in the task of educating children unless one has an insight into the meaning of adult human existence; and Harwood then proceeds to describe the three soul-forces of thinking, feeling and willing and their foundation in our physical organism. In the following chapter he traces the child's journey of incarnation in relationship to these three soul-forces; and he then examines the problems associated with a premature awakening of the intellect (a theme with which several of his articles in *Child and Man* are preoccupied). The core of the book, in a certain sense, is the long chapter on 'The Heart of Childhood', where Harwood briefly describes the class-teacher years and the historical themes and scientific subjects recommended by Rudolf Steiner as appropriate for the curriculum in the respective years between the change of teeth and puberty. The subsequent chapters look beyond this mid-point of childhood to adolescence and adulthood, when the individual ego begins to identify its true destiny; and there is a separate chapter on the temperaments. A further chapter examines how a school may best be organized in order to implement these insights into child development. The final chapter on 'Education and Society', which contains a clear, succinct summary of Rudolf Steiner's advocacy of the crucial importance of recognizing the individual integrity of, and the mutual interplay between, the three spheres of society, seems no less relevant to our time than to the end of the 1930s, in that—even though the outward circumstances may have changed—the source of the problems besetting the world has not:

> ...a society which does not... recognise that man has become an individual ego is merely a relapse into former conditions of life when individual freedom had no meaning for the majority of mankind. Unhappily in the present [20th] century Europe experienced a very relapse in this respect. The liberal

idealism which seemed to have been gathering more and more strength during the nineteenth century was for a time pretty well exterminated in most countries of Europe, and is now on a highly precarious basis... (*The Way of a Child*, seventh edition, Sophia Books (Rudolf Steiner Press) 2013, p. 89).

As a last example of Harwood's literary contributions to Michael Hall in its pre-war incarnation in Streatham, I shall cite here the words of a quintessentially characteristic poem probably deriving from his years as a Class Teacher:

A Song of King Arthur's Castle

King Arthur's walls are strong and steep,
By Western seas they stand,
Three sides sheer down upon the deep,
And one upon the strand.
And cliff and tower and crag resound
To Hail or Farewell shout,
As on that adamantine ground
The knights ride in and out.

White waves on Arthur's castle wall
And Sun-gold in the spray,
And knights like stars in Arthur's Hall
And he like Sun of Day.

In Arthur's Hall with bread and wine,
The feasting-board is laid,
And they who at that table dine
With Spirit strength are stayed,
While music, like the cleansing sea,
Does so renew their heart,
That who sits down in misery,
In steadfast joy shall part.

White waves on Arthur's castle wall
And Sun-gold in the spray,
And knights like stars in Arthur's Hall
And he like Sun of Day.

The knight that rides from Arthur's court
Rests not save in the field,

Till fiend or foe be all down fought
Or sorest quarrel healed,
And wild men see the armour gleam
As through the wood they range,
And stand and gaze as in a dream,
And feel a blessing strange.

White waves on Arthur's castle wall
And Sun-gold in the spray,
And knights like stars in Arthur's Hall
And he like Sun of Day.

Or when he wrestles, fiend beset,
At midnight hour malign,
He feels the splendour o'er him yet—
Arthur's seven-starred sign,
Then round him shines that castle tower,
And in its might he stands,
And all King Arthur's men with power
Strike battling in his hands.

White waves on Arthur's castle wall
And Sun-gold in the spray,
And knights like stars in Arthur's Hall
And he like Sun of Day.[67]

7. Prelude to Chairmanship of the Anthroposophical Society in Great Britain

Cecil Harwood's connection with the Council of the Anthroposophical Society in Great Britain lay through his teaching and administrative work with The New School in Streatham. At the AGM of the Society on 28–29 January 1928 he had joined the Council as a representative member of the Shakespeare Group of the Society in Streatham; and on 3 March 1928 he was appointed as a member of a special committee whose task it was 'to consider the constitutional questions raised at the General Meeting [of January 1928] and report back to a special meeting of members as soon as possible after the World Conference [on Spiritual Science in London at the end of July 1928]'. The nature of these 'constitutional questions' was not specifically addressed, but they clearly had a connection with the storm-clouds hovering over the Dornach headquarters of the Anthroposophcal Society (as discerned by Daphne Harwood, see above) which were to burst forth in the mid-1930s in a destructive tumult, as will be chronicled later on in view of Harwood's (and Barfield's) close involvement with it. At the Extraordinary General Meeting that was convened on 20–21 October 1928 to consider the Special Committee's Report, the idea of an Executive Council of twelve (as opposed to a Council consisting of representatives of groups) was introduced for the first time; and Harwood was elected to serve on this Executive Council initially until January 1930. It is apparent from the Annual Report for the year 1928 that the Special Committee was unable to arrive at a consensus; and a group of some 63 members (out of a total of around 640)—including about half of the members of the Zarathustra group, which met at Herbert Heywood-Smith's home in Redcliffe Square, South Kensington—had by the time of the EGM separated off from the Anthroposophical Society in Great Britain (AS in GB) to form a so-called Rudolf Steiner Fellowship. The writer of the report offers the following despondent comment:

> When we survey the work of the year 1928 [and it should be noted that this had included the large-scale and successful public World Conference in London referred to earlier and the grandiose Opening Conference of the Goetheanum] we cannot escape the impression that the internal crises through which our Society has passed have definitely affected the development of Anthroposophy in this country. Greater efforts have never been expended; but the effects of misunderstanding, mistrust and fear are paralysing; and, to mention only this outer aspect, many of our most active members have spent

hours and days in dealing with internal difficulties, sometimes—as they them-selves will be the first to admit—on a comparatively unreal basis, where they would otherwise have spent their time and energy in the deepening and in the spread of true anthroposophical life.

However, even during 1928 Cecil Harwood's wider work within the Anthroposophical Society in Great Britain was not confined to his respon-sibilities as a member of the Council; for, amidst his busy life at The New School, from Sunday 14 October he gave a series of nine public lectures at Rudolf Steiner House on the overall theme of 'The Spirit of Man in the History of the Earth'. The course was divided into three groups of three lec-tures entitled, respectively, 'Man in the Bosom of Nature', 'The Descent of the Spirit' and 'The Responsibility of Human Freedom'. On 20 September he wrote a letter about this course 'to the members of the English Society':

Dear Friends,

I was asked last July by the Executive of the English Society to give a course of lectures in the Rudolf Steiner Hall during the autumn, and I have been able during the summer holiday to prepare the brief summary of the lectures enclosed with this week's News-sheet and entitled: 'The Spirit of Man in the History of the Earth'. In such a Society as ours it is happily possible for me to ask quite impersonally for the help of the members in making the lectures known, and it is my hope that the brief summary may be of use in introducing strangers to the scope and general nature of anthroposophical ideas in the field of history. I am well aware that public lectures are only one—and not even the best—of the many ways of arousing an interest in anthroposophy. But I believe there are many men and women in London who would welcome an opportu-nity of hearing in a fairly comprehensive way of a philosophy of history—if it may be so called—which would give them back the clear consciousness of their own manhood, in the face of the confused, degrading and pessimistic beliefs generally accepted today. And for those who have already become interested in anthroposophy the coming together in a meeting may awaken a spirit which will work very strongly for the future of the whole movement.

Many members of the Society will remember as vividly as I do myself the terrible sense of desolation in life which we experienced before we had the good fortune to become acquainted with Rudolf Steiner; when the practice and theory of modern civilisation seemed united to put out the light of the spirit which burned so feebly within us. I suppose the least return which our present gratitude can make is to endeavour to bring to others also the light-ening of the load which has been taken from our own shoulders.

Yours sincerely, Cecil Harwood

51 Angles Road, S.W.16

In the course of the following year (1929) Harwood continued to be in demand as a lecturer. On the 5 and 12 May he gave two lectures at Rudolf Steiner Hall on 'The Education of Children and the Education of Humanity', and on 17 July he gave a lecture at The New School on 'English Poetry and its Relation to Religion and Practical Life'. Then in August he was speaking (probably for the first time) at the Goetheanum in Dornach, first on a 'Historical Subject' in the course of English Week (3–11 August) and shortly afterwards on 'Anthroposophical Education' at the Summer School between 13 and 19 August. His next public lecture of which there is a written record (i.e. a record that it took place as opposed to a transcript or even detailed notes, of which there are none in this period of his life) was in Cardiff on 29 November 1931, when his theme was 'The Religious and Moral Basis of Education'.

Meanwhile, at the AGM of the AS in GB on 25–26 January 1930 not only was Cecil Harwood confirmed or re-elected as a member of the Executive Council but his close friend Own Barfield was also elected for the first time; and they both continued in this role for the remainder of the period covered by this section of the book. Further events of note over the ensuing four years included the publication of Harwood's first article (for Barfield this had already become a more habitual event) in the journal *Anthroposophy* (a Quarterly Review of Spiritual Science)[68]; a course of three lectures by Harwood on 'Aristotle and Alexander: the Birth of a New Culture' at Rudolf Steiner Hall on consecutive Sundays from 2 October 1932[69]; the first performance in English[70] of the Oberufer Paradise Play and Shepherds/Nativity Play at the Christmas Festival, Rudolf Steiner Hall, on 22 December 1933 by the teachers of The New School; an exhibition of children's work at the Town Hall, Haverstock Hill in February 1934, sponsored by the Hampstead Educational Council, at the end of which Harwood lectured on 'Rudolf Steiner: Founder of a New Education'; and further lectures by Harwood, two at the Second Educational Easter Course at The New School, 29 March–2 April 1934, the overall theme of which was 'The Individual in the World Today'[71], and a further talk at the Summer School at Westonbirt in the same year (21–31 August), where he was principally representing The New School.

At this point it is essential—if one is to be able to appreciate the nature of Harwood's preoccupations on behalf of the Anthroposophical Society in Great Britain especially from 1934 onwards—to consider at somewhat greater length the tensions and struggles which were now beginning to come to a head.[72]

The first indication of what was to come appeared in the form of what can only be described as an 'edict from headquarters', namely, the announcement in September 1933 from Dornach that in future any English translations of Rudolf Steiner's lectures were to be confined to a new central organ for English-speaking members throughout the world to be known as the *Anthroposophic News Sheet*. Daniel Dunlop, as General Secretary, vehemently protested about this decree, especially because of the limitations that it placed on anthroposophical periodicals sold to the public (specifically, the journal *Anthroposophy*).

The next step was taken at the Annual General Meeting of the Anthroposophical Society in Great Britain held on 10–11 February 1934. At this meeting, many hours were devoted to a discussion of one item on the agenda, which was formulated as follows: 'To consider the serious relations at present existing between the Headquarters of the General Anthroposophical Society at Dornach and this National Society, and to decide what action, if any, shall be taken.' There were clearly strong feelings about the withdrawal of the permission hitherto granted to publish translations of lectures by Rudolf Steiner. However, the Resolution which formed the outcome of the weekend's deliberations, and which was moved by Owen Barfield and seconded by Harwood's colleague at The New School, Arthur Sheen, also expressed other, and essentially more serious, concerns:

> We, the members of the Anthroposophical Society in Great Britain present at this AGM wish to assure the Vorstand of the General Anthroposophical Society of our earnest desire to co-operate with and support them individually and as a collective body.
>
> We are aware that under the existing administration of the Goetheanum, two members of the Vorstand [these were Ita Wegman and Elisabeth Vreede], recognised as such by Rudolf Steiner, have been progressively excluded from the counsels and active leadership of the Society. We regret that this has been so and welcome the stand taken by the Executive Council of the Anthroposophical Society in Great Britain in co-operating with all sections of the anthroposophical movement.
>
> We confirm and support our General Secretary and Executive Council in an unqualified assertion of our autonomous freedom as a Society to welcome any other members of the General Anthroposophical Society in our midst, and we express our approval of the manner in which they have conducted the affairs of the Society in the difficult events of the past few years.
>
> We desire the General Secretary and Executive Council who have been elected at this meeting [and this included both Cecil Harwood and Owen Barfield] to maintain the freedom of the Anthroposophical Society in Great Britain within the General Anthroposophical Society, while still endeavouring to find a basis of mutual co-operation with the administration at Dornach.

Shortly after this Resolution was sent to the Goetheanum, a proposed motion to change the Society's Legal Statutes at the forthcoming AGM prompted a further Declaration submitted by the Executive Council of the AS in GB[73]; and this was considered at the AGM of the Anthroposophical Society which was held in Dornach on 27–28 March. At this meeting decisions were taken which exacerbated the growing divisions within the world Society, eliciting accusations of inconsistency and failing to practise what one preaches from Harwood and a despairing comment—tempered by a vision of eventual unity—from Dunlop at the news that a majority of members had in effect rejected the plea of the AS in GB's February Resolution that divisive forces should not hold sway within the Society. As the AS in GB, together with other national Societies, supported a so-called Declaration of Will presented to the March AGM on behalf of a minority of members (and specifically two members of the Vorstand, Ita Wegman and Elisabeth Vreede), this meant in effect that it was placing itself outside the wider framework of the world Anthroposophical Society. Thus, for example, the three members of the Vorstand who were by now exercising dominant control (Albert Steffen, Marie Steiner and Gunther Wachsmuth), who had previously made the decision to visit London in May, refused to use Rudolf Steiner Hall for their conference but used another location. The practical consequence of the decision of the General Meeting in Dornach was that an Extraordinary General Meeting of the Anthroposophical Society in Great Britain was convened on 10 June 1934, which confirmed the Resolutions formulated in February and March and sought ways in which to deal with the new reality that the AS in GB was now, whether it liked it or not (and it clearly didn't), 'an independent group of the Anthroposophical Society' which would henceforth itself admit new members as opposed to being a vehicle for their admission to the world Society. (It should be emphasized that there was a much smaller group—carrying the impulse of those that had left the AS in GB in 1928—which continued to have a direct relationship to Dornach. This was known under a variety of different names.)

It is significant that, as a background to these difficult and turbulent negotiations, several articles were published in the journal *Anthroposophical Movement* during this period on the theme of the consciousness soul and the task of England and also Britain as a whole. Prompted in part by Owen Barfield's thoughts on this theme, as expressed in articles published in the quarterly review *Anthroposophy* at the end of the 1920s,[74] Mary Kaufmann (Adams) wrote an illuminating article on 'Human Relationships in the Age of the Spiritual [Consciousness] Soul' which appeared in the issues dated 22 March and 5 April 1934; Cecil Harwood, in an article entitled

'Tendencies to a Threefold Social Order in English History' that appeared in the issue dated 7 February 1935[75], summarized some thoughts regarding the importance of realizing the potential inherent in, on the one hand, the prevalence of English Common Law over Roman Law and, on the other, the commitment and devotion to individual freedom in England through an embracing of Rudolf Steiner's insights into the threefold ordering of society; D.E. Faulkner Jones wrote a thought-provoking article on the theme 'England and the English-speaking Peoples' that appeared in the April 1935 issue; and Owen Barfield wrote a two-part review of Miss Faulkner Jones's book *The English Spirit*—published in June 1935—for the issues dated May and June 1935. It was in the latter issue that the death of Daniel Dunlop, the General Secretary of the Anthroposophical Society in Great Britain, on 30 May 1935 was announced; and it also belongs to this whole theme that in the issue that followed (July—August 1935) there was, in addition to many tributes to Dunlop himself, an obituary note by Dorothy Osmond marking the death of his lifelong friend, the poet A.E. (George William Russell).

By the time of Dunlop's death events in Dornach had proceeded relentlessly to their anticipated conclusion at the General Meeting of the Society on 14 April 1935. Before this AGM in Dornach an Open Letter dated 29 March was sent by the members of the Executive Council on behalf of the AS in GB:

Open Letter

to all members of the General Anthroposophical Society and especially to those Members attending the General Meeting at Dornach on 14 April 1935

The Agenda of the forthcoming General Meeting, published in the *Nachrichtenblatt* of the 17 March 1935, contains proposals for the exclusion of two members (Dr. Ita Wegman and Dr. Elisabeth Vreede) from the Vorstand of the General Anthroposophical Society, for the expulsion from the Society of six other members (Messrs. D.N. Dunlop, George Kaufmann, Dr. F.W. Zeylmans van Emmichoven, P.J. de Haan, Jürgen von Grone, Dr. E. Kolisko), and for the severance from the Society of a number of important Groups, among them the Anthroposophical Society in Great Britain, represented by the undersigned Executive.

The peculiar wording of these resolutions, which speak of 'actions bearing the character of self-exclusion' from the Vorstand, or of persons 'having ceased' to be members of the Society, cannot conceal the fact that the members concerned are to be expelled against their own will and judgment, from the Vorstand and from the Society respectively.

The motions are followed by an explanatory paragraph purporting to outline the reasons for these extreme measures, and making grave and sweeping accusations against those concerned, as of deliberate untruthfulness, or of pursuing for years past, from the responsible positions they occupied in the Society, 'private aims and ambitions of power by every means at their disposal'. Further, a Memorandum bearing on the events of the last ten years in the Society and obtainable through the Secretariat of the Society at the Goetheanum, is announced. This Memorandum, the signatories of which are among the proposers of the motions, became available barely three weeks before the Meeting at which the decisive steps are proposed to be taken. Claiming to place before the members facts upon which a true judgment can be based, the Memorandum, which, as it says at the close, has taken months to prepare, is at the same time avowedly an *ex parte* statement. Incidents to which the signatories attach historic importance and of which, in many cases, they can have had no direct personal knowledge, are described by them without calling in the evidence of the immediate participators, unless the latter were of like mind with themselves.

On the strength of evidence thus compiled and presented, the members assembled in [the] General Meeting are asked to take a decision, the immediate effect of which, if it takes effect at all, can only be to sunder the community created and confirmed by Rudolf Steiner at the Foundation of this Society. By whatever arguments these measures of expulsion are advanced; by whatever legal formulae they seek enforcement; for the members concerned they cannot possibly have the effect of severing them from the Foundation which was laid by Rudolf Steiner in the hearts of all Anthroposophists, at Christmas 1923. The suggestion that a comparatively small number of members are concerned, enhanced on this occasion by the way in which a few individuals are singled out for special mention and punishment, can but create a dangerous illusion in this regard.

No fundamental change in the relation of these members to Rudolf Steiner and to Anthroposophy, only the line they have sincerely taken in the midst of differences and difficulties, the existence of which on both sides is admitted, is the real reason for the proposed exclusion. The difficulties are not solved thereby: they are only evaded. Some among those whose expulsion is proposed—notably the two Vorstand Members, Dr. Vreede and, above all, Dr. Wegman who is also the most severely attacked—stood in a very near relation to Rudolf Steiner and played no little part in the resolves and actions of the time of the Foundation. The recorded words and the remembered deeds of Rudolf Steiner on that occasion are in overwhelming contrast to the decisions we are now called upon to take, which the proposers and the authors of the Memorandum seek to justify by presenting a most derogatory picture of these Vorstand Members, not only of their actions but of their character and motives. The picture thus presented is not the Truth. It does the greatest injustice to Rudolf Steiner himself, and it will not go down in History save to the shame of those who now put it forward.

In justification of these exclusive measures, much is made of the Declaration of Will in which we ourselves (not only Mr. Dunlop and Mr. Kaufmann) took the initiative last year in consultation with members in other countries, and which we signed (with the exception of Mr. L.F. Edmunds, who since February, 1935, has taken the place of Mr. Arthur Sheen on this Executive) as the responsible Executive of this national Society. The negative and destructive light in which Dr. Wegman, Dr. Vreede and other leading members and their activities are looked upon by some of our fellow-members at the Goetheanum, is revealed to the full extent in the articles, paragraphs, motions and memoranda now placed before us. If, in effect, these adverse judgments underlay the treatment—the cold-shouldering, the disdain and even active opposition—which our best efforts and initiatives received increasingly as the years went by, any impartial observer might understand the protest, the assertion of our will and presence which we voiced in the much maligned Declaration and by which we stand today. That Declaration called for recognised differentiation within the one Society. Even the union of already existing Groups in different countries, which is now made the basis of the proposed expulsions, even this free and loose association was only entered into during last summer after our request for mutual agreement and for a place within the Goetheanum had been denied.

We affirm that the measures now proposed, and above all the procedure which has been adopted, are contrary in spirit not only to the Foundation Statutes of our Society but to elementary principles of justice. We shall demonstrate our absolute rejection of this procedure by absenting ourselves from the General Meeting, so far as any official representation of this national Society is concerned. It is to be hoped that members who are still capable of looking upon recent history with some degree of detachment will realise that there must be two sides at least from which the events of the past ten years may be viewed and examined. Not a few of those members who adhere to the present leadership must to some extent be disconcerted at such ruthless methods as are now propounded.

The truth will only now begin to emerge when the two sides of the story are available. Moreover, if and when there is a *will* to settle differences on *both* sides, the way can be found. Is it too late to suggest that there is a better way, leading to work carried on 'in peace and without fighting' in the future? We think there is, and we are prepared to assist in finding it, if given reasonable opportunity and if we find any degree of readiness on the other side.

Finally, we must declare that the motions, if passed by the General Meeting, will receive no recognition from us. We shall continue with our tasks for Anthroposophy inspired by Rudolf Steiner's life-work, on the basis of the spiritual freedom embodied in the Foundation Statutes, and we shall continue to regard the Goetheanm as 'there for *all* members'. In the absence of justice in any procedure, there can be no respect for merely legal clauses. We regard as *invalid* any decision which would make the Foundation Meeting ineffective.

Executive Council of the Anthroposophical Society in Great Britain

D.N. Dunlop, *General Secretary*

M. Wheeler, *Treasurer*

Owen Barfield

Andrew Curtis

L.F. Edmunds

E.S. Francis

G.S. Francis

A.C. Harwood

George Kaufmann

Mary Kaufmann

Michael Wilson

Theodora M. Wilson

After the predictable outcome of the General Meeting of 14 April, Owen Barfield (who edited *Anthroposophical Movement* at this time) felt moved to write—and sign—the following contribution to the issue of the journal that appeared in May 1935:

The Anthroposophical Society

Since the separation of this journal from the fortnightly News Sheet, which is now sent to all Members of the Anthroposophical Society in Great Britain, it has fortunately been unnecessary to refer to matters which are subjects of dissension in the General Anthroposophical Society. I cannot help feeling, however, that there would be a sort of affectation in passing over without any comment at all the fact that the Anthroposophical Society in Great Britain was, on April 14 last, declared by a large majority in [the] General Meeting at

Dornach to be no longer a recognised Group of the General Society, while our own General Secretary, Mr. Dunlop, and Mr. Kaufmann were (with five other leading Members), declared to be no longer Members.

While the identity of the Society which passed this resolution with the Society founded by Rudolf Steiner is no longer admitted, it would, nevertheless, be stupid to make light of this event, idle to pretend that the manner in which it has been brought about does not affect our spirits and tend to sap insidiously our very faith in the power of Anthroposophy to mould character and foster community. I do not feel called upon to expatiate further on the event itself or the long disputes which preceded it, but as editor of an Anthroposophical Journal I do feel disposed to comment briefly on the document entitled *Denkschrift*, 154 pages long, which has been translated into English under the name *Memorandum*, and is, I am told, receiving an extensive circulation among Members in this country and elsewhere.

In truth, comment is difficult enough. What can one say of a *book*, signed by twelve well-known anthroposophists and purporting to give a sort of inner history of the Society for the last ten years, which is, nevertheless, pervaded throughout by a sustained ebullition of personal rancour that would be disgusting even if the facts were as represented? Nor is this the whole of the matter. Those who have not actually seen this astonishing 'White Book' will hardly believe that the plentiful charges which it brings against named individuals (serious charges of more than one of the seven deadly sins) are interlarded with (*horresco referens*) playful, almost kittenish, slaps of sarcasm embodied in epithets, asides, dashes, exclamation-marks and inverted commas. The style in which this affair is conceived and written is to me the most baffling thing about it. It is not content with insinuating clearly and repeatedly that the persons against whom it is directed are unmitigated egoists and liars; it cannot refrain from poking them simultaneously in the ribs; it chucks them under the chin; it taps them archly on the shoulder with a fan and looks coyly away with a side-glance down. I have never met anything like it before and hope never to do so again. Here is one example of the way in which ill-nature, in its anxiety to lose no opportunity of stinging, degenerates into a positive silliness that is unanswerable because it is unintelligible.

On page 96 a Report signed by eight members of the Executive Council of the Anthroposophical Society in Great Britain of a meeting held in Dornach on November 29th, 1930, is quoted in full. This Report contained the following sentence:

'With great earnestness Dr. Wachsmuth placed before the members the picture that had never been absent from the minds of many—the Goetheanum—the needs of the Goetheanum on the physical plane and the liability of the Society for its maintenance.'

On the next page of the *Memorandum* this sentence is described as 'a peculiar example of Mr. Kaufmann's sentimental style'. Nothing more is said of it. Just that. No reason is given for saying it: no inference drawn; no suggestion made. Simply: 'There follows a peculiar example of Mr. Kaufmann's sentimental style'.

I confess that this sort of remark produces in me a great[er] sense of hopelessness than do the pointed, and of course libellous, comments which precede it, accusing the eight signatories to the report of conspiring to deceive the English Members; for this sort of remark appears to me to be not only motiveless, but actually meaningless. I simply do not understand it at all. I follow the grammar and syntax: everything else about it is totally incomprehensible to me. Of what kind of consciousness can it be the expression? One can remonstrate even with malignity. One can respect indignation—and endeavour to avoid irritating it further. One can argue with a person who has lost his temper, for one is at least still in communication with him. But to those who speak as if they had lost their reason at the same time, there is no reply but silence. Incidentally, I happen to have not merely signed, but written this Report myself; but I do not think that is of any particular importance.

As to the facts alleged it requires no legal training, the most rudimentary sense of justice will dismiss this *Memorandum* as worth considerably less than the paper it is written on. If the authors themselves believe what they say (and I must believe that they do), there is reason for a proper judicial enquiry at which both sides would be heard. Meanwhile, calumnies uttered not in the presence of the accused by witnesses who have not stood up to cross-examination are not evidence one way or the other. They are simply mud.

Here at any rate I am concerned with this ill-starred *Memorandum* only from the point of view of the object for which this journal exists, that is, the furtherance through the Anthroposophical Society, founded by Rudolf Steiner, of the spreading of the knowledge of Anthroposophy among English-speaking peoples. Now this knowledge is also spreading in other ways. Rudolf Steiner's books are published and their greatness is such that it cannot fail to be perceived more and more clearly as time goes on. It cannot be doubted that there are already in this country many close students of Rudolf Steiner's writings who take no notice whatever of this Society or any other. It is possible to look, say, fifty, say one hundred years ahead and to ask oneself whether by that time what is now known as the Anthroposophical Society will have anything more than a historical connection with the main stream of Anthroposophical thought in this country. Will it still comprise the main body of the students of Rudolf Steiner's work or will its membership be limited to a small and outlandish sect? If the Anthroposophical Society becomes identified in any way with documents of this amazing description, the answer to this question admits (the English temperament being what it is) of no doubt whatever. When mud is thrown, some of it always sticks. But the most powerful and the only lasting effect of this very very muddy *Memorandum,* so far as England is concerned, must be to render Anthroposophy both ludicrous and odious in all eyes. If it is placed by well-meaning zealots in the hands, let us say, of people who are deliberating whether to join the Anthroposophical Movement or not, then the difficulty will be, not to convince these persons that Herr this did really (or did not really) say this that and the other to Frau so-and-so, and all the rest of it (a question in which they will not be in the slightest degree interested)—the only difficulty will be to reassure them that it is possible to become an Anthroposophist working in association with other Anthroposophists without going completely off one's rocker. Reputations, especially questionable ones, are easy to acquire, hard to dispel. Artillery which destroys the base from which it is discharged is not worth employing, even if it does some damage to the target. Will not the authors, publishers and disseminators of this deplorable document think carefully whether the damage which they hope to inflict on their openly declared enemies is worth the damage which they *must* inflict on themselves, on the name of Rudolf Steiner, on all of us? I do not know whether this is 'a peculiar example of Mr. Kaufmann's sentimental style'. I do know that I mean it.

The month after this article appeared, an Extraordinary General Meeting of the Society took place in London (on 22 June) where the following Resolution was adopted:

The Members of the Anthroposophical Society in Great Britain in Extraordinary General Meeting assembled hereby declare:

1.　The Resolutions passed at the General Meeting of the General Anthroposophical Society held at Dornach on the 14 April 1935, do, in our judgment, violate the principles given by Rudolf Steiner in the Statutes which were adopted at the Foundation Meeting of the Anthroposophical Society, Dornach, Christmas, 1923.

2.　We desire to dissociate the Anthroposophical Society in Great Britain from the general administration of the General Anthroposophical Society by the three leaders who are in charge at Dornach and who have identified themselves with the above-mentioned Resolutions.

3.　We accordingly desire that the Anthroposophical Society in Great Britain, having upheld its existence hitherto as an autonomous national Group in the sense of the Foundation Statutes, shall continue from now onward as an independent Society, to be maintained, so far as in us lies, in the spirit of the aforesaid Statutes and of the Foundation bequeathed to us by Rudolf Steiner. We instruct the Executive Council to prepare for submission to the next Annual Meeting such alterations of our Statutes and Bye-laws as shall give effect to this.

4.   We bear goodwill to Anthroposophists in all countries who may now or at any future time desire to co-operate with us in all anthroposophical work in the spirit of the Foundation Statutes.

Amidst all these difficulties it must have been a heartening experience to participate in the Anthroposophical Summer School at Harrogate (12–23 August 1935), where Cecil Harwood spoke on 'Imagination in the Consciousness Soul'. The event was also attended by many speakers from abroad, including Dr. Wegman, Count Polzer-Hoditz (whose theme was 'England and Bohemia in the Age of the Consciousness Soul'), Dr. Herbert Hahn, Sigismund von Gleich, Maria Röschl, Dr. Vreede, Dr. Zeylmans van Emmichoven, Caroline von Heydebrand, Dr. Karl Schubert, Dr. Kolisko and Dr. Ernst Lehrs (I mention these names to give an indication of the extent to which the AS in GB was not an isolated entity).

The text of the Resolution that was adopted on 22 June, and also of the suitably amended Statutes, Rules and Bye-laws, was included in the News Sheet sent out on 5 February 1936 announcing the AGM and weekend gathering on 24–25 February 1936 at Rudolf Steiner House and Hall. Also included in this News Sheet was an Explanatory Letter from the Executive Council, which reminded members of the reasons why this Resolution was to be presented at the AGM.

The report of the Annual Meeting published in the March 1936 News Sheet confirmed that the Resolution and the associated amended Statutes and Bye-laws were carried at the AGM 'with only a few dissentients'. It is also of interest to note that Dr. Wegman, Dr. Vreede, Dr. Zeylmans and Maria Schindler, the Swiss authoress, were all present at the meeting.

The only observation of significance to make about the AGM held the following year, on 27–28 February 1937, when the major preoccupation was the rebuilding and extending of Rudolf Steiner House, is that both Cecil Harwood and Owen Barfield were re-elected as members of the Executive Council. What could not have been anticipated, however, was the death in September that year of the Chairman of the Executive Council, Montague Wheeler (who was also the architect who had designed Rudolf Steiner Hall and House); and his fellow Council members accordingly nominated Cecil Harwood to take his place.

This appointment was confirmed at the 1938 AGM, which was held in London on 15 January. On the same evening Harwood gave a lecture on the theme of 'The Spiritual Task of England in the Present State of the World'. (There was no report of what he had said, except for the observation that it was 'very inspiring'.) However, it was clearly in the Society's interest that, in Harwood, they had a Chairman who could enthusiastically throw himself into the practical implications of the re-building work that was proceeding apace and which, inevitably—not least because underground water had been discovered—would cost more than expected. On both fronts he was equal to the demands of the task, inviting members to visit the site with him over the AGM weekend and subsequently agreeing to become Hon. Treasurer on a temporary basis (Montague Wheeler had also carried this role and no one else had come forward).

In addition to carrying responsibility for these roles, Harwood gave his particular stamp to a leadership quality that the AS in GB greatly needed at this time when storm-clouds were again gathering over Europe.[76] The following message to members printed in the April 1938 issue of *Anthroposophical Movement* was typical of this leadership quality:

> Dear Friends,
>
> In the present times we must all give anxious and devoted care to the spreading of anthroposophical spiritual thought in the countries where there is still freedom to do so. The Executive Council want to urge members to begin already to investigate what they can do to make anthroposophy better known in the district where they live, during next Autumn and Winter Sessions. We should like to be able, during the summer, to mature a plan for steady, co-operative work in all parts of the country. The good success of the public week-end of a month ago at Manchester will, no doubt, encourage other provincial groups to arrange similar week-ends. We feel, however, that the time has also come when anthroposophy should be heard of in many more parts of London than at present. The membership of the Society is scattered over all London and over all England. It must, surely, be possible for many members, in many districts, to arrange locally public or private meetings where some aspect of anthroposophy could be presented to a fresh audience.
>
> We therefore appeal to members to let us know what they can do in their district, whether by public lectures, drawing-room meetings, or by securing the inclusion of a lecture on an anthroposophical theme in some established and reputable local society. We are convinced that if we can plan a united effort for next year we shall be able to reach many more people who are in reality waiting for the teachings of anthroposophy. It is naturally of great importance that where meetings are arranged there shall be some

opportunity of following the initial interest with an enquirers' group or some other means of developing a sustained study.

Please, therefore, create new opportunities, and let us know what they are, and in what way you would like us to help. We must surely feel in the present time the urgency of developing all the opportunities for the working of spiritual forces which courage and foresight can open out.

A.C. Harwood

The following brief excerpts from the Report of the Summer School[77] published in the September 1938 issue of the same journal testify both to Harwood's many-sided activities on behalf of the Society—and the same issue included a 'Notice to Members' from their Treasurer politely but powerfully requesting prompt payment of membership subscriptions—and also to his greatly valued personal qualities. Thus in addition to leading (together with Caroline von Heydebrand) a well-attended study class on behalf of the Education Section, Harwood was active in a lecturing capacity:

> Mr. Harwood gave a course of three lectures on English Literature which were a delight. He showed how in Chaucer and Langland we have representatives of the southern and northern streams respectively, and traced in what way these streams had united in English literature. He had to make one mighty leap from Chaucer to Shakespeare and thence to the poets of the Romantic Revival, but he was, nevertheless, able to show us how uniquely English literature reveals the development of the consciousness soul. It is to be hoped that, busy as he is, Mr. Harwood will find time to give us more of these lectures.

But then we are also told that Harwood's commitment to the Summer School went beyond making contributions of his own:

> For the second year in succession the Conference has been presided over by Mr. Harwood who, by his unfailing serenity and good-temper, guided us skilfully through troubled waters. His rare capacity for seasoning his own earnestness and that of other people with the salt of a little humour was greatly appreciated, and we owed it to him in no small measure that so many people expressed at the end of the Conference the feeling that it had been a particularly happy one.

Towards the end of 1938—on 8 December, to be precise—another figure who was to play an important part in Cecil Harwood's life and in the life of the Anthroposophical Society in Great Britain as a whole arrived in London. This was Dr. Karl König, an Austrian Jew who had at the last moment made a dramatic escape from Nazi Germany and Austria. König's arrival in

Britain formed part of a general effort by members of the Anthroposophical Society to help members and friends of the anthroposophical movement in Germany and Austria who were of Jewish descent to be welcomed as refugees in Britain (an intention that was specifically circulated through the January 1939 issue of *Anthroposophical Movement*). König had, 'to [his] great astonishment' (as he wrote in his diary), received a letter from the British Consulate in Bern indicating that he and his family had been granted permission to enter the country and to settle down permanently. He never discovered who had made the application to the Home Office on his behalf; but it seems highly likely that Cecil Harwood's friendship with Eric Beckett (who worked in the Foreign Office) and his family connection through his father-in-law Lord Olivier with Sir Samuel Hoare, who was Home Secretary at the time, had a lot to do with it. According to an unpublished memorandum by John Baum,

> Elisabeth Swann (née Lipsker) relate[d] a conversation which took place while she was a student of eurythmy at the London School of Eurythmy in the late 1960s: 'Cecil Harwood once said jokingly to me that of course he was really the founder of Camphill'. He was referring to his quiet help in obtaining permission for Karl König and the Youth Group [his future Camphill colleagues who were at the time likewise based in Vienna] to enter Great Britain. Being an English gentleman he would never have dreamt of mentioning it to Karl König.'

Harwood and König may well have met before through their both having participated in conferences: the World Conference on Spiritual Science in London (July 1928), a conference with a similar theme in Stuttgart (4–9 January 1933) and a conference in The Hague on the Psychology of Nations (31 October – 4 November 1934). However, König formally 'arrived' within the orbit of the Anthroposophical Society in Great Britain only at the AGM held at Rudolf Steiner House on 14 January 1939, when:

> he told us briefly of the work he had planned two years ago in Vienna, which he hopes now through the strange workings of karma to be able to carry out in the north of Scotland where Mr. and Mrs. Haughton's deep interest in the care of backward children and their generous hospitality [are] making it possible for Dr. König to carry out the work previously planned and to have with him many of his original co-workers.[78]

He was, in addition, a special guest as a lecturer at the Summer School in Cambridge (29 July–8 August), having in the June of that year previously become a member of the Anthroposophical Society in Great Britain.

Meanwhile, Harwood—in his combined role of Chairman and Treasurer—was leading a major drive to use the newly available extended facilities at Rudolf Steiner House to the fullest possible extent by, for example, asking for members' help and support for the Whitsuntide Conference at the House from 31 May to 4 June; and in the May issue of *Anthroposophical Movement* an extended accommodation list for members visiting London was published. Plans for the autumn were, however, put into disarray by the onset of war (whether or not Harwood was able to give his scheduled lecture on 24 September to mark the beginning of the autumn term on the theme of 'The Spiritual Basis for Life in the Present Age' is not clear), as stated in the following message from Harwood published in the October 1939 issue of *Anthroposophical Movement*:

> Dear Fellow Members, May I please send you a message of greeting in these tremendous days, in the confidence that we shall not forget each other or the spiritual task which we have been called upon to fulfil. All that had been planned for our Society for the rest of the year is for the moment overthrown; but its foundation is in the hearts of the members, and however much we may be separated and thrust into urgent practical affairs, we shall not forget that what the world needs most urgently of all is the revelation of the spiritual worlds. In different forms, in different countries, will now—has now—come that chaos out of which new life is born. It is for us to be thankful that we do not enter that chaos with unclear minds or wavering convictions; and to hope that the knowledge we share will enable us to work actively in the destiny of our age.

PART TWO

1. The Minehead Years

The move of Michael Hall to Minehead at the beginning of September 1939 had a significance not only for the school but also—because of the vulnerability of Rudolf Steiner House to bombing raids—for the Anthroposophical Society in Great Britain. In both respects, Harwood's presence played a key role throughout the war-time years.

In the October issue of *Anthroposophical Movement* (vol. XVI, no. 10) it was cheerfully announced that the approximately 'hundred and thirty of the children of Michael Hall' had been met with 'the kindest reception from the residents on whom they are billetted' and that 'a large and romantic house on the hill (just above St. Michael's Church) has been secured for the School'. However, as Joy Mansfield describes (see op. cit., pp. 33–35), the whole process was a magnificent example of improvisation. Not that careful plans had not been made; it was simply the case that in war-time nothing could be expected to proceed as had been intended. The 'large and romantic house on the hill', which had previously belonged to the eccentric wife of a rich Belgian Baron, was—while being thoroughly suitable for the school's purposes and had been miraculously discovered when the County Secondary School intended for Michael Hall suddenly became unavailable—almost derelict and needed much work to make it habitable. And yet both teachers and children responded so strongly and remarkably to the common need that, in spite of everything, the term was able to begin only one day late; and the Harwood family was accommodated in a servants' flat at the west end of the house.

There is a brief paragraph in Joy Mansfield's book *A Good School* describing the actual opening of the school on the first day of term in its new home. However, a fuller description—including the words of the opening ceremony—is given in the report in the preliminary (November) issue of a Monthly Journal which Francis Edmunds initiated and edited for the duration of the school's Minehead years. Indeed, he introduced this preliminary issue addressed 'to parents, friends, union members, and others interested in the work of Michael Hall' with a stirring and passionate evocation of the school's educational task at a time of renewed outward chaos and materialistic darkness. He concluded his introduction with the following thoughts:

> In view of the exigencies of the moment, it is time to take stock of what has been done and of what may yet be done. Limiting ourselves more especially to the tasks of education, we shall endeavour to show, in the coming pages of

this proposed monthly issue, how we may truly serve our children, that they, in their turn, may be capable of still greater service.

The riddle of man is before us all. It is our conviction that the solution of this riddle is to be sought only along the paths of exact spiritual science as taught us by Rudolf Steiner. We shall have articles dealing with fundamental problems of human nature, and other articles showing how these problems may be met in education. We shall hope to have articles, also, throwing light on many spheres of human knowledge, and showing how this new light may illuminate and transform what we have to teach to children as knowledge for life.

What was begun in our School magazine, *Child and Man*, we shall now seek to carry further in these monthly issues. It will be our hope that these issues may be a help to many; that they will encourage activity in spreading the knowledge of this education—that this activity may spread further and further afield and on into the future, leading men to a new social era that shall be based, not on conundrums, platitudes and theories, but on a spiritual knowledge of man. We shall be grateful if all those wishing to receive these monthly journals and so to help us to pursue and further this work will kindly write to us.

The report given in this November 1939 issue is unsigned, but it was in all probability written—at least in part—by Harwood, who throughout the Minehead period—and most especially at this early stage—carried overall responsibility for administrative matters at the school. As for the words of the opening ceremony itself, these unmistakeably bear Harwood's distinctive stamp. The writer—whoever it may have been—speaks about the strong spirit of collaboration that lived in the school at the last Summer Festival (with the pageant and the St. John's Fire) to take place in Streatham, the crisis leading to the sudden evacuation from London and the eventual arrival in Minehead of a party numbering a little over 60, although when school did finally open 'we were 150 strong'. The report concludes with a strongly affirmative message that gives expression to the qualities that enabled the very real, initial practical difficulties, including the implications of having lost some 100 children as a result of the evacuation from the school's original Streatham home, to be overcome:

We cannot tell what the future will bring, but this we know, that the work begun by Rudolf Steiner, above all, his work with and for children, was never more needed than it is today. Amidst all the destructiveness that besets us, we have been given a positive, creative task; in the struggle with forces that debase the human being, we have been blessed with a renewed ideal of man. We wish our children to grow up with this ideal in their hearts, an ideal of man filled with the power of Christ. We think with gratitude of all who are standing by us at the present time; of all our parents and friends who are making every endeavour that the work shall go on; we look with the deepest thankfulness to the children who are with us in this strange and difficult time and our hearts long that they shall grow strong to change the evils that would bind mankind. We think with regret of the many children who are not with us today, and shall carry the thought of them with us wherever they may be. We wish to feel, not that we are isolated in this little town of Minehead, but that we have brought something of all England here, and that, from all England will flow to us the help and good-will which alone can carry the work into the future.

And the words of the opening ceremony then followed:

Ceremony for Taking Possession of The School Building At Minehead

(The children, after marching through the town, and up the North Hill, were assembled outside the East entrance of the building. The doors were shut. It is to be noted that the building had not been occupied for several years.)

Leader: Children, you are no doubt very glad to have arrived here at last. Are you glad?

Children: (with a shout at the end of their long journey) Yes!

Leader: Now we must gain entry, and, if we can, take possession of this mansion. Is it your will that we try and take possession of this mansion?

Children: Yes!

Leader: Is it your will that we choose this place for the future home of our School?

Children: Yes!

Leader: Then let us ask one of our champions, let us ask champion Harry to deliver three strokes upon that ancient door. Let us bid him strike.

Children: Strike! (He strikes three times.)

Leader: No reply! Let us bid him strike again.

Children: Strike again! (He strikes three times.)

Voice from within: Who comes to disturb the peace of this ancient place? The windows rattle and the doors shake! The owls go hooting up the chimney! Who is there?

Children: (after their leader)

               We come from afar,

               We follow our star.

Voice: Whence do you come?

Children: From London we come

               To seek a new home.

Voice: London indeed is far!

               I know you what you are,

               Vagrants, wanderers,

               Vagabonds, beggars,

               Begone from this door!

Leader: Sir, your words are harsh,

               We bring you no trash,

               But more goodly treasure

               Than kings may measure.

Voice: Treasure I love—

               Your words do me move:

               Bring me your treasure—

               I'll open with pleasure!

Children: We bring you a treasure

               So fine and so rare,

               The eye may not see,

               Nor the ear may not hear—

               More precious than gold,

               Yet the hand may not hold.

Voice: Aha! I have you there—

               Your treasure is mere air!

               Not thus will I be fooled,

               Begone and seek elsewhere!

Leader: Have you a heart,

               Then know right well,

               The treasure we bring

               Is of Michael!

Children: Thou herald of Light,

               Thou forger of Might,

               Come now to our Call,

               Thou Michael.

Voice: If he be your guide,

               Then open I wide,

               To one and all,

               This house and hall.

               Welcome ye are

               From London afar.

               Here ends your quest,

               Here find you rest,

               Here may you dig

               And delve and learn,

               And goodly reports

               You here may earn.

Doors slowly open. Children enter and file into the Main Room of the house.

Leader: In the name of the teachers and children all,

               In the name of our own dear Michael Hall,

               We thank the powers that have hither led

               Our School to its new home in Minehead.

Leader proclaims: Hence forth be it known

                         Through Minehead Town

                         This house shall men call

                         Michael Hall .

Children: Michael Hall,

                So be it known

                Here finds a home

                In Minehead Town.

(The children were then told how we came to find the house, and something of its history. The ceremony concluded with the saying of the School Michael Verse.)

(An old Celtic Verse)

Thou Michael the Victorious,
I make my circuit under thy shield.
Thou Michael of the white steed
And of the bright, brilliant blade,
Conqueror of the Dragon,
Be thou at my back.
Thou ranger of the heavens,
Thou warrior of the King of All,
Thou Michael the Victorious,
My pride and my guide,
Thou Michael the Victorious,
The Glory of mine eye.

★

Francis Edmunds, who had—in the words of the upper school pupil who later became his wife—appeared in the school 'like a fireball'[79], not only zealously ensured that the Monthly Journal continued to appear with absolute regularity (war-time supplies of paper notwithstanding) until September 1946, when the school community had completed its move from Somerset to Sussex, but also contributed in addition to the editorials also a regular spate of well-researched, full-length articles about Waldorf education, general anthroposophy and the Christian festivals.

In addition to his overall administrative responsibilities,[80] Harwood also made frequent contributions to the Monthly Journal. In the course of the first academic year in Minehead, he wrote a series of articles on child development ('The Threefold Being of Man in Childhood', 'The First Three Years of a Child's Life', 'Children in the Fourth and Fifth Year', 'Children between Five and Seven', 'Children from the Seventh to the Fourteenth Year', and 'Children from the Ninth to the Twelfth Year') in successive issues. However, his name also appears as the author

of other contributions. Here, for example, is a characteristic poem written for the January issue of the Monthly Journal:[81]

O man, lift up your voice,
In you all creatures call,
Then send to Heaven their joys,
Who are the word of all,
O man, lift up your voice.

O man, lift up your hand,
And bring a blessing down,
Beneath the stars you stand,
Dishonour not your crown.
O man, lift up your hand.

O man, lift up your head,
For you are made the stair,
Where Heaven's angels tread
That unto earth repair.
O man, lift up your head.

 Man, lift up your heart
Where God lies sacrificed,
So bear you His own smart,
So lift you up the Christ.
O man, lift up your heart.

For the following, February, issue, he made the following contribution in
honour of Rudolf Steiner's birthday. This is worth including here because
of the insight that it gives into Harwood's ability to relate Rudolf Steiner's
cultural and social ideas to what was going on around him:

The Anniversary of Rudolf Steiner's Birth

Rudolf Steiner was born on February 27th, 1861. As we enter more deeply
into the present war it is both tragic and inspiring to look back on his hopes
for what might have arisen for the world out of the last war, during the whole
of which—a symbol of the aspirations of all mankind—members of pretty
well all European nations were working with him in Switzerland building
together the first wooden Goetheanum.

He was then perhaps the only person in Europe who could foresee with spiritual vision the coming of those vast new inhuman forces which were to plant their hold on mankind during the next twenty-one years; the ideologies, for instance, which like real beings have obtained a demonic mastery over the human mind. Consequently he also foresaw that their menace would only be met if new spiritual forces were released in the world to overcome the demon. Your old sword will not bite into your new dragon.

It is true as Tennyson wrote that:

> ... God renews himself in many ways
> Lest one good custom should corrupt the world;

but the spiritual renewal which can enter the world must enter through the activity of human thinking and the force of human consciousness. Race was once a good custom; nationality was once a good custom; but racialism and nationalism are fast corrupting the world.

For these reasons Dr. Steiner based his hopes for the future not on a better working of existing institutions, but in the formation of altogether new forms of life born out of a new consciousness of the nature of man himself. Consider only that the entity we call a nation was not born out of any conglomeration of existing baronies or boroughs, but was rather something that cut across older feudal institutions and was based on a new sense in the individual of being a Frenchman or an Englishman, etc. The startling nature of this new national consciousness has been well emphasised by Shaw in his play of St. Joan.

In the 15th century came the new consciousness 'I am a citizen of France or England', which superseded the old 'I am a member of the feudal system and of the Roman Catholic Church'. In the 19th and 20th centuries was born the consciousness 'I am a citizen of the world'. This last had its origin in two different sources. Firstly, a large and increasing amount of cultural and scientific knowledge and artistic experience was becoming the common property of everyone; and secondly, economically all nations were becoming interdependent. Every child was taught that the whole world had now to work to produce his breakfast table; though this had not been the case a few centuries before when the little innocent got up in the morning to swill down his hunk of home-cured bacon with his quart of home-brewed ale. The feeling of world citizenship rested on these two opposite poles of life, and had little or nothing to do with the political state, in which national character and customs were most marked and individual, and which was eminently worthy of being retained, not for the unity but for the diversity it introduced into world affairs.

Dr. Steiner therefore hoped and worked for the establishment of new institutions which would embody the cultural life of the individual on the one hand, and the economic life of the world on the other, independent of political states.

Such a step, however, could hardly be made without an advance in the nature of man's thinking about himself and about the world. Intellectual thought can only conceive of things in their physical or logical unity and division, imaginative thought can see the interpenetrating processes which follow different laws and yet harmonise in a unity. Intellectually, a man is bone, blood, muscle, fat—mutually exclusive substances: imaginatively, he is a statue of salt interpenetrated by a column of water and a pillar of fire. Such an advance to imaginative thought Dr. Steiner wanted to bring about in the education of children. But the same advance in the sphere of world affairs would have enabled men to see that the economic and cultural life could follow their own laws independent of the political state, and would have led to a corresponding threefold organisation of economic, cultural and political life.

In actual fact the reverse happened. The whole structure of the League of Nations was such as to place the political element over the other aspects of life; and, for a variety of reasons, economic and cultural life became more and more rigidly contracted within national boundaries. Both thoughts and products had to be stamped with the national mark to secure circulation.

This war has already shown some remarkable contrasts with the last; perhaps nowhere more or better than in the treatment of individual aliens. There is on the one hand a general desire abroad to distinguish between the individual and the system into which he has been caught and there has been no branding of true German culture or banning of German music because we are at war with Germany; and on the other hand there is much talk abroad of ways to make the best use of the world's resources, the better distribution of raw materials etc. Whether these aspirations to an independent cultural and economic life can be helped to grow into a sufficiently mature form to influence a new peace time alone will show. Such an end will not be attained without a new force of creative thought. Whether in education or self-education we can all strive to create that force; and in both spheres Rudolf Steiner is the teacher of the present age.

The April issue of the Monthly Journal (no. 5) featured an article by Harwood on Shakespeare:

Shakespeare and England

It is the common tradition that Shakespeare was born and died on St. George's Day, April 23rd. In the register of the Parish Church of Stratford-on-Avon his birth is recorded in Latin and his death in English—a fitting symbol of the work he has accomplished in the making of the English language, the English character, and the English nation.

Shakespeare's plays as a whole fall roughly into three periods. Amongst the first plays written from about 1592 to about 1598 a very important group is formed by the plays on English History, a group which became something like the history book of the population of London in the days of Elizabeth and James.

What did the citizen and his wife and 'prentice find in this book? Firstly he found a national hero, who is unlike any hero who appeared in history before. Henry V, the plain blunt king who has sown his wild oats, but who is religious withal, who is not offended that a humble subject has promised him a box on the ear, who can act his part in life and yet see it all objectively from without, is the typical bearer of the consciousness which was to create a new age.

Secondly, as he watched the sequence of the plays from *Richard II* through the two parts of *Henry IV* and *Henry V* the ordinary citizen saw the spectacle of a nation, which had been divided by the wars of Scotch, English and Welsh, becoming united in a single resolve: Welshman, Scotchman and Irishman quarrel together in their talk before Agincourt, but in one thing they are united—they are all determined to fight their hardest for the English king.

Thirdly, although the wars were wars of conquest in France—if they were to be histories they could not be otherwise—the plays are full of references to the state of England as an island separated and defended from the continent by the silver sea:

> Which serves it in the office of a wall
> Or as a moat defensive to a house.

The work which Joan of Arc had done towards driving the English out of France had been accomplished, and the separation from Europe, which had been Queen Mary's shame, had become Queen Elizabeth's glory.

Thus citizen, wife and 'prentice learnt from Shakespeare to see England historically and geographically as an independent nation; and, flourishing in that nation, the typical English character. For not only the country, but the individual within it also came to bear the character of an 'island'. First, the Englishman's island is his castle; then his house; and finally his own individual body, through the windows of which he looks on the world and builds up the philosophy based on what he sees through the windows of his five senses.

Shakespeare thus first created the ideal consciousness of the English Nation. What did he pour into the vessel he had created in the second period of his plays? The great Tragedies are the essential plays of this second group of Shakespeare's dramas. In them the individual man, living by the powers of his island soul and isolated from the world of the spirit, is represented in his battle with the life which destiny has brought him. It seems as though the greater the force, the less the success: men who live by the powers of their own ego alone cannot save even their own souls.

Three of these great tragedies have been commonly given an outstanding position—*Hamlet, Lear* and *Othello*. Hamlet is the man who lives by the human power of thinking, but the force of thought fails him and the certainty which he endeavours to attain turns into its opposite—doubt. Lear lives by the pure force of the will: never was there a man who acted in a more arbitrary and unreasonable way, 'the cause is in my will, I will do so'. But the will cannot achieve itself, any more than the thinking in Hamlet: its energy turns into raving madness. Othello tries to live by the passion of love. But this personal passion cannot succeed, either; love is converted into jealousy and hatred, and becomes the bringer of death.

Thinking whose certainty becomes doubt: will whose energy becomes madness: love whose selflessness becomes hatred and murder—such is the fate of the soul which tries to live by its own incarnate ego alone. It is a picture which stands alike for the individual as for mankind. Since Shakespeare's time men have tried more and more to live by the powers of their own unaided human souls. The result which they now see around them is Doubt, Madness and Hate.

Shakespeare does not leave his plays at this point of man's development. Three plays, and three plays alone, belong to the last period of his writings,[82] *Cymbeline, The Winter's Tale* and *The Tempest*. These are the only plays of Shakespeare in which human affairs are brought from chaos to order by the intervention of the spiritual world. It is indeed a crude intervention in *Cymbeline*; but anyone who has seen *The Winter's Tale* well acted must have marvelled at the rebirth of the Queen as a gift returned to mankind from the world of the spirit. It is as though the pure forces of the human soul had been laid up in heaven during a dark and stormy period of earth history, to descend once more in all their heavenly freshness with the gift of healing and sanity to mankind. In *The Tempest*—the last and loveliest of all the plays—Shakespeare shows us a vision of man again achieving spiritual powers and controlling the forces of the elements, Ariel and all his quality. But the vision is only momentary—the time is not yet ripe, and Prospero burns his wand and 'deeper than ever plummet sound' he sinks his book. Thus the picture of mankind with which Shakespeare takes his leave of the stage is that the human soul again enters the world of the spirit, and finds there the healing and wisdom which it needs. The dragon of doubt, madness and hatred is slain and the mission of St. George's Day is fulfilled. St. George is the patron of all England and all Englishmen. England too must fulfil the mission of its patron saint.

★

The following academic year (September 1940–August 1941) was one of remarkable stability for an evacuated school, both in terms of overall pupil numbers and of staff. It began on 5 September with a festive opening of a school hall, which children and teachers had throughout the holidays been working to complete from a converted stable. Cecil Harwood had written a play in four scenes especially for the occasion: 'The play was moving not only through its simplicity of representation but in the way it seized on the actual moment, for it led up through three scenes taken from different periods of English history to the last scene, that of the children themselves at work on the hall and the driving in of the last nail. The theme throughout was the search for that freedom which we associate with the Spirit of Michael—it was, in every sense, a Michael Hall play...' In his Editorial, Francis Edmunds then went on to quote some appreciative words spoken by one of the teachers in the course of his closing speech: 'What more beautiful picture can we have at the beginning of a new school year, a year that will undoubtedly be filled with great trials and difficulties, than this, that in a place that had been abandoned and cast aside as of no further use, a disused stable, out of old boards and rotting nails a stage had been erected on which could be performed the shining works of God, that which can come to life out of the freely-creative spirit of man?'

It must also have been a great source of encouragement that it was possible to report in the October 1940 Monthly Journal that the Teachers' Training Course had re-commenced at the school (with seven regular students). There was, in addition, a successful conference at Easter on the theme of 'The Formative Elements in Human Life and Society' arranged by the Michael Hall College of Teachers. (The Summer Conference at Minehead in August will be referred to in greater detail in the next chapter.)

Harwood continued to contribute to the Monthly Journal during this academic year, although after two further articles on child development ('Children from the Twelfth Year to Puberty' and his two-part article on 'The Birth of Thinking') he passed responsibility for encompassing children of Upper School age (14 to 18) to the tireless Francis Edmunds. Instead, in subsequent issues he wrote a series of articles on other themes pertaining to English Literature and History; and whether he was writing about the fourteenth-century English poets William Langland and Geoffrey Chaucer, Lord Byron (focussing more upon the man himself than upon his poetry) or Robert Owen, he always fully related poets and writers to their historical contexts and these historical vignettes to an overall conception of the evolution of national and human consciousness. Of all these articles, 'The Birth of Thinking'[83], with its vivid discourse about the essential quality of imaginative thinking (as distinct to abstract reasoning), is especially pivotal as a key to what he went on to write over the course of this period. It will therefore be reproduced in full here:

The Birth of Thinking

Puberty is the time when normally the birth of critical intellectual thought takes place. It is a specially important time for modern children, because all modern life is founded on intellectual thinking, and the experience of this type of thought, therefore, comes with great intensity to the children. It also throws its shadow before it, and children will endeavour to experience the world in this way even years before they have the real basis in their physical development for doing so.

The most important thing that a parent or a teacher can realise at this age is that intellectual thought, as we know it today, is not the final end of human evolution, nor has thought always appeared to people of past ages to have the same character as it does at the present time. We conceive of thought as something cold, dependent upon the lifeless brain, and apt to be destroyed by anything like the warm surge of feeling. The old Greek people, however, described thought as existing in the *fire* element, and among the human organs dependent upon the heart—or even sometimes on the liver, one of the hottest of all human organs. It is ridiculous to say that the Greeks were simply mistaken in holding a view so different from the modern one. They had a different kind of thinking, and naturally experienced it differently, even as far as its connection with the physical body.

Rudolf Steiner always insisted that in the crisis which he foretold humanity was reaching, the only fundamental cure for the intolerable illness of mankind was the development of a new type of consciousness; and the first step in this direction he called Imagination—thinking in concrete images, and not in abstract generalisations. It is not surprising, therefore, to find that for the stage of a child's life which he so often characterised as the time of intellectual thought in the child himself, he insists that the character of the teaching shall be Imagination and again Imagination. For it is only imaginative thought that can fertilise the sterile intellectual thinking which children only too easily fall into at this stage of their lives. Every teacher, therefore, in the subject in which he specialises must endeavour to create such imaginative thoughts. We will therefore first of all consider the nature and character of such thought.

First, it is the nature of 'imaginative' thought to be entirely inclusive of everything which concerns the matter in hand. Actually every time you think in concrete pictures you inevitably embrace aspects of the matter which will elude the more selective abstract thought. It is not necessary to depart from the most practical and mundane matters to discover this. Some years ago

I gave the following typical and local example of the distinction between imaginative and abstract thought to a class of older children. Milk bottles had recently been introduced to take the place of the old milk-cans. They were originally sealed with a cardboard disc inserted within the rim of the bottle—no doubt a perfectly good way of sealing a bottle considered alone and on its own merits. Had the inventor, however, perceived with the eye of imagination he would have seen the actual picture of the bottle standing on the doorstep of a London house; he would also have seen the traffic rolling past, he would have noticed the dust blowing down the street, and he would not have failed to observe the dust settling snugly in the little dust trap on the top of the bottle, all ready to fall into the milk itself when Mrs. Jones levered up the disc with a skewer—as she had to do in those almost prehistoric days. Because, however, the inventor did not see these things, but saw the milk-bottle alone and abstractly, much machinery had to be replaced in order that the flush metal top, proof against the accumulation of dust, might replace the old sunken disc.

Another aspect of this comprehensiveness is that the imaginative consciousness will not shrink from apparent contradictions. Rudolf Steiner said there are actually always twelve points of view on any question, and these points of view will not all seem at first to agree. Imaginative thought is always stimulated by such apparent contradiction which preserved thinking from the 'inevitable conclusion' reached by logical thought. An example of such an apparent contradiction may be taken from the history which the children study at this age. Most modern Protestant children find it natural to sympathise strongly with the Protestant revolt from the old Catholic Church. They are on the side of the new progressive faith as naturally (and perhaps as irrationally) as Disraeli was on the side of the angels in the great controversy of ape or angel. It is very good that they should come to sympathise to the fullest and most conscious extent with this assertion of individual conscience and responsibility in its highest and noblest form. But it would be useless to abstract the individual and not see him in the whole European situation in which he existed at the time. It was then that the tables had been fairly turned on the Crusaders, and the Infidel was threatening to invade Europe, as Godfrey and Richard had once invaded Palestine. Once more the old Catholic Church stirred itself, and the Pope called a last Crusade, but a Crusade of defence and not of attack. What was the response? From Northern Europe—full of Protestant religious quarrels and 'texts and aching eyes'—nothing. Only Spain and Austria rallied to the cause and the Turks were driven back again by Don John at Lepanto. Thus was Protestant Europe saved by the very power which it set out to destroy. From the one standpoint it would be easy to condemn what from another standpoint it is only too easy to applaud.

These are fairly prosaic examples of the wholeness of the imaginative faculty, and can easily be appreciated by ordinary thought. A final example will lead us to another stage of imaginative thinking and prepare the way for the next article. Imaginative thought sees the operation of cause and effect in far more subtle ways than is generally the case. The connection between old age and childhood, by which disease in old or middle age can be traced to mistaken education in childhood, is an example from the life of the individual. In the same way in history, what appears in one century is not always to be traced to events immediately before, of which the effect is at once apparent. But just as thoughts arise from past times in the individual consciousness, transformed by their long sleep in the mind, so the character of one historical epoch will often be the result of another epoch far separated from us in time. For there is a sleep and waking also in the whole life of humanity, which is not apparent to ordinary perception and thinking.

In the last number we gave some examples of what was meant by imagination in the teaching given to children over fourteen. The progress in these examples was probably plain. The first step in imagination is to see a thing or event in a complete concrete picture, as was suggested in the very prosaic case of the milk bottles at the door. But once we start seeing life in pictures the question will inevitably arise, pictures of what? For it is the nature of pictures in some sense to represent or express something. There must be something *behind* a picture, so to speak, otherwise it would not be a picture, but only an object (as some supposed pictures undoubtedly are). Not that a picture is a symbol or a photograph—but it is what it is because it is created so by forces which transcend itself. To treat a picture as a thing-in-itself is to fall into the deadly Victorian materialism of art for art's sake. True art exists to express or incarnate the spirit. To take an analogy from portrait painting, a camera will no doubt suffice to establish physical identity but an artist will express what he has perceived of the character, which is the formative power making the features what they are. It is the same with all aspects of life; when we approach them as artists, seeking to find pictures, we will be driven to ask what are the formative powers making the pictures what they are.

The supreme example of such a picture in life—commonly treated as a thing-in-itself—is man. By analogy based on sense perception we can relate man as a thing to the animals as things, placing bone by bone, and organ by organ, and drawing conclusions from the comparison. Such a process, however, can never make man more than a higher animal—which is not only an obviously incomplete view as far as man is concerned, but even absolutely untrue. For we should expect a higher animal to have finer sense-perceptions than a lower one, and to be better adapted to its environment—things which, in point of fact, man has not and is not. But once we begin to approach the human body as picture, we shall have to ask what formative powers have made the characteristic structure of the head, the heart or the limbs; and we shall be led to seek these outside the body itself, just as we seek for the character in something other than the face which reveals it.

It is therefore wonderfully fitting that just at the time when children have entered the deathlike consciousness of puberty, and experience the world merely by 'the light of common day', Dr. Steiner has placed in the curriculum a long period for the study of the history of painting and sculpture which (until quite recent times) means fundamentally the representation of the human form. In such a study the children are bound to look on the human form as picture, expressing in face and gesture the whole stage of human evolution at the time, or the state of soul of the individual. They inevitably see the human form as moulded by spiritual forces, and are saved from materialism in the most crucial place of all, the experience of their own manhood.

Such a study also brings to birth the faculty of imagination which can afterwards have such far-reaching effects on human knowledge by treating as picture what is commonly regarded merely as thing.

No one has been more conscious of the deathlike consciousness of adolescence and the need to spiritualise it through Imagination than the poet and artist William Blake. In all Blake's work he is constantly returning to this theme, with which he really first found his own poetic genius. If the *Songs of Innocence* are read side by side with the *Songs of Experience*, it will be found that the first represents the happy confiding innocent imagination of early childhood and the second the doubts and despairs and disbeliefs of adolescence. The secret is at once revealed by the title pages, in which Blake often gives the key to what is obscure in his writings. One such title page for the *Songs of Innocence* shows a pair of children reading out of a book on the lap of Dame Nature; their backs are turned on the Tree of Knowledge of Good and Evil round which the serpent is coiling itself. The companion picture for the *Songs of Experience* shows two young people bending over a bier on which two dead figures are laid—youth coming to the first experience of death. The poems in the two books are mostly in contrasting pairs. Innocence sees on Holy Thursday the company of little boys and girls like 'multitudes of lambs' flowing beneath the huge dome of St. Paul's; experience sees on the same day 'babes reduced to misery in a rich and fruitful land'. For innocence, 'Where Mercy, Love and Pity dwell, there God is dwelling too', but experience suggests that:

> Pity would be no more
> If we did not make somebody poor;
> And Mercy no more could be
> If all were as happy as we.

The Lamb is the picture of innocence, and the Tiger of destructive experience, and for Blake the great question of life became: Can God be the creator
both of the positive vision of innocence, and the negative view of experience?—'Did he who made the lamb, make thee?' There was no doubt in
Blake's mind that to remain at the stage of experience was to remain with the
forces of death. He was consumed with hatred for the sense-bound thinking
('single vision' he called it) which had produced the knowledge of life represented by John Locke, Newton and Dr. Johnson. This limited knowledge he
called a sleep—the sleep of death. 'God us keep' he exclaimed, 'from single
vision and Newton's sleep'. To this sleep he later gave in his prophetic books
the name Sleep of Ulro, and he made himself the prophet of the power which
would awaken man from this sleep and restore to him again the 'fourfold
vision' by which he would see into the spiritual world. This power was none
other than Imagination which is the force of resurrection planted in the place
of death, the power which for Blake was nothing other than the risen body
of the Christ.

Immediately after the first part of Harwood's article 'Essays in English Literature', where he gave examples of the characteristic alliterative metre in
Langland's great poem The Vision of Piers Plowman,[84] we find another of his
poems written for special occasions. This is his 'Birthday Song'[85]:

Childrens' Birthday Song

Many the stars that stand over the earth,
And the days as the year goes by,
But one star over the place of my birth,
One hour, when first was I,
Looked for the light where the new child lay,
Listened and heard the sign;
And the great sun rose on my life's first day,
And the glory of earth was mine.

Fine things, O Earth you have shown to me,
Fine things from you I have heard,
The laughter of light on the splendid sea,
The song of the covert bird;
And I have dreamed with the dreaming rose
Whose slumber the butterfly shakes,
And wakened and watched with the silent snows
When the whole world watches and wakes.

And once and again in the dance of the days
Leaps out my day and my hour,
And I see above me the one star blaze,
And its presence I feel like a power,
And I cry to that steadfast star I see
'O star, be my light like thine,
The sun in the heavens thy comfort be,
And the Christ on earth be mine'.

★

1942—the middle year of the war—witnessed significant further developments in the life of Michael Hall. One important step was the proposal—announced in February 1942—to inaugurate an 11th–12th Class that autumn, while another was the opening of a new hostel at 'Little Odell', a house with the potential to accommodate about 25 children which had been acquired for the school by one its supporters. (Harwood wrote a verse 'For a New House' for the House-warming, which was recited by the children.) Cecil Harwood continued to be what one might describe as the school's public face (just as Francis Edmunds was the principal spokesman for the College of Teachers). Over the academic year in question this was manifested principally in two ways. Firstly, it was his role in the Developments Committee to notify parents and friends in June of the decision that the school would not return to its Streatham site once the war was over and to inform them subsequently of the alternative possibility then being explored of a 'beautiful estate of just under 300 acres' near Newbury. Secondly, he wrote an article for the May issue of the Monthly Journal on 'Recent Movements in Education'. As it concerns an on-going debate as to the wider social context of Rudolf Steiner schools in this country, Harwood's article is of continuing interest even in the present political climate. However, it will be of value to preface this article with a brief extract from his three-part article about Robert Owen, where he places the familiar (and necessarily very limited) left/right-wing political debate in a threefold social context. This is the concluding section of the third and final part of the article:

> Superficially it would appear that [Robert] Owen's economic theories were in complete opposition to the doctrines of Laissez Faire, which actually won the day in the England of the nineteenth century. But in the nineteenth century especially it is often the case that a deeper unity underlies two apparent antagonisms... In the case of Owen and the Laissez Faire School, the latter held that economic processes alone must determine human life, while the former held that human labour alone created value. What is the point in

which they are united? In the fact that they both deny any effectiveness to the spirit.[86] They recognise no independent sphere of the spirit to balance the economic sphere in which man is immersed; and because there is no polarity to the economic sphere there is no life of rights to hold the balance between the two. The life of rights was in the nineteenth century left to struggle for existence by way of a perpetual battle in the economic sphere itself between Capital and Labour, Trade Unions and Combines, Strikes and Lock-outs. Rudolf Steiner, however—the champion of the spirit—restores the effectiveness of the spirit as a creator of values in the economic sphere itself. He shows that value arises not merely as a result of human labour but through the spiritual thinking-activity of man as well. The man whose spiritual inventiveness creates a device that serves labour is creating value no less than the man who labours with his hands or at the machine. But this value is created not from the economic sphere but from the independent spiritual life of man. And it is for the life of rights to see that every man enjoys conditions of life which give him reasonable access to the spiritual life on the one hand, and to the goods which industry creates on the other. Labour alone does not create value, except for those who believe, like Owen, that man is a product of his environment. Perpetual struggles between Capital and Labour are not the means of establishing human rights, except for those who believe, like the Laissez Faire School, that human labour must enter into industry as a commodity and be bargained for like raw materials. For a healthy society it is essential to have a true conception of man. And this is not possible to even the greatest ethical idealist if he denies the reality of the spiritual world.[87]

The issue of the funding of education likewise cannot be resolved on the basis of economic criteria alone (as continue to provide the context wherein it is debated) but belongs rightly within the realm of the spirit, where freedom holds sway:

Recent Movements in Education

Since the outbreak of the Second World War, a good many new tendencies have shown themselves in the sphere of education, on which it may not be out of place to add some comment. The first and greatest is the enormous advance of opinion towards the socialisation of education and the bringing of all schools within the framework of the State.

Anyone who remembers the arguments brought forward by those who advocate this reconstruction, and is sensitive to the tone which lies behind them, will be struck by the fact that they are chiefly concerned with the social and economic advantages which are said to be enjoyed by those who have been educated in special schools [i.e. outside the State system]. What is in itself a purely educational question is transferred to social and economic spheres. But supposing we could keep the question in the purely educational sphere and ask simply: 'Is it better for this child to be educated in a Secondary School, or a Public School, or—shall we say—a Rudolf Steiner School?'— then we should first have to decide to whom the question should be put. For in such immediate concrete cases we are at once brought up against the contradiction, which Rudolf Steiner often pointed out, between Socialism and Democracy. Socialism would say: This question must be put to the State and the State must decide what type of education it will provide, allowing perhaps for some experimental schools on sufferance. Democracy would say: The object of Society being to secure the maximum amount of freedom for the individual, this question must be put to the parent, who is responsible for his child and therefore has the right to send him to what school he pleases.

If we take the democratic point of view and ask the parents it is obvious that we shall get a variety of answers but that the answers will be practically conditioned by the financial circumstances of the parents. Some will be free to send their children to the school of their choice, others will not. Here is a manifest inequality which is genuinely felt to be an injustice. The Socialist solution is to abolish the inequality by driving every child into the State school. But there is another solution, equally egalitarian and more truly in accord with British individualistic tradition, namely to extend to all the privileges now possessed by the few, to make it possible for all parents to choose, and therefore to have sympathy with, the schools to which they send their children. As long ago as 1855 Disraeli wrote:

'The basis of English society is equality. But here let us distinguish: there are two kinds of equality; there is the equality that levels and destroys, and the equality that elevates and creates. It is this last, this sublime, this celestial equality, that animates the laws of England. The principle of the first equality, base, terrestrial, Gallic and grovelling, is that no one should be privileged: the principle of English equality is that everyone should be privileged.'

We are already very far advanced into the Socialist state, and it will not of course be possible suddenly to establish all schools on a freer basis. But it is possible tentatively to suggest a means by which a beginning might be made. The education of children costs the State or public authority, say, thirty pounds a year for each child.[88] That means that the individual is entitled if he chooses to thirty pounds' worth of educational services each year for each of his children. It will cost the public purse no more for the authorities to say to the individual: If you choose to send your child to a non-State school which has justified itself by reaching a certain size, and existing for a certain number of years, we will pay an equivalent (or possibly somewhat smaller) sum of money for his education in that school, as we have ourselves been relieved from the expense of educating him. I believe that if this could be done an enormous number of people, who at present have to send their children to State schools, would wish to co-operate with an equally large number of teachers who would be eager to found such free schools. In some districts it would come about that the free schools would absorb the State schools; in others they would continue to exist side by side, while in others there might be at first no impulse for a free school at all. But the interest in, and enthusiasm for, education for its sake would be everywhere immeasurably enhanced. For the individual would be exercising the equality of privilege—he would be more a man and less a unit within the State...

One significant feature of the proposed unification of education [i.e. State education for all] is that, in attempting to abolish one form of class distinction, one would in reality substitute another and an even more terrible one. For it is an integral part of the whole idea that there should be different schools for children of different abilities and capacities. You would thus have (as you have already to a large extent in State schools) a class system based on supposed ability instead of on social tradition or money. This is the efficiency view of education: it is assuredly not the spiritual view, or the civic view. It would immeasurably increase that gulf between the more highly and less highly educated which is such a distressing feature of modern life and has led to the dreadful categories 'high-brow' and 'low-brow'. Already the gulf between Public School and State School is being rivalled by the gulf between Secondary School and Elementary School. A division of life based on intellectual intelligence is perhaps the worst from which any community can suffer...

In the Waldorf School—which was a kind of pattern for all schools in the modern age—Dr. Steiner set his face against all such divisions and separations, including the class division. Children of all abilities learnt together—and even in the upper classes where there was naturally more specialisation, certain common cultural subjects, which are the language between soul and soul, were studied together as the common inheritance of all mankind... And rich and poor, aristocrat and plebeian, sent their children together to the school, not because they were forced to do so by the Almighty State, but because they regarded it as the best school they knew of. They were exercising the equality, not of regimentation, but of privilege.[89]

Harwood the story-teller and literary historian was also prominently featured in the Monthly Journals during this academic year. We have a glimpse of his lighter side in his entertaining account of a children's party on 14 February. On a (slightly) more serious note, he wrote a two-part article for the November 1941 and February 1942 issues on 'The

Moral Effect of Stories on Children', describing his efforts to make up stories to help particular children to work through their difficulties (notably a girl who staunchly resisted any form of social engagement and a boy who resorted to stealing sweets in order to win popularity). And then in the July–August 1942 issue of the Monthly Journal we find a full article by him on the theme of the Nordic sagas which—because of its inherent interest and because of what it reveals about Harwood's awareness of these archetypal stories—it has not proved possible to abbreviate or summarize:

Sigurd and Siegfried

A citizen of ancient Athens would have been very surprised if someone had suggested to him that he might be entirely ignorant of the stories of Achilles and Odysseus, but deeply versed in the old Indian myths of Rama, or of Nala and Damajanti. He would have thought it very peculiar to be ignorant of the stories of his own people, and well acquainted with those of a foreign race. Nevertheless such has been the case until recent years of the Northern peoples, who were educated for centuries on the stories of Greece and Rome, but never heard of Odin and Sigurd, of the steed Sleipnir or the sword Gram.

The ancient story of Sigurd or Siegfried, which was in the very blood and bone of our Northern ancestors, has been preserved for us in two different countries and in two different forms belonging to two different ages. In the latter half of the eighteenth century the transcript of the Niebelungenlied was brought to light in Germany.

This is a mediaeval version of the story in which the setting is the castles and forests of Germany, and the actors are knights and kings and high-born ladies. But in the nineteenth century there was discovered in Iceland, still existing in living tradition, the far older version of the Volsung story, where the scene is laid in wooden halls, and the actors are kings of the heroic age— that is, kings who plough their own land and steer their own ships, and build their houses with their own hands.

All children in a Rudolf Steiner school hear the Northern myths and stories from their Class Teacher when they are in the fourth class. But for the tenth class Dr. Steiner wanted a comparison to be made between the two versions in order that the children should understand a very important step in human evolution—the change from love based on family and kin to love between individuals. It is a change which can be illustrated from the stories and history of many countries, but it is particularly striking in the metamorphosis of the Volsung Saga into the Niebelungenlied. Wagner made a blend of both versions in his opera of the Ring through which more people probably know the story than through the noble epic version of William Morris. It may therefore be necessary somewhat to disentangle the two versions in making the comparison between them.

The preservation of the story in Iceland and the Faroe Islands is one of the miracles of history. All the conditions for preserving an ancient tradition seem to be brought together in these remote lands. They are far removed from foreign disturbances, the soil affords only a primitive life, there are long winter nights in which the only entertainment was the saga-man. The miracle was that when far richer lands had so scanty a population they came to be inhabited at all.

Like many other miracles it was wrought by a woman—one who deserves to be as well known as Helen of Troy. Gyda was her name, and she lived in Norway in the ninth century and was exceedingly good to look upon. The fame of her beauty reached Harold, the most important king in Southern Norway, and he sent some retainers to ask her father for her hand in marriage. The maiden, however, told the ambassadors that she marvelled no king had ever thought to put all Norway under his sway. If there was such a one, he might be worth the marrying. The retainers returned in some alarm as to how the king would take the message. But Harold replied that they ought not to be angry with the girl, for she had put something in his mind which he wondered he had not thought of before. He at once took a vow not to shave or cut his hair till he had made himself master of all Norway. For nine years he was called 'Shockhead', but by the tenth he had conquered all Norway and Harold Shockhead became Harold Fairhair. But hundreds of sturdy bonders or farmers, rather than lose their independence, migrated to Scotland and the Northern Islands, and when Harold drove them from there to the Faroes and Iceland. They were pagans still and when they reached the coast the leader cast the sacred posts of the high seat on the waters and built his farm on the bay where the tide and currents drifted them ashore.

We do not know what happened to Gyda, but all unwittingly she had preserved one of the greatest works of human genius, the story of Sigurd the Volsung.

The differences between the stories of Sigurd and Siegfried may perhaps be grouped under three main heads, and to discuss them it will be necessary to epitomise some of the story. The first of these main heads is that the Volsung saga is essentially the story of a family, the Niebelungenlied of an individual. In the former we hear of the ancestors of King Volsung; of the great hall he built round a central tree, the Branstock; of the betrothal of his daughter Signy to King Siggeir; of how Odin, 'one-eyed and seeming ancient', planted a sword in the Branstock at the wedding feast, and Siegmund, Volsung's son, alone could pull it out. We hear of Siggeir's anger when his offer to buy the sword is refused, of how he invited the Volsungs to his house, and treacherously sets upon them, while Siegmund alone is saved by his sister Signy; of how in his old age Siegmund marries Hjordis, but is killed in battle and his sword broken by Odin before his child is born.

We are told how Hjordis takes the shards of the sword, and is carried away as a serf by King Alf to Denmark—and then, and only then, are we told of the birth of Sigurd. All this is entirely missing from the Niebelungenlied, which begins by telling us of a beautiful maiden, called Chriemhild, living in a rich castle at Worms, and of a noble young prince, Siegfried, living in an even richer castle in the Netherlands.

The interest in the family history has entirely disappeared and chapter one begins with the hero and heroine. It is something like the change from Greek tragedy, whose theme was blood guilt descending from generation to generation, to the tragedies of Shakespeare, which deal with the destiny of the individual man. But in two versions of the same story it is a very striking change to observe.

The second significant difference lies in the loyalties which are held up for our approval in the two stories. In the Volsung Saga Signy, married against her will to King Siggeir, is loyal to her brother and treacherous to her husband. She saves Siegmund from her husband and keeps secretly in touch with him when he is hiding away like an outlaw in the forest. She sends him her two sons, as they grow up, to be taught the arts of hunting and war, but both children are frightened by a snake in a meal-bag, which Siegmund tells them to untie, and are rejected as cowards. Finally with the help of the witchcraft of a 'shape-shifter' she visits her own brother in disguise and bears a child by him who later passes the test of the snake and helps Siegmund to avenge the death of his brother and his father. It is Signy who lays the plot for a treacherous attack on her husband, and who, when the attack has failed, enables her brother to escape from the living tomb in which Siggeir has immured him; who counsels him to set fire to the house and destroy her husband and all his tribe. She herself perishes in the flames, triumphant in her vengeance on her husband and her loyalty to her kin.

This theme which begins the story is repeated again at the end. For when Sigurd has been killed and his wife, Gudrun, is married to King Atli, who plans to get the ring-gold from her brothers, Gudrun murders her children by her husband, and helps her brothers against him.

There is no incident sun the Niebelungenlied corresponding to the loyalty of Signy to Siegmund because this piece of family history is not included in the tale of Siegfried. But the consciousness of a new age has completely reversed the loyalties of the tale of Gudrun. For Gudrun (now called Chriemhild) passionately longs for vengeance on her brothers for killing her husband Siegfried, and she uses her marriage to King Etzel (Atli) to invite them to her home over the Danube and spring a treacherous attack on them. We sometimes see the consciousness of an individual completely reversing the facts—with no intention to do so—to get what he desires; here is the consciousness and feeling of a new age demanding—equally unconsciously—the reversal of an ancient story: the old wine is to be put in new bottles and given a new flavour.

This later reversal of the story, however, is already foreshadowed in the Volsung Saga itself. For to wield the sword which the God had brought from Heaven, and to win the gold which the Dwarf has fashioned beneath the earth—this is not the task of the powers which work in the blood and the generations but of the ego itself. Hence comes a surprising and dramatic turn in the story of Siegmund. When Signy bears a child to her brother Siegmund, we expect that this child, born of the closest connection as was common in the ancient world, will prove to be the successor of Siegmund in the wielding of the sword. But it is not so. Sinfiotli dies, and in his old age Siegmund woos Hjordis the daughter of a king over the seas. But another king is already wooing Hjordis, and her father leaves the matter to her free choice. She chooses Siegmund and departs with him; but before she can bear him a child, he is defeated and killed in battle by the rival king, and in the battle Odin himself appears to break the sword he brought to the earth.

Hjordis gathers the shards of the sword, and is carried away a serf by a Danish king who finds her on the battlefield. Thus the ultimate wielder of the sword is not the child born within the Volsung blood, but the offspring of a marriage freely chosen; and he is born an outcast in a strange land with no family or kin to back him. The sword, too, the power by which he achieves his greatness, has to be welded anew before he can use it. Inheritance is useless except when its gifts are re-created by the individual.

Even in the older story, therefore, Sigurd breaks like a comet into a world ordered with all the fixedness of the stars on kinship and blood relation. It is not surprising that in the later version this new force has turned the story inside out, making the crooked straight and the rough places plain.

The third great distinction between the two versions is that in the Niebelungenlied the splendid myth of the Gods has shrunk to a confused and atrophied memory. The tale-teller is in the position of the people who say 'Good-bye' and never know that the words they use once meant 'God be with ye'. He has heard of the sword, but knows nothing of Odin and the Branstock. He brings the gold into his tale, but where is Andvari and Otter and the Dragon?

Siegfried is riding past a mountain one day when a company of men are bringing a store of gold out of a hole in the hill, and 'oddly enough, they were about to share it!' Siegfried seizes the gold from them, and appoints Albrich as its guardian, and Albrich is at one moment a dwarf and at the next a feudal underlord. The tale has become pathetically human, and the divine workings of the Gods are no longer understood.

We are approaching the age when physical things will be the only reality and men will live, or try to live, by bread alone.

Mankind is now emerging from that age, and not one of the least signs of that emergence is the fact that the ancient myths have been rediscovered and people are deeply interested in their significance.

What Rudolf Steiner has contributed so powerfully to this understanding is to reveal the way in which they are related as prophetic imaginations to the coming of Christ. So it is with the Volsung Saga.

For centuries before the birth of Christ we see the principle of individuality arising. The old objective State religious rites, the common oracle and the civic altar, lose their hold on men, and a kind of personal mysticism trickles in little streams down the muddy estuary their receding has left behind. We see this principle becoming more and more earthly; we see it above all in the Roman people where finally the Emperor becomes the God. And at the moment the Christ is born who redeems and spiritualises the human ego, who recognises his father and mother, his sisters and his brethren, not in the family related to him by blood, but in those that do the will of the Father.

What did he say of this power which he brought into the world? 'I come not to bring peace but a sword.' It was the sword which the prophetic imagination of the old Norse people perceived standing in the stem of the Tree of Life for him to take who could grasp it. So Sigurd takes the sword, but cannot use it aright. Brynhild is lost, the gold is lost. For the true wielder of the sword has not yet appeared on the earth, and no earthly man can yet say with St. Paul, 'Not I but Christ in me'.

★

The school continued to expand its numbers over the next academic year (September 1942–August 1943), largely because of the fulfilment of the impulse to extend the upper school provision to what turned out to be a post-matriculation Senior Leaving Class or Twelfth Class, which attracted pupils from other Steiner schools lacking this facility and was, moreover, the only Waldorf Class 12 in existence anywhere in the world (owing to the closure of the German schools by the Nazis). Because no examinations were taken, the pupils followed a curriculum that was wholly based on Rudolf Steiner's indications for that age, and they received a certificate that gave an outline of the syllabus that had been covered. The subjects included Literature, History, History of Art, Music (including its practical applications), Physics, Chemistry, Zoology, Mathematics, Religion, French, German, Latin, Modelling and Wood Carving, Water Colour Painting, Speech and

Dramatic Art, Eurythmy, Bothmer Gymnastics, Bookbinding, Perspective Drawing, Elements of Double-Entry Book-keeping and Shorthand. Harwood's particular areas included—under Literature—'The Development of English Literature to Modern Times and Some European Influences' and—under History—'Main Trends in World History and the Great Cultural Epochs'. He also offered an advanced reading course in Latin from some Classic authors.

Harwood's contributions to the Monthly Journals during the academic year in question were mainly associated in one way or another with history. Only one brief article in the March 1943 issue entitled 'Two Practical Questions' reflected his 'public face' position at the school.[90] A very capable and dedicated group of colleagues carried not only much of the core teaching work of the school but also some aspects which he had formerly been responsible for, such as writing pageants and plays. And yet a brief sentence in the report of the Midsummer Festival in the July - August 1943 issue characterizes Harwood's stature and the nature of his presence at the school: 'Before closing with the traditional Chorus and 'Awake' from *Die Meistersinger*, Mr. Harwood spoke a few words to the occasion, giving added point and meaning to the whole Festival...' It is also of relevance to point out here that his chosen theme in a course of educational lectures given by some of the Michael Hall teachers in Bristol during May and June 1943 was one that reflected the thoughts expressed in his article 'Recent Movements in Education' (May 1942) cited above, namely 'The School and the State' (given on 7 May 1943).

With one exception, Harwood's articles on history were all associated with the history curriculum for Class 10, which entails a review of ancient history extending to the time of Alexander the Great. These articles, which were three in number, appeared successively in the April/May, June and July/August issues of the Monthly Journal under the title 'From East to West'. It is not possible to reproduce these articles here in their entirety, but Harwood's introduction and the general direction of his thoughts may serve to indicate something of the scope and essential purpose of these studies which Rudolf Steiner deemed to be appropriate for 16-year-olds:

> The history curriculum for the tenth class in a Rudolf Steiner School is a review of ancient history as far as the time of Alexander the Great. The fundamental ground for choosing this period is that it corresponds to the development of the children themselves. Alexander, the world conqueror with a passion for knowledge, who founded centres of learning in every corner of the known world and who tried to break down the barrier between East and West, represents the highest ideal which could be attained in a world which

as yet knew not the Christ. In Alexander's time knowledge and power became the possession of earthly man. This is also the experience of the individual child at this epoch of his life history. World history shows him the steps by which this stage in human life was reached.

At the same time, however, it is impossible to teach ancient history without discovering how topical it is. The trend of civilisation was—and perhaps is—still westward, but the West in Alexander's time began to turn back upon the East. Alexander goes in turn to Egypt, Persia and India—the homes of the greatest ancient civilisations, and the problems of East and West, which our own penetration of the East has made so formidable, begin to arise. To know something of the origins of the Eastern mind and character is vital for any new understanding of the East and West today.

Harwood then proceeds to speak of the ancient civilizations inaugurated—'as the tradition goes'—by Manu [Noah] in India, Persia, Mesopotamia and Egypt, dwelling quite especially on the story of Gilgamesh, which, he says, 'shows us perhaps the first occasion on which man becomes puzzled by death'. In the second part of his article, he reflects at some length on the contrast between the *Iliad* and the *Mahabharata*. His comparison is from a certain point of view so arresting that it warrants quoting this excerpt here:

> If... we look at the two epics from the point of view of moral content and teaching, we shall discover an immense superiority in the Indian story. The background of the *Iliad* is the fear and hatred of death, anger, jealousy, fraud, cruelty, the lust to kill, and rancour pursued beyond the grave. The background of the *Mahabharata* is a noble courage rising above the fear of death, generosity, honour, princely behaviour, hatred of killing, the forgiveness of enemies. And if we look a little closer in the stories, we shall understand why this degradation of moral virtues had come about in the time and people of the *Iliad*. For the Greeks had no compelling spiritual tradition behind them [unlike the Indians, as Harwood has already explained]. They were to develop the individual intellectual consciousness; their patron Goddess Athene sprang fully armed from the head of Zeus. But it is a long business for the self-conscious, self-governing individual to develop as fine a behaviour as is to be found in ancient spiritual traditions. It is not easy to found your morality on your own moral intuitions.

The third part of the article describes the transition from the story of Achilles (the Greek hero who is himself contrasted with the more spiritually and morally attractive figure of the Trojan Hector) in the *Iliad* to that of Odysseus in the *Odyssey* and the latter's ability to resist the temptations to abandon full consciousness and thus fall back into states of consciousness which belong properly to an earlier human condition. Harwood then concludes his article as follows:

> Thus it is that as civilisation moves from East to West we see on the one hand the loss of ancient and noble spiritual powers and traditions but on the other the rise of intellectual thought which has made modern life and modern science possible. But the Greeks themselves still stood too near the East to take the content of their thoughts from the material world [as] revealed to sense perception. The process of thought itself was still as vital in them as the old clairvoyant pictures had been in the East. They were translating these ancient pictures into ideas—and to a Greek like Plato an Idea meant a living archetypal force which gives form and meaning to the objects in the physical world. It is a mistake to imagine that the Greeks invented their thoughts out of nothing, that there could have been a Greece without an Egypt, a Persia or an India. Aristotle teaches the doctrine of the Mean, of right conduct being a middle course between two extremes.
>
> But Odysseus sailed between Scylla and Charybdis, long before Aristotle was born. The Ideas themselves were metamorphosed memories of Group souls and the formative forces directly visible in ancient times to clairvoyant sight.
>
> In advancing to conceptual thinking, in using the power of Athene, the Greeks were for the first time making consciousness depend upon the brain and nervous system. It is just in this that there is so remarkable a parallel between the process of thought initiated by the Greeks and the development of their history. The real relation of thought to the brain is not that the brain thinks—how can matter think?—but that the brain substance acts as a reflector to the spiritual activity of thinking, and in this reflecting of the thinking process thoughts become objective and conscious to the thinker. Just as you cannot see yourself except in a mirror, so you cannot perceive your thinking process in which you live just as truly as you live in your skin—unless the brain acts as a reflector and enables you to see your thoughts. The whole of Greek history, however, is itself a reflection—a reflection back into the East of the wisdom which had once lived there, and in the process of reflection that wisdom is metamorphosed into conceptual form.
>
> What impressed the Greeks so much about their own history was that they were able to overcome the East and carry their own form of life and knowledge thither. It began with the half-mythological war against Troy: it was carried further in the Persian wars, when Greek intelligence outwitted Eastern tradition and numbers: it reaches its culmination in the conquests of Alexander, who carried the teachings of his master Aristotle to the homes of the ancient civilisations, to Egypt, Persia and India. It is a great reflecting process carried out on the stage of the world. The history of individual consciousness is writ large in the history of the race.

The Greeks had their own way of recording the fact that the new Western way of thinking was to supersede the ancient Eastern clairvoyance. Plutarch records that they were astonished that two catastrophic events in their history took place in the same year and in the same night. The great temple of Diana at Ephesus—the greatest remaining home of ancient initiation—was burnt down to the ground on the very night on which Alexander the Great was born.

Alexander and Ephesus—conscious thinking and ancient initiation—could not exist side by side in the same world. Civilisation would still move westward but the thought life of the West would lose the power to comprehend the sources from which it sprang. The Greeks could not travel west and conquer the world as the Romans and later Western peoples did. Their task was reflection. Their very harbours look east, their land still preserves that close connection with the East which is to be found also in their thought. But the harbours of England and the Spanish peninsula look west. They were waiting to be used. But the Greeks had first to do their work and fulfil the promise of their own epics, to overcome the traditions of the East and find in consciousness their own soul.

The other article referred to earlier appeared in the September—October 1942 issue of the Monthly Journal (nos. 34 and 35). Entitled 'The Thirty Years' War and the Wars of This Century', it reflects the tragedy that the wars engulfing the twentieth century might not have happened had Rudolf Steiner's advocacy of the threefold social principle, with in particular his insistence that economic affairs should on no account be determined by nation-states but should be the domain of—in Harwood's words—'an independent world-wide economic life', been listened to by the warring powers as they were still embroiled in the closing stages of the First World War. Against this background, the conflict of the Second World War can be viewed not so much as a war between nations but as a battle between such a vision of the world economic order and the tyranny of those political forces seeking to prevent it coming into being. These are the thoughts that are implicit in the latter part of the article. The first part is an account of the Thirty Years War and of the profound changes that it brought about in religious sensibilities and political allegiances:

> After the Thirty Years' War every man was to be free to have his own independent religious and spiritual life, to think his own thoughts, to worship as he wished, or not to worship at all. To the mediaeval mind such a state of affairs would have meant the disruption of society—even our own diarist Evelyn in the late seventeenth century expressed the fear that religious diversity would make law and order impossible. We now know that this is not so; but we must not think that it was easy for this new idea to be born. The Thirty Years' War is the proof that it was not.

Equally, Harwood is saying, it is not easy to see how the further step that he envisages can be born out of the present war; but this is what he clearly advocates at the conclusion of the article:

> Such [dictatorial] politics take no account of the human individual who exists for the State, not the State for him. In outstanding contrast to this way of approaching social questions is that of Rudolf Steiner, who began not with the State, but with man. What he sketched in the threefold state as the right social solution for Central Europe in 1918 we can now see on a broader stage as the need of a world convulsed by war. We may work for it, or we may reject it, but we can no longer deny that it is a view of society which is rooted in human nature itself. It struggled towards realisation in the Thirty Years' War. It is struggling still in our days.

★

Plans had been developed for a post-matriculation 11th–12th Class during the academic year from September 1943 until August 1944; and on the strength of this the school continued to flourish in exile, as it were. By the beginning of the Summer Term 1944 there were over 200 pupils in the school, and there were many applications for the coming autumn (there would have been more pupils had it been possible to open more boarding houses). Harwood's presence would seem to have been comparable to previous years. On 20 January 1944 he opened the festival in celebration of the school's 19th birthday and expressed the hope that by its 21st birthday 'we should be installed in a new and permanent home' (which was indeed to be the case). He also wrote an account in the June issue of the Monthly Journal of the Midsummer Festival. I include it here not least because it is a beautiful example of Harwood's distinctive mixture of gravitas and humour:

The Midsummer Festival

> Every year the Midsummer Festival takes on a different form, the English summers are not more different, the English skies are not more variable. This year saw a practice which has not been followed since the days of Streatham—a full-length play acted by the Tenth Class, whose recent performance of a French play aroused considerable expectation in the audience.
>
> The younger half of the school saw the play first in the afternoon, and then had tea—which means the kind of lemonade which does not mean lemons—in

groups on the terrace. Then came games and side-shows, this year on a modest scale. The queue of serious-faced children waiting their turn for the Fortune Teller was a sight for to see. The faces generally seemed even more serious when they came out than when they went in. Who shall say what frightful destinies had been revealed to them? Then, after some country dances to a small orchestra on the lower terrace, we climbed to the second terrace and sat or stood to watch a fairy tale performed by some of the teachers.

The woodcutter who would not believe in fairies—and whose manners at breakfast left much to be desired—neglecting the most sinister of warnings, cuts down the tree he has been told to spare, and is at once transmogrified into a spider. His little daughter—who does believe in fairies—sets out to rescue her true father with the spider for her guide. A little gnome (who is pulled up the bank by his beard), a fish, a bird, and an old man fishing in a very broad river—which has to be crossed—all play their part in showing the woodcutter's daughter the way. At last the woodcutter is restored to his devoted daughter, and sanity is restored to him. We have no doubt that in future he will believe in fairies, and pay due heed to their warnings.

After the fairy tale play, the younger children went home, and the older ones ate their supper. Then came the second performance of the play.

The actors had now an older audience, who were more understanding of such a play as *Twelfth Night*, though hardly more appreciative—and they warmed to their work. The Duke spoke his opening words richly against the background of a string quartet playing a stately Elizabethan air. How often Shakespeare uses music to create atmosphere where a modern playwright would employ lighting; and nowhere with greater effect than in *Twelfth Night*. Indeed a rich musical quality pervaded all the poetical scenes, in which there was some speaking of pure poetry as exquisite as you will hear in a life time. It would indeed have been difficult for Olivia not to fall in love with so handsome a young man who spoke such beautiful lines so beautifully.

Olivia's household were as riotous a company as anyone could desire to drink with. Sir Toby had a great gusto for the part and a rolling threatening walk which he used with great effect; Sir Andrew was throughout in admirable fooling, not without much subtlety—witness the face with which he listened to the clown's singing of 'O Mistress Mine', half vacant, half conscious of his ale and yet wholly in the song; while Malvolio really managed the difficult task—some have held it impossible—of meriting at once our contempt and our sympathy, our laughter and our tears.

Four of the main characters were changed after the first half of the play, but the continuity was not broken. The new actors had a standard to live up to, but they wisely acted in their own way, and the play was sustained. The piling up of situations in the last act was well-managed on a small stage, and

Malvolio's exit had all the intensity it should have. It was very pleasant to see so many of the minor parts carried off so well, and the singing by the Clown of the beautiful contemporary settings to the songs was most moving. 'A mellifluous voice, as I am a true Knight'.

After the actors had been enthusiastically acclaimed, Mr. Darrell [who had, together with his wife Dorothy, suffered the tragic loss of their only daughter, Bridget, on 14th August 1943, shortly before her twelfth birthday] spoke of the contrast between the happy summer day we had enjoyed together, and the terrible tragedy of the present events in Europe and the world. How could we understand the contrast between this time of light in the year, and this season of darkness in the history of mankind? Only if we could come to see the light which is beyond all light, the light of which Angelus Silesius wrote in the dark times of the Thirty Years' War:

> Who in this mortal life would see
> The Light that is beyond all light,
> Beholds it best by faring forth,
> Into the darkness of the night.

The day concluded with singing, and the singing ended once more with the chorales from the Mastersingers which many old scholars and parents will recollect. When shall we be able to sing them together again round a St. John's Fire? Will it be next year [as indeed it was]? And where will it be? Who can tell? But it is for that happy occasion that we hope and pray.

Harwood made several other contributions to the Monthly Journals during this academic year. For the September and October/November issues he wrote a two-part article variously called 'A New View of England's European Wars' and 'Another View of England's Foreign Wars'. The combined articles present an analysis of English history from the sixteenth century onwards in the light of Rudolf Steiner's view of soul-development from the sentient soul through the intellectual soul to the consciousness soul. The whole article is too long to include here, and in any case the most pertinent part is its concluding section, where Harwood reflects on the challenges of the twentieth century with respect to that country with which England (he refers consistently to England rather than Britain) was then at war:

In the 20 century, England no longer lives in splendid isolation as far as European wars are concerned [he had previously argued that this had been more or less the case since the Napoleonic Wars]. From the beginning of the century it was plain to most people that the new continental enemy was to be Germany. It only remains in this article to ask: Have we in England some inner relation to the soul of Germany at the present time such as we had to the souls of Spain and France when these countries were our paramount enemies [his point here is that at these former times England was going through, respectively, a 'sentient soul' and an 'intellectual soul' phase]? The question is not so easy to answer because we are in the midst of events and even see them obscured by the smoke of battle. But it is important to remember that the great danger, the characteristic vice, of the consciousness soul is to be void of content. The mere conquest of matter has ceased to provide that stimulus to the soul which filled the nineteenth century with the optimism of people confidently striding forward to newer and better things. Nor can objectivity alone do more than observe the processes of life—it cannot create the thoughts by which they are mastered, controlled and formed. There is a universal demand at the present time for more activity of thought. Traditional things, things that previously seemed to settle themselves, or were taken for granted—education, religion, town planning, morals, finance—have all become problems demanding an immense amount of thought and spiritual activity. How simple and straightforward by comparison seem the great aims for which our grandfathers and great-grandfathers fought! The abolition of slavery, mankind suffrage, elementary education for all, prison reform—they are plain objectives which a child could understand. But how are the raw materials of the earth to be got to all who need them as the Atlantic Charter declares they should? How are we to avoid the vicious circle of boom and slump? How is education to raise the general level of culture and the standard of taste? These are not simple questions, they call for much activity of mind, they demand some general philosophy of life before the first beginning can be made to answer them.

It is just at this time, when this general demand on the power of thought is being made, that our enemy is the nation which is pre-eminently the nation of thinkers and philosophers. It does not, perhaps, matter that the nation has, for the time being, abdicated its true function, that the places of Goethe and Schiller are occupied by Goebbels and Rosenberg. The true soul of a nation is not extinguished by a fit of frenzy, however terrible and devastating it may be. We may yet live to be amazed that we have had to fight Germany, just at the time when we are called upon to develop a new faculty to which that country has pre-eminently pointed the way, and to convert the consciousness soul—the soul of the spectator—into the spiritual soul—the soul of the creator. Certainly more and more people today are reading the works of that greatest modern representative of the old cultural traditions of Germany, who caused the title of his first book to contain in its English translation the words *spiritual activity*'.

For the March 1944 issue (no. 52) he wrote an extensive article about the new Education Bill entitled 'The Education Bill and Rudolf Steiner Schools'. Predictably he fulminates against some ideas—sharply at variance with the approach in Rudolf Steiner schools—which already then had become dear to the British Government, such as beginning formal school education at five and persisting in drawing an absolute line at the age of eleven. However, the bulk of his article is a critique of prevalent psychological distinctions between what are seen as being three categories of children (A, B and C), who go respectively to Grammar Schools, Secondary Technical Schools and Modern Schools. I shall again cite the concluding section of this article, as it clearly presents his view of a much better alternative:

> There are several minor reasons also why this segregation is inadvisable. A good many children do not markedly belong to any of the types. Nor have all children declared their type, even by the age of fourteen. I know of several cases of children who would certainly have been classified as type C who have made a most surprising development at the age of sixteen. I do not doubt that the presence of the other kind of children, and the sharing of common lessons with them, has helped them to do so.
>
> This is not to say that in the 'multi-lateral' Rudolf Steiner School there will not be specialisation. There should be, and, but for the war, there would already have been much greater specialisation than has yet been achieved at Michael Hall. We need libraries, engineering shops, kitchens, laundries—and far more specialist teachers. But the picture will always remain of the common study of all children together in the first long main lesson, when they approach the subjects suitable for their age, not only for their intellectual, but also for their moral and cultural content. Then, having made a unity, you can make such diversity as is needful. But, thanks to the unity, the lawyer, the technician and the carpenter will not speak different languages when they meet in the train together. Democracy will become more than voting, it will be the possession of a common cultural inheritance.
>
> It is in this sense that, to the divided humanity and the separate experience of the new education proposals, we oppose a common humanity and a united experience. Happily there are good signs that we shall be allowed to do so. The nation has not yet so far become a State that everything is to be cut to a pattern. And the Board of Education likes to be able to watch experiments for which it need take no responsibility. I do not doubt that the Rudolf Steiner Schools will continue to grow, and I believe that in them the real picture of man can be fostered for the future.

The last major contribution by Harwood during this academic year was his long article on Wordsworth included in the April/May issue of the Monthly Journal (nos. 53–54). This is important because it is an extended example of Harwood writing on a theme arising from English Literature, regarding which he gave a considerable number of lectures—of which no records (other than brief virtually indecipherable notes) exist—and wrote no books (other than his short monograph on Shakespeare).

William Wordsworth

The popularity of anthologies—useful enough in an age when literature has to be taken hurriedly like a meal in a snack bar—is no doubt responsible for the common belief that Wordsworth was a mild and placid soul, who spent most of his life sitting among celandines, or laying on his bed and meditating on daffodils.

Actually he was a man of austere will, who saw the stirring life of his time at a pretty close quarters, who made heroic walking tours and was an active fisherman and gardener, who went through a profound crisis in his inner life, who worked himself to the point of illness, and who was described by Carlyle as 'a man of immense head and jaws like a crocodile's, cast in a mould designed for prodigious work'. He was also a man who, at a fairly early age, discovered that he had a certain task to perform for his generation, and who stayed at that task through the whole of a long life. Unlike most poets, he deliberately set out to be a teacher and a reformer.

What did he set out to teach and reform? He wanted to reform the whole relation of man to nature, and to teach his generation to receive the moral impulses and spiritual impressions which he felt nature could give. In particular, he revolted against the peculiar relationship of man and the natural world which had been accepted in the eighteenth century. Newton, at the end of the seventeenth century, had finally destroyed that time-honoured belief of our ancestors, that the whole universe worked in miniature in man, that the macrocosm reflected itself in the microcosm. Professor Tillyard in his recent interesting book, *The Elizabethan World Picture*, has shown that this belief still pervaded the whole of our life and literature as late as the Elizabethan age. Shakespeare takes it for granted that the planetary forces work in metals and plants, that earthly music is a copy of the harmony of the spheres, that man is composed of the four elements, and catastrophes in the heavens presage and reflect crises in human life, that human society is a copy of divine society, and that each kingdom of nature has its 'king' (how else should it be a kingdom?)—lion, eagle or dolphin, resembling the human king or the sun's majesty in the heavens. When Newton reduced the planets to purely physical bodies motivated by a First Cause and controlled by the laws of gravity, he destroyed all that ancient belief. Man became a unique being, alone possessing feeling, freedom and intelligence, walking about in an alien and mechanised universe.

Yet not quite alien—for so strong is the natural desire to feel some sympathy and correspondence between man and nature that Pope, in his *Essay on Man*, gives an account of human character which is nothing more than Newton's Planetary System in miniature.

> The general order since the world began
> Is kept in Nature and is kept in Man, [Epistle 1,V]
> Two principles in human nature reign
> Self-love to urge and Reason to restrain,
> Nor this a good, nor that a bad we call
> Each works its end, to move or govern all. [Epistle 2, II]

Self-love in the human being corresponds to the First Cause in Nature, and reason to the force of gravity, which keeps the planets in their courses. There is the same order in Pope's man and in Newton's nature. Apart from the correspondence, however, both the poetry and philosophy of the eighteenth century regarded sense-perception as the only link between man and nature. When Locke described the human mind as a *tabula rasa* on which the senses wrote their impressions, poetry took up the tale and concentrated almost exclusively—as far as nature is concerned—on description of what the senses perceived. A work like Thompson's *Seasons*, with its clear and somewhat flat painting of the countryside and its activities throughout the year, provides the type of this descriptive poetry. The mind has become a mirror, and by *reflecting* on what it sees may be moved to emotion, but nature does not directly communicate passions and impulses to the human soul.

Wordsworth's experience as a child was quite different from this. In the wild nature of the northern hills, where he was born and bred, he felt Presences, Beings, Powers. Sometimes he was so exalted in his soul that on his way to school he had to hold on to a gate to keep himself down on earth; the mountains spoke to him like the voice of conscience; the sounding cataract haunted him like a passion.

His first aim was comparatively simple. With his love of nature he had acquired an eye for 'the infinite variety of natural appearances which had been noticed by the poets of any age or country', and he made it his task 'in some degree to supply the deficiency'. He therefore began where the eighteenth century left off—with description. But it was a description of humbler things and based on very different feelings from those which occupied the minds of the descriptive poets of the eighteenth century.

The next step came when Wordsworth met Coleridge, and together the two poets planned the *Lyrical Ballads*. The theory of poetic language which Wordsworth now evolved—that the poet should use, as far as possible, the language of everyday speech—need not here concern us. It was, however, a fairly natural corollary to his main intention which has been expressed by Coleridge in the following words:

'Mr. Wordsworth was to propose to himself as his object to give the charm of novelty to things of every day, and to excite a feeling analogous to the supernatural by awaking the mind's attention... to the loveliness and the wonders of the world before us'.

Here is at once something which goes beyond mere description. The poet is to awaken in the reader the experience of things beyond the senses, which eye has not seen, nor ear heard:

> The light that never was on sea or land
> The consecration, and the poet's dream.

Wordsworth was not left to pursue his aim in peace. The French Revolution took possession of his mind and heart. He travelled in France with the Deputies returning from the First Revolutionary Assembly; he saw in the towns the enthusiasm for the dawning of a new age; he endorsed with his whole being the feelings of that revolutionary friend who, pointing to a poor abject woman pasturing her cow on the grass verge of the highway, proclaimed: 'We are out to put an end to that!' Even when the first atrocities broke out, his faith was not shaken. He was in Paris the month after the September Massacre, and in a magnificent passage of the *Prelude* he describes his conviction that blood will bring blood, that 'the earthquake is not satisfied at once'. But it was not until Napoleon arose, and in place of the free spirit of the early revolution he saw 'an Emperor crowned by a Pope', that Wordsworth's faith broke. His whole life broke with it, and he went into that death-in–life, that negation of all hope and belief, through which, perhaps, all great spirits must pass at one time in their lives. In Wordsworth's case, however, the crisis was particularly acute: for, more than any other man of his time, he had experienced in his personal life, concentrated into a brief span, that darkening of spiritual consciousness which is the story of humanity at large. As a boy he had known spiritual visions; as a youth he had felt the 'shades of the prison house' beginning to close around him; as a man he lost faith even in the human spirit. It was a real death of the soul.

It was his sister, Dorothy Wordsworth, who brought him back to poetry. She awoke in him the old passion, the old faith in himself as a poet and as a man with a mission. But when he began to write again there was a difference. In his earlier poetry, Nature alone is sufficient. Now Nature is not complete without the visible presence of man. Even the majesty of dawn will no longer do alone. We must have:

> Dews, vapours, and the melody of birds,
> *And labourers going forth to till the fields.*

It is interesting to note in Dorothy Wordsworth's *Journals* that the scenes and moments by which she and her brother were most moved were those in which some human feature appears in the landscape, or a human voice greets them in some wild spot almost with the voice of nature itself. The solitary singing reaper, or the woman's greeting on the lonely road, 'What, are you stepping Westward?'—these are the scenes which are 'felt along the blood', the moments of which poetry is made.

This placing of the human being into the scene of nature was only a picture, or visible expression, of a philosophical view of man's relation to nature which Wordsworth, now risen from the death of his despair, had begun to develop. There are two sides to this philosophy. Man must receive from Nature, and in order to do so he must first repress the critical spirit.

Wordsworth refers in the *Prelude* to the time when he confronted Nature as a critic:

> Bent overmuch on superficial things,
> Pampering myself with meagre novelties
> Of colour and proportion: to the moods
> Of time and season, to the moral power,
> The affections and the spirit of the place
> Insensible.

This critical habit he was able at last to overcome:

> I shook the habit off
> Entirely and for ever, and again
> In Nature's presence stood as now I stand
> A sensitive being, a creative soul.

If you are to learn from nature you must develop the mood of pure reception for what she has to offer. It was because he wished to bring this lesson home that Wordsworth delighted so much to paint those simple rustic characters, shepherds, packmen, and leech-gatherers, who were truly receptive of Nature's influences—and for whom he was so much laughed at by Byron and other of his contemporaries.

But this is only one half, and the most obvious half of his philosophy. The other is much more difficult to comprehend. It was not properly understood by his contemporaries, perhaps not fully even by himself. Had it been understood and appreciated, man would not have exploited nature in the way he has done. For this other half lies in the belief that man has not only to receive from Nature, he has something also to give back to her, a debt which he owes, and without which Nature is not complete. You must first be the 'sensitive being', but afterwards you must become the 'creative soul'.

When you have done this you can begin to give back to nature what you owe. Nature is incomplete and imperfect until man restores his debt. That is why the natural scene is incomplete without the central human figure—nature needs man to love her.

From the practical point of view it is plain that Wordsworth was trying to build into his generation a feeling of responsibility to nature. He wanted men to ask not only, 'What can I take from nature?', but 'What have I to give to nature?'

Of course he failed for his generation, and the whole of our modern exploitation of nature is based purely on the question, 'What can I take?'. There are not wanting signs, however, that man is becoming conscious of this terrible one-sidedness in his relation to nature, and begins to feel as well his responsibility to his mother, the earth. We are still far from treating the earth as a living organism as Wordsworth treated it, but without doubt there is a new spirit abroad.

Wordsworth, however, was not a practical but a philosophical reformer. What he reverts to again and again is that *creative* power of the mind which he calls Imagination.

> which in truth
> Is but another name for absolute power
> And clearest insight, amplitude of mind,
> And Reason in her most exalted mood.

This is the power by which we unite ourselves again with the spirit of nature. Nature speaks to us directly when we are children: in growing up we lose the contact with her divine essence; as men there flashes up in us the power of philosophic imagination which enables us to enter again into her mysteries.

Philosophically also, Wordsworth has had a long time to wait for his fulfilment. That fulfilment came, however, with Rudolf Steiner's *Philosophy of Spiritual Activity*, the completely philosophic and reasoned expression of what Wordsworth was trying to grasp by concrete poetical experience. Here also, in a still more wonderful form, we have man torn from nature, receiving only one half of the world from his senses, and restoring the other half through his ability to enter the purely spiritual world of thought—to unite the pure percept with the pure concept.

It is because of this fundamental sameness of their philosophy that in reading what Rudolf Steiner has to say of Nature we are so constantly reminded of Wordsworth. I will conclude by quoting two passages which contain the essence of much of the *Prelude*.

'As long as man gives himself up to his mirror-thoughts about external nature he does nothing but repeat the past. He lives in corpses of the Divine.

When he himself brings life into his thoughts, then, giving and receiving communion through his own being, he allies himself with the element of Divine Spirit.'

'As he quickens the Divine Spirit in himself, he charms it also into the dead and dying matter which surrounds him.'

★

The last academic year of Michael Hall's evacuation to Minehead began with the uplifting news that there were now about 230 children in the school with a growing waiting list. There remained two major unknowns. When would the war end? And: Where would the future home of the school be? Perhaps because of these two uncertainties, it proved all in all to be 'a heavy year in many ways, the heaviest we have had to face since we evacuated from London'.[91]

When these words were written, the first question had, of course, resolved itself (the war ended in May 1945). But the second still had no answer. After the initial exploration of a site near Newbury (referred to earlier) had come to nothing, high hopes had been placed on Ottershaw College near Woking, Surrey; but after the school's offer to purchase it had been accepted by the vendor, in May 1945 the County Council implemented a Compulsory Purchase Order originally drawn up the previous August. The dramatic story of the purchase of Kidbrooke Park, Forest Row, Sussex is not related at all in the Monthly Journals (doubtless everyone was too busy trying to cope and not even Francis Edmunds could find a moment to write about it) and is summarized in Joy Mansfield's book *A Good School* in the form of retrospective reports from the Michael Hall Old Scholar magazine and from a meeting in the summer of 1946 of the Friends of Michael Hall.[92] These dramatic events took place in August 1945 shortly after the beginning of the school's summer holiday; and, because of Harwood's pivotal role in the proceedings, they warrant outlining here. Kidbrooke Park had been investigated as a possible site shortly after the news about Ottershaw College had come through in May, but the initial reports had not been favourable. However, when Harwood and William Mann visited another possible property in Tunbridge Wells, Harwood 'felt strongly urged to go and have another look at Kidbrooke Park' (from the description it would seem that he had not himself visited it before); and despite the somewhat forbidding nature of its current disorder and unprepossessing aspect, he formed the clear conviction that 'this was the future home of Michael Hall'. An offer was accordingly made (by telephone) on the spot and was accepted, subsequently increased because of Francis Edmunds's foresight in single-handedly committing the school to purchasing much of the adjacent land belonging to the estate. What then happened was that the Upper School moved to Kidbrooke Park for the Autumn Term 1945 to make preparations for the exodus of the Lower School from Minehead and for the re-opening of the entire school at its Sussex location more or less to coincide with its 21st birthday (details will follow in part three).

It is perhaps a reflection of this uncertain and stressful period that Harwood did not make contributions on literature or history to the Monthly Journals during the academic year from September 1944 to August 1945. This must also partly have been associated with the coming into force of the new Education Bill on 1 April 1945. In this connection, the thoughtful Editorial—unusually, signed by the Editor, Francis Edmunds - for the June/July 1945 of the Monthly Journal (nos. 67–68) continues to be of considerable relevance to the situation of Rudolf Steiner schools (and indeed of all schools) in this country, now that, through agencies such as OFSTED, State control of education has—despite the good advice of many educationalists—increased to a wholly unwarranted degree. It is good to remind oneself that this situation is of relatively recent origin and arose when the country was gripped by a bitter military conflict; and there is no justification for regarding it as a normal or acceptable state of affairs.

The New Education Bill

On April 1st, the New Education Bill came into force. So much was happening at the time that this fact was scarcely noticed by the general public though it preludes a radical change in the cultural life of this country, a change the effects of which will be felt increasingly as the years go by and long after the great emergencies of the present war are ended. How far the new bill will take effect in all its details, how far it may yet be modified, only events will show, but it means that henceforth no educational enterprise, new or old, can go forward without a good-will passport from the government in power: no school is guaranteed to continue on the basis of its own life, and government policy is liable to shift and change with party influence. Ostensibly the Bill offers greater advantages to all; education is now free to the extent to which the individual is able to receive it; the condition, however, is that it shall be the education the State offers.

Already even State schools, especially the former Secondary Schools, are experiencing a considerable curtailment of liberty; the enterprising headmaster feels that a great measure of his initiative has been taken from him. As for the 'independent' schools, their continuance no longer rests solely on the will of the people concerned, on the founders of these schools, on the teachers working in them, on the parents who send their children to them. We cannot judge of the ultimate effects of the Bill which to begin with may be persuasive rather than coercive. The important point is that the Bill introduces a new era in government control over the educational and cultural life, and that politicians rather than educationalists have the final word. This is no less than a revolution and the wheels do not go back. How are these new measures likely to affect the Rudolf Steiner Schools,[93] if not immediately then by degrees?

Hitherto our schools have started as and when there were a group of teachers there to start them. Often they have made very small beginnings, perhaps no more than a private house that has had to be adapted gradually as the numbers grew. Sometimes there have been friends to stand by at the beginning; generally new friends and supporters have come forward. The teachers have not only been people with scholastic and academic qualifications but have included men and women who, out of their experience of life, have come to feel that work in such a school was their life's task—they have come out of a human impulse and not in the first place professionally and they have often been amongst the best teachers.

It was the responsibility of the group of teachers taking the initiative in starting and fostering such a school to win the interest and support of parents—to convince those around them of the need for schools founded on Rudolf Steiner methods. They have had to work hard, to take personal risks, to make considerable sacrifices, and they have succeeded and won children for their schools. All internal problems, questions of fees, salaries, extensions, the appointment of new teachers, even the training of new teachers, have been dealt with by the teachers themselves. Each school has worked as an entirely separate and independent unit; each has striven to retain maximum freedom of initiative for the development of its methods and ideas; each has sought its own means for the closest possible co-operation with the parents. The only common ground between the various schools has been the common source of inspiration in Rudolf Steiner's teaching. There has been no interference of any kind from outside; there have been no governing bodies of any kind outside the schools themselves; within the schools there have been no headmasters but each has its College of Teachers, co-responsible for all the life and business of the school. There have been instances where a friendly inspection by public educational authorities has been invited; there have been cases where educational authorities have visited us, out of their own interest. These were the simple and open conditions of the past. The tendency throughout the war years has been for Rudolf Steiner Schools to grow; today they are all meeting a growing stream of enquiries and applications. There is every evidence of increasing interest in the work of these schools.

The education has proved to many that it has life in it; out of its own powers it gives hope and promise for the future. This is how things have been. How are they to be now?

To begin with we must expect much closer scrutiny of premises. This will probably be the first major official demand. We may expect a reasonable attitude from the inspection boards, especially so long as there is an actual shortage of schools, but the power is in their hands to say yea or nay. Where previously parents and teachers were content to make do with moderate housing conditions, improving them stage by stage as monetary resources became available, now they may be faced with considerable initial outlays before the means are there to effect them. Thus on physical grounds alone the opening of a new school is likely to be a much harder venture than it has been. Also there will be conditions about midday meals and related problems which all schools will have to meet; this will mean adequate kitchen space, dining space, rest rooms, house staff, and so on.

Another point of control will be in the proportion of teachers to children, or in the maximum number of children to a class. Our work is so many-sided that we tend to have a higher proportion of teachers especially whilst the schools are small. Conversely, our methods make it possible to cope with larger classes—in fact, we prefer big classes. In the Waldorf School [the original Stuttgart school founded in 1919] it was a common thing to have classes of 50 and over. At Michael Hall the largest number we have had in a single class was about 40 and this was not thought to be a hardship. We shall be fortunate if we can have our own way in such things.

Most important of all will be the question of teachers. In choosing teachers we have always judged first and foremost by the *person*. According to our methods we can make no use of youngsters fresh from the universities and training colleges, however excellent their diplomas and degrees. For our younger children especially it is *life experience* that ranks as the highest qualification; we have always looked first for the requisite *human gifts* and only secondly at the academic qualifications. We have sometimes found even that just where a person is best 'qualified' he is most stereotyped and least creative. A trained specialist in a given subject might serve best as a Class Teacher. Someone trained in his younger years in one sphere might do his most fruitful work in another where he can apply his own original and more mature gifts. Or again someone might have natural genius as an educator without any previous training at all, might even come out of the business world or out of some other work to become a teacher. With us it is the will for self-education, for self-development that counts for more than the ready qualification. In a Rudolf Steiner School it is in the appointment of teachers that the greatest freedom of all is called for. But in future it is more than probable that an 'unqualified' person will simply not be allowed to teach. This may not be an insurmountable difficulty in every case; it may, on the other hand, be a serious hindrance in other cases and hampering to free decision and initiative. At any time the authorities may turn round and say: 'We cannot recognise your right to exist as an independent school because such and such conditions are not being fulfilled. We cannot recognise so and so as a teacher because he lacks this, that or the other.' Thus an outside judgment, formed from quite other premises, would be imposed upon the free working within such a school; once such a judgment is admitted there is no knowing where it may not lead.

The officials concerned in such a matter will be doing their duty; within the limits of their function they will be doing what they believe to be the best—but the effects may be disastrous. No one can demand of them that they should interest themselves in the Rudolf Steiner or in any other unorthodox method. They may or may not be so interested. A friendly and interested inspector may be able to help much. Someone more critically inclined may cause considerable complications. Thus, apart from general legislation, local influence may play a big part in regard to any particular school.

These are some of the first implications of the New Education Bill so far as they may affect us in the near future. There will be other difficulties too arising out of the nature of the education itself... [Edmunds goes on to spell out some of the particular strengths of the Rudolf Steiner approach to education and some of the areas of potential conflict with the approach outlined in the Education Bill.]

We have tried to select the salient points where we are likely to encounter increased difficulty. To the difficulties themselves there can be only one answer. Rudolf Steiner education is based on a new conception of man; it is a conception that strives to give man his rightful and meaningful place in nature and in history; it is a profoundly Christian conception in that it seeks to reach the innermost creative forces in human nature; it conceives of man as a threefold being of spirit, soul and body and seeks to relate itself to all three and to teach in accordance with all three; it works for the strengthening of the life of thought, for the deepening and enriching of the life of feeling, for releasing and fortifying the life of will; it works for the individuality of man as the source and mainspring of all social and cultural evolution. There are many today who seek such a conception before all else. Many a parent will have to face the difficult choice of taking the easy way the world offers or the difficult way of his own free judgment. Because our education is not based merely on theory but grows out of life itself and out of the deeper needs of the time we live in, we believe that we shall not lack supporters and that children will come to us.

But we are challenged and we shall be challenged as we never have been yet. The New Education Bill will affect us in two ways; first, by showering material benefits along its own path of extending its form of education to the many, and secondly, by increasing directly or indirectly the restrictions on free endeavour. It is for us to appreciate the good impulses that underlie the former whilst working courageously to counteract the latter. Since we serve a spiritual end we shall hardly be discouraged by outer difficulties. We must be on our guard, however, against a policy that tends to become too protectionist [a word that has acquired other meanings since Edmunds was writing: he means, I think, an over-anxious wish to placate the authorities]—for protection in one sense may easily become prohibition in another, and then freedom is denied in the very act of proclaiming it. That is a moral danger which we may not overlook for a single instant. By freedom we mean above all freedom of self-expression, freedom of initiative. Too much State protection must inevitably lead to the weakening of the forces of individual initiative and then the whole social structure grows weak. The New Education Bill will be a truly progressive measure provided it allows for and even encourages the maximum freedom of choice. Since all parents are tax-payers and have equal rights within the community of the land, it is not unthinkable that at some future time parents will have the right to apply for an educational grant with freedom to choose their school; that would dispose of party politics from the sphere of education and foster a free cultural life. It is something to hope for but it lies far ahead. In the meantime we must take circumstances as they are and persevere in good faith for the truth that we know.

Harwood subsequently echoed the central thought in this article with a brief note in the October Monthly Journal written from Kidbrooke Park on 'Freedom in Education', where he introduced some words on this theme taken from the last chapter of John Stuart Mill's essay *On Liberty* (1859). This is a brief extract from Mill's thoughts on the subject:

If the government would make up its mind to require for every child a good education, it might save itself the trouble of providing one. It might leave to parents to obtain the education where and how they pleased, and content itself with helping to pay the school fees of the poorer classes of children, and defraying the entire school expenses of those who have no one else to pay for them. The objections which are urged with reason against State education do not apply to the enforcement of education by the State, but to the State's taking upon itself to direct that education; which is a totally different thing. That the whole or any part of the education of the people should be in State hands, I go as far as anyone in deprecating...

Significantly, over Easter weekend that year the Michael Hall teachers resolved to strengthen and celebrate their educational work by means of the first Education Conference at the school since 1940. The invitation to participate was shared with parents and other friends. Harwood participated in this conference, which had the theme of 'The Education of the Will', and on Easter Saturday gave one of the five evening lectures entitled 'Education and the Destiny of the Individual': how can education help the individual to discover his true powers and through these powers his special tasks in the world?

Harwood additionally wrote a two-part article (a continuation had originally been planned but it never emerged amidst the pressure of events) on the theme of 'Studies in Rudolf Steiner Education'. This appeared in the December 1944–January 1945 and the February–March 1945 issues of the Monthly Journal (nos. 61–64). This constitutes an essential element in the foundations that he was active in establishing for the future of Rudolf Steiner education in this country. The first part bore the sub-title:

The Background

Every theory or system of education has behind it a background of thought which consciously or unconsciously forms and colours the practical measures which it adopts. The great flogging schools of the seventeenth and eighteenth centuries had behind them a vast respect for classical knowledge, which was to be acquired, if no other means would do it, *a posteriori*. 'A great man', said Sir Roger de Coverley in front of the monument of Dr. Busby in Westminster Abbey, 'he whipped my grandfather; I should have gone to him myself if I had not been a blockhead—a very great man'. The public schools of the nineteenth century were built on a deep sense of imperial responsibility and the call to fulfil tasks for which a steady code of conduct rather than imaginative or intellectual brilliance was necessary. The new Education Act is undoubtedly principally aimed at fitting the individual into the structure of economic society; there is a good deal of lip service paid to the importance of a cultural education but the whole structure of the new schools is based on destinations which fundamentally lead to different kinds of careers.

In the forefront of his new education Dr. Steiner recognised that there would be 'concrete and individual measures in teaching and education'. About these measures it is fairly easy to speak or write. But no one can begin to appreciate the meaning of Rudolf Steiner's education unless he penetrates into the background, which it is not nearly so easy to describe. This is partly because it is profoundly philosophical, and partly because it is so different from anything conceived in any other educational circles today that to speak of it is like throwing down the gauntlet to the whole world of established opinion. And it is not easy to tell the Emperor that he has no clothes. There is certainly a general belief abroad that some fundamentally new impulses are needed not only in education but in life as a whole. As long ago as 1921 Professor J.H. Robinson wrote: 'It is quite true that what we need is education, but something so different from what now passes as such that it needs a new name.' Yet when something appears so fundamentally new that it really fulfils Professor Robinson's postulate, the natural conservatism of the mind asserts itself, and the new thing is not dispassionately examined.

It is easy to gauge the importance which Dr. Steiner himself attached to the background of his education from the circumstance that he devoted to it the very first lecture he gave to the newly assembled teachers of the Waldorf School, and that he again and again reverts to the importance of the kind of thoughts the teacher has in his mind, about the child, about life and death, about the universe. In the first lecture to the Waldorf teachers he describes the main task of education in a most arresting and novel way. He says it fundamentally consists of teaching the children how to breathe rightly!—an idea so strange and unexpected that it fairly takes the breath away.

Such a description of his task would probably suggest to the modern educator, either some form of breathing exercises—which Dr. Steiner was emphatically not in favour of—or possibly some kind of Yoga training, which he regarded as entirely unsuitable to the present age. No school of modern thought has any key to unlock the meaning contained in such a sentence. But, when deeply considered, breathing contains the profoundest mysteries and miracles of our existence.

In the first place breathing continuously brings us into union with the world outside us. When we are in a room with other people we may be thinking our own thoughts, or digesting our own food, but we can never be breathing our own air. The mantle of air is common to all mankind; it is essentially the social element, blowing over the frontiers of all nations with universal benevolence. It is not for nothing that when we are in a tense social situation, when we expect some terrific quarrel to blow up, we feel constricted in our breath, and, if the situation happily resolves itself, we 'breathe freely' again. You can never really 'breathe freely' in the company of people you dislike, or who bore you, or whose intentions you suspect. Who has not found himself drawing a deep breath on shutting the door after an unpleasant interview? But supposing you had such sympathy with all people, such insight into their difficulties and limitations, that no one was really intolerable to you, what would be the result? You would 'breathe freely' all the time. To learn to be social is a way of learning to breathe. To teach children to be interested in each other, to have all sorts and types and kinds of children together in a school, in a class, is one way of teaching them to breathe.

There is, however, another direction of thought which is essential for the first understanding of what Dr. Steiner meant by 'breathing'. Most people today are familiar with the mediaeval picture of macrocosm and microcosm. Indeed Professor Tillyard has shown in a recent book that such conceptions last far into the Renaissance, and that the belief that man is a miniature of the whole universe is an unquestioned article of faith in Shakespeare. This is a belief which it is possible to visualise; one can see, as in a picture, all the forces of the stars, of the planets, the elements, raying themselves into the being of man. But transfer the same thought into the sphere of time and you have something more difficult to imagine, a great rhythm—a cosmic rhythm—and a host of intermediate rhythms sounding their music between the music of the spheres and the little octave of man. It is to those encircling orbits of rhythm that Dr. Steiner chiefly referred when he spoke of the process of breathing.

To take the orbits at their two extremes, he often drew attention to a majestic relation between the movement of the sun and the rhythm of the breath. It was well known even in the ancient world that when a certain moment of the year comes round again, the sun, which, during the twelve months has fallen behind the fixed stars through all twelve signs of the zodiac, does not return to precisely the same point as before, but is actually a little behind that point. It is plain that, in the course of time, all these little distances will slowly cause the sun to traverse the zodiac in a much greater space of time than the yearly rhythm. This time, often called the Great Year, or the Platonic Year, is no less than 25,920 ordinary years. This number, however, has its reflection in every day of our human lives. For the average rate of our breath—one breath to every four heart-beats—is eighteen to every minute, which is 1,080 in an hour, and 25,920 in a day. That the sun should give us in this marvellous way the measure of our constant breath will not surprise us so much if we reflect that it is from the sun that we receive all the other rhythms of our lives; the procession of the seasons; night and day; sleeping and waking—indeed, if we accept the traditional norm of threescore years and ten as the life of man, even the span of our existence on earth, the time during which the sun lags the distance of his own circumference behind the fixed stars, and after which he no longer 'covers' the star under which we were born.

To experience the seasons, or the rhythm of sleeping and waking, in the right way is, then, to learn to breathe rightly.

We should live through the year with the living earth, we should feel the earth becoming more conscious in the cold of winter when all its forces are contracted into it, we should feel it passing into sleep in the summer, when 'the high midsummer pomps come on' which are the bright dreams of the sleeping earth. Or, when we sleep, we should know that we are breathing out into the spiritual world the thoughts and experiences of the day, and breathing in the forces of renewal which can only truly come to us if we are in harmony with the divine powers.

If we give children in their lessons such thoughts as are welcome in the spiritual world, so that they learn to sleep rightly, we are also teaching them to breathe.

Breathing, however, also takes us directly into the sphere of the soul; for the systole and diastole of the breath is reflected in the contrasting experiences of joy and sorrow. When we cry it is on the in-breath; when we laugh it is on the out-breath. Joy and woe are an out-breathing and in-breathing experience both of soul and body. To people of more ancient times, or of more simple [undeveloped] countries today, it was and is as necessary to cry as to laugh. 'When they had taken their fill of sweet lamenting' is a constantly recurring line in Homer; the keening in Ireland may express genuine sorrow, but it is a sorrow which the people 'enjoy', as a tragedy or a piece of mournful music is enjoyed, not an experience they run away from.

It is most important for children to live in this alternation of sadness and joy, as indeed their natural instinct—playing weddings and funerals—prompts them to do. We have forgotten this today. We laugh, for instance, at the pathetic passages in Dickens, and they are no doubt overdone. But Dickens and his contemporaries were right. They could no more laugh without sometimes crying than they could breathe out and not in.

To learn in a childlike way to experience these contrasting moods is also to learn to breathe rightly, to be in harmony with the world.

> Joy and woe are woven fine,
> A clothing for the soul divine,
> And when this we rightly know,
> Safely through the world we go.

When we think of in-breathing and out-breathing, our thoughts also turn to birth and death. The first breath we draw at our birth is an in-breath; when the spirit departs from the body at death, we breathe out. It is not an accident that in Greek and Latin the words *pneuma* and *spiritus* mean both spirit and breath. We breathe in at birth—and immediately we begin to cry: we breathe out at death, and, if our life has been a worthy one, we shall do so, if not with actual mirth, at least with a happiness and serenity akin to it. This has been beautifully expressed in a poem of the seventeenth century.

> On parent knees, a naked new-born child,
> Weeping thou sat'st while all around thee smiled;
> So live, that sinking to thy life's last sleep,
> Calm thou may'st smile, whilst all around thee weep.

The picture of earthly life as an in-breathing of the soul from pre-existence and an out-breathing again into the spiritual world is a very ancient one, familiar both in the Eastern and Mediterranean world, where it was still taught by Plato. It was obscured in Europe with the coming of Christianity which, for its own good reasons, concentrated men's thoughts exclusively on the life after death. This was no doubt due to the moral impulse which the Christian Church wished to bring into the world; but it inevitably produced a vein of egotism. Man spent his life preparing for a happier state in the future, not putting right unhappy relationships and imperfections which may have been the consequence of his misdeeds in the past. The founding of charities for the singing of Masses exclusively for the soul of the departed shows how far this one-sided thought about the soul would go. It was the final culmination of that conception of the soul which looked only to the life after death. The living were to be harnessed to the work of securing the happiness of the souls of the dead.

But from the sixteenth century onward here and there the thought and experience of pre-existence began to appear again.

Wordsworth expressed it magnificently in his famous *Ode on the Intimations of Immortality*, and though in his old age, when he had become an orthodox High-Churchman, he claimed that he was only expressing a poetical idea, there is no doubt that when he wrote the Ode pre-existence was not merely a belief but an experience to him. Yet the belief has never become effective in life generally; and in education the fundamental aim is still to draw capacities out of children (the highly doubtful derivation of the Latin *educo* is often quoted in this connection), never to enable the soul and spirit to enter properly into the body.

Now to draw out is an important thing to do; but it is only one half of the matter; and Dr. Steiner wanted his teachers to draw in as well: not only to bring children up but also to bring them down.

That is why the Curriculum for the first seven years of school life always proceeds from the spiritual to the material, from movement to stillness, from the living to the dead. It is part of the process of incarnation, the slow breathing in of the soul and spirit in order that they may permeate the whole man.

There is much interest in the West today in the ancient Yoga practices of the East. Yoga also teaches how to breathe; but it begins with the training of the physical breath so that from a controlled breathing spiritual experience may arise.

The effect of such breathing exercises is to loosen the psyche from the body, and was an important training for the ancient East. But it is also the opposite of what Dr. Steiner himself wished for the children of the present age. Work rightly with the rhythms of soul and spirit and they will then penetrate the body and bring about a right breathing. Birth and death, night and day, the seasons of the year, sleeping and waking, joy and sorrow, remembering and forgetting—experience these rightly and you will breathe in full measure the breath of life.

In the second part of his article, Harwood takes up a particular aspect of the breathing process, namely, our faculty of perception, which likewise is of a twofold nature:

The Polarity of Intellect and Senses

The idea—it might better be called the picture—of *polarity* is an essential element in Rudolf Steiner's view of education and indeed of the world as a whole. It is a very rich and living idea; it implies not merely opposition and contrast, but also a fundamental unity which makes it impossible for the one pole to appear without its opposite, and it implies the creation by the two poles of a fruitful medium between them, which at the same time keeps them apart and enables them to send their influences to each other. It was natural for such an idea to find expression in a man like Coleridge, whose belief in the formative power of thinking was so very much greater than his capacity to give form to his own thoughts. This is what Coleridge writes in his *Aids to Reflection* about the principle of Polarity in the human organism:

'The cerebral system of the nerves has its correspondent antithesis in the abdominal system: but hence arises a synthesis of the two in the pectoral system as the intermediate, and, like a drawbridge, at once conductor and boundary. In the latter, as objectized by the former, arise the emotions, affections, and, in a word, the passions, as distinguished from the cognitions and appetites.'

This is, of course, neither more nor less than a description of the threefold organism so magnificently developed by Dr. Steiner a century later. Outside Anthroposophy I imagine it is the best account of the more obvious aspects of threefold man—the things that most strike the eye—ever given. These stand in the forefront of our education and have often been described in this journal; but in the background stand many other polarities which can only be reached through a general comprehension of the threefold man, and of which the polarity of intellect and sense-perception is one.

In the theory of the senses which developed from the time of John Locke onwards, the senses were regarded as passive instruments through which the pictures of the external world were written on the mind. Locke described the mind as an empty slate—a tabula rasa—with no content of its own, on which, little by little, the sense impressions are written. Concepts are afterwards formed by abstraction from the data given by the senses. The eye sees, for example, a lot of balls or spheres, and gradually the mind abstracts the idea of a uniform smooth undifferentiated surface which forms the concept of a sphere.

The part of the senses is to be merely passive and record the images as a kind of camera. Indeed this view of the senses probably made possible the invention of the camera, and the camera, once invented, in its turn provided so plausible an image of the eye that the idea of passive senses has become deeply ingrained in the popular as well as in the scientific mind. It is therefore something of a shock to find Rudolf Steiner describing the senses not as passive but active, and the image formed by sense perception as arising not from nerve but from blood activity.

It is not very easy to accustom the mind to such a revolutionary idea; perhaps one way to begin is to observe how much activity there is to be found in ordinary sense-perception. Let us take a few examples. You are looking idly from the window of a stationary train at a crowd on the platform. Your eyes are fully open and if you were a passive camera the scene would be fully recorded on the plate.

Suddenly, however, you think you see someone you know. Immediately that point in the crowd grows clear and vivid, while the rest fades away in a kind of mist. You have begun to see actively, and a really clear sense-image only arises when you exert the force of your will. Or you are at a party and you are cornered by a lady whose conversation is excruciatingly dull. Suddenly you hear some remarks that interest you in another part of the room. You immediately almost cease to hear the voice of the lady a few inches from you, and (God forgive you) answer Yes, or No, at random to what she is saying. The other voice is quite distinct above the general hubbub of conversation, because you have willed to hear it—you are not merely registering sounds passively like a machine. Notice again that when you look at a picture—even a small picture—you never see all the picture at once. It is a great mistake to imagine that you passively receive a sense-impression of the whole picture. Actually you direct your eye from one part to another, bringing now this part, now that into relief. The mere sense-impression of the picture—apart from the memory-image which remains when you go away from it—is an act of creation. Indeed Dr. Steiner said that even in so simple a thing as seeing a square picture-frame the eye really creates the image of the squareness by unconsciously following the outline round. You are really always *feeling* the things you see with your eyes, just as children love to feel all objects with their hands. If you only see square things—like modern houses or blocks of flats— you suffer from an appalling monotony in the activity of the eye, which has ultimately a stultifying effect on the creative power of the mind. Remember also that in sight you are always actively focussing with two eyes on the point of observation. It is as though two arms go out from your eyes, with which you grasp the object in much the same way as you grasp something with your two hands. The more you study the question the more unreasonable it seems to believe that the senses are only passive recipients. How, then, did such an idea become so firmly fixed in the modern mind?

The mistake is, I believe, one particular example of a general misunderstanding of the human organism which has grown up since the age of modern science. For it has become customary to believe that only the head and nerves are concerned with the activity of the soul or mind, and that other parts of the body have a purely physical function. The heart, which was once regarded as the seat of emotions, is merely the distributor of the blood. The fact that your heart beats fast when you meet a lion round the corner is one of Nature's devices for the preservation of the species by enabling you to run away faster—though it is not quite obvious why Nature should not be equally interested in the preservation of the lion. It was against this limitation of soul function to the nerves and brain that Rudolf Steiner fought with his picture of the threefold man.

He reasserted in a new and scientific fashion the old belief that the heart is the centre of feeling, and the metabolism—and especially the blood as the bearer of metabolism—is the true vehicle of the will. Now if you examine a sense organ, the eye for instance, you will find in it very fine nerve ends, and, side by side with them, the ends of very fine blood vessels.

Modern science thinks that the blood vessels merely feed and build up the physical organ. In the threefold view of man the fine blood vessels appear as the means by which man develops the will in sense-perception, by which he creates the sense-perception image.

What, then, is the function of the nerves? It is to enable you to become conscious of, and conscious in, the sense-pictures *created by the will*. It is a process analogous to the real function of the misnamed motor-nerves, which modern science supposes to conduct the will activity from brain to muscle. In reality the activity arises through the blood—the muscle is essentially a blood organ—and the nerve only contributes to that amount of consciousness, that awareness of the organ, without which the will could not function. If you did not know you had fingers you would not be able to move them, and you are aware of your fingers through the nerves.

But being aware of them does not by itself enable you to move them. On the contrary, too much awareness will often inhibit movement and action. Every sense-image is really a little work of art—you create it first and are conscious of it after. But the creation and the consciousness spring from different poles of the organism.

Along the nerve stream down which comes the awareness in sense-perception comes also intellectual consciousness, the concept. Fantasy or Imagination—the power to make mental pictures—is brother to the blood power of creating sense-images.

It makes, therefore, a very great difference whether you approach your sense-perceptions from the side of concepts or of concrete fantasy. From the side of the concept a thing will be 'only a cloud' or 'only a tree': from the point of view of your fantasy its form will be unique, all the more different because it is the same as other clouds or trees, eloquent of its inner nature like a human face. Blake, with his customary power of bringing contrasts to vivid expression, has written a little conversation on this point. Two men are talking about the sun:

'When the sun rises do you not see a round disc of fire somewhat like a guinea?'

'O, no, no, no, I see an innumerable Company of the Heavenly Host, crying: Holy, holy, holy, is the Lord God Almighty.'

The first man fastens on the abstract idea of *roundness*—anything round may fairly be compared with the sun. The second sees that the sun is not merely the disc—it is also the light of the sun in all its manifestations of colour and power.

Blake is, of course, speaking as a seer; but the eye of an artist like Turner saw pretty much the same thing—certainly not the round disc 'somewhat like a guinea'.

In a Rudolf Steiner School all learning is approached—especially among the younger children—from the point of view of the will. That is why fantasy and imagination play so important a part; and why, in the early stages of teaching the sciences, children are shown the pure phenomena without theoretical explanations. So few people today can really see something without being interfered with by a theory. They see the stars, but always in the back of their minds is the thought of the immense distances to which modern astronomy has relegated them. They see a fire, and, because they have a general idea of combustion, do not notice the unique quality of the flame.

It is a far more living experience to see what is unique than what is generalised, and children, who live by the will far more than adults, have a natural genius for clear individualised sense-images. We ought not to dull this power by calling too early on the opposite power of abstraction, on the system of the nerves. But there is more at stake than merely keeping children's sense-perception healthy and vivid. Important questions of scientific method arise in this connection, which will be dealt with in the next article.

★

As already indicated, the next article did not appear in the Monthly Journal during that academic year. But even the excerpts that have been given from these Michael Hall Monthly Journals emanating from the Somerset town of Minehead during the years of the Second World War will have given some indication of the astonishing wealth of committed study and research that was taking place amongst the teachers during that time. Cecil Harwood was, as has been made clear, not alone in this by any means. And yet whereas most of the other teachers devoted all their time and energies to the school and, where applicable, their family lives, Harwood continued throughout this period to carry an additional heavy burden of responsibility for the Anthroposophical Society in Great Britain. The details of this will now be explored in the chapter that follows.

1. *Harwood with his birth family: (left to right) Gwen, Arnold, Eric, mother, Hilda, Maurice, father with Cecil on his lap*

2. *Lord and Lady Olivier (Daphne's parents) at their home in later life in the village of Ramsden, Oxfordshire*

3. *Daphne as a girl*

4. *Daphne on horseback in Jamaica*

5. *Daphne as a young woman before meeting Cecil*

6. *Daphne with a child (probably John)*

7. *Harwood, Passport Photo, 1951*

8. *Harwood sitting on the steps of the school in Streatham*

9. *Pushing Laurence and Mark in a wheelbarrow*

10. *With a group of children playing a musical game*

11. *As a cheerful cricketer at Streatham*

12. *Walking tour in Wales, mid 1930s (photographed by Owen Barfield); from left to right: Cecil Harwood, C.S. Lewis, W.O. Field, W.E. Becket, Arthur Hanbury-Sparrow*

13. *At the seaside (date and place unknown)*

14. *Daphne with (left to right) Laurence, Sylvia and Mark*

15. *With Owen Barfield at Bee Cottage, Beckley, Oxfordshire c. 1921*

16. Laurence Harwood as a young man

17. Daphne, Lois and Cecil, probably around 1947

18. Cecil cheerfully armed with a pile of books (1949–50)

19 and 20. Rehearsing Laurence's Class 11 play 'King Midas' (written and produced by his father) in summer 1949

21. *The last Michael Hall Training Course before relocation to Emerson College (1963). It was run by Harwood (Libby Sheen is on Cecil's left)*

22. *Cecil up a ladder doing maintenance work at South Harbour 'with family approval' in July 1967; left to right: Nancy (cousin to the Harwood children), Lois, John, Cecil, Mark*

23. *Harwood family in 1945; from left to right: Sylvia, Daphne, Mark, Louis, Cecil, Laurence*

25. *Marguerite Lundgren as a young woman*

24. *Lecturing in his later years*

*26. Marguerite and Cecil in Ireland
(photographed by Christine Hebert)*

27. Out walking with Marguerite

28. At an amphitheatre in Greece

29. By a waterfall in Norway

30. *Smoking his pipe at a round table in Norway*

31. *Cecil and Marguerite at South Harbour*

32. *In conversation with Sir George Trevelyan on the lawn of Wallington Hall, Northumberland. He began to go blind the next day*

33. *The last photograph*

2. The Anthroposophical Society in Great Britain in a Time of War

It was noted earlier that, in the October 1939 issue of the Society's journal, *Anthroposophical Movement*, Cecil Harwood had announced the cancellation of the proposed Autumn Programme at Rudolf Steiner House owing to the House's vulnerability to the effects of war. However, some activities at the House continued; the Bookshop, for example, remained open and a 'kindly placed bus-stop and sheltering doorway' encouraged many passers-by to examine the books and exhibits and sometimes to come in to buy a few postcards.

This information derives from the November issue of the journal, where there also appeared a brief notice from Herbert Heywood-Smith, leader of the Zarathustra Group of the Society which, as noted earlier, had in 1928 separated in part from the Anthroposophical Society in Great Britain. The notice included these words: 'We feel that the time has now come when breaches which have hitherto existed in the Society should be healed and some form of free co-operation should be found, so that Rudolf Steiner's work may spread more rapidly and securely. A cordial welcome will be given to all who are able to come to the group meetings.'[94] Thus whereas the wider world was being engulfed in a second major conflict, the Anthroposophical Society was registering the intention of trying to do the opposite. Heywood-Smith was as good as his word, and both Cecil Harwood and Owen Barfield (who remained a member of the Executive Council and edited its main journal throughout the war) heartily welcomed this gesture.

Despite the continuing threat of enemy action, a normal timetable of events at Rudolf Steiner House resumed in January 1940. Indeed, as this year proceeded use of the House was extended to the feeding and accommodating of those engaged in arduous war-service; and, with the encouragement of Harwood and the Executive Council, a Canteen—requiring a Food Controller's Certificate betokening a Catering Establishment—and Rest Room were opened in August.[95] In the October 1940 issue of *Anthroposophical Movement* the following report on Rudolf Steiner House appeared:

> All who live and work at Rudolf Steiner House are greatly encouraged by the many letters and messages of good cheer which are received daily from members throughout the country. The house stands firm and strong, and is filled with activity both day and night. With the new phase of the war we

have been called upon to offer hospitality to many people both from the immediate neighbourhood, and from the East End of London, who have lost their homes and almost all their possessions. This work is gladly undertaken by members and friends in addition to the work for which the Canteen was first opened—that of providing meals and rest for war workers who in increasing numbers are depending on us for their needs, before going to duties that have become so arduous and dangerous.

Side by side with all this, the work entrusted to members of the Anthroposophical Society goes on steadily. Small but eager groups of people meet almost every day of the week for lectures and classes. The Library, Bookshop and Office are all centres of steady work, and the number of new members and enquirers is in no way diminished.

For the opportunity to work in these ways we are all deeply thankful, and our gratitude goes out to those members who help so much by their thoughts and messages, though they may be far away to share in the immediate tasks with which we are faced.

We do not hesitate, in these days, to send out a further appeal for help, feeling confident that any who can do so will respond, in however small a degree. We need camp beds, mattresses, blankets, pillows, cushions and armchairs for this special work. Fruit, vegetables and flowers are always welcome, and gifts of money will help in endless ways. All gifts in money and kind will be gratefully acknowledged and should be sent to Miss [Dorothy] Osmond or Miss [Lilian] Short at Rudolf Steiner House.

Rudolf Steiner House continued thereafter to be used as normal by the Anthroposophical Society in Great Britain for Annual General Meetings and all sorts of other events (but not for Summer Conferences) until July 1944, when the opening of the Second Front on 6 June (D-Day) had led to anticipated reprisals and the AGM planned to take place at Rudolf Steiner House on 8–9 July was postponed. As it turned out, the House had by September that year suffered only slight damage during recent air-raids and no other cancellations proved necessary.

By the time when the postponed AGM took place on 6 January 1945, it had become urgent to focus on the future of Rudolf Steiner House and Hall; and this was the main item on the agenda. The issue was now no longer so much one of trying to avoid direct hits but something altogether different which Harwood, as Chairman, outlined at the meeting. Essentially, this had to do with facing the reality that the Society's Headquarters had been funded during the 1930s by interest-bearing loans (technically referred to as Debenture holdings). Before the war the Society had paid rent to the Anthroposophical Association Ltd. (a non-profit-making business company whose sole function was to own and manage Rudolf Steiner

House and Hall) for the part of the building which it occupied (and during the war this continued to happen), but the greater part of the outgoings had to be met by letting the Hall, chiefly to dramatic societies having little or nothing to do with anthroposophy. 'This main source of income was', in the words of the report of this 21ˢᵗ AGM of the Society,[96]

> affected by several crises preceding the war, and practically ceased at the outbreak in 1939. The Debenture holders, in many cases at great personal sacrifice, agreed to renounce their interest, and for some time expenses were helped by the fact that the Royal Air Force hired the Hall for lectures. This tenancy had now expired and at present, apart from occasional lettings, the Association's only source of income was the rent paid by the Society. The main question was, therefore, what to do with this situation after the war, when there would arise the Association's moral and legal responsibility to resume the payment on Debenture interest or to repay capital.

After an extensive discussion around four options presented by Harwood, the resolve was made to try to extend the Society's activities so that the entire building could be used for anthroposophy (in preference to resuming the letting of the Hall to theatrical businesses); and at the next AGM on 15 September 1945 this resolve was confirmed and the decision was also made to convert the Debenture holdings into a new loan secured on the property as an interim step to maintaining the whole building as defined above.

Throughout the war Harwood, because of his role of Chairman, carried a major share of responsibility for the building that served as the home of the Society. He also continued to be the Hon. Treasurer until October 1942, when Edward Bailey took over this task. But he was also frequently cast in the role of Chairman or presiding figure for several other Society events, including Summer Conferences, quite apart from giving lectures in a variety of places throughout the country.

★

In the absence of any surviving people who can speak of their personal experiences of these times,[97] the best way of forming a picture of the Anthroposophical Society in Great Britain during these war-time years is through reviewing the written records. I shall inevitably be giving a personal impression and moreover, one that is inclined towards chronicling the activities of its faithful Chairman. The aim is, nevertheless, to paint a somewhat broader canvas and give some kind of idea of what was living in the members of the Society during this tempestuous time. As with the Minehead Monthly Journals, I shall try to achieve this for the most part by treading an approximately chronological path through the issues of *Anthroposophical Movement*.

★

It had become a practice—one that was presumably an impulse of the Editor, Owen Barfield—to allow a great variety of different individuals to express their deepest thoughts and concerns where otherwise an Editorial would introduce any particular issue. In January 1940 this task was allotted to Karl König, whose name featured prominently in the closing pages of Part One. His contribution was entitled simply:

1940

'Rudolf Steiner is a Festival in the life of humanity!'

These words still echo within me as if they had been spoken only yesterday. They were the words with which Dr. Rittelmeyer[98] opened his lecture to the World Conference on Spiritual Science organised by the Anthroposophical Society in Great Britain in the year 1928.

'Rudolf Steiner is a Festival in the life of humanity!'

The words were resounding as I was nearing the shores of England last year. The waves were dashing against the ship, the wind beating across the deck, the clouds rushing over the sky—all were speaking, singing, these same words.

'Rudolf Steiner is a Festival in the life of humanity!'

And now they are resounding, have been resounding for days, since the world has stilled in order to prepare for the approach of Advent.[99] The Earth is calm, the life-forces are quiescent; even the heavens seem higher and the air more pure. The voice of the spirit can thus be heard more clearly. Again and again the hosanna sounds:

'Rudolf Steiner is a Festival in the life of humanity!'

Let the name of Rudolf Steiner not be forgotten amid the racket of war, the blast of attack and defence, the blind fury of hate, the fear of destruction, the grip of death and annihilation.

Well-nigh everyone in this country today realises that the present war is to betoken a change reaching into the innermost nature of the individual, that each human being who passes through this war will emerge at the end as one who has been baptised. But the *kind* of baptism which the individual will receive will depend upon *himself*. Will it lead to the heights or to the depths?

Moreover, who does not realise that this war is the first to be waged not by the will of men alone, that machines have proved mightier than the human will and that today it is the machines that are leading men to battle?

It is for the human being to choose whether he will receive baptism from the machines or from the heavens.

The machines came into being because science was unmindful of her true mission. But science was unmindful of her mission because the human beings who inaugurated her no longer understood her innermost nature.

England was the birthplace of Charles Darwin's *On the Origin of Species by means of Natural Selection*, published in the year 1859. What the human mind construed from the ideas contained in this book is reacting in the form of the armed force of Nationalism. Darwin founded a theory of selection which is bearing fruit today as political Nationalism.

Thus science has two aspects: that of the machine and that of the political delusion of race. When this fact is realised, words of Rudolf Steiner spoken in England in London, 24th April 1922, become prophetic:

'We have a grand and lofty science, but a science not yet 'christened'. We speak of culture, but nobody feels the urge to christen this science. This, however, is what must be done. If science is not christened, everything that the human being needs from the cosmos will be lost.'

If we make a beginning with this christening of science, the features of the countenance of modern nature-knowledge which confronts us as war, will change. A menacing, cruel countenance will give place to one of loving tenderness, bearing within it the beams of the Cross and the roses of the Resurrection.

If we succeed, man will receive the true baptism of this war, for it will be enacted by the forces which he 'needs from the cosmos'.

Well may the year 1940 be begun with these thoughts. For if they are strong enough in individual souls, the Festival 'Rudolf Steiner' will be celebrated by far more human souls than it is today.

König followed up this article with three lectures that he gave on 20–21 January at Rudolf Steiner House on the theme that he had highlighted in his article, namely 'The Christianising of Science in our Time'. He spoke especially out of his knowledge of anatomy and physiology in addressing the fields of psychology, zoology and embryology. Science, he said, is at present connected only with thinking; it must be brought into relation also with feeling and will. The lectures attracted a large and highly appreciative audience, and further lectures by him on a similar theme were planned for the end of March. That the interest in König's work was no passing phase is further confirmed by the fact that he was invited to give two further lectures out of another area of his research at the AGM in June 1941 (of which more will be said later). In the meantime he had—together with several of his Camphill colleagues—been interned on the Isle of Man at Whitsun 1940 (i.e. on or around 12 May) as an 'enemy alien' and—as one of the first internees to be freed—subsequently released on 4 October.[100] He wrote the following words about his period of internment for publication in *Anthroposophical Movement*[101]:

> I want to tell you a little about the inner side of our life in the Internment Camp. It was wonderful. Dr. [Ernst] Lehrs, Mr. [Willi] Sucher and I formed a very strong working group, and worked out some very important things. Our work was especially connected with the St. Michael's day of this year, and with the working of Elias and St. John in world history... Apart from this work, we gave many lectures to lots of people, and the extraordinary circumstances made them much more open to these things than in normal times. I also had the privilege of speaking at the Camp University on embryology and anatomy. So it really was a good time, not only for us, but also for some of our fellow internees. I also worked as a doctor and was able to help many people. On the other hand, it was often very hard—without beds, tales, chairs etc., but I think this will be forgotten soon and the other part will remain through life and beyond it. I felt that much new karma in connection with anthroposophy had come into existence, and I hope that we made the best of these times.

Owen Barfield's article in the May 1940 issue of the journal reflects the distilled experience of an anthroposophist who—in contrast to König—was neither Austrian or German nor—through ancestry—a refugee.[102] Barfield was, it is important to stress, a convinced Germanophile:

Some Reflections arising out of the War

Those who are old enough to remember the outbreak of the war in 1914 will have been struck by many wide differences between the psychological atmosphere which prevailed in this country then and the atmosphere which prevails today. Those who are not so old will perhaps scarcely believe that a serious press campaign was launched for suppressing the performance of German music at orchestral concerts—not merely modern German music, but German music of all time, including Bach and Beethoven.

At the beginning of the present war Mr. Chamberlain announced that we have no quarrel with the German people. Lately a pronounced reaction from this view of the matter has been apparent, not only in the press, but in the utterances of Government spokesmen. This is hardly surprising, and I for one think that the Prime Minister overstated the case. Having heard many of Hitler's broadcast speeches, and read still more of what he has said and written, I find it difficult to believe that an unwarped mind could fail to perceive that the whole inspiration of his life is hatred. I find it equally difficult not to 'have a quarrel' with a people whose majority approve, acclaim and virtually worship precisely this man. It would have been more correct to say 'We do not hate the German people'.

I think the real distinction lies, not between Hitler and the German people, but between the noble and the ignoble elements in the German soul. We may recognise this dispassionately without any priggishness and in the full knowledge that our own souls both as individuals and as a nation are compounded of the same mixed stuff. Anthroposophists in particular should be able to adopt this detached attitude without its misleading them into a superior and supine attitude of inaction. For there should be no danger of our identifying our true and ultimate selves with any nationality. We think of ourselves as having been incarnated in many nations and as destined to incarnation in many more. Yet it is a very superficial inference from this, to claim that one has risen above national feeling, patriotism and all such childish taboos. We may know that our spirits are free of nationality. We also know that our souls are not. Our soul-life is the process of our karma in any one incarnation, and it is connected in the most intimate and sacred way with nationality.

What is a Folk-Soul? This article does not claim to be more than a loose assemblage of personal reflections, and I hazard the suggestion that it is something which bears the same relation to that being of the hierarchies, called by Rudolf Steiner in some places a Folk-Spirit, as the soul of a man bears to his ego. It is not of itself eternal. It is for the time being the process of the karma of that spirit. As such it must have the most subtle and delicate connection with the karma of individuals...

Karma works strangely. How much does the English Folk-Soul owe to Joan of Arc? Sometimes the best service one person can do to another is to ensure the failure of that other in what he has undertaken.

It has been said that the English would have had no army at all in 1914 if it had not been for Lord Haldane. If there had been no English army the Germans would probably have broken through in Flanders in the first months of the war. Haldane was by temperament a philosopher, but he made it his life's work, in the face of apathy and hostility, to provide a sound basis for the British regular army. Work under these discouraging conditions can only be carried on when strength is found from inner sources. To what source did Haldane himself attribute the strength of his inner life? To Germany. The notoriousness of this fact is the subject of an anecdote in his biography. Besides being a philosopher, Haldane was addicted to wearing very ancient hats, and it is related that once King Edward VII, seeing him approaching across the lawn at a garden-party, turned to the bystanders with the remark: 'Here he comes in the hat which he inherited from Goethe!'

Later, after the outbreak of war, the gutter-press fastened on an old remark of Haldane's to the effect that Germany was his 'spiritual home' and hounded him out of office on the strength of it as being 'pro-German'!

Karma works strangely and we may ask ourselves whether the high purposes of that great human spirit which clothed itself in the German body and soul of Goethe in the eighteenth century of the Christian era would have been furthered—or foiled—by an overwhelming victory for the Prussian arms in 1914.

I am not in a position to dogmatise on this subject. My thoughts can only pass from it into a rather awed contemplation of the whole mystery of the mutual relations of souls; of human souls to one another; of human souls to nation-souls, their own and those of other nations; of nation-souls to one another. What can be said of this? 'One word is too often profaned for me to profane it'! But there is, as we know, only One way in which this relation can be transmuted from mere self-centred co-presence into that selfless intermingling, by virtue of which soul somehow becomes spirit and clothes itself with the spirit's attribute of eternity. Before, however, relapsing into silence and an O altitudo! there is one rather more definite thing which I would presume to say.

Rudolf Steiner did not confine himself to general observations on this matter. In the lectures which he gave upon the relations between the living and the dead, and elsewhere, as in the Mystery Plays, he sought to depict how such an intermingling as I have referred to may be of importance not only to the particular souls concerned, but also to the whole of the earth. For where a soul is cut off, as by death, from the normal means of outward expression, it may, nevertheless, speak out into the world of action from the heart of a free and living man. Perhaps by now my drift has become clear enough to enable me to summarise what I have to say in a couple of sentences. I am sure that we (that valiant 'we' of the middle-age civilian) must fight and win this war; but I am sure also that we must struggle to keep the soul of Germany close-hid with Christ in our hearts. For whether we win or lose, the time may come when that will be the only home left for it on earth.

The articles by König and Barfield may serve as a contextual background for a brief summary of Society events in 1940, highlighting especially those in which Cecil Harwood was involved. Thus on 24–25 February Harwood gave three lectures at Rudolf Steiner House on 'Athens, Rome, London'; and on 13 April he was invited to lecture in Dorking on 'Education as an Art'. The AGM for that year took place on 29–30 June, when Harwood's role as stand-in Treasurer seems to have especially featured in his sense of urgency on behalf of Rudolf Steiner House and Hall. It is also, I think, important to mention that Dr. Alfred Heidenreich, who on Rittelmeyer's death had become joint Leader (Oberlenker) of the Christian Community, apparently gave an outstanding address on living in apocalyptic times. As noted earlier, there was what must have been a fairly low-key, but nourishing and nurturing, Summer Conference at Minehead (2–12 August), advertised as a 'Meeting for the Study of Rudolf Steiner's Work'. It was an evident delight for the 50 or so participants to be able to enjoy the sea-girt environment on the border of Exmoor. Cecil Harwood gave an address on the opening evening.

★

The overall structure of the Society's life in 1941 was not dissimilar to the previous year, except that the Michael Hall teachers additionally arranged an informal Easter Conference for members of the Society from 11 to 14 April at Minehead. There were Whitsun conferences both at Wynstones School and at Camphill Aberdeen, the latter being the first occasion when 'Camphill opened its doors to the public on a grand scale'[103]. The AGM was over the same weekend as the previous year (28–29 June), when Karl König lectured to full houses on St. John the Baptist and St. John the Evangelist. There was a full report of this Annual General Meeting, where—as before—Harwood officiated as both Chairman and Treasurer, in the August and September issue of *Anthroposophical Movement* ably written by Miss Connie Winney. In the October issue of the Society's journal there were three interesting reports of conferences, in each of which Harwood was fully involved. He had himself published a full announcement of the Summer Conference in Minehead in the July issue and was most likely its principal organizer. This is the report that subsequently appeared:

Conference at Minehead

Owing to the indefatigable efforts of the teachers of Michael Hall, Minehead, a great number of members and friends from all parts of the country were able to attend the summer conference which took place from August 16th—24th at the school in its beautiful surroundings of sea and hills.

This year the new assembly room (created out of an old stable by Mr. Mann and his helpers) provided a perfect setting for the lectures and activities that took place. Day after day the hall filled, often to full capacity. Many newcomers had their introduction to anthroposophy and one feels that seeds have been sown which may bear fruit for the future.

An expectant audience gathered for Mr. Edmunds's fine opening lecture, which laid a firm foundation for the subject of our study: 'Knowledge of Man in the Making of the Future'. This was developed from a number of aspects and in great depths, during the following days. Dr. Nunhofer's two lectures on 'The Nature of Blood and its Relation to the Spirit', and Mr. Duffy's talks on Dr. Steiner's teaching in relation to the cultivation of the earth, which today appears to be gaining marked appreciation in the agricultural world, aroused much interest. Dr. [Walter Johannes] Stein's four enthralling lectures formed the central part of the conference. After he had spoken on the evolution of nationalism, revealing the deeper aspects of this country's history in connection with present events, he went on to the development of man's thinking. He led us through the different stages of consciousness and initiation as experienced throughout the ages, and gave us an understanding of the form that the latter must now take for humanity. This deeply interesting and illuminating cycle was brought to a close by a lecture on reincarnation as understood in antiquity, the Middle Ages, and as it can be comprehended by man today.

Mr. [George Kaufmann] Adams spoke to us on 'The Christ Impulse and the Social Future' in a way that left a lasting impression on those who heard him, and Miss Groves approached one of the aspects of the social future in a talk on 'Money and Democracy'.

Friday and Saturday were devoted to the Arts. Mr. Michael Wilson's two talks on music and Mr. Mann's illustrated lecture on Leonardo, Michelangelo and Raphael—representatives of man's thinking, willing and feeling—were much appreciated. The lovely eurythmy performance arranged by Mrs. Mann included a rendering of a scene from *A Midsummer Night's Dream* with incidental music by C.R. Yuille-Smith, Schumann's *Papillons* and other items which were a joy to behold.

There were opportunities for practical activities, such as Mr. [William] Mann's modelling class, Mrs. Darrell's painting and Mrs. Mann's eurythmy lessons. Mr. Adams's geometry classes (illustrated by Miss [Olive] Whicher's drawings) were well attended and proved of great help to many in furthering their understanding of anthroposophical teaching.

On the last Sunday of the conference a lofty spiritual experience was brought to our understanding when Mr. [Leo] Baker spoke to us of the Second Coming of Christ. In the afternoon, after tea, hospitably offered us by the teachers of Michael Hall, we had the treat of a concert by Mr. Wilson and Mr. and Mrs. Kobbé.

Mr. Harwood's closing lecture in the evening made clear to us how vitally our thoughts and our deeds can contribute towards the making of the future, and, after further lovely music, we parted, filled with profound gratitude for so much that we had experienced and with a deepening sense that each one of us should carry over into our various spheres some of the spiritual gifts that have been given to us.

The report was signed 'A.I.'

In the following month Harwood travelled up to Aberdeen to participate in an event initiated by Dr. Ernst Lehrs and Dr. Karl König. Before the event itself, however, Harwood spent a few days visiting Camphill (arriving on 9 September according to the diary of Irmgard Lazarus[104]) and also, as noted in Mrs. Emily Haughton's guest book, must have visited Kirkton House, the birthplace of what became the Camphill movement, between 11 and 12 September. The event in Aberdeen itself—Camphill Estate lies a few miles outside the city centre and Kirkton House some distance away in rural Aberdeenshire—was described in the October issue of *Anthroposophical Movement* by Harwood himself:

Educational Lectures in Aberdeen

An exceptionally fine opportunity for introducing Dr. Steiner's educational movement to Scotland occurred in Aberdeen on September 13, when, through the initiative of Dr. Lehrs and Dr. König, the Aberdeen Branch of the Scottish Teachers' Association invited Dr. Lehrs and Mr. Harwood to lecture at a session of the Association specially convened for the purpose. The lecture room was packed, about 260 people being present, including the Director of Education and numerous Headmasters and Headmistresses as well as people of importance in other walks of life.

There is no space here to speak of the content of the lectures, but it was evident from their reception that they aroused not only interest but enthusiasm. Indeed the interest in anthroposophy aroused by the work of Dr. König, and now also of Dr. Lehrs and Dr. Röschl-Lehrs, is quite phenomenal in the history of our movement, and has been compared by one member who knew of it to the enthusiasm in Germany in the opening days of the Waldorf School. All members will desire to send their warmest wishes for the extension and consolidation of this brilliant opening of anthroposophical work in the North of Scotland.

This event partially coincided with a Members' Conference on 13 and 14 September at Rudolf Steiner House on a theme of great topical importance. Harwood must have travelled back to London on the night sleeper, as he gave the concluding public lecture. A report was written by Frances Melland:

The Members' Conference of Mid-September

'The Task before us at this Moment in History' proved to be such a wide and varied one that the three sessions for the conferring together of members carried us on a far range of subjects and into the deepest aspects of spiritual science. It began with what Rudolf Steiner has called the central aim of anthroposophy—to prepare for the re-appearance of Christ amongst humanity in a new and supersensible form in the near future. It led us, in an endeavour to understand further the mission of our own peoples, through the realms of world economy, regional survey, and the problems of ownership or the use of land for its true purpose. And here, as in the third subject—the building of a new social life, together with those who have died that it may come about— we sought for *the way* of doing it, the 'how' even more than the 'what'.

There was a sense of real thankfulness for the opportunity of conversing together on such subjects; and the efforts made through previous study by many members, and by others simply in the journeys undertaken from the country, all shared in bringing about an experience of unity in the deep things of life, and the feeling of having moved a step further in our common work.

The Conference subjects were very ably introduced by Mr. Adams [his theme was 'The Social World on Earth and Human Souls in Spiritual Worlds'], Mr. Bittleston ['Rudolf Steiner's Words of Prophecy about the Etheric Christ'] and Mr. [Charles] Davy ['The Fulfilment of the Threefold Commonwealth']; and, in addition, so many good contributions were made by those attending that it is hard to know what to cite in a short space. But perhaps the key-notes sounded in Mr. Davy's address, through his moving Imagination of 'the power of the Christ crowned with thorns' as over against the power of Hitler working through cruelty and tyranny.

Mr. Harwood's public lecture [on 'England and the Belief in Freedom'], which completed the weekend's meetings, put a high ideal before the audience—an unusually large one in this House—in translating the belief in 'freedom' vividly into that of 'spiritual activity'. Time, only, was all too short for what we attempted in the confines of two days; and it is clear from the wide response among the membership that there is a need for gatherings of this kind to be held in future at more frequent intervals.

Two articles from the issues of *Anthroposophical Movement* have a particular importance as regards an impression of what was living amongst members of the Anthroposophical Society during 1941. They were both written by men who were subsequently to have a close involvement with the annual journal *The Golden Blade*, which was founded in 1949 mainly at the instigation of one of them, Arnold Freeman. The other—Adam Bittleston, a priest of the Christian Community—was its editor for a number of years and always reflected a deep awareness of the times in which he was living. Adam Bittleston's article was included in the June 1941 issue (vol. XVIII, no. 6).

Threefold Impulses in World Conflict

In this war three distinct forms of civilisation are struggling for Europe—the Soviet Russian, the Nazi and that of the English-speaking peoples. Passive or active, allied or 'neutral', Soviet Russia is a very real participant throughout. It is worth seeking again and again from different points of view to understand these three with the aid of anthroposophy.

In *The Karma of Vocation*—which is among the books by Dr. Steiner specifically banned in Germany by the Nazis—Dr. Steiner describes the danger of a wrong inner relationship of the human soul to the beings of the Third Hierarchy. It is possible for souls which have not found a true relationship to Christ, the Spirit of all mankind through all human history, to look too exclusively to their own Angel, or to the Archangel of their country, or to the Arché of the time in which they live. If they look towards any of these three with the mood with which men should look only to the Divine that works through the whole universe, they lose from sight after a time the true being from the Third Hierarchy and a misleading spirit stands before them. The consequences of such a mistake are terrible.

The official thought and a great deal of the practice of Russia for the last twenty years are based on a fanatical devotion to that which the *present* has produced—the technical achievements and the theories of the nineteenth and twentieth centuries. They cut away most of the past of mankind and that which is most essential for its future. The Soviet system may be called, from this point of view, the worship of an ahrimanic spirit of the age. Here we have the mistaken relation to the realm of the Archai.

In Germany the one-sided nationalism which has done so much to poison the life of this century reaches its most extreme form. It is a worship of the Archangel; though we cannot believe that it is directed towards the Folk-Spirit, but an appalling caricature.

In the West we find much more marked—in place of the mass egotism of Russia and the national egotism of Germany—individual egotism. This is a characteristic of the 'shadow side' of the English-speaking peoples; an individualism that *can* find expression in true freedom, but can also take the form of a narrow sectarianism, or the assertion of the right to business selfishness. We know something of the many practical difficulties that this mood causes. Particularly in the economic life, the rights of the individual—or of some individuals—have been very much exaggerated in the West to the detriment of wider needs. Behind this is a wrong Angel-worship, and individualism where each seeks his own Divine, forgetting the true Divine Powers that unite mankind. This real danger in Western civilisation has often been pointed out—though in other words—by those in Middle and Eastern Europe who wished to make the West appear hateful; and they have had some success.

But Western individualism offers the greatest opportunity for the wide development of a free spiritual life. This is the great positive scope for individualism. A spirited cosmogony, which should become a strong and living element within the intellectual life of the future, can only be acquired and developed by free individuals. This flower and fruit of the future society—what should be its content? To form a picture of the spiritual life that should be attained by this age, we may again look to the cosmos beyond the Earth. Rudolf Steiner pointed out that the spiritual life of the age should be inspired by the forces of the outer planets, Mars, Jupiter and Saturn. So rich and colourful should the spiritual life of the age be; so violently does our age sin against itself, when its spiritual life remains a sphere of Moon-like shadow-pictures. In religion, in science, in history, should work these forces of courage, of light, of awareness of the rhythms of time. (We may take the picture given elsewhere by Rudolf Steiner of Western man as a 'spiritual giraffe' and say: The giraffe will find proper use for his long neck when he learns to browse among the outer planets!)

If the power to acquire and develop a spiritual cosmogony, of which the basis has been given in anthroposophy, exists particularly in the West—however little evidence can be shown for this yet—can we find any possible tendency today in Middle Europe?

Far more deeply founded in the souls of Middle Europe than that terrible structure which has been erected by the Nazis is the longing for a law that springs from the heart. This was one of the baits that ensnared Germany into accepting Nazi leadership. The Nazis held out the promise of a truly social, Germanic—as opposed to Roman—system of law, which would help and protect all members of the community. Many Germans have found since how deceitful that promise was; but they are helpless to a degree that English people find hard to understand or believe. But one day this longing for a healing law may find expression; and this we may perhaps express cosmically as a transmutation of law, from its dominance by decadent Mars forces, by the healing impulse of Mercury. We see everywhere tendencies towards this transmutation; in penal law, for instance, we grope towards methods that would cure instead of punishing. We may say, I think, that in this realm we need those forces of the inner planets which serve true human evolution, not only Mercury's healing, but also the loving warmth of Venus, the moral wisdom that belongs to the holiest forces of the Moon.

If we compare the spiritual life of the future society to the flower and fruit of a plant, we may compare this realm of law to the leaves; and remember that Tree described in the Apocalypse, whose leaves are for the healing of the nations. For to this realm of law also belongs the critical sphere of relationships between the Rights-States of different countries. War has its origins far back in the spiritual and economic conditions of the world; but it is in this sphere of Rights that it actually breaks out. War is always a failure to find agreement about the Rights of peoples.

In international relations today we are very far from embodying these healing forces. And it may seem the maddest paradox to say that the nation whose leaders have most violently destroyed in recent years what there was of truth and humanity in international relations, have an especially strong impulse towards the healing of them. Yet if we look beneath the surface we can see the truth of this. In a materialistic world it may often happen that a group, which possesses individually the strongest impulses towards a certain virtue, may by its external organisation do the uttermost to destroy this very quality. The youthful impulses towards the good are held back from realisation in the physical by the maya of appearances; they are *confused* by Ahriman. If the West fails or refuses to understand this, later on it may do itself and the world great harm by cutting itself off from these sources of strength.

Something similar has happened in the East. The positive force that has been misled into Russian Communism is an impulse towards economic brotherhood—the root of the future social order. We may describe this cosmically as the expression of the spiritual Sun-forces that have been united by Christ with the Earth. In what has been carried out in Russia, we see the expression of the opposing forces of earthly demonic powers.

To carry the Christ impulse into the economic relationships of the world would be a true service to the Archai, the Spirits of the Age; to evolve in each country a law that sprang really from the heart, a true service to the Archangels. If spiritual science lives in human minds, Rudolf Steiner has told us, it means for the Angels themselves that their sphere of life reaches further into the cosmos.

In Nazi-controlled Europe and in Russia political life has hardened into forms which offer great hindrances to any *visible* progress towards such true relationships. Progress can only go on in secret places—in the 'catacombs' of the modern world. The West has the mighty opportunity, that progress can go on openly in the light of day, in places where English-speaking peoples prevail against their enemies. Hindrances in the social order exist here, too; but they can be overcome or disregarded in a way not possible in Germany or Russia as they are. And what England is now suffering may help in the overcoming of their hindrances, so that there may well be approaching us one of the greatest opportunities in the history of the world.

Arnold Freeman's article, published in the next (July) issue, tackles a similar theme in a totally different way:

The Task of the English-Speaking Peoples

The English-speaking peoples have set themselves an aim; they have made up their minds to free human affairs from the 'curse of Hitler'. Very slowly and reluctantly—and therefore very deeply and tenaciously—they have accepted the hellish ordeal of modern warfare.

I raise here no interrogation upon the legitimacy of this war effort. Anything I propose is intended not as an alternative to the prosecution of the war—in which we are irrevocably engaged—but as an additional method of achieving our aim. And yet, I confess that at times this other method looms up in my mind so massively that I ask myself—as many others are asking also— whether it does not after all amount to a vast alternative.

Clear-sighted observers of events have already long been asking large and bold questions: Can this war be won in the military sphere alone? Are we not face to face with issues that transcend those of the battlefield? Has not this war (and that of 1914-18) arisen, as it were, inevitably out of the conditions of modern civilisation? And can the war in any fundamental or final sense be brought to a conclusion except by the discovery of new political and social arrangements? Is there any way of shortening the war and saving from torment and slaughter multitudes of human creatures other than by making up our minds in all earnestness to the re-shaping of the world?

Reflections such as these, it will be said, are the platitudes of every estimable paper and periodical. I nevertheless defiantly bring them forward in this place in order to remind myself and others of the implications of these facts for anthroposophists. We believe we know the right answer to Hitler's 'new order'. We believe it to be all-important that mankind should discover this answer. We believe that if this answer could arise in the hearts and minds and wills of human beings all the world over, we should find ourselves miraculously creating cities instead of destroying them.

The war aim of the English-speaking peoples is as yet little more than a negative. Should it not be the task of anthroposophists to try to convince them that the only fundamental way to get rid of Hitlerism is to set up a world-wide Threefold Commonwealth?

I feel we ought to be able to argue on some such lines as these: 'The war has inevitably risen out of the way in which human beings in these later centuries have chosen to order their civilisation. The world in modern times has come to consist of a medley of nation-states, bound together by no inner relationships; none of them acknowledging any sovereignty greater than its own will. Each of these states is in the last resort concerned with its own existence and its own interests. Each sets up its military frontiers and its tariff barriers. Each manufactures its own psychology of nationalistic exclusiveness. Not only are inner relationships impossible among communities so organised; wars between them are inevitable.

It is these unitary systems, these totalitarian monstrosities—each arrogating to itself absolute control over every aspect of its social and individual life, none of them knowing any law other than its own survival and expansion that degrade and devastate man's existence. It is the very institution of the nation-state itself that must be brought to the judgment bar of mankind.[105]

Hitler's crime against humanity is that he is striving to develop and maintain and extend the absolute authoritarianism of the nation-state; he would like to totalitarianise the entire world on nation-state lines. And the task of the democracies is not merely to oppose and measure Hitler upon the battlefield, but also to repudiate outworn political and social arrangements and set themselves to the realisation of that newer and nobler world-order towards which deep underlying historical forces of the times are impelling us.

The close of the war will see the English and American peoples in a position of immense power and immense responsibility. What will then be required of them is not so much a treaty with the vanquished as an invitation to mankind to participate in a far-reaching experiment upon democratic lines. The English-speaking peoples are becoming re-integrated. Many other ...peoples are anxiously looking to them for help and leadership. It is imperative that within the vast territories controlled by the democracies every effort should be made to meet the social demands of evolving humanity. In order that human beings may have the 'freedom' for which they ask, it is essential to institute throughout the New Democratic World a spiritual sphere entirely free of all state interference in which the inviolability of the selfhood of every human creature is, as it were, an accepted social axiom; in which there is the utmost liberty of thought and expression; in which there are the fullest safeguards to the spiritual and cultural rights of minorities and groups; in which there is every encouragement to personal initiative and creativeness. In order that human beings may solve their economic problems satisfactorily in the New Democratic World it is essential further to institute an independent economic sphere in which the entire Anglo-American democratic world resolves itself into a great free-trade area; in which there is a free flow of economic activities; in which there is a single network of communications and in which English and Americans and Norwegians and Greeks and Czechs and all others who decide to participate shall associate together to provide themselves with the paraphernalia of their material sustenance. And it will be necessary in a third and likewise separate and independent rights sphere for the New

Democratic World, through the parliaments and other such organs of the various constituent states, to give in every direction full effect to the irresistible modern demands for human equality.

The elucidation and elaboration of a Threefold Social Conception such as this is the true war aim of the English-speaking peoples. This is the programme of democracy. In such arrangements as those here hinted at, the social strivings of the age could be satisfied. Here would be the true beginnings of the world 'Commonwealth of Mankind'.

I make no pretence of being able to say these things as they ought to be said. But are there not others who can adequately give them utterance? Cannot anthroposophists somehow set about the supreme task of convincing the English-speaking peoples that it is towards the Threefold Commonwealth that their path lies?

★

I shall not give such a full synopsis of the Society's life over the remaining years of the war, since the yearly pattern of events was maintained more or less in accordance with the picture that has emerged so far. Instead, I shall focus for this period (1942–1945) more narrowly on specific contributions by Cecil Harwood himself.

The first of these was a short article in the February 1942 issue of *Anthroposophical Movement* on 'Evil and the Devil', in which he writes about the recently discovered importance of presenting the harrowing events of the Oberufer Three Kings Play to the children, with its depiction of the ahrimanic devil of Satan as opposed to the luciferic devil who tempted Adam and Eve in the Paradise Play. He continued (until October 1942) to carry the responsibility of Hon. Treasurer, and at the AGM that year (4–5 July) confirmed his willingness to continue beyond the three-year period previously agreed. A further item of significance agreed—at his request—at this AGM was that he should henceforth be known as the 'Chairman of the Society' rather than—as hitherto—'Chairman of the Executive Council'. His chairmanship role at meetings and conferences remained and effectively intensified; and he continued to lecture widely (thus, for example, in the autumn of that year he spoke in Llandudno, Manchester, Sheffield and York).

In 1943, when at the AGM on 13–14 March he was re-elected as Chairman of the Society, two significant deaths occurred on the world-stage of the Anthroposophical Society: Dr. Ita Wegman died on 4 March and Dr. Elisabeth Vreede on 31 August. Perhaps it was not unconnected with especially Ita Wegman's death that the working relationship between Harwood and Karl König was re-awakened and further intensified through König's visit to Minehead in August (he arrived in Minehead on 3 August) prior to the Summer Conference on 'Man as a Being of Body, Soul and Spirit' at which he was lecturing (7–14 August). And Harwood again visited Camphill in December that year for an intimate gathering focussing on Rudolf Steiner's lectures on *Occult History*, when Steiner spoke openly about certain themes pertaining to karma and reincarnation in Stuttgart at the end of 1910.[106]

In the May-June issue of *Anthroposophical Movement*, there was a notice regarding the AGM and weekend gathering of 8–9 July, when Harwood was to give a public lecture on 'The British Genius in the Mission of Europe'. As indicated earlier, this event did not take place when intended, and there is no outward evidence that Harwood gave the proposed public lecture. There was, however, a series of Summer Meetings at Minehead from 5 to 13 August on the general theme of 'Some new aspects of Science, Art and Religion', and Harwood was one of the speakers. It was also mentioned in the September issue of the journal that there were at the time 774 members, the highest to date.

As the issues and proposals centring around Rudolf Steiner House and Hall in 1944 and 1945 have already been briefly summarized, I shall conclude this chapter about the life of the Anthroposophical Society in Great Britain during the Second World War with some extracts from a report of the 22 Annual General Meeting of the Society which took place on 15–16 September:[107]

> The twenty-second General Meeting of the Society was held in Rudolf Steiner Hall on 15 September, 1945. The chair was taken by Mr. A.C. Harwood, who welcomed about 176 members representing nearly every group and activity... Mr. Harwood reported that the total membership was now 838. Since January there had been 28 new members, two resignations and three deaths. He then spoke of the members who had died and read a verse given by Rudolf Steiner.
>
> The meeting then proceeded with the election of the Chairman for the coming year. Mr. Harwood said that no nominations had been received and he would like to make clear to members the conditions under which he could put forward his name again. In view of the new responsibilities in connection with the removal of Michael Hall to Kidbrooke Park, he might not be able to come to Rudolf Steiner House as often as he felt it right for the Chairman to do. He was, however, experienced in the Chairmanship of the Society and as we were going through a critical period he would, if members so desired, continue to hold office. Miss Garrett proposed and Miss Bonny seconded the re-election of Mr. Harwood. The proposal was carried unanimously...

There then follows a lengthy section of the report (by Miss Winney) about the proposals regarding Rudolf Steiner House and Hall, which do not need to be recapitulated here. And the report ends as follows:

> The attendance throughout the weekend was most encouraging. On the Friday evening, Mr. Adams lectured on 'Atomic Energy', to an audience of 346 people who not only filled the entire hall, but were seated on the stage.
>
> A somewhat smaller, but deeply appreciative audience consisting mainly of members, listened on Saturday to Dr. Lehrs's inspiring lecture 'The Impulse of the Shepherds and the Impulse of the Kings in Human Understanding'. Each day there were opportunities for social gatherings and the excellent teas so well organised by Mrs. Goodman and her helpers added greatly to the general enjoyment. There were many new members present. For others it was the first visit to Rudolf Steiner House since the outbreak of the war and the happiness of reunion in the building which had so miraculously escaped the effects of bombing was felt by all. It was a meeting which will be long remembered as one of the most important in the history of the Society.

3. Family Man, Advocate and Adviser

It cannot have been lost on Harwood that during these war-time years he was in a certain sense in a state of triple evacuation. Not only was Michael Hall evacuated from Streatham but the Anthroposophical Society in Great Britain could be said to be exiled from its world headquarters in Dornach. Moreover, Britain was at war with the countries of Central Europe whence anthroposophy had derived through the work of Rudolf Steiner. That he and his colleagues in Minehead were able not only to sustain this but also to transform such a situation into an oasis of invigorating and renewing forces (as has been made apparent in the two previous chapters) is a deed whose effects cannot fail to have profound consequences for the future. But none of this would have been possible without the support and sacrifices of his family. Because of this, it will be of value at this point to quote further from Lois Olivier's memoir of her father, beginning from the point where she begins to describe the family's Minehead home located in the former servants' quarters of the main house:

> Our new home was somewhat cramped, with no bathroom either. This was remedied when the entrance 'bothy' was partitioned, a bath installed and a cauldron with a gas ring beneath it. Water was conveyed by hosepipe from the cold tap. There were numerous occasions when either the water overflowed, or was allowed to boil away merrily, filling the whole place with steam. Father had a narrow den off the sitting room, lined with his books. I used to practise the piano after lunch, but at a given signal I had to abstain, as father was about to embark on his 'forty winks'. This habit of taking a nap after lunch probably enabled him to maintain that air of 'imperturbability' he was noted for, in spite of a very full daily schedule. He would start the day by getting the breakfast ready, putting the porridge on before shaving.
>
> Despite the rationing and other trials, the duration was a very happy time. On washing days we were sent down into the town to be fed at the British Restaurant. This was often combined with a visit to the local library. The cinema was quite popular, and there were sometimes concerts in the rather garish Regal Ballroom. But there was also a deal of entertainment in the school stable-theatre: plays, music, and parties with hilarious skits when some of the teachers let their hair down.
>
> Father joined the Home Guard—and looked very uncomfortable in his uniform and stiff boots. Often on night watches overlooking the Bristol Channel he would be asked by his companions for 'some of they stories'. He in fact broadened their horizon by regaling them with the adventures of

Odysseus. CSL[ewis] visited us now and then, though he must have put up elsewhere, as there was no spare bed. There was an occasion when father took him on a cliff walk in the direction of Bossington, and some of the path had been precarious. We were given to understand that CSL had not liked it—and did not have a head for heights. Father would take it in his stride—for so often in Cornwall he had had to guide us elder ones up steep cliffs, after being cut off by the tide on a shore-line exploration.

We had a pony, mainly in my charge. Father would take his turn at exercising her, but could not always be said to be in control, particularly when she decided to turn round and head for home at a canter. In Somerset there were also countless outings on bikes, with our little sister [Sylvia, born in May 1937] installed on father's cross-bar—to the delightful valleys and moors in the vicinity. Although Michael Hall teachers had subsistence salaries, we never seemed to miss out on summer holidays. We would stay in Guest Houses in various parts of Exmoor. My mother would sometimes ride the pony over the moors to join us at the chosen hostelry. (She was already in her fifties, but a good horsewoman, having been brought up to play polo in Jamaica.) As the car was laid up, we must have covered the distance on our bikes. The Cornish cottage was no longer at our disposal, as the farmer had been detailed to take on an extra labourer to dig for victory. But we did visit the cottage in North Wales belonging to my mother's Cambridge friend, Eva Hubback (later the principal of Morley College). That idyllic place inspired father to write his play *A Rope their Pulley*. Father led many a mountain trek. Occasionally we would find a dead sheep in the stream that ran down the mountainside and supplied our drinking water! After the war, there were holidays further afield: in the Lakes, on Mull, in S. Ireland.

Father had his vegetable bed on the terrace near our 'quarters'. There was a greenhouse with a mildew vine. This was a useful retreat—with a novel— from the clamour of younger siblings, warm in the winter sunshine. Next to it was the workshop where father produced many a toy, including stilts and a sledge.

Christmas was always an especially happy time in our household—starting with the excitement of finding one's stocking bulging at the foot of the bed. There was the candle-lit tree always, and father accompanying carols on the piano. People used to *make* presents in those days, which were well appreciated.

We never returned to the house in Angles Rd.—probably much to everyone's relief. After hostilities ended, it was decided to re-locate Michael Hall nearer London, in the Home Counties. A property was sought suitable to accommodate boarders. Ottershaw College was on the cards, but the deal fell through. Eventually father and William Mann, also a teacher, reported favourably on Kidbrooke Park, in Sussex. And so in 1945 the numerous containers with school equipment took to the road, heading for Forest Row. The school moved in two stages, with the upper school being installed first. Hence mother and the younger ones remained longer in Minehead, while father and I had our first (and only) taste of being boarders. (John had already left school.) The 'mansion', a fine post-Georgian building, had been used by the Alliance Co. during the war. They had put up some useful large huts of timber, which served well for classrooms. But there was also a lot of practical work to be done. We were all given turns at scraper duty to remove the ubiquitous black-out paint.

A cottage beside the back drive entrance was allotted to us. The rooms were rather small, so after a while an extra sitting room was built on, clad in wood. It was here that father turned his hand to building the fireplace. He was somewhat put out when a tradesman who happened to see it remarked: 'Who laid those bricks? Ought to be shot.' Father made a splendid shoe cupboard for our numerous footwear. After improving the coal-shed also, the coalman was heard muttering 'Nice coal-hole spiled'. Both parents were fond of gardening. There were roses, as well as sundry vegetables. When my mother was ill, father had an extra window put in her room so that she could see the garden better and have more sunlight.

As Lois implies, Daphne Harwood was very anxious that their new home should be as warm and welcoming as possible, and she was fastidious about domestic details. She must have visited Kidbrooke on at least one occasion before the latter part of November, when she wrote two letters to Cecil which give expression, on the one hand, to her deep love for her husband and children but also to her concerns and, quite possible also, to her growing physical frailty. These letters are undated but must have been written towards the end of November 1945. They were in the end sent together prior to Daphne's visit to Kidbrooke on 6 December. She writes appreciatively about the recent school assembly at Minehead and about the stresses experienced by some of the teachers. The second letter includes a passage typical of Daphne's writing:

Sylvia haled me out over Hopcott and down Alcombe yesterday afternoon ... I was most grateful to her—golden and tawny leaves still hung on the branches, and there was a lovely misty peace on the hills and in the woods— and a good smell of damp earth. We chased down the wood's path, steep—and Sylvia said 'I'm so happy, I'm so happy'—and every now and then she turned aside and went under a clump of young spruces with their tent-like branches: 'This is our house—you must come in, isn't it *lovely*, Mummy'. It is a joy to go a walk with her and see her deep love of trees and moss—and wood sorrel—and sheep—and streams ('I kissed the stream goodbye, Mummy, feel my nice fresh mouth'—and she gave me one of the most blessedly cold kisses I have ever felt)—and the four goats...

Twelve-year-old Laurence, meanwhile, was having a flute lesson at the teacher's house they visited on their walk, while his younger brother Mark was entertaining a little girl called Angela with a game of marbles.

Much of the rest of both letters consisted of practical plans for gas points in various rooms of the new house and thoughts about all their furniture which had been stored at Streatham and which was now going to be very useful ('O goodness—how I blessed you and any others concerned that we don't go back there'). And she emphasizes the importance of keeping the PIANO (in capital letters) free from damp and in a place it doesn't have to be moved from more than necessary.

And then after writing that she is glad that 'an extra room is being seriously considered', she goes on to say:

> No—I don't think I take a black view—not on the whole. I was feeling unwell last weekend at Kidbrooke and hence felt, more than I should have done perhaps, the fact that not only your mind but your heart and soul are so entirely filled by your life and work there—that to maintain intimacy of soul—let alone to develop it—is hard, because it seems like intruding where there is no room. I mean—of course we may exchange views about stoves—and even attend reading of anthroposophical lectures—but it is what lies between these... It is only too natural that things should be like this now... I have hope and faith that there is a way through and out.

John Harwood, Cecil and Daphne's oldest son, would have still been a pupil at Minehead when he wrote a lengthy letter to his father dated 13 January 1943 from the address of his maternal grandparents at Wychwood, Selsey Avenue, Bognor Regis (his grandfather, Lord Olivier, died shortly after in February 1943 not long after the last of their frequent visits to Minehead in the summer of 1942). This would have been during the Christmas holidays, as the new term that year began only on the school's birthday, 20 January. This is not the only letter from his children that Cecil kept amongst his papers: there are also two newsy letters from Laurence when he would been, respectively, eleven and twelve, and one other from John. But this long letter gives an intelligent and critically-minded sixteen-year-old's impression of a war-time London that is full of active cultural life. He spends his first night in London at the Rudolf Steiner House canteen and has supper with Owen Barfield and his daughter Lucy, goes to see *The Marriage of Figaro* at the New Theatre, then visits his school's former haunts in Streatham where a party is taking place and the next day attends a local performance of an excerpt from the Coventry Cycle of the Mystery Plays. Returning to the middle of London (which, he says, 'is a very small place after all') he meets up with his Uncle Arnold (one of Cecil's brothers), who is an architect with an office in London. He then meets up with his mother at Victoria Station (Daphne must have been spending time with her parents at Bognor) and attends another performance at the New Theatre which, as it happens, his mother's sister Noel has also gone to see. The following day he goes to see a play called *The Doctor's Dilemma* and after that attends a concert at the National Gallery. After spending time shopping with his mother in Bognor they go to Arundel and then Chichester they both return to London, hear another concert at the National Gallery and then see *The Magic Flute*. After going to another concert he then goes together with some others including Maisie Radford to hear Vaughan Williams lecture at Morley College on 'How to write an Opera' (John comments: 'I don't think I could write an opera from what he said although he said quite a lot and cracked a lot of jokes'). I include a brief impression of this 14-page letter because it somehow makes one aware of some of his parents' rich cultural life and connections even as the country was in the midst of war. (If this book was about John, the letter itself would be included here in all its entertaining eloquence.)

Mention should be made in view of the reference to Maisie Radford of a letter from her to Cecil. The letter is undated, although it is clear it was written during the war in response to one from Cecil. Despite the fact that St. Anthony in Roseland, being right on the coast, was vulnerable to raids from sea and air, she was still very busy with concert parties. The letter is imbued with the endeavour to sustain musical life at a time when so many people were having to experience evacuation and enforced migration, which—quite apart from all the horrors of destruction that war brings—she sees as a not unmixed blessing.

★

Because of his role at Michael Hall and his position as Chairman of the Anthroposophical Society in Great Britain, Harwood must have received a lot of correspondence; and the letters that he kept from the war years are probably the merest fraction of what must have been generated by his extraordinary ability to enter into people's situations and problems and to try to find satisfactory solutions. Some of these letters are simply from former pupils (including at least one on active military service), others are from friends and acquaintances wanting his advice or asking his opinion of something that they have written. There are several letters from the grateful parent of a boy whom Harwood agreed in 1941 to take on as a pupil and whose situation was, evidently, not straightforward. In one letter dated 2 November 1941 the father of this boy describes Harwood as follows: 'You are indeed a redeeming feature on that blot called England [this gentleman, Charles Ellis, lived in Forres]: I am even encouraged, against all the evidence, to hope that the few good Englishmen (who are *very* good) will be sufficient to leaven the many (who are so ghastly)—with the help of course of the Scots and perhaps an odd American or two.' There is one lengthy letter from Charles Davy dated 4 May 1943 about ideas regarding higher education, a theme which—as already indicated—was very important for Harwood. Some letters are quite specific in their content, as, for example, Herbert Read's letter of 22 December 1940 expressing his warmest appreciation for Harwood's book *The Way of a Child;* and there is also Walter Johannes Stein's grateful letter of 10 November 1940 in response to Harwood's efforts to secure for him a position within the Anthroposophical Society that could enable him to carry out the work—and it turned out to be very considerable—that he wished to achieve. He continued to correspond with Eric Beckett and with Owen Barfield, and there are a few interesting letters from Barfield which help to identify where he was living during these years.

In one of these letters, dated 6 February 1944 and written from Long Crendon, Barfield writes about the background to his book *This Ever Diverse Pair*:

> About my Preface [this may possibly have been his introduction to the collection of his essays published under the title *Romanticism Comes of Age* later on in 1944]: I will really try and get on with this now. I suppose I had better make a clean breast of it and admit that one of the things that has kept me from it is the fact that I have been writing something else. A number of serio-comic studies concerning my experiences as a Solicitor, rather personal—egocentric, but I really think the alternative would have been a nervous breakdown at some time in the period 1941–43. It got near enough completion about the end of last year to make me very anxious to get it really finished and put out of the way. You might regard this information as confidential since, if it is published, it will be under a strictly preserved pseudonym and the identity of the author only disclosed to a few selected friends. Friends who are also clients will be selected with even greater care! Lewis and [Eric] Beckett have both seen or heard parts of it and seem to approve. The characters and events are of course all imaginary and it's not for *that* reason that I should want to preserve the anonymity. No doubt you will say, if I could find time for that, I could have found time to write stuff to help the A.S. [Anthroposophical Society] instead. But it doesn't work out quite that way. Writing from pure inclination is a form of relaxation and

there are times when I can write this stuff though too tired to read. Actually most of it was scribbled in pencil in trains and it is only the transcribing and tidying up for the typist which is using up the little bit of spare time I should otherwise have for the Preface.

And he adds in a 'P.S.': 'I am of Daphne's way of thinking about the *Abolition of Man*. I read it twice and found it one of the most faultless things [C.S.] Lewis has done. Very pertinent indeed to the current climate of thought and beautifully expressed. Them's *my* sentiments.'

In connection with his correspondence with Barfield during this time, there was one matter that had arisen which well illustrates the lengths that Harwood would go in trying to help someone in their difficulties. That the person concerned was a close friend from his Oxford days, namely Leo Baker, must have added to the energy that he devoted to the affair in question, which came to a head towards the end of 1942. Suffice it to say that Baker, who was at the time employed by Wynstones School, was responsible for an act of indiscretion when, in Barfield's words (Barfield was involved as the Anthroposophical Society's legal adviser, because the affair threatened to mushroom into a major scandal), 'he was in a suicidal frame of mind with toxic poisoning'. It would appear that the school massively over-reacted (it is of no significance for present purposes what this act of indiscretion was) and the whole affair threatened to blow out of all proportion. To make matters worse, relationships between Leo Baker and his wife Eileen were at the time not as harmonious as they might have been. Harwood initially offered Leo and Eileen a cottage at Minehead where they could live and send their children to Michael Hall, but there was a fear that the explosive nature of the situation would follow the Bakers there; and so Harwood made the suggestion that he might try to speak with Miss Margaret Bennell, who was ultimately responsible for the line that Wynstones was taking. However, Baker was worried that this might be construed as an attempt on his part to use Harwood's (and Michael Hall's) prestige to his own personal advantage. And then he makes the following comment about Harwood's skills in negotiations of this kind: 'You are one of the very few people whose reputation etc. is such that we could ask you to serve as a watching and advising third party. There is hardly anyone else with sufficient experience, authority and unquestioned impartiality...' (from a letter dated 26 November 1942).

The other item in the correspondence that Harwood kept consists of letters from Dr. Ernst Lehrs. The background to the first—and very long—letter from Lehrs that Harwood retained, dated 13 January 1941, is the reference in the November 1940 issue of *Anthroposophical Movement* to letters that had been received from 'enemy aliens' in the Internment Camp on the Isle of Man. Karl König's letter, testifying to his release from captivity, has already been referred to earlier; but at the time Lehrs was still in confinement, together with his wife, Maria Röschl-Lehrs:

> Dr. Lehrs, with little emphasis upon his own position in an Internment Camp, writes to say how glad he is to hear of the work upon which we are engaged and how deeply he would like to be together with us in the 'actual Front', as he puts it. He also writes of the work among young Internees in the Camp during the time when Dr. König was also there with him and which he will continue alone now that Dr. König is happily released.

Lehrs and his wife must have been working at Wynstones when they were interned. Harwood, as Chairman of the Anthroposophical Society in Great Britain, must have devoted considerable energies to campaigning for the release of anthroposophists who were suffering from the internment policies of the British Government, and Lehrs refers to a memorandum which he wrote on their behalf (for which he was very grateful). Lehrs's own situation was further complicated by the extreme anti-alien sentiment around Wynstones (though doubtless not at the school itself) and by his wife's need to take advantage of an offer made by König that they join him at Camphill Aberdeen. This seven-page (and the pages are large) letter from Lehrs is for the most part a detailed description of the complicated endeavours on the part of many people, and not only Harwood by any means, which finally led to his and Maria's arrival at Heathcot House, Blairs, Aberdeen in January 1941. At times during Lehrs's letters his choleric nature manifests itself in the form of impatience at Harwood's inability to reply to his questions more or less immediately, but this is tempered by his awareness of 'how pre-occupied you usually are and how many different threads are pulling at you' (letter dated 10 May 1943). What is so amazing is the way in which all this sorrow and frustration was transformed into a constructive and loving working relationship based on mutual respect. This quotation comes from Lehrs's letter of 14 May 1941:

> Dear Cecil, Tomorrow will be the anniversary of our unhappy tribunal where you so gallantly fought for us. In vivid recollection of that event and of the following most unhappy day of my life—which then was to bring about such an exceedingly fruitful time—I am writing to you taking this opportunity for telling you that I have just finished reading your book *The Way of a Child*. It must be the result of my internment that I had no knowledge of its publication up to quite recent weeks. Then I ordered it from London and read it at once, as I must confess, with the utmost delight.

This little book is a deed. I am sure it is exactly what Dr. Steiner so badly wanted us to do but what never anyone of us managed. It is absolutely astonishing in what concise form you get expressed all those fundamental things. Everything is put forward in a lucid way so that the reader can feel to gain definite knowledge and yet can feel eager to know more from the original source. It is a masterpiece how you have distributed the name of Rudolf Steiner throughout the book and how you have pointed out the relation of the following contact to him in your Preface. I am sure the existence of the book will be of great help for our work where first information is wanted about our Education, as e.g. here in Scotland...

Through this correspondence with Lehrs, the initial contact already strongly formed with König was able to blossom. As already indicated, this bore fruit in Harwood's fleeting journey northwards in September 1941 (Lehrs had hoped that he might have been able to attend the Whitsun Conference in Camphill that year, but it was not possible for Harwood to squeeze this into his busy schedule). I shall conclude this section with some thoughts about educational policy that Lehrs expressed in the last letter of the series that Harwood retained and left for posterity (or maybe it was altogether the last that he received from Lehrs). This letter was dated 10 May 1943:

Dr. Steiner once said to us in a College meeting that with time only three forms of education will remain—the Socialist... [or] Western one based on materialism (for notwithstanding the great variety of theories and methods in this stream, it will finally be one single one only)—then the Catholic, and between these two powerful currents the tiny seedling of the anthrop. education. Now my 'vision' of the post-war situation is this: that immediately Germany has been occupied and the Nazi domination abolished, the R.C. Church, represented by their bishopry in Germany on the one hand, and the Socialists, backed by the British Minister of Education, the Soviets etc. etc. will take matters into their hands and divide the prey between them and it will be extremely difficult to find any 'gap' between them for the re-establishment of a free education. For they will both function as the official representatives of the world's 'decency'; and who will be able to deny this to them?—It will be therefore very important to raise our voice in good time that a gap be left for the re-establishment for what one could term free education based on spiritual principles (Christian)... However, will it not sound rather ridiculous to claim the backing for something as essential for the reconstruction of the German people which is not even properly backed in this country itself?! And here, we feel [by 'we' he means he and his wife], lies the real problem. When people ask us here what the British people could do to help Germany to get back to her true educational spirit, our answer always is: first to arrive at it themselves! There cannot be any salvation spread elsewhere which one has not first applied to oneself. Thus let Britain give after the war a fair chance to the R.St. Education for developing in her own country, then the rest will come quite by itself.

There is still another possible picture of the future, and a very much more tragic one. I don't know whether I have ever mentioned these things to you, or whether you have learnt of them through other channels. I mean the picture Dr. St. has drawn of Germany's inevitable future in the course of this century. I will quote it to you as it has been written down by Count Polzer [Ludwig Polzer-Hoditz] immediately after a conversation [that he and some others had] with Dr. St. about these matters: 'The towns in Middle Europe will gradually perish, an agricultural population will remain and a few spiritual centres where the West will send [its] sons for their education. These spiritual centres will foster the spiritual life in a monasterial form. The industrialism has ruined Germany; its chimneys will fall.' At an entirely different occasion, at a different time Dr. Steiner said exactly the same words in [Ehrenfried] Pfeiffer's presence about the spiritual life, speaking of these centres as cultivating the spiritual life in the way 'of the Waldorf School'.

It is, of course, impossible for us to know whether this applies already to the end of *this* war, or only to a time after other such catastrophes have swept over Europe. In this case a 'gap' might be granted to us, as it was after the end of the last war, of a number of years during which we will enjoy comparative freedom to build a little further what has been founded during the last gap.

PART THREE

1. The Destiny of Britain within Europe and the Wider World and the Individual Human Spirit

Hitherto, the main focus of this book has been upon Cecil Harwood's personal journey—largely prompted and facilitated by the meeting with Daphne Olivier in September 1922 in Cornwall—in helping to found and then play a crucial role in developing and bringing stability to the first Rudolf Steiner School in Britain, Michael Hall. He did, of course, continue to be actively involved with Michael Hall and with Steiner Education for the rest of his life; and when, for example, it was decided to resume publication of the Waldorf periodical *Child and Man* after the war-years in June 1947, it was Harwood who was chosen to be its editor.[108] However, from approximately the time when the school found sanctuary and a sense of permanency in Sussex after its war-time exile in Minehead, Harwood's considerable creative powers were devoted among other things to identifying and—in a particular context—endeavouring to fulfil a much wider task. This task concerned Britain's place in the wider world (especially in Europe) as discerned from an anthroposophical perspective; and the context in which Harwood was able practically to implement something of this broaching of the question 'What are we—in Britain—here to do?' was given to him through the longevity of his Chairmanship of the Anthroposophical Society in Great Britain.

It is not possible to appreciate the full significance of Harwood's endeavours in this connection without viewing his contribution alongside that of his close friend Owen Barfield. Except for the short period when Barfield taught at The New School in Streatham, he and Harwood were never professional colleagues. However, they were both members of the Council of the Anthroposophical Society in Great Britain continuously from January 1930 until Harwood's retirement from the Chairmanship in 1974 (Harwood had joined in January 1928), while Barfield 'gracefully retired' at the Annual General Meeting in March 1976 following Harwood's death. Barfield also served as Treasurer of the Society for six years, from his appointment in May 1961. In this capacity and in other respects in their writing and lecturing activity, each of the two men brought a different—but intimately related—element to bear. Harwood, with his seemingly infinite sociability and gregariousness, tended to view matters of social and cultural development in terms of social groupings (such as nations) and through an understanding of folk psychology, whereas Barfield's more universal approach lay primarily through the individual, through addressing the fundamental issues lying at the root of modern cultural dilemmas enshrined in a question such as 'Do I exist?' Because of this, Owen Barfield will feature more prominently in this part of the book than he has previously; and there is even a sense in which some of his thoughts point towards cultural and social developments that have the potential to build further upon what Cecil Harwood actually achieved in his life.

Harwood published very little in the way of books. Apart from *The Way of a Child* (1940), his only other books were *The Recovery of Man in Childhood: A Study of the Educational Work of Rudolf Steiner* (Hodder and Stoughton, London 1958) and *Shakespeare's Prophetic Mind* (Rudolf Steiner Press, London 1964). He mostly contributed his thoughts by way of copious lectures. From the evidence of such of his lecture-notes that have been preserved, all his lectures were meticulously prepared and he never simply 'winged it'. Moreover, this preparation was itself founded upon extensive annotations from Rudolf Steiner's books and lectures, to each of which he would devote a separate exercise-book. As his lecturing activity largely preceded the advent of tape-recorders (although I know of at least one recording of two lectures that he gave in Northern Ireland, on 'The History of Man' and 'Karma'), and no one saw fit at the time to appoint someone to record what he said in shorthand, one is limited to a perusal of his notes in an almost illegible hand. From these extant notes and from the titles of many other lectures that were announced in issues of anthroposophical publications, it becomes apparent that especially towards the end of his life he tended to focus mainly upon historical themes (although he continued to be asked to lecture about Steiner Education, most notably in Colleges of Education). Typical examples of the scope of Harwood's lectures on history are courses that he gave at Rudolf Steiner House in 1958 and 1965. Thus between 22 January and 26 March 1958 he gave a course of ten lectures on the overall theme of *'Man's Search for Himself in History'*, the individual titles of which were as follows: 'Egypt and the World of the Dead', 'Chaldaea and the World of the Stars', 'The Human Soul in Mythology', 'Greek Philosophy: from thinking in Pictures, to thinking in Ideas', 'Saint and Ascetic: the early Christian Ideal', 'Chivalry and the Orders of Knighthood', 'Faith and Knowledge: the Dualism of the Middle Ages', 'Knowledge for Power: the Signature of Bacon', 'Evolution and Dialectical Man' and 'The Recovery of Man in Spiritual Science'; while in the spring of 1965 he shared with William Mann in giving a course of twelve lectures between 19 January and 7 April entitled *'Man's Destiny with the Earth: its Impress in History and in Art'*, with Harwood addressing the historical themes of 'Egypt and Sumeria: the Stars and the Tomb', 'Egypt reaches its Agony: the Climax of an Empire', 'Reaching for the Logos: Christians before Christ', 'Athens, Jerusalem, Rome: Life Struggle and Death Struggle', 'The Light and Darkness of Mediaeval Man' and 'The Last Inheritance: the Discovery of the Earth and its inner Meaning'. With respect to themes in the specific area of this chapter's title, reference has already been made in Part 2 Chapter two to a lecture on 'England and the Belief in Freedom' that Harwood gave during a members' weekend conference at Rudolf Steiner House in mid-September 1941 on the overall theme *The Task before us at this Moment in History* and also to a public lecture on the theme 'The British Genius in the Mission of Europe' that he had intended to give at a weekend gathering at Rudolf Steiner House on 8–9 July 1943 (the event was cancelled owing to war-time activity and there is no evidence that the lecture was given in the form intended). Another characteristic contribution was made at the Summer School in The Hague (14 July–9 August 1958) on *The Social and Cultural Rebuilding of Europe*, where Harwood's responsibility was to speak from a 'West-European' perspective. Much of Harwood's lecturing activity on this theme arose from his deep knowledge of history (as already noted) and his awareness of the stream of the evolution of consciousness. This was exemplified by his lectures on English History at Rudolf Steiner House in May—June 1959 with the general title *From Spectator to Stage*, repeated as three public lectures given in Glasgow (24 November, 1 and 2 December 1959) on 'Man before Christ', 'Man in the Middle Ages' and 'Modern Man', and his lecture in Brighton (31 October 1961) on 'History and the Individual'. In the period leading up to the four hundredth anniversary of Shakespeare's birth (when his own book on Shakespeare was also published), he was working with questions such as 'Shakespeare's Image of Man: a Study in the Development of Consciousness' (a lecture given at Rudolf Steiner Hall on 25 April 1964) and 'The Mystery of the Spiritual [Consciousness] Soul', which formed his main contribution to a Whitsun Conference (16–18 May 1964).[109] The same year saw Harwood leading a weekend conference at The Old Manse, Lumsden, Aberdeenshire (11–14 September), where he was lecturing on the overall theme of *From Mediaeval Man to Modern Individual*, giving four lectures on the birth and development of the consciousness soul as it can be observed in English literature and history: the Canterbury Tales, Shakespeare and the Aptitude of the British for a Threefold Way of Life. More broadly, perhaps, he gave a pair of lectures in Bristol (4 and 11 May 1966) on 'The Idea of Man in the Technological Age'[110] and 'Accident or Centre of World Events'; and in the next month his theme at Ardleigh, near Colchester on 9 June was 'The Chaos in the World and the Chaos in Man'. Similarly, he would not infrequently address the subject of Rudolf Steiner's central contribution—as he saw it—to the modern world. Towards the very end of his life he gave numerous lectures on the general theme of Britain and the Consciousness Soul especially to young people—most notably at Emerson College from the time of its move to Forest Row in the summer of 1964 and until the early part of 1972 but also at a Youth Conference at Michael Hall in 1968, where his theme was explicitly that of 'The Consciousness Soul'.

However, Harwood found time to write several articles for the most part published in the *Anthroposophical Quarterly*, which he co-edited with Mildred Kirkaldy from its inception in 1956 until the autumn of 1975, and *The Golden Blade*. While virtually all his contributions to the former periodical were reviews or comments upon books that had been published, the annual publication of the latter—its first issue appeared under the editorship of Arnold Freeman and Charles Waterman (Davy) in 1949—gave him the opportunity to give freer rein to some of his deepest thoughts and insights; and it was in a pair of *Golden Blade* articles written (or at any rate published) 25 years apart that he gave the fullest testimony to his deep affinity with the theme of Britain's place in the world. These were entitled 'Tendencies to a Threefold Social Order in English History' (1949) and 'Threefold Ideas in English Life: the Organic Society' (1974). It is also of significance that when he came to edit a volume of essays in 1961—thus approximately mid-way between the appearance of these two articles—commemorating the centenary of Rudolf Steiner's birth,[111] Harwood chose to contribute not something about Waldorf education but an essay brilliantly summarizing the evolutionary journey of humanity through the post-Atlantean age from the time of the Indian cultures of pre-history to the modern age.

Because of their importance and relative inaccessibility, I propose to reproduce these two *Golden Blade* articles here. The first contains several little gem-like insights about England (or Britain) and the consciousness soul, while the second in particular has some ideas which are by no means out of place in today's social and political climate. Both articles owe much to Charles Waterman/Davy's book *The Three Spheres of Society*, published by Faber and Faber in 1946.

Tendencies to a Threefold Social Order in English History

The threefold order of society envisaged by Rudolf Steiner is based on a division of function, not on a division of classes.

It therefore represents something new in history, and, like all new things, is born out of a change of human consciousness. Plato's Republic had its divisions, but they were class divisions of much strictness; in this they merely reflected contemporary society which made an absolute distinction, for instance, between freeman and slave. A similar absolute distinction between the serf and the various classes of freemen (themselves fairly rigidly distinguished) survived into the Middle Ages, and was reinforced by the great distinction between secular and clerical society. It is only in recent times that the same man has had the ability to think of himself as belonging to the various spheres of society, and acting differently in a variety of capacities.

It is easy to recognise and acclaim the great discoveries and inventions that belong to the modern age. It is far more difficult to characterise the change in consciousness which has made these discoveries possible. Since the Renaissance a new type of mind has been born, or has been undergoing a slow process of birth, to which Rudolf Steiner—the first person fully to recognise and describe it—has given the name of 'consciousness soul'. One characteristic of this consciousness soul is that it moves freely and easily among material things and the forces of the physical world; another is that it can live outside time and so develop a historical sense; a third—which in reality underlies the other two—is that it endows a man with the capacity to see himself from outside, even in the engrossing moment of action. It has been called the spectator consciousness; it could be called the Hamlet consciousness—for who has not sometimes felt that the very play in which Hamlet is the principal actor takes place in his mind, that the play is in him no less than he is in the play?

This new consciousness belongs to all Western Europe since the Renaissance, but it is most deeply implanted, penetrating to their very blood and bone, in the Anglo-Saxon races. It crops up in the earliest stories of English history. There is something of it in the attitude of Thomas-a-Becket, who served the King when he was Chancellor, but the Pope when he was Archbishop. It was there when Drake played out his game of bowls. It shines brilliantly by reflection in the story that Napoleon, after Waterloo, said to one of his captors: 'What will Wellington do now? I suppose he will make himself King of England'—unaware that the Duke put on his civilian clothes as fast as he could, and that when he had them on, he put on also a civilian mind which could never even have conceived such a thought. Chesterton has put this attitude (perhaps a little early) into the behaviour of Alfred the Great, when his first thoughts, on being slapped by the woman whose cakes he had burnt, are of torture:

> and the evil things
> That are in the childish hearts of kings –

but in a moment his mood changes, he goes out and the woman looks

> On a stranger sight than sylph or elf,
> On one man laughing at himself
> Under the greenwood tree.

This ability to put oneself outside oneself—which includes, of course, the ability to laugh at oneself—is, I repeat, something new in human history. The Romans had a touch of it in some outstanding personalities, but it did not become a common possession of mankind until the Renaissance, and then only gradually, and principally in this country. Historians are sometimes puzzled by the fact that former civilisations did not invent the idea of representative government. But to be a representative you must be prepared and able at the right time to forget yourself and act as a representative—and you are not likely to be chosen unless other people believe that you will do so. Your representative may announce that he represents your interests and not your opinions, but they are at least *your* interests and not his. You do not expect he will use his position to make himself King of England. He must see himself from outside acting as a representative. Without this ability, and general confidence that it will be exercised, representative government is impossible.

It is this ability which has made representative government possible in England during the past few hundred years; it is lack of this ability which has made it impossible in other ages and other countries. Rudolf Steiner relied on it when he proposed the threefold social order for Central Europe after the First World War. Hitler (and before Hitler, Woodrow Wilson) denied it. If you cannot separate yourself as economic man from yourself as spiritual man or man of rights, you will be a German or an Italian or a Russian in all three spheres. This is the final conclusion of nationalism which Wilson preached and the dictators materialised.

The consciousness soul was not born even in this country in a year, a decade, or even a century. The Englishman whom we regard as typical (he belongs perhaps more to the last [19th] century than to this), with his inexcitability and detachment, his dislike of extremes and of display, his toleration and spirit of compromise, his Roman solidity and Greek love of understatement, was simply not to be found in the sixteenth, seventeenth or eighteenth centuries. The Elizabethan gentleman would sell an estate to provide himself with a suit of clothes; he was personally dirty and covered up the smell with a plentiful use of civet; he was indifferent to cruelty; he delighted in the affected and extravagant in art; he paid outrageous and sycophantic compliments unblushingly; his immediate descendants were often religious fanatics. In other words, he exhibited most of the traits that we would today think characteristic of the Spanish or Italian peoples.

Similarly, his followers of the eighteenth century, with their wit, their satire, their love of reason and proportion, their elegance and their rhetoric, were more akin to the French than to the modern Englishman. Yet through all this exotic vegetation there is always springing up the new native growth of the consciousness soul, destined to destroy alike the good and the bad in the earlier character. With this growth comes an instinctive feeling towards the threefold social order; the man of the consciousness soul wants to see himself as a different being acting under different principles when he is a producer or consumer, when he is obeying the laws, when he is engaged in public controversy at Hyde Park Corner, or writing a book, or founding a university.

It is always hard to know where to begin in tracing a new movement. Critics who seek the origins of the Romantic Movement are apt suddenly to find themselves way back in the spacious days of Beowulf. So with the consciousness soul you can point to such a change in the law as Elizabeth introduced, when the Papists were no longer persecuted for their beliefs but fined for not attending church—the law no longer enquiring into your opinions but concerning itself only with your practices—a distinction of very great importance for a country which was to introduce the new scientific views of the world against a background of traditional religion. You could no doubt go back earlier still; but, for the present purpose at any rate, perhaps the best beginning is the time of the Civil Wars of the seventeenth century, so closely parallel and yet in such contrast to the Thirty Years' War in Central Europe.

The Thirty Years' War began as a religious struggle; it ended as a purely secular fight for the dominance of Europe. At first Catholic troops fought Protestant—both sides almost in the spirit of a crusade; but Wallenstein found that all he needed were soldiers—of whatever religion; and Richelieu, though a Cardinal of the Roman Church, was prepared to back either side if it were profitable to France. The incidents of the war are of great complexity; the political development simple and uniform.

The English Civil Wars, on the other hand, present from the very beginning a much more complicated picture. From the first the quarrel takes place on three levels, and in three spheres. There is the trade and economic quarrel. It does not matter whether the interference of the early Stuarts with trade by means of monopolies and imports and controls was a good or a bad thing; the new trading and manufacturing communities believed that it was not the function of the King to interfere with trade and manufacture. Then there is the legal quarrel. It does not matter whether Ship-Money was morally right or wrong; the legal community believed it represented one more act of the King against the law—and they believed (unlike the Stuarts themselves) that the King was under the law no less than the humblest of his subjects. Finally, there was the religious question, not altogether accidentally bound up with the other two. For the trading communities were naturally Puritan. The practice of trade produced the puritan virtues of thrift and economy rather than the older ideal of giving your coat to the beggar or your estate to the church. And these virtues again worked back on commercial ability and astuteness.

The Stuart Kings stood for the divine right of kings, which was really a renaissance of ancient Egypt, where the Pharaoh was high priest and judge and economic administrator in one. Like Kepler, they 'stole the golden vessels of the Egyptians', but not to the same satisfactory end. For, by their policy of the unified State, they had the misfortune to unite against them all the elements of a threefold state struggling to be born. They were not fighting against men alone, but against those impersonal forces in history which achieve so quickly such unforeseeable results.

What was the position when the struggle was over? How different was the social England to which Charles II returned from that which he left? It would be idle to pretend that spiritual freedom had been obtained. Books and newspapers had still to be licensed; religious toleration was of the most fitful kind, and then granted for political rather than spiritual reasons; but monopolies had gone and, in spite of some forced loans, the trading community had achieved a far greater measure of independence than it enjoyed under Elizabeth. It was in the sphere of rights, however, that the position appeared most consolidated. Probably as much through the experience of military government under Cromwell as through the old resistance to the Stuarts, a temper was abroad apt to resist any infringement of the law except by full constitutional procedure. It was this temper which made it impossible for James II's nominee President to find a blacksmith in Oxford willing to open the doors of Magdalen for him. It was this temper which drove James himself from London almost without a blow. This temper—reaching the remote islands of Scotland and undermining the very party of divine right—caused the Highland fishermen guarding bonny Prince Charlie in the island of Raasay to call through the door: 'You are the King—but we are the parliament—and you must do as we say!'

After the bitter experiences of the seventeenth century the law was especially regarded in the eighteenth as the guardian of individual rights and liberties. The extent to which it protected privilege is in our days almost incredible. Landlords who pulled down whole villages because their roofs offended the eye that viewed them from the Great House; parcels of uninhabited land which sent a member or two to parliament; professors who never taught, lectured or studied; vicars who never saw the parishes which gave them their comfortable incomes—all these were supported and maintained by the law. This very support of the freedom of the individual to enjoy his own had, however, one unexpected result. The great individuals whom this system encouraged were certainly not going to have their mouths muzzled. Wherever they were, they spoke out their minds—and it is not a far step from speaking to writing. Thus it came about that, whereas Gibbon thought it advisable to veil his attack on Christianity under the elaborate irony which he so much enjoyed, by the end of the century the licensing of books and newspapers was a thing of the past. The reaction against the French Revolution was to produce some fierce pieces of intolerance, but virtually freedom of speech and thought and religion was established during the eighteenth century.

The nineteenth-century historians, brought up in this freedom, appreciated to the full its virtues, but not perhaps its difficulties. Seen from the other side of the Thirty Years' War, liberty of speech and religion must have appeared almost incompatible with a coherent society. To go to a ruler of the sixteenth century and propose him to take away his controls over the spiritual life was much the same as to go to a modern ruler and propose the removal of all controls over economic life. The one would have replied, as the other does reply, that Society would go to pieces without such controls. It took much experience to discover that a nation could cohere even though the individual spoke and wrote as he liked. This possibility had become plain to the nineteenth century. What the 20 century is discovering is that this spiritual freedom is untenable unless it is supported by a pervasive and absolute belief in equality before the law. You cannot grant freedom of speech to people who believe that they are the only ones who should enjoy it. No single part of the Threefold State can stand for long alone.

For it was just at the end of the eighteenth century, when the new industries in England were beginning to call for a new and more conscious organisation of society, when England was first fully realising the consciousness soul, that the French Revolution by a characteristic flash of genius produced the three watchwords, *Liberté, Egalité, Fraternité*. The crowds who shouted them probably never reflected that the three ideals were incompatible with each other; that equality denies liberty, and fraternity equality. Because they never sorted them out and applied them in their different spheres, because they did not produce a balanced organic society, within a few years they were to suffer a rigid military dictatorship. The experience of Europe at large has been slower but not less sure.

The beginning of the nineteenth century—after the Napoleonic Wars—found England, for the first time since it became a nation, without any effective enemy on the Continent. The political situation coincided with the swift development of industry on a mechanised basis, which gave England power abroad, but, at home, presented her with problems of social organisation new in the history of the world. If mechanised industry had come in the days of slavery, the right organisation for it would have been at once apparent. Gangs of slaves would have worked the machines as they worked the plantations and the ergastula and the galleys. But the very consciousness soul which brought mankind into such close touch with the physical world that he could explore its latent forces had also produced a sense of the ego in man which precluded slavery. The great question for England, and for the world which was to follow in England's footsteps, was, under what sign will the new industries be established? Was it inevitable for them to be built up under the sign of *laissez-faire*, with its corollaries of buying in the cheapest market and selling in the dearest, and of equating labour and raw materials?

Laissez-faire is really nothing more than an extension of the eighteenth-century individualism into the factories of the nineteenth, without the aristocratic sense of social responsibility which had so often kept the great house in friendly connection with the cottages clustered outside its gates. It is therefore interesting to see from what side opposition to it arose.

Take, for instance, the Machine Wrecking Bill, which was to make machine-wrecking a capital offence. Through the pressure of the new industrialists it passed the House of Commons; but largely under the influence of a speech by Byron—who contrasted the industrial North highly unfavourably with the Turkish East—it was thrown out by the more aristocratic Lords. Then there is the strange case of Robert Owen and his 'villages of co-operation'. Owen is perhaps the first case of an industrialist with a conscience who hated the doctrine of 'buying cheap and selling dear'. His idea was to establish the new industries on a co-operative basis in communities to be financed indifferently by rich individuals, by corporations, by townships or by the Government. Profits were to be limited, the workers were to have access to the land, living was to be partly communal, and the general lay-out of the buildings somewhat like a College—without the chapel.

The great practical success of his mills at New Lanark attracted an immense interest to Owen's plans. The royal Dukes, the Archbishop of Canterbury, ambassadors and visiting Royalties, all admired and patronised his schemes. At one time it looked as though 'villages of co-operation' might have been generally established over industrial England. Indeed, the sudden dropping of Owen's schemes by his influential supporters was not due to anything inherent in the schemes themselves. Like many self-made men, Owen fancied he had discovered the secret of the universe—in the fact that man is the product of his environment. This led to the corollary that religion is inherently untrue and the root of all evil. Owen carefully staged a public declaration of this startling truth at a mass meeting in London. It was too much for the Archbishop, for the royal Dukes—and for *The Times*. Owen's schemes were dropped, and he turned his attention to founding an ideal community in America.

But the very name he wished to give to his industrial communities, 'villages of co-operation', showed that Owen was conscious of a most important fact about the new industries. Intrinsically the old craftsman had not been co-operative—he had done the whole job himself; the old serf or peasant had not been co-operative—he had ploughed *his* strip of the great field and kept *his* geese and *his* swine on the common pasture. There was social organisation for a variety of reasons, but the organisation did not arise from the actual act of production. Under the new machine industries the common work of many men was necessary to produce a single piece of cloth, a single pair of boots. The work of the world was calling for co-operation in a sense it had never done before. The new industries were asking to be started under the sign of fraternity.

Unhappily, eighteenth-century individualism proved too strong. The fraternity which afterwards arose in the industrial world—represented by the trade unions—was not directed to economic production but to the securing of rights. Industry begot battlefields rather than villages of co-operation.

Yet never had the power of free association and the forming of societies been so strong as in the nineteenth century. It had never, in fact, existed in the same way in the history of the world. No free association was allowed under the Roman Empire, and governments had hitherto regarded it as no less incompatible with social existence than freedom of speech. Association had always been regulated by charter. But now, quite suddenly, labour combinations and societies of all kinds became legal and flourished. If the eighteenth century is the great age of the individual, the nineteenth is that of the Society. Scientific, literary and antiquarian Societies, Old Boys' Clubs and Ancient Orders of Buffaloes, missionary and philanthropic Societies, Trade Unions and Freemasons—all of them had, if not their actual foundation, at any rate their flowering time in this century of association. With this came two other things—the full realisation of free trade and the urge towards universal education. Everyone was to have access to the best books, and the result was to be something like an earthly Paradise. It seemed as though the ideal of a Threefold State was about to be realised.

Here again, however, the canker of the century was at work and the buds were blighted. Free trade was not in reality free trade. It was based on the temporary and artificial conditions of a monopoly. England was, for practical purposes, the only manufacturing country. All countries that wished to be in the swim were compelled to buy from her. There was no freedom about it. With individualism rampant at home, and monopoly entrenched abroad, it was no wonder that the economic system grew up askew. We have now reached the polarity of nationalisation at home and State bargaining abroad. When Byron was a small boy a quack doctor applied an apparatus to his twisted foot which bent it an equal amount in the opposite direction. The theory was plausible, but the foot did not improve.

With the advent of the nineteenth century we enter the stage of the awakening of the working classes. They not only organise themselves in Trade Unions, but they assert their existence—for the first time—in the political and spiritual spheres, represented chiefly by the Vote and by Universal Education. The experience of education for all is a very recent one and can hardly yet be said to have succeeded. But it is interesting to observe that one at least of its earliest advocates would regard our present school system as entirely on the wrong lines. John Stuart Mill was wholeheartedly convinced that the State should pay for the education of all children whose parents could not afford to pay themselves. But he was equally convinced that the State should not provide the schools. It would be a sad day for England, he said, when individuals did not rise up to create schools, provided the necessary funds were available.

This was the ancient tradition of the independence of the spiritual sphere from the political. We still instinctively apply it to those educational institutions whose origin lies before the nineteenth century—the Universities and the Public Schools. Particularly with regard to the Universities we plume ourselves on their independence of the State, and deprecate the central control of the German Universities from Berlin. But in many quarters it would be regarded as heresy to give a similar independence to our elementary or secondary schools. In fact, the grammar schools are rapidly losing their old independence, and the turn of the Public Schools may soon come.

Those who complain that universal education, so far from producing an age of sturdy independent thought, has led to an epoch of mass suggestion, should remember that the schools have not thought for themselves. Freedom and independence are guaranteed by free institutions, not less than by free individuals.

A hundred years ago Cobbett was touring Europe and preaching Free Trade. He was able to do so because there was a general admiration for English institutions, social and economic. That admiration vanished with the First World War, and no amount of advertising the 'British Way of Life' will bring it back. But a genuine step forward in social organisation could recover it. More and more people are asking themselves if there is a way between Scylla and Charybdis. It would be a magnificent fulfilment of the tendencies of English history for England to realise it in a balanced Threefold Commonwealth.

Harwood's other article on this theme covers a roughly similar ground but has the benefit of a lifetime's research into the historical background; and it takes fully into consideration developments in the wider context of society over the intervening 25 years. (I shall include the subtitles scattered through the article, even though these may be editorial.)

The Organic Society: A Brief Historical Sketch of Steiner's Threefold Social Order

At the time of the Peace Conference of Versailles there were two contrasting views as to the settlement of Europe. The first was that of President Wilson, based on the self-determination of separate nations, essentially a spatial conception; the second was Rudolf Steiner's view of a functional division of European Society, in which the nation-state would be concerned only with the question of Rights as between its citizens, while responsibility for production and industry would be assumed by economic associations working across political frontiers, and the sphere of culture—religion, education, the arts, etc.—would be based on the free initiative of individuals and groups of individuals specially concerned for these matters.

Steiner knew his Europe—which Wilson did not—and recognised that its complex distribution of peoples and their interdependence in economic affairs made the picture of a group of neatly divided omnicompetent States an absurdity. But Wilson's view had behind it the enormous prestige of America's decisive entry into the war, and was easy to grasp in terms of traditional politics: Steiner's had some influential, and not a little popular, backing in Central Europe—he was a public figure and large audiences flocked to hear him wherever he lectured—but a functional division was difficult to grasp, and the idea probably never reached the Council table of Versailles. Steiner recognised the immediate failure, but he believed that his threefold distinction corresponded to basic needs of human nature, and that in some form or other it would evolve out of the difficulties of the next hundred years, if the western ideal of man were to survive.

Organism or Organisation

Steiner's functional division depends on regarding society as an organism rather than an organisation. An organisation, like a machine, can be separated spatially into its parts. An organism cannot be so divided into its functions. But, as Coleridge observed, it is often necessary to distinguish where we cannot divide. Steiner took the functions of the human being as an analogy—actually more than an analogy—for the distinctions he made in the functions of the social organism. You can distinguish the conscious function (of head and nerves) from the rhythmical processes (of breathing and circulation) and from the metabolism (of the digestive organs)—but you cannot separate them spatially. They follow different laws, and it is precisely because they do so that they work harmoniously together.

The three spheres of society also have their own laws and characters, and can work harmoniously only when they are so far distinguished as to react properly on each other. The keynote of each has never been better or more pithily expressed than in the inspired cry of the French Revolution: Liberty, Equality, Fraternity—ideals naturally incompatible within one polity.

The keynote of the cultural life should be freedom in the highest degree; that of the sphere of rights, the equality which guarantees a reasonable share in the advantages of society to every citizen; while that of industry, considered in its proper role of production, is patently in the modern age fraternity. For in modern industry no man produces by or for himself—thousands must co-operate to make and market even one pair of shoes.

The Threefold Idea in English History

If the French nation produced an inspired threefold slogan, it may be said that much of English social history has witnessed an instinctive struggle towards a threefold ideal. It was a struggle out of the old conception of a separatist society—in which a man was either bond or free, either a secular or a religious etc.—into one where every man had a place in all functions of society. Steiner recognised the leading position of England in this struggle when he said that in 1848 England might have established something of the nature of a threefold State. For even then the political State was losing its hold on the cultural and religious life, which was passing into the freedom of the individual, and on the economic life, which was developing international finance and world trade.

This development had depended on England pursuing over many centuries an evolution largely independent of the rest of Europe and at a different tempo. Serfdom, for instance, disappeared from England during the fifteenth century—well ahead of most of Europe. Or again, the English Reformation and the separation from Rome was of a totally different order from that of the Protestant States of Northern Europe. The Thirty Years War, which convulsed Europe in the first half of the seventeenth century, left England to its own affair of a private civil war, basically concerned with the question of sovereignty and law. Kings returned after Cromwell, but monarchy was never quite the same again, and by the end of the century Parliament demonstrated its supremacy by creating a king. Moreover the indifference of the first Georges to English affairs fostered the establishment of a parliamentary government in which the king, like his subjects, was under the law—and under the Parliament. It was in the eighteenth century, especially, that England felt itself as the country of freedom, fulfilling the claim already made by Shakespeare:

> Slaves cannot live in England; if their lungs
> Receive our air, that moment they are free.

Of course the freedom was of limited application, but it prepared the way for claims of freedom in the world of ideas and in industrial action which would have horrified most of those who first sang 'Britons never shall be slaves'. For the Industrial Revolution, which gave England an unparalleled supremacy in the world for a whole century, brought to the surface aspirations which had shown themselves here and there even in the confused times of the struggle between king and Parliament. The evolution to the world which first trade and then manufacture had brought about had been accompanied by an even more tremendous involution towards man himself. The ordinary worker, living in concentrations of a size unknown before, was no longer content to accept a status confined to his work. He wanted to share the life of ideas through education; he demanded the right to send members to Parliament; in industry he claimed the freedom to combine in Trade Unions. By 1848 he had in a large measure attained all these things. He was transcending the separatist society and was already standing in all three spheres of the social life. He had reached this stature of involution at the time when John Bright was preaching to foreign Governments and Heads of State that the new conditions of industry were demanding free trade over all the Earth.

All this was stirring in the England of the mid-nineteenth century, but there was no one to give conscious form to the new impulses or to show how they were related. The result was that in the century when 'something like a threefold State' seemed possible, the three spheres had the misfortune to become entangled in a new and disastrous way, even though in many respects a natural instinct continued to move on the lines of a healthy separation. This may be illustrated for the cultural sphere in the development of education, and for the economic in the growth of the Trade Unions.

Freedom in the Cultural Sphere

The struggle for freedom of religious belief, freedom of speech and of printing was a long one, and was not finally successful in England until the beginning of the last [19th] century. It was then also that the ideal of universal education first took shape. But the exponents of this ideal did not generally advocate the provision of schools by the political State. J.S. Mill, for instance, wrote that the State should assist parents who could not afford the necessary fees, but should never trespass into the sphere of education by itself providing the schools. It was felt that freedom depended on free institutions, as well as on the vigilance of free individuals.

The middle decades of the century saw unparalleled activity in the founding of independent schools of all types, and the Registrar General's Certificates report 80% of the male populace as literate before the Forster Act of 1870 established the National Board Schools.[112]

This Act killed many independent schools, but the English feeling for independence has kept not a few alive, often through great sacrifice on the part of the fee-paying parents. The avowed Socialist aim is to incorporate all independent schools in the State system. The Conservative aim seems to be to tolerate them while in some way regulating their intake. But there is a body of opinion, occasionally but increasingly heard, for devising some way of assisting parents to send their children to independent schools if they so wish, either by some form of tax relief, or by a 'voucher' system entitling to a grant.[113]

The Butler Education Act encourages local authorities to assist parents to send their children to the school of their choice, but they have proved very reluctant to do so. Many continental countries assist independent schools (such as Steiner schools), both in the matter of teachers' salaries and of capital outlay. England has—temporarily it is hoped—forgotten its tradition of fostering privileges rather than strangling them, to which Disraeli referred when he wrote: 'There are two kinds of equality; there is the equality that levels and destroys, and the quality that elevates and creates. It is this last, this sublime, this celestial quality, that animates the laws of England. The principle of the first equality, base, terrestrial, Gallic, and grovelling, is that no one should be privileged: the principle of English equality is that everyone should be privileged.'[114]

Not every parent would wish to send his child to an independent school. But monopoly is as dangerous in education as in industry, and there should always be sufficient independent schools to challenge, if not to overthrow, any monopolistic system.

In general, however, England is par excellence the country in which the freedom of speech, of religion and of ideas has been fostered and maintained. It is no doubt difficult to get a hearing on the media for ideas (such as Steiner's) which are drawn from unrecognised wells of thought; true originality is choked by the sensational and ephemeral, and there are certainly very powerful background pressures of both a positive and a negative kind. But at least the ideal of freedom is recognised, even if in practice it may call more than ever for the proverbial eternal vigilance.

Trade Unions and the Sphere of Rights

Theoretically, and to some extent practically, English law since Tudor times had forbidden combinations of workmen, but had compensated by empowering magistrates to fix wages. Pitt's Anti-Combination Act of 1800 brought this to an end. Its repeal in 1824-5 saw an enormous burst of 'combination' activity of all kinds, especially among the working classes. For just at this time the new industries were forcing cooperation on society in a way unknown in the old hand industries.

The fundamental question was in what way and under what sign these new industries would be inserted into life. Unhappily the feeling for liberty, which had become so strong in the eighteenth century, was carried over into the nineteenth, and applied not so much to the cultural sphere, where it belongs, as to the industrial sphere, where it does not. The new industries were inserted into life under the sign of liberty, which basically meant liberty for the industrialist. The doctrine of *laissez faire* prevailed over the efforts of men like Robert Owen with more idealistic views.

This *laissez faire* attitude, which regarded human labour as a commodity to be purchased as cheaply as possible in the labour market, produced intolerable conditions, and it was only very slowly that Parliament, which should be the custodian of human rights, was induced to intervene in the matter of hours and conditions of work—beginning with child labour. It is not surprising, therefore, that the industrial workers saw in the new right to form associations a bargaining weapon against their employers. Trade Unions became, not unions of managers and workers for developing production, as Robert Owen advocated, but unions of employees alone, fighting for better conditions and higher wages. Fundamentally this is still their character.

Wages, however, represent the individual's claim on the current production of society. What that claim should be is a matter for the Rights State (Parliament) to decide, not for individual trade unions concerned only with their own members. The absurdity of our present succession of strikes, or threats of strikes, and of a fixed percentage of wage rises irrespective of the existing anomalous scales, is becoming increasingly evident. In a threefold State, the Rights sphere—Parliament—would make an overall survey of wage levels, and decide the appropriate amounts for all basic industries. The Trade Unions would have to give up their vested interest in the present strike-bargaining (no easy thing) and in return they would demand some amendment of the present function of capital (also no easy matter). Not a few firms today are seeking for new conceptions of the role of capital in their industries.[115]

Recent events have shown how deeply the workers resent uncontrolled dividends and capital appreciation for absentee shareholders, who know nothing of the business but exercise a final control over it. If capital is only attracted by the prospect of a large return, it is a fairly obvious answer that labour will be attracted only in the same way. It would be the task of a real trade union to bring together the three parties in every industry, the management, the labour force and the suppliers of capital, to work out a harmonious relationship. But industry exists for the consumer, and the consumers' interests must also be represented in all industrial planning.

To bring about such changes will admittedly be a matter of enormous difficulty. For the Trade Unions, the right to free collective bargaining has become a matter of faith. They resist any attempt to restrict it and at present would not dream of giving it up. The Union leaders feel that their authority and prestige depend on their success in battling for the men's demands. It is hard to imagine them surrendering this role to any kind of government authority. We must, however, begin to envisage a system of economic production which will not be a battlefield, but will fulfil its real function of producing and distributing commodities by methods which would be generally accepted as rational and fair. The present system is rapidly becoming lethal.

All modern forms of social security are a step towards establishing the means of living as a fundamental 'right' for those who cannot (and sometimes will not) work. The next step is surely for a 'Rights State' to take over the whole sphere of the level of wages, i.e. the right to call on current goods and services. This emphatically does not mean that the political State should take over the management of industries. The political State running an industry is always in an ambivalent position. As employer, it must be interested primarily in industrial efficiency; as guardian of human rights, in the well-being of the workers—and the two by no means always coincide. A dialogue between the two interests is essential to strike the right balance. Moreover the union of political and industrial power, like the union of political power and educational control, is a fairly safe way to some form of totalitarian regime. The Rights State would, of course, continue to lay down conditions of labour, and would be ceaselessly active in enforcing regulations against pollution. In its working it would reflect the peculiar genius of each country. There is something of a true instinct in the fact that not a few people are especially afraid of the effect of the European Common Market on our political institutions.

The Economic Sphere today

The economic sphere is the *enfant terrible* of the modern age, making the greatest demands and causing the greatest trouble. This is not only because it provides the products for what has come to be regarded as the good life, but largely also because it is regarded as the principal provider of the purchasing power necessary for the consumption of what it produces. It is largely for this end that every country now must produce more, every country must find new markets. Even in the eighteenth century a Bishop interested in space travel expressed the hope that, if we reached the moon, we might find there 'a new vent for British woollens'.

We have inherited this conception of wages—that if a man shall not work, neither shall he eat—from an earlier economy. It is a point at which we need a radical change of thinking. We must conceive the worker as performing his work not for himself but for others (which is actually the fact). He receives his financial claim on the general products of society because he is a man and a member of that society. This does not mean equal wages for all, as advocated by Bernard Shaw—one kind of work requires greater economic freedom than another—but that the final arbiter of that measure of freedom shall not be the economic sphere itself. It is a matter which belongs essentially to the sphere of Rights.

Economics is now a world question, and its problems will ultimately be solved only on a world level through economic associations with the imagination and expertise to relate world production to world consumption. A competent international body is needed to make, and to make continuously, a survey of world resources, world power and world productivity. Perhaps the first attempt towards this was made in 1924, when Mr. D.N. Dunlop, Director of the British Electrical and Allied Manufacturers Association, with the support of the then Prince of Wales, founded the original World Power Conference.[116] Dunlop was an ardent admirer of Rudolf Steiner, and regarded the World Power Conference as a first step towards a world economy as Steiner conceived it. Such a survey would then be brought into relation with a similar survey of world needs, and one of its objects would be to anticipate the tensions between the so-called 'developed' and 'under-developed' countries.

Heroic as such a world basis for production and distribution may appear, it is the only way in which the 'brotherhood' of the economic life can ultimately be realised. Indeed—as more and more people are realising—the only solution to our industrial problems is by way of the ideal. The ordinary workers especially have a natural feeling for brotherhood over the world. They know subconsciously that they are working for others, even though, under the existing system, it appears that they are working for themselves. It may be that the Marxist cry 'Workers of the world, unite' has turned a little sour, but it did—and still does—represent a form of idealism very precious to the common man.

Of course it will be objected that such an ideal is well enough on paper but impossible to effect. The fact is, however, that modern evolution has already made the world an economic unity. Those who wish to preserve national economics are the modern inverted Don Quixotes, trying to preserve the windmills in the face of atomic power.

Naturally the drive towards a world conception of industry can be supported by whatever can be achieved along the same lines within a single state or group of States. Economic blocs, however—such as the Common Market—can face two ways: either towards a wider world economy, or towards a more potent exclusiveness. At all costs they should avoid the latter danger. And they should not enforce, or be confused with, a political union. Rather should they give rise to an increasing awareness of the distinction between the Economic Sphere and the Rights Sphere of Parliament.

It is noteworthy that Churchill realised the essential difference of these two spheres when, in a lecture at Oxford in June 1930, he said of the prevailing economic difficulties: 'It would seem, therefore, that if new light is to be thrown upon this grave and clamant problem, it must in the first instance receive examination from a non-political body, free altogether from party exigencies, and composed of persons possessing special qualifications in economic matters.' He then proceeded to advocate the forming of an economic sub-Parliament, which might 'for the time being command a greater interest than the Political Parliament'. He was no doubt thinking in terms of national economy, and he probably conceived such an Economic Parliament too politically in structure; but he certainly thought it should be entirely independent of the political State, to which it should pass its recommendations.

In a short space it is possible only to mention an important financial proposal for the economic sphere, which might have a profound effect on the apparently insoluble problem of inflation. Steiner pointed out that whereas capital goods—buildings, machinery etc.—decay and become obsolescent, and consumer goods disappear even more quickly, theoretically the money which they represent remains constant. He therefore called money the 'unfair competitor' and strongly advocated introducing into the financial sphere the principle of 'dying money'. At present money does indeed die by the simple process of inflation, bankruptcies, etc., but in such a way as to cause the maximum social disturbance and injustice. Steiner recognised that the principle of 'dying money'—not merely transferring money as in the case of death duties—could be worked out in a variety of ways. But he plainly thought it was a necessary element in a stable social economy.

The idea of dying money, however, is closely bound up with Steiner's recognition of three types of money. Purchase money, loan money and gift money, each with its peculiar nature and laws. There is a natural progression from one type to the next and it is when money reaches the stage of gift money that it properly dies. It is gift money through which the cultural and spiritual activities receive their support. For these complicated matters the reader must be referred to Steiner's *World Economy*.[117]

Interplay and Interpenetration between the three Spheres

From one point of view the responsible bodies in the three spheres would represent the interests of their respective spheres alone, and would make demands of other spheres at 'summit conferences' which Steiner described as 'not altogether dissimilar to those between nation-States'. But there would be an important difference. In a confrontation between nation-States each party is seeking its own interests alone. In a meeting of representatives of the three spheres of society there would be the moderating influence of the knowledge that each shares in the other spheres as well, and not merely in the one he is particularly representing.

For instance, the cultural educational sphere is primarily concerned with the building of man. Steiner stood modern educational assumptions on their head when he stated that the true task of education is to decide what experiences are necessary for a child to grow to full manhood. Industry, he said, must then adapt itself to the nature of the fully realised man. But education requires its due share of the products of industry, and summit conferences would have to settle the level of that share.

Moreover, the conception of society as an organism demands that the individual shall always stand within all spheres because he is human and indivisible. The saying of the monarch: *L'état c'est moi* has now become the saying of every man, *Moi, je suis l'état.*

Thus the worker in the production line of a factory must always be something more than a mere manipulator or manufacturer, as he was originally and correctly called. His intelligence must be called on in the matter of practical arrangements at his level of work. He should be cognisant of the problems of his industry in production, marketing etc., and be free to express his opinion. In one form or another he should be interested in the disposal of profits, not necessarily in the form of a bonus for himself but perhaps in the support of local cultural and recreational activities. He must no longer be regarded as a 'hand', and his labour should cease to be a commodity in the labour market. But the inventor, the production manager, the sales director, though standing squarely within the economic sphere, represent within that sphere the principle of creative thinking, and, as doing so, they must be given the maximum amount of freedom. It is the great gift of capital that it emancipates itself from direct contact with particular forms of labour and production, and accords the freedom which the entrepreneur needs.

The days of personal ownership of large concerns are over—the director and the manager are increasingly salaried professionals acting as trustees for the capital at his disposal. There must be mutual recognition of the worker as a man and of the manager as a free agent. Only in this way will the trade union, as we know it today, develop into a true economic association.

In a former age, when Plato set out on the search for the nature of Justice, he felt impelled first of all to create the picture of the just State, which would then play into the life of the individual. Today the situation is reversed. The State must be created in such a form that within it the individual can realise his full potentialities as a man.

> The age of instinctive social organisations is past. A truly human society must be consciously formed on the recognition of the separate roles of economic production, of human rights and spiritual freedom. The first is a world question, the second reflects the peculiar genius of a nation, the third is the stamp of man.

Although it is possible to discern evolutionary trends that underlie the historical development of mankind, what actually occurs as regards human progress has never simply proceeded along straight and steady paths. A modern observer[118] might well discern little or no progress as regards the implementation of a threefold vision of society in Britain since Harwood wrote the second of these two articles some 45 years ago. The intrusion of State domination into education has enormously increased, not least through the ministrations of OFSTED; and the continuing prevalence of neo-liberalism in the economic sphere ensures that the economic order serves the betterment of the few rather than addresses the needs of the world, to say nothing of the urgent situation of the Earth as indicated in the climate emergency. Moreover, recent developments on the political scene have not only led to a threat being levelled at the realm of law and at the sovereignty of Parliament (which, as Harwood has so clearly indicated in these articles, has been consistently and exemplarily nurtured in these islands over recent centuries) but to the wilful disregarding of the concept of responsibility for a wider whole—as opposed to a narrow interest-group—which especially in his 1949 article Harwood justly delineates as the mark of what Rudolf Steiner referred to as the consciousness soul. Although this is a trend that has been gathering momentum over the last few years, it has—with the outcome of the General Election on 12 December 2019—now been enshrined in something that those who, like Cecil Harwood, lived through the years leading up to and encompassing the Second World War would find it difficult to imagine could ever happen in this land, namely, a regression (however temporary) to a pseudo-regal concept of sovereignty which has rather more to do with Steiner's concept of the sentient soul. One figure who has in political circles consistently epitomized a resistance to such a regression to narrowly personal interests is Caroline Lucas, who in a Party Political Broadcast for the Green Party in the month prior to the recent General Election (i.e. in November 2019) did not mention the Green Party at all but spoke of the crucial importance of joining together in the attempt to meet the challenges posed by the impending climate emergency. She ended her brief address by trying to envisage how future generations will look back upon us now in their endeavour to assess what we did or failed to do with the knowledge with which we have been authoritatively provided—that we cannot continue to regard the natural world, and the great majority of its human inhabitants, as a resource to be exploited or simply ignored. Her last words were at once enigmatic but also profoundly meaningful: 'Who were we?'

At such times as this it is necessary to try to remind ourselves—or to discover for the first time—who we really are as individual human beings. In an article published in the 1970 issue of *The Golden Blade* entitled 'The Disappearing Trick', Owen Barfield ventures into this difficult but essential territory of philosophical enquiry, attention to which is a prerequisite for finding meaning and inspiration in a world where the mysteries of human existence are often assumed to be secondary in importance to the latest technological innovations. As this important article has not, to my knowledge, been republished elsewhere, I shall reproduce it in full as a means of shedding further light upon the aspirations that Harwood expressed regarding the distinctive cultural and social contribution of Britain in the modern age out of his understanding of indications given in various contexts by Rudolf Steiner. It is also worth mentioning that this article—and the lecture on which it was based—was one that Barfield himself regarded as especially important.

The Disappearing Trick[119]

In my opinion a great deal of what is going on around us today can be traced to the presence in very many minds of an unspoken question and an unspoken answer to it. For the most part both question and answer remain not merely unspoken; they are not even consciously formulated. The answer, if it *were* formulated, would be either 'No' or 'I don't know'. As to the question, in the ordinary life of society perhaps the nearest it usually comes to formulation occurs in early adult life in the shape of what is sometimes called 'the identity crisis'. In circles interested in philosophy or metaphysics however it is sometimes explicitly formulated and as explicitly answered in the negative. The question is 'Do I exist?'

In almost any modern American university one of the most popular and flourishing departments is likely to be the Department of Sociology; and if we look a little into what is meant by 'sociology', if we meet the Professors for example, and see the books on the shelves of the students' book-store, we quickly learn that what is meant is 'behavioural' sociology. The label reminds us that, for the purposes of sociological study, human beings are normally taken to be simply their external behaviour. Should any student be inclined to wonder at all *why* human beings behave as they do, he is likely to seek the answer in the Department of Psychology; and when we have pursued the same line of investigation here, and this time have met not only the Professors but also the rats, with which they spend the bulk of their time experimenting, we shall realise that academic psychology is hardly less exclusively behavioural than academic sociology. Not only human beings in society, the student learns, but each single human being really *is* his physical behaviour.

Look for instance at the book *Walden Two*, which appeared three or four years ago. It is a utopia on the lines of *Brave New World*, but, unlike *Brave New World*, it is not intended as a satire. Perhaps it is an extreme case, but its well-known author, Professor Skinner, is a leading Professor of Psychology at Harvard University and, if we read that book or hear him lecture or broadcast, we shall soon grasp that the basic assumption underlying all he thinks and says is, that the question 'Do I exist?' has already been answered in the negative. If you actually asked him the question, he would tell you that you had 'missed the point'. Nobody doubts his senses; for the rest, there is response to stimulus, there is motivation, there is aversion, there is habit, and all this adds up to behaviour. To raise any question about 'I' or 'me' is to miss the point.

It follows of course that to raise the issue of 'responsibility' is also to miss the point; and, lest it should be thought I am tilting at American universities or unfairly singling out sociologists and psychologists, let me also mention a broadcast talk on Criminal Law, which was heard on the BBC a year or two ago. It was called 'Dispensing with Responsibility' and was summarised in the *Radio Times* as follows:

> The most challenging and interesting critics of the law believe we should eliminate or by-pass the question of an individual's responsibility.

Reflect for a moment on all that that implies. No one is likely to dispute that the question of responsibility is a difficult one. Justice, wisdom, psychology, human sympathy and understanding and the quality of mercy all enter into it. But, unless that other question has first been answered in the negative, a proposal to ignore responsibility altogether, although it may indeed be 'challenging', can hardly be described as 'interesting'.

Of course the root question is not always answered so emphatically in the negative. Uncertainty, anxiety about the proper answer are a much commoner condition. Psychiatrists are familiar with that uncertainty and the existential psychologists among them have already traced a good deal of anxiety to its source in the unanswered question (see, for instance, R.D. Laing's *The Divided Self*). Examples are all too easy to find. It is just a question of selection. In Canada one naturally thinks first of the startling réclame achieved by Marshall McLuhan with his prophecies. Individuality, he assures us, was a by-product of the invention of printing and is now on its way out. And he, too, is rather fond of replying in advance to any reader who may be showing signs of disagreement, that he has 'missed the point'. But I put his answer, with some hesitation, among the 'Don't knows' rather than the 'No's', because, though he makes it quite clear that he knows where we are all going, and generally seems to welcome the prospect with enthusiasm, he does very occasionally speak as if we had some choice and even as though he intended a warning rather than a prophecy. At least he does so in *Understanding Media*.

After all this are there any indications that the question is being answered anywhere in the third possible way, that is, in the affirmative? Of course there are any number of individuals and small groups scattered about the world who do so answer it—who have no doubt that they exist and will continue to do so whether they like it or not. There are many such in the Churches, though it is not so with everyone who goes to church, and there are many others outside them. But my concern here is with general trends, movements of thought or of impulse (which is often potential thought) that are 'contemporary' in an easily recognisable sense (such as determine for instance the flavour of contemporary drama), trends which are as broadly tangible as those I have already chosen as examples in the other direction.

I believe there *is* one rather important indication, though perhaps it has not yet been very much noticed; and I refer to the marked increase during the last few decades in people's concern with history—and with the past of mankind in general—but also to a subtle change in the *nature* of that concern. Side by side (and they may even exist side by side in the same personality) with an almost aggressive tendency to reject the past as irrelevant, to deride it, to resent any sort of preoccupation with it as a clog on 'progress', one notices an enormous increase in the number of paperbacks and other books of a historical nature now being sold. It includes historical fiction, but it is not only that. Both in the New World and in Europe popular historical magazines appear and are successful. Young people, who have no intention of becoming archaeologists, spend their vacations joining in a dig somewhere, and so on. Other examples could be added. I am convinced that what I am talking about is something real.

Moreover it has been observed, and I think with justice, that this modern concern with history is of a different nature from the older kind. You may be fond of history for antiquarian or nostalgic reasons, reasons of a sentimental nature; but what people are obscurely seeking today is something more like an existential encounter with the past, while still remaining in the present. It was summed up by the Dutch historian, Johan Huizinga, in the striking phrase: 'Today historical thinking has entered our very blood'.

At this point I have to digress for a while and interpose a few observations on a different topic altogether. If you want to observe what is going on in the general consciousness at a particular time—or at all events in a large section of it—it is sometimes a good thing to look carefully into a particular word that keeps on cropping up all over the place. Such vogue-words may often furnish a key to what is working, not so much on the surface where the ideas and slogans are bandied to and fro and back and forth, but a little below the surface. When I was a young man, one of these key words was 'functional'. One suddenly found every writer who was up-to-date, or wished to be thought so, edging it in at every possible opportunity, and without perhaps having a very clear idea of what he meant by it. I want for a moment to take a look at one such word which I keep on coming across today, and which shows signs of becoming one of those key words, if it has not done so already.

The word 'psychosomatic' is of course derived from two Greek words, one of which means 'soul' and the other 'body'. It was originally used by doctors to denote the kind of disorder that is both physical and mental in origin. It marked a reaction against the typical nineteenth-century view of the body as a mechanism and of the soul or mind (if there is one) as quite separate from it, like a sort of ghost in a machine. If you want to understand such disorders, it was implied, you must accept the fact that the human being is a 'psychosomatic' organism. It began with medicine; but it has spread to wider circles; and it is evident that emphasis on the fact that man, as a whole, is a psychosomatic organism (in which it is impossible to distinguish between mind and body) gives some sort of satisfaction to large numbers of writers and thinkers today.

That is why it is important to examine the word rather carefully. And as soon as we do so, we discover that what it necessarily implies is, not that mind and body—or soul and body—cannot be distinguished (though that is what it is generally taken to mean), but that they cannot be separated. If they could not even be distinguished, the word itself would have no meaning. It would not be there. For what it signifies is that the speaker's mind has united two components of the human being which the mind has first distinguished. Yet if you watch it carefully, if you pounce upon it and consider it in its context, you are as likely as not to find that what it is *intended* to imply is that psyche cannot meaningfully be distinguished from soma at all.

One could add here that this confusion between distinguishing and dividing—the tacit assumption that we cannot distinguish what we cannot divide—is a weakness that has been growing increasingly prevalent in the thinking of the western world throughout the last three or four hundred years. We first decide that A cannot be separated from B; and then, especially if it happens that B is something we perceive with our senses or of which we can at least form a visual image with sharp outlines, we go on to the second stage, which is to suppose that A cannot be *distinguished* from B. From there the step is a short one to the third stage: the conviction that B is 'real' and A is 'unreal'. This, in spite of the fact that the whole function of what we call our reason, our thinking power, *is* to distinguish and then again unite what cannot be physically separated. The other we can do with our hands and our tools.

Now this fact has very much to do with the question whether I exist or not; and therefore the realisation of this fact has very much to do with the question whether I can feel convinced that I exist. If I am indeed indistinguishable from my senses and my muscles, whose sole business is to register and respond to external stimuli, I am clearly not responsible for my actions; or, to put it another way, I do not exist.

These considerations may seem a very long way removed from a popular concern with history. There is nevertheless a connection between them. For the study of history is, by its nature, a way out of just that paralysing inability to distinguish what we cannot divide, in the particular case of the distinction between soul and body, between psyche and soma. Or, if not a way out, it is at least a step in the direction of the door marked EXIT.

Of course it is only one way out. Another way is the way of intelligent reflection. But any such reflection is commonly, perhaps rightly, labelled 'philosophical', and not everyone is inclined for it. Not everyone is anxious, or even willing, to switch off the radio, sit still, and reflect that consciousness itself depends on two elements that must always remain distinguishable, though they are never divisible... the distinction between 'that-which-is-conscious' and 'that-*of*-which' it is conscious... or to reflect that this is a distinction which we re-affirm by the very act of denying it; or, putting it another way, that a theory about the brain, or about behaviour, can never (no matter what microscopic details it reduces to) perform the disappearing trick of vanishing into the brain, or into the behaviour about which it is a theory.

It is one thing to realise such a crucial truth by reflecting on it; it is another to discover it for yourself when you are not even looking for it—to have it positively forced on your attention. But that is just what his concern with history may do to a man. As soon as he becomes really interested, not only in things as they are, but in how they came to be what they are, quite practical distinctions between inseparables are forced on him. Take language for instance. It is perfectly true to say that written or printed language cannot be separated from its meaning without ceasing to be language, and becoming mere ink shapes. Nevertheless the history of the alphabet is a different study from the history of meanings of words and cannot profitably be pursued until we have accepted that fact. Again, in a successful work of art, say a statue, the nature of the material, as is often pointed out, is inseparably fused with the form of the work and the quality of expression achieved. But the history of marble, or of that particular piece of marble, is widely divergent from the history of sculpture, or of that particular sculptor and his art. However far back you trace the history of sculpture, you will not find it emerging from the geological adventures of marble. So it is with the psychosomatic organism called 'man'. If you wish to seek its history, you must distinguish its components, because they have different histories and moreover different kinds of history.

Furthermore it is just a fact that history *is* all about the human psyche distinguished from the human soma. No doubt one may not improperly use the word 'history' in connection with marble, but the provenance of marble is not in fact history. It is geology. That is what made the well-known professor of history, J.R. Collingwood, go so far as to say that 'All real history is history of thought'. Whether or not one goes as far as that, or even if he does not trouble himself about the nature of history at all, the fact of the distinction is being forced all the time on anyone who is concerning himself seriously with the historic past.

Moreover—and this is particularly significant—the converse is equally true. It has been proved by experience that, if you start so to speak from the opposite end; if you are mainly interested in things as they are, so that your whole intention is to be a scientist rather than a historian; but if you have nevertheless chosen to focus your attention on the psychic rather than the somatic aspect of the human organism; then, you are simply driven into the past, you are driven into all manner of historical theory. This is what happened in the case of psycho-analysis, and particularly in the case of Sigmund Freud. Interesting himself, as he did, in certain disorders whose origin appeared to be predominantly psychic, he was forced, in the first place, to go back to a point in the individual's past life beyond the reach of memory. But then he found this was not far enough. He could not explain the disorders to his own satisfaction without going farther back still—back to experiences had before the patient's birth. These could not, as he believed, be experiences of the patient himself, since those could only have begun after his physical birth. Therefore they must have been the experiences of his ancestors, feelings of guilt, for instance, which each of us 'inherits' along with his physical heredity, by a kind of 'inherited memory', which is nevertheless unconscious memory.

As a good Darwinian Freud assumed as a matter of course that psychic symptoms originate in physical causes; but, as his investigations proceeded and his experience increased, he found himself driven further and further back into history in his attempts to reach a point at which the divergence could be deemed to have first begun. Even the primordial guilt-feelings, which at one time he derived from crimes committed by primitive hordes against the father of the tribe, he later ascribed, not to actual crimes but to a repressed *desire* to commit them. However far back he went, the distinction was already there—until he was reduced to talking about 'hordes of wild cattle and horses, where conditions regularly lead to the killing of the father animal'.

Here is a very revealing example of a conflict between a motivated refusal to distinguish and a factual compulsion to do so. As a faithful observer and thinker he found himself more and more obliged to insist on the distinction. But as a good Darwinian he was obliged to assume that, if you go far enough back in history, you will reach the point at which psyche performs the disappearing trick of vanishing altogether into soma. The ultimate and effective cause of all mental phenomena must be physical! This is also the conviction, or the presupposition, which is sometimes taken as justifying the psychedelic movement, and is the tacit assumption that has given such alarming strength to it in our time.

What is perhaps especially remarkable is the way in which that slovenly concept of 'inherited memory' was allowed to slip in, and then to become the central pillar of his own theory, by one who frequently emphasised his loyal adherence to the Darwinian theory of evolution. For any idea that memories could be 'inherited' is in fact totally incompatible with the Darwinian theory. The biological theory of evolution is based, fairly and squarely, on the maxim that no qualities, not even physical ones, acquired by a single organism during its lifespan can be passed on by heredity. But this radical inconsistency is not peculiar to Freud, nor even to psycho-analysis. Even a biologist like Julian Huxley is not above using the notion of inherited memory, when it is convenient for explaining something. As to popular science, and all kinds of current writing in journalism, fiction and so forth, how often we are told of obscure recollections arising in the man of today of the experiences of his 'tree-climbing' ancestors! And yet... if the ancestors really *were* tree-climbing animals, *and no more* (as Darwin for instance propounded), there can be no such thing as inherited, or 'racial' memories. It was because he was absolutely convinced that there could be no such thing that Darwin invented the 'tree-climbing' theory.

But how else are we to explain the evolution of consciousness—particularly of our modern consciousness? How else are we to explain it, if we insist on assuming that there is no real distinction between mind and body—if we insist, not only that we are unable now to separate the two, but that we are unable to distinguish them, and that the mind comes into existence at birth as an attribute of the body? If the statue grew somehow out of the geological nature of the marble, from which it is now inseparable, and had no independent source?

I find this all very relevant to the unspoken question with which I began. You can say that 'history has entered into our blood'—or you can say that evolution has entered it. It is the evolution of modern consciousness that people are interested in, when they become concerned with history today; when they begin to make the existential encounter with it. How did we get to where we are... and *what* we are? That is the question. Because evolution is in my blood, I shall feel convinced that I exist when—and only when—I have some understanding of how I came to be what I am.

Many books have been written from different points of view to show that our modern consciousness (which can only be termed 'self-consciousness', whether or not we afterwards go on to claim that the 'self' is illusory) has gradually evolved from a less individualised consciousness—such as is manifested at the stage of mythical thought, or by tribal consciousness. The picture such books evoke is of our present, sharply-defined, isolated and isolating self-consciousness gradually, in the long course of pre-history and history, emerging from a dimmer and vaguer kind of consciousness, a consciousness shared by many human beings and extending over a wider area. It is a convincing picture for many different reasons; but on closer examination it proves to have one very serious flaw in it.

If self-consciousness can truly be said to have 'evolved', it must have increased gradually. But what does it mean to say that self-consciousness must have 'increased', or must have 'emerged' gradually from another kind of consciousness? If self-consciousness can accurately be said to have 'grown', or 'evolved', from what it was, say, in 10,000 BC to what it is, say in AD 1970, then the *same* self must be assumed as present in both periods. The same self, though not the same organisms (bodies). What does 'evolving' mean? It makes sense to speak of the species horse 'evolving' through the ages, though individual horses have perished utterly; because there is something that has persisted through all these perishing, namely the species. But if it is individuality itself, selfhood itself, that is to be conceived as 'evolving', what then are we to say has persisted? It can only be the individuality. In other words something called individuality has taken the place of species in the process of evolving. In this case, then, it is not the same species but the same individual that must have persisted through those successive embodiments that reveal its evolution to an observer—becoming, in the process of transformation, gradually more recognisable as what it is today.

And this is something you do not find in the books to which I referred. Not yet.

It is quite extraordinary how many of these inconsistencies quietly disappear if we accept the fact of successive embodiments of an individual human spirit. No need now to play about with hopelessly unscientific fantasies of physically inherited memories in a psychic Unconscious—since the Unconscious brings its own past with it into embodiment. And in that individual spirit—in the ego as the unconscious kernel of conscious personality, in the trans-biographical ego, which persists from life to life—we have a unity that is capable of actual, and not merely metaphorical, evolution.

There is of course no doubt that what we call 'personality' is psychosomatic. It is inextricably involved with the body and its functions, and particularly with the sense-organs. Men have been well aware of this ever since the study of psychology began. The Greek philosophers were well aware of it, and before then the Hindu sages, and others. What distinguishes our time is our overwhelming awareness of the contribution of the physical component; so that, if we were quite honest, we should be speaking, not of 'psychosomatic' but of 'somatopsychic'. The real issue today is the existence... or not... and the nature of that kernel of the personality of which we are normally unaware, and which persists through historical and biographical changes. If there is in truth no such kernel, then personality itself is a kind of illusion; and it would really be better that it should perform the disappearing trick, for it can only be a kind of grit in the smooth machinery of life. So it is felt in many quarters, and with a good deal of justification. So it is argued by the behaviourists, so it is felt, by and large, by those who fall for such movements as the Hippy cult; so it is felt and argued in a good deal of contemporary art and theory of art.

This acute awareness (which we all have, if we are honest) of the extent to which our consciousness is dependent on the brain and nerves and senses and other bodily functions, is making it particularly difficult for us to conceive of any element in the personality having existed before birth, and perhaps still more difficult to conceive of any persisting after death. Yet if we distinguish, or if we merely remember how we do constantly distinguish, between psyche and soma, the difficulty begins to disappear. For we do distinguish. If we converse with someone who is awake, and then afterwards see him asleep, we cannot help making the distinction. The psyche is still there; but it has ceased to manifest. Psyche and soma, we observe—or soul and body—are differently related at different times; so it is clear that, whatever the relation between the two is, it is not that of indistinguishableness; and it need not, and should not, be so very difficult to conceive of the converse happening in the case of death; or that, because the soma disappears, it does not follow that the psyche disappears with it.

The truth is that the human psychosomatic organism is one in which two elements are interrelated in an infinitely subtle way. In point of fact there are more than two, for we have already had to distinguish between the personality and the 'kernel' of the personality, but let us leave it now at two elements, which are related in a subtle way, and moreover in a way that varies rhythmically with the course of time. An adequate psychology of it would have to pursue the subtlety of that interrelation as far as possible into its physiological and psychological ramifications. It would have to pursue it by *everywhere* systematically distinguishing what cannot be divided. It would have to distinguish—and then show the relation—between not only psyche and soma in general, but between their different interrelations with each other at different times; to show the different relations between the different parts or functions of the one and the corresponding parts and functions and systems of the other, and, in doing so, to distinguish and relate those parts and functions and interpenetrating systems themselves, as they are within the one system (the physical body for instance) considered apart from the other. And I must say without hesitation that the only psychology I know which even begins to fulfil those exacting requirements is Rudolf Steiner's psychology and physiology of threefold man. To expound it would need a lecture to itself, or several lectures. Here I am merely stating my opinion that his is the only psychology and physiology on the basis of which it is possible to understand in any detail the rhythmical variations in the complex interrelationships between soul and body which manifest themselves in the sequences of sleeping and waking, of life and death—and indeed of other sequences also.

I regard it as a matter of great importance that we should never lose sight of the vast difference between the oriental concept of reincarnation and the occidental one. The occidental idea of successive embodiments of the individual human spirit is by no means the same as the oriental one of 'reincarnation', though unfortunately it is in the latter form that most people in the West are introduced to it. Whereas the oriental doctrine looks primarily towards the past, the occidental one looks primarily towards the future. This characteristic was clearly stamped on it from its first appearance in the speculative utterances of many western philosophers towards the end of the eighteenth century; but it remained almost wholly speculative until Steiner, by integrating it with his threefold psychology, transformed it into a firmly based interpretation of human existence.

Part and parcel of this integration are many features which markedly distinguish his treatment of repeated terrestrial lives, not only from oriental teaching but also from any other of which I at least have ever heard. As an instance of these, his alone pays as much attention to periods between death and rebirth as it does to periods of life in the body. And this appears to me to be, both psychologically and historically, significant. With the rise of depth-psychology there appeared for the first time in history an attempt, at least, to investigate the sleep-relation between soul and body, as well as their waking relation. We very badly need a similar move towards focussing on the pre-natal and the post-mortem relation between the two—on the discarnate relation as well as the incarnate one. Indeed, I doubt if anything less than this can re-establish western man's confidence in his free will and the personal responsibility which that alone entails.

At the centre of all Steiner's teachings (or, as I prefer to say, his 'findings') there stood what he always referred to as the Mystery of Golgotha; and it follows from almost everything he said that it is because the Being whom Christians call the Christ and others have called by other names united Himself with the Earth at a definite moment of time, and as a historical fact, that history may now be said to be 'in our blood'—or that evolution is in our blood. For Christ actually *is* the past, not dead, but living in the present and on into the future.

Just because of the heavy pressure technological civilisation is constantly exerting on us to identify with the present moment, that is, to identify with happenings to our senses, happenings of our bodily functions, and even with happenings in the world around us—and thus to disappear as responsible persons—it is essential that the Christ impulse should be increasingly realised in experience. Nor need we absolutely despair of this coming to pass. For what is it that sets us free for that realisation, for that existential encounter? If we look well into it, it is that very pressure of the present moment, of which I have just spoken.

That is the other, and less oppressive, way of looking at what is going on all round us. We are assailed... hammered and clamoured on all hands... by ever-multiplying sense-impressions and popgun impacts on our nervous systems. Thought perceptions, brief memories light up in us and as quickly vanish again. They are dependent on our brains and nerves and senses; and we are aware of this dependence as perhaps never before in the history of humanity. But it is just because of this *fleeting* nature of our thoughts and perceptions that, although our personalities may seem to consist of them, we are not *determined* by them—that we, in ourselves, are not determined by them—that we ourselves are free. But this freedom is rapidly becoming useless, and even menacing, to us; because, overtly or covertly, we draw from the fleeting nature of our conscious experience the conclusion that we have, as individuals, no real being. But real being is precisely what is secured to us by our having already existed as units in the past. It is because of this that we are, whether we like it or not, not merely Spirit (as most, though not I believe quite all, of the Buddhist sects, for instance, maintain), but individual spirits. The sense of not-being from which we suffer in our present selves... and which gives rise to the anxious question: Do I exist?..., is the indispensable foundation of our freedom. That this is so was first fully realised by an appreciable number of people only comparatively recently; and the discovery was called Existentialism.

But this freedom gives us no assurance of reality. That is because we should in fact have no reality—we should be mere bundles of stimulated behaviour—if the self had to rely on its present experience for its being. But it does not have to. It experiences its freedom in the fleeting present. It is a real Being because it has an immemorial past and has slowly evolved to be what it is. The moment we recognise and realise this, the rudderless and helplessly drifting 'Do I exist?' is converted into the very guarantee of our freedom and of our obligation to steer; we become, not the free nothings of Sartrian Existentialism, but free spirits deep-rooted in the past, and responsible to it, growing thence towards the future and responsible *for* it. It was Rudolf Steiner's conviction, and it has long been mine, that much, if not everything, may depend on how soon the generality of mankind comes to a realisation of this fact. Much that has happened since his death and much that is happening today has contributed to reinforce that conclusion.

★

Cecil Harwood would have wholly agreed that implementation of the aims of which he consistently spoke and wrote in connection with especially the history and potential future of this land and the wider world required a 're-establishing [of] western man's confidence in his free will and the personal responsibility which that alone entails'. Without the kind of awareness of what the personal self truly is, without such a grappling with questions of the nature of 'Do I exist?' or 'Who were [are] we?', any attempt to break free from a perpetual round of infringements of personal rights and opportunities for responsible social engagement will be doomed to failure. Nevertheless, Harwood did indeed act in the limited sphere where his responsibilities allowed in a manner that exemplifies what he—and Barfield—were writing about; and in the chapter that follows an attempt will be made to chronicle the achievements in the later part of his life in connection with his chairmanship of the Anthroposophical Society in Great Britain.

2. The Anthroposophical Society and the Healing of Divisions

By the time of the 22nd Annual General Meeting of the Anthroposophical Society in Great Britain in September 1945, Cecil Harwood had already been its Chairman for nigh on eight years; and he could look back over a period when, under his wise and energetic guidance, a Society that had some ten years previously been severed against its will from the world Anthroposophical Society with its centre in German-speaking Dornach had during the war years also found itself to a certain extent also exiled from the Germanic culture through which anthroposophy had come into the world. A new phase was now being inaugurated under Harwood's leadership whereby the tragic splits that had wrenched deep cleavages in the Christmas Conference Society founded by Rudolf Steiner in 1923–24 began to find healing, both within Britain and within the world Society as a whole. It is worth emphasizing, however, what was noted earlier at the end of Part Two Chapter two, namely that, because of his close involvement with launching Michael Hall in its new home at Kidbrooke Park, it was only with a certain temerity that Harwood agreed to continue in his role as Chairman. What follows is not so much a history of the Society during the years of Harwood's Chairmanship but, rather, an attempt to trace chronologically the story of the social healing process within the Society, for the guidance and leadership of which he was largely (though not of course solely) responsible.

After the intense challenges and privations of war, the year 1946 was a quiet year in the life of the Anthroposophical Society in Great Britain. There was no AGM, although there was the usual round of conferences at Easter and in the summer, and Harwood gave a lecture in connection with the Threefold Social Order on 'The Spiritual History of the Free Human Being' at Rudolf Steiner House on 21 March. But Charles Davy's book *The Three Spheres of Society* was published by Faber and Faber (under the pseudonym of Charles Waterman) and elicited a glowing review by Adam Bittleston in the July 1946 issue of *Anthroposophical Movement*, where he wrote that he proposed to give a copy of the book to the Governor of his school who, when Bittleston was a pupil, had 'tried, with kindly interest in my future, to convince me that I was wrong in valuing these books [of Rudolf Steiner] so much'. The Governor had added: 'And as for this Threefold Commonwealth idea—why, it has nothing to do with the real problems, it is quite irrelevant.' Bittleston was of course not dissuaded by such remarks from his course either then or subsequently, and in the light of the new possibilities that the end of the war had opened up felt able to write:'Much has changed today. Do we realise how great our opportunities are, if only we have done enough to digest and transform Rudolf Steiner's work in our own thinking and life, and have been awake enough to what is going on in the spiritual atmosphere of the time?'

A further matter of particular interest reported during this year was George Adams's visit to Switzerland (and Dornach in particular) reported in the following issue. George Adams had been one of those individuals selected, for whatever reason, for expulsion from the General Anthroposophical Society, and in his usual graceful style gave his impressions of which the following words may stand as a reflection:

> I was hospitably received by many friends and conversations reached across the grave difficulties of ten to fifteen years ago. Our Dornach friends themselves have been through deep waters during the last three or four years. Many of these see now that when differences arise in an occult movement the Gordian knot cannot be cut so easily by the summary expulsion of those with whom one disagrees.Valiant work is being done in spite of painful divergences and the material exigencies resulting from the war. At the end of the present month there will be the Conference—the first to be held for some time in the Goetheanum Building itself—which has already been announced in these columns[120]. Great difficulties had to be surmounted in bringing this about. Our friends are bearing a heavy burden. Returning late one evening, passing these beautiful dwellings with so many evidences of new and sincere striving and hard work, I felt that this is a place of inner suffering. In times of bitter estrangement, individual anthroposophists, however deeply each may feel that he is right and his opponent wrong, are in their natural relations again and again confronted by the reverse of the ideals they have set before them.

The 23rd Annual General Meeting of the Society duly took place in Rudolf Steiner Hall on 4–5 January 1947. At this meeting, a plan was proposed for joint use of Rudolf Steiner House together with a group known as the Arts Council. Harwood did not support this plan but wanted the Executive Council alone to carry responsibility for maximizing use of the House by a wider group of eurythmists and other aspects of anthroposophical work. On these grounds he indicated that, as he didn't want to stand in the way, he would offer to resign the Chairmanship. However, at an ensuing Extraordinary General Meeting on 22–23 March it became apparent that the Arts Council had withdrawn its proposal. In the meantime, too, Harwood had made many connections during his visit to Germany the previous month and had held conversations with people in Dornach, thus becoming engaged in the affairs of the Society on an international level. 'Our friends in Germany,' he said, 'though obliged by present conditions to work in small and isolated groups, had an intense desire to create the whole Anthreoposophical Society again, in spite of difficulties. They looked to England and Holland as sources of spiritual and material help.' He thought that these connections had an important bearing on the future, and that as he had been destined to make them, he could, if members so desired, continue as Chairman of the Society and try to offer a useful contribution to the future of the work. The members assented to this and supported Harwood in his plans for the House (which were explained in further detail the following month).

Towards the end of 1947 there was a Members' Weekend Conference on Social Questions, to which both Harwood and Barfield (among others) contributed. The following report of these contributions—and of course of the remaining sections of the Conference—appeared in the January 1948 issue of *Anthroposophical Movement*:

> Under the title: 'The Slaying of Leviathan', Mr. Harwood gave the picture of Hobbes' 'Leviathan' as the omni-competent State, towards which we have been tending historically ever since Henry VIII fused Church and State, and thus destroyed that principle of duality, with its delicate balance of political and spiritual powers, which had hitherto preserved our social equilibrium. Yet Leviathan was never accepted. Inherent in our national character was, and is, the passion for individual liberty and spiritual freedom, so that the tendencies towards a State monopoly of power were constantly and often successfully opposed. One could indeed trace throughout English history a potential threefold form, which partially merged yet was as often beaten back. The monster, Leviathan, was continually opposed; on the one hand, by the representatives of individual conscience, and on the other hand by the growth of international trade, and of necessities developing out of the broadening of our economic life. Picturing this equilibrium as it is reflected in our code of law, Mr. Harwood described the distinctive features of English Law in contrast to European Law derived from Roman sources: how the one protects the rights of the single individual, and thus gives the basis for his spiritual freedom, whereas the other protects more the rights of princes, thus increasing the power of the State. Picturing developments in our history towards a more true social form of economic and spiritual life, he instanced the experiments of Robert Owen towards industrial co-operative fraternity, which had achieved so much success before it was superseded by 'laissez-faire' with its resultant human misery; and again on the spiritual side, the wise foresight of John Stuart Mill who had pleaded that the State should never develop schools of its own, but should only devise a system of paying for children who could not otherwise afford to attend. Mill's warnings, as Robert Owen's example,

have been neglected, so that today we have State ownership of both industry and schools. Whilst in the 19th century, an abnormally favourable economic situation existed for us which masked the potential dangers, in the twentieth century these artificial industrial conditions have broken down, and the problem of Leviathan arises in all its undisguised menace. Mr. Harwood finished his address by indicating that the initial error of thought which resulted in a concept of matter divorced from spirit underlay the thought of Hobbes and his contemporaries, and was directly connected with that concept of the omni-competent State which failed everywhere to recognise the significance and value of the individual human spirit. In his address on the forces of law which may ultimately control Leviathan, Mr. Barfield vividly contrasted the two kinds of law which have grown up in England, the one which he likened to a 'Roaring Lion' or Law of Force, and the other which he likened to a 'Gentle Mother' or protective law of love for our fellow-men. Between these two forms of Statutory and Common Law, 'where,' he asked, 'are we to find the promise of a new and finer form of law which can control the tyranny of the State?'

In the May 1948 issue of *Anthroposophical Movement* Harwood wrote that he had agreed to take over its editorship (formerly carried by Miss Winney). He also added in a section entitled 'News from Dornach' that at the General Meeting in Dornach that year, despite threatening deadlock and renewed struggles among the remaining members of the Vorstand (Executive Council) —Ita Wegman and Elisabeth Vreede had both meanwhile died in 1943—

> the exclusion of the various individuals effected by the meeting of 1935 was annulled. Some who were present describe the spirit of the meeting, the sense that the Society had been re-born on a truly universal basis, as more impressive [and probably more realistic] than any of the resolutions taken. While it appears that nothing was said about the position of this Society and the Dutch Society, it is plain that these unexpected and fortunate new developments may profoundly affect the relation of this Society to the General Society. Much will yet have to be worked out, and the Executive Council [of the AS in GB] will consider the next step with great earnestness. But I do not think that this Society will wish to play a passive role in the new situation.

During the summer of 1948 Harwood had again visited Germany, and described a land still in ruins and with considerable shortages of food and other resources. He had been invited mainly in order to attend an Educational Conference in Hanover and spoke about education in England, but 'in such a way as to bring as much support as possible to the aims of our [Rudolf Steiner] schools', which in Germany fell into a group of independent schools that was less prevalent than in England. He concluded his report with these evocative words:

> Already the ruins of some of the cities begin to have a slightly mellow and softened appearance. Flowers grow in the rubble, and small trees and bushes appear in the skeletons of houses and offices. Walking in the late evening in such a town as Düsseldorf I already felt a little as though they were the remnants of some ancient civilisation. So must the Northern invaders have walked once among the wrecks of the Roman cities, which they were destined to build again on the basis of their understanding of the Christ impulse. Our own destiny is not far different.

Harwood (together with Francis Edmunds and Adam Bittleston) had also attended a series of meetings in Arlesheim in June 1948 with members from different countries regarding the future of common work within the anthroposophical movement in the world. In his report Adam Bittleston included these thoughts:

> Again and again we saw how decisive it is for the progress of anthroposophical work to find the right mood and suitable forms for common work. And it was clear almost at once that wide agreement was present among those who had come together in these meetings, right down into particular tasks of our movement. We all saw that much needs to be done before we can have a General Anthroposophical Society in the comprehensive, genuine sense intended by Rudolf Steiner.

However, a measure of the difficult path that still lay ahead was expressed only a month later by Harwood himself as part of his introductory editorial article to the September issue of *Anthroposophical Movement*:

> It was a great disappointment to find on visiting Dornach in June that the promise of a new understanding and co-operation between the conflicting parties there had not been fulfilled. There is an enormous will among anthroposophists all over the world to work together, and the impulse to a new co-operation is brought to Dornach every time members from abroad come there. But among the leading personalities in Dornach itself there is such a tangle of ancient difficulties that it seems impossible to make the 'spring to freedom' which life is calling for.

At the 25th AGM of the Society on 7–8 January 1949, Harwood—who as usual had been unanimously re-elected to serve as Chairman for the following year—spoke of meetings that he had attended at the Goetheanum, whence he had only just returned (no doubt partly to attend the funeral ceremony of Marie Steiner, who had died on 27 December 1948). Indicating that 'the shadow of recent conflicts loomed heavily' over the Goetheanum, he made it clear that efforts made after the 1948 General Meeting in Dornach to bring some solution of the difficulties had 'produced no result'. It was therefore his view that 'he must regretfully recommend to the members that the Anthroposophical Society in Great Britain should not, by any official step at present, change its independent status'. He also informed the meeting of what Albert Steffen had told those who had attended the meetings in Dornach after Christmas, namely that it had been hoped it might be possible to open the Goetheanum for performances of *Faust* during this year of the bicentenary of Goethe's birth, but that the present serious financial difficulties were hindering these plans. Albert Steffen had also pointed out that, in view of Marie Steiner's death, it would be necessary to appoint at least one other person to the Dornach Vorstand; and it was noted in the May issue of *Anthroposophical Movement* that one of those people appointed at the April General Meeting to fill this vacancy, Dr. Hermann Poppelbaum, had announced that all the signatories to the so-called *Denkschrift* or Memorandum published at the time of the expulsion of leading members of the Anthroposophical Society in Great Britain had agreed to withdraw it from circulation.

The year 1950 saw the death of Cecil Harwood's beloved wife and colleague Daphne. She had been taken ill shortly after Michael Hall's 25th birthday celebrations on 20 January, and died on 14 July. A deeply appreciative summary of her life and her contribution to the Waldorf School movement in Britain by Jesse Darrell appeared in the October 1950 issue of *Anthroposophical Movement*.

For 1951, I shall confine myself to mentioning three symptoms of an underlying mood of anxiety and suffering that seems to have been particularly characteristic of this year. The first of these is Harwood's reference at the 27th AGM of the Society in January to the fact that, of the 1178 current members, some 400 were paying no subscription and had not responded to letters asking them to contribute something (even if not the full recommended amount). No doubt this was not a unique situation, but it was in this year that the Chairman made a special point of it. The second symptom appears in the course of a plea made by Harwood in the March-April issue of *Anthroposophical Movement* that members should where possible attend a major conference at the Goetheanum (29 July— 12 August), when all of Rudolf Steiner's Mystery Plays were to be performed. In the course of his description of the event Harwood writes (and this is the symptom to which I refer): 'In the present state of the world nobody knows for how long it may be possible to visit the Goetheanum.'

The third symptom is a lengthy poem by Owen Barfield in the July-August issue of the News-sheet which constitutes an uncharacteristically scathing attack on modern poetry (which Margaret Bennell—understandably—subsequently felt moved to moderate to some extent). Entitled 'History of Poetry in the Second Half of the Twentieth Century', it culminates in the following deprecatory words:

> When the half-century turned, most of the wise feared she [Albion's muse] was done for:
> There was no life in the Earth, none. With a sharp eye for the outside,
> The bards make a polite noise: in the background are the bright boys,
> Who observe nature and make notes.

These sentiments are corroborated by the knowledge that Barfield's writing and publishing his humorous treatise on legal practices *This Ever Diverse Pair* in 1950 had effectively rescued him from a mood of even darker despair.

As an initiative which can, in a certain sense, be seen as a means of transforming this underlying mood, Harwood announced in November 1951 that there would be a Public Conference in London (at Bedford College, Regents Park) between 28 July and 5 August 1952 on the theme of 'The Awakening of the Twentieth Century'—awakening, as he put it, from the sleep of the nineteenth century. He quoted the following familiar lines from Christopher Fry's play *A Sleep of Prisoners*:

> The human heart can go to the lengths of God.
> Dark and cold we may be, but this
> Is no winter now. The frozen misery
> Of centuries breaks, cracks, begins to move;
> The thunder is the thunder of the floes,
> The thaw, the flood, the upstart Spring.
> Thank God our time is now, when wrong
> Comes up to face us everywhere,
> Never to leave us till we take
> The longest stride of soul men ever took.
> Affairs are now soul size.
> The enterprise
> Is exploration into God.
> Where are you making for? It takes
> So many thousand years to wake,
> But will you wake for pity's sake?

The London Conference of 1952 was very much Harwood's initiative, and in the January issue of *Anthroposophical Movement* he clearly set forth the aims and overall structure of the event:

> The sequence of the main evening lectures is intended first of all to open up some of the fields of knowledge and experience which are challenging man with the riddle of his own being and destiny. First must naturally come a review of the shattering events of the century; then a consideration of the Earth in its relation to the universe, and of the sphere of the senses on which so much of modern knowledge is based, will lead to the question of man himself and the eternity of his being. After this central point is passed the lecturers will rather show how the spiritual knowledge, which man can win once he realises his own spiritual being, can illuminate such questions of the day as education, national and social problems, and the great cleavage between East and West. Dr. Zeylmans has kindly agreed to give both the opening and concluding lecture in which he will be able to knit together (as only he can) the threads of the intervening discourses and discussions... The success of the Conference must ultimately depend on the good will and energy of members in making it known. This will require active work from everyone.

Not since the World Conference on Spiritual Science in 1928 had such a large-scale public anthroposophical Conference been planned in Britain. The Conference would appear to have fulfilled Harwood's expectations, at least to some extent, even though it could not emulate the World Conference in terms of its international context or public acclaim. Mabel Cotterell wrote a thoroughly appreciative report in the News-sheet for August-September:

> Our long-awaited Summer Conference was a success from the very beginning. More than 600 people attended Dr. Zeylmans's opening lecture and the following seven crowded days seemed to accumulate a crescendo of interest and enthusiasm. The members came from many dfferent countries, many enquirers came to whom anthroposophy was a new experience and the beautiful grounds of Bedford College and the sunny weather made a perfect setting. Months of hard work by the Secretariat had gone into the preparation and all the arrangements went without a single hitch...

Harwood was asked to speak at a Public International Conference to be held in The Hague from 24 to 30 August 1953, which could in a sense be seen as a development of what had been achieved the previous summer in London, though expanding it to encompass a pan-European dimension. Entitled 'The Birth of Europe: A Spiritual Problem', it turned out to be—in

Harwood's phrase (for the unsigned report in the November issue of *Anthroposophical Movement* was clearly by him)—

> a very great event... one experienced it as a spiritual deed, erecting a strong, firm pillar within the restlessness of present-day Europe. The path which European evolution has taken so far, the different stages of its development, the many contributing factors which have led to the bewildering situation of today, the spiritual goals which begin to appear like stars on the distant horizon of the future, illuminating the paths along which we have now to travel and thereby showing us the tasks of our present incarnation—all these, through the united efforts of all the friends, we became able in the course of the Conference to see more clearly than ever before...

Some 1,200 to 1,400 people from 18 different nations attended throughout, and 'several hundred of those present were new to anthroposophy'.

The 1950s were as a whole a time of gradual consolidation of the Anthroposophical Society in Great Britain, and several important new initiatives were taken and institutions established in various fields throughout the country. It is also significant that several important books by anthroposophists were published by 'mainstream' publishers such as Faber and Faber, Hodder and Stoughton and Victor Gollancz.[121] The tone for these years was reflected—and probably to some extent influenced by—Harwood's editorial comment in the January 1954 issue of *Anthroposophical Movement* entitled 'Some New Year Reflections', where he posed the following four questions (and went on to muse at length about the second): 'What exactly is the Anthroposophical Society in Great Britain?'; 'Why am I a member of it?'; 'What ought it to be doing?'; and 'Is it doing it?'. He concluded his article by indicating that his reflections had arisen from deliberations within the Executive Council regarding 'ways and means towards achieving greater unity within the Society'. The implied emphasis here was on the nurturing of the Anthroposophical Society in Great Britain as opposed to trying to address the—still intractable—issues of the relationship with Dornach and the healing process which it is the main purpose of this chapter to trace. Within this period of the 1950s there continued to be much involvement with anthroposophists in the rest of Europe, as exemplified in the Summer School in The Hague on 'The Social and Cultural Rebuilding of Europe' (14 July—9 August 1958), at which Harwood contributed from a West-European perspective between 28 July and 2 August. Also in 1958, Owen Barfield wrote about a meeting at Scheveningen (Den Haag) at the end of 1956 attended by himself and Harwood of anthroposophists from different Northern European countries, out of which an International Whitsun Conference at Odense (Denmark) between

23 and 27 May 1958 had arisen. Throughout this period, member numbers steadily grew (despite the consistently applied policy of 'lapsing' members who neither contributed financially nor communicated) and Harwood was always re-elected as Chairman at each successive AGM.

The first indications of renewed efforts to heal the divisions within the Society appeared in Harwood's editorial message entitled '1961' in the December 1959 issue of *Anthroposophical Movement*. Harwood noted that in order to secure the maximum possible publicity for events and publications marking the centenary of Rudolf Steiner's birth, 'the Council are seeking the cooperation of the English Section of the General Anthroposophical Society as well as of the Executive of the Goetheanum. Some Council members had a meeting with Dr. Poppelbaum during his recent visit to England, and he very kindly promised his cooperation in the preparation of the Exhibition [for the centenary celebrations]...'.

The approach of the centenary year of 1961 coincided with—and doubtless in part promoted—a renewed endeavour on the part of Harwood and his Executive Council colleagues towards the union of all groups and sections of the Anthroposophical Society. To this end, Harwood and Frank Newell had visited Dornach to speak with the members of the Vorstand. Subsequent to this, the following letter dated 21 September 1960 was written to the Vorstand at the Goetheanum. It was signed by Harwood and the Secretary, Roma Browne, on behalf of the Council, which then consisted of G. Adams, E. Bailey, K. Bayes, A.O. Barfield, Lady Chance, J. Davy, G. Eedle, Mrs. Francis, J. Jeffree, Mrs. M. Kirkaldy, F. Newell, Miss D. Osmond, Mrs. V. Plinke, R.M. Querido, A.P. Shepherd, and Miss C. Winney.

> Dear Friends,
>
> We are writing to you consequent upon the report given to us by Mr. Harwood and Mr. Newell of their recent conversation with you in Dornach. We would first of all like to express our gratification at the friendly nature of the conversation in spite of Mr. Harwood's frank statement of our difficulty in the present situation of the Society, especially with regard to the Nachlassverein [of which more below].
>
> With regard to the connection of this (or any) National Society with the General Society we have always regarded this as a matter of mutual recognition based on confidence between the leaders of each Society, rather than as the relation of a subordinate part to a whole. We refer in general to Dr. Steiner's insistence on the autonomous character of the National Societies, and to his particular statement in a lecture given on April 16th 1924, that only individuals can become members of the (general) Society, not Societies. We think therefore that it would not be a right expression to speak of this Society joining or re-joining the General Society, but rather of a mutual recognition

out of which individual members may, and we hope will, decide in increasing numbers to join the General Society through this Society as was originally envisaged at the time of the Christmas Foundation.

We consider, however, that owing to the history of the last thirty years and the lack of effective communication between this Society and the General Society during that time, this process must and will inevitably be a gradual one. As a first step towards such a reunion, however, we would be glad to encourage both our existing and future members to join the General Society through this Society, to forward their names to you for ratification and to collect their subscriptions for periodic despatch as was previously done before our separation. We do not, however, think that the time has yet come when we can make it a condition that any present member or any person wishing in the future to join this Society shall necessarily become a member of the General Society. We would hope that this transitional arrangement would lead to a renewed intercommunication through which the membership of our Societies would later become fully integrated...

We must, however, stress that in making you this proposal we do not in any sense support your present attitude to the Nachlassverein and its publications. We consider one of our most important tasks to be the publication in English of Dr. Steiner's books and lectures and their dissemination throughout the British Commonwealth.

To this end we look forward to a continuance of the friendly co-operation of the Nachlassverein which we at present enjoy. In the same way we would warmly welcome a renewed co-operation with you in our common and all too urgent task, the deepening of our own experience of Anthroposophy and the spreading of the knowledge of Rudolf Steiner's work throughout the world.

This letter elicited a reply confirming the substance and agreeing to the proposal regarding gradual reunion through the will of individual members. Regarding the matter of the Nachlassverein, however, there remained an absolute divergence of views, as is clear from the following extract from this letter from Albert Steffen, Guenther Wachsmuth, Hermann Poppelbaum and Rudolf Grosse dated 16 November 1960:

But we must make it quite clear that our attitude towards the Nachlassverein rests on the firm conviction that this organisation is in blatant contradiction with Rudolf Steiner's clearly expressed intentions. But this attitude can in no way mean that we regard the dissemination of Rudolf Steiner's books and lectures as less important than anybody else...

Another point requires to be clearly stated. We must place the utmost value on the fulfilment of Rudolf Steiner's will as laid down in the principles and guiding lines of the Christmas Foundation. This we regard as a most important part of

> his legacy to our Society...The common determination to this fulfilment is for us
> the true and only real foundation on which a spiritually fruitful and an inwardly
> sincere co-operation between the parts of our Society should be based...

Harwood and his Council colleagues responded on 2 December by welcoming what appeared to be an acceptance of their proposal, while noting the difference of view regarding the Nachlassverein and also 'the highest value' that they placed 'on the Christmas Foundation'. They also made the request that this correspondence be publicized through the News-sheet, which was agreed to. Subsequently, at the AGM in March the arrangements that had been agreed with the Vorstand were formally ratified by the members, in that the Council was empowered to work out means whereby individual members might rejoin if they wished to do so. This would appear to have been a relatively simple process; and following the AGM all members were sent a letter explaining the situation and offering them the possibility of taking up membership as individuals of the General Society based in Dornach. By early the following year a steady stream of members had began to do so.

Before proceeding any further with an account of what happened next, it is clearly essential to try to understand this matter of the Nachlassverein, or Rudolf Steiner's Literary Estate, which was proving so divisive. For the following analysis I am indebted to Crispian Villeneuve's Foreword to his compilation of Marie Steiner's introductions to her publications of Rudolf Steiner's lectures, Marie Steiner, *Esoteric Studies: The Flaming Word*, Temple Lodge, London 1993. The story is taken up from the time when, following the period which had led to the shattering events of 1935 already recounted in this book, prior to which Marie Steiner, Steffen and Wachsmuth had in 1933 signed a pact of mutual collaboration, Marie Steiner herself began, in Villeneuve's words, to 'feel herself somewhat shouldered out by the other two surviving Vorstand members from the effective leadership of the Society'. By 1942 this breach had become fully public; and in relation to the current difficulties within the General Society Marie Steiner published a moving appeal for forgiveness among Society members in the December 1942 News-sheet. However, the only reply of any substance that she received was from the 'long-since outcast' Ita Wegman, who was to die shortly afterwards. Hence:

> in the depths of [her] anxiety about the future of the Anthroposophical Society Marie Steiner now decided to take an important further step. On 3 June 1943 she founded the Rudolf Steiner Nachlassverwaltung in order to ensure that the legacy of Rudolf Steiner's both published and unpublished literary estate, which had been bequeathed to herself, might be rescued from the Society's seeming collapse and properly safeguarded for posterity.

Steffen and Wachsmuth opposed this move and refused to give this body—the administration carrying official responsibility for Rudolf Steiner's Literary Estate—any formal recognition. A sizeable minority of members supported Marie Steiner's views; and in 1947 she transmitted her rights to Rudolf Steiner's estate to this Nachlassverwaltung. Villeneuve goes on to state that:

> an attempt at reconciliation between the opposing sides was made at the Society's Annual General Meeting in April 1948, and in the good will then engendered the expulsion decisions of 1935 were somewhat awkwardly repealed [as noted previously]. But by the autumn it had become clear that the still existent differences within the General Society between the majority supporting Steffen and Wachsmuth and the minority who continued to support Marie Steiner had come to a total impasse.

On 11 September of that year Marie Steiner made a last will in which she named the Rudolf Steiner Nachlassverwaltung as sole inheritor to her own estate; and she died soon afterwards on 27 December. Matters came to a head the following year, when the Anthroposophical Society's so-called Philosophic-Anthroposophic Press (a term that Harwood regarded as utterly opaque and meaningless to the 'non-initiated') published several lecture-courses by Rudolf Steiner without permission from the Nachlassverwaltung, which thereupon took the matter to the Solothurn cantonial court. Legal wrangling continued for three years, with the official Society line that the copyright of Rudolf Steiner's works had been transferred to the Society being disseminated throughout the world Society. However, in June 1952 the five Swiss judges delivered the unanimous verdict that there was no concrete evidence since Rudolf Steiner had made his will in 1915, making his wife the inheritor of his estate, that the actual copyright had been transferred out of her jurisdiction. Villeneuve concludes the story as follows:

> The copyright to Rudolf Steiner's works had been personally vested in Marie Steiner at the moment of her husband's death and had remained so thereafter until the contract of transference of 1947. Since that contract remained unrevoked in Marie Steiner's last will it followed that the still subsistent copyright had now passed to the Rudolf Steiner Nachlassverwaltung, while the previous entitlement of the Anthroposophical Society to publish the works of Rudolf Steiner was now abrogated. For it was not the Anthroposophical Society but the Rudolf Steiner Nachlassverwaltung who were successors in title to Marie Steiner.

Meanwhile, the centenary celebrations centred around February and March 1961 gathered apace, with Harwood the principal motivating figure in everything. T.S. Eliot, Basil Spence, Kathleen Raine and William Golding had agreed to take the chair for various lectures in Rudolf Steiner Hall, *The Faithful Thinker* (a volume of centenary essays edited by Harwood) was to be published on 25 February, accompanied by two Press Conferences (also for the exhibition in the House). There was a centenary broadcast on the Home Service (Radio 4) on Wednesday 1 March from 9.30 to 10 pm. Articles on Rudolf Steiner appeared in journals such as the *Hibbert Journal* and the *Contemporary Review*. Lectures were given in numerous other places all over the country, not a few of them delivered by Harwood. In the April issue of *Anthroposophical Monthly* it was reported that:

> the centenary celebrations have succeeded probably beyond what their most sanguine promoter could have hoped... *The Faithful Thinker* has already received some very positive reviews in papers as widely different as *The Times Literary Supplement* and the spiritualist organ, *The Greater World*. An excellent account of Steiner appeared in *The Observer*. There was an appraisal of Steiner education in *The Times Educational Supplement*, and a great many papers had notices of the Exhibition and lectures. Most of the Press notices were favourable, though there were exceptions. One paper wrote: 'The Steiner Centenary Exhibition attempts the impossible and *fails to achieve it*'. The Broadcast was at a peak listening period, and judging by comments received both from members and the public, made a good impact. It was repeated on the Scottish Regional Programme a fortnight later. The Centenary also received notice at other times, and short accounts with photographs of Dr. Steiner or the Goetheanum appeared in *Radio Times* and the *Listener*...

Harwood went on to say in this account that the exhibition was greatly admired and attracted considerable interest on the part of people outside the movement, that the lectures were very well attended and that the eurythmy performances were sold out and had to be repeated.

Possibly the first formal step towards greater communication and collaboration between the Anthroposophical Society in Great Britain and the English Section of the General Anthroposophical Society was a Christmas and New Year Festival arranged jointly by the two groups. This was held in Rudolf Steiner Hall on 30 December and included a talk by R.G. (Dick) Seddon entitled 'The Birth in the Cave'. Notification of events organized by the English Section, which had its base at 38 Museum Street, also began to appear in *Anthroposophical Movement*. These events included the annual 'Leicester Conferences', the first of which to be announced in the News Sheet was scheduled for September 1962 (this was the third of these Conferences).[122]

In the course of announcing the next AGM of the Society on 12 and 13 January 1963, Harwood inserted two notices relevant to our principal theme. The first concerned membership of the General Society:

> I would like to remind members of the arrangement which was recently made with the Executive (Vorstand) of the General Society in Dornach, Switzerland, by which members of this Society can join the General Society through our organisation. So far the response has been somewhat disappointing. I would urge all members who have not taken this step to consider whether they should not do it forthwith, as a practical means of showing our goodwill towards the fine and incessant work which goes on at the Goetheanum. If any members have lost the particulars sent them with regard to this matter, fresh copies will gladly be sent by the Secretary.
>
> We are in the unfortunate position of not knowing how many of our members belong independently to the General Society, and a recent request in the News Sheet for information brought a minimal response. Is it possible that a reminder will do better, or are members still determined (like the Scotch lady when the Guard asked her destination) not to tell 'yon spearing body'?

The second related to a proposal for the amalgamation of the AS in GB with the English Section:

> Some members of the Society may have seen, or may be seeing, a document which has been put into circulation among its members by the Trustees of the English Section of the General Anthroposophical Society, particularly as some members belong to both Societies.
>
> This document contains a rather detailed scheme of the fusion of the two Societies in a New Society with a new constitution. It has been examined by the Council of this Society only as far as its preliminary conditions, which brought out some fundamental differences between our points of view. I therefore proposed to our Council that we should invite the Trustees to a joint meeting with us to discuss these matters in the frankest possible spirit. Meanwhile, however, without consulting with us, the Trustees decided to hold a meeting of their members to discuss the proposals—a decision of which I was informed—and to circulate the proposals to all their members. We had no information of this latter decision, and as far as this Society is concerned the proposals must be regarded as entirely unauthorised.

The next step in this saga was prompted by a Resolution, proposed by Alan Howard, seconded by Kenneth Jones and signed by 29 members, favouring the forming of a united English (this was the word used in the Resolution) Anthroposophical Society on the basis of some detailed proposals as to how this idea might be implemented in practice. This elicited a lengthy letter from Harwood published in the December 1962 issue of *Anthroposophical Movement*, which because of its importance is reproduced in full here:

Dear Fellow Members,

As the question of my election as Chairman will again be before you at the Annual General Meeting (even though I am informed no other has been nominated), I feel I ought to state clearly for your full consideration the position I hold in relation to the unhappy differences of opinion which have arisen from, or crystallised round, the Proposals for Union with the English Section, of which you have read in the News Sheet.

Of the ultimate ideal that there should be, as there once was, One Society in Great Britain (not I hope in England alone), I think there need be no question. What is in question is, firstly, whether other considerations are of equal or greater importance, and, secondly, what are the best means of attaining to such a Society with the greatest measure of goodwill from all concerned?

To take the first question, I think it is agreed that there would be little meaning in the One Society unless it were a National or Territorial Society within the General Society as envisaged at the Christmas Foundation Meeting. We have therefore immediately—and rightly—not to concern ourselves with Britain alone but to look at the General Society also with its Headquarters in Dornach. Unfortunately when we do so look, we find at those Headquarters the still prevailing division (already described in my letter in the October News Sheet[123]) between the Vorstand or Executive of the General Society and the Nachlassverwaltung, who administer Rudolf Steiner's Literary Legacy under his will. We have important and fruitful connections with both these bodies. Moreover, we have in our Society and on our Council members who feel deeply on each side of this question, to whom indeed it is an important moral issue. I hope we shall be able to continue to conduct our affairs in such a way that our present practice, which gives the Society a truly 'Universal' character, may continue, and to this end I am sure that we must preserve the present freedom of choice to belong or not to belong to the General Society for present and future members, and the freedom to recommend either course to those introducing new members. I have myself rejoined the General Society and urged others to do so, because of my admiration for its many fine activities, but under prevailing conditions I could not be a party to any compulsion in this matter. The present arrangement is working well, and when I had the privilege of a long talk with the Vorstand early in November they expressed themselves as satisfied—indeed more satisfied than was—with the working of the arrangement and the numbers of members joining through us.

At the same time I am convinced that our Bookshop and Publishing Company should remain an integral part of our Society's activities under the control of the Council, and that we should continue our open and friendly relations with the Nachlassverwaltung to whom we are indebted for our rights to publish Rudolf Steiner's works in English.

I realise that unhappily the principles I have here briefly re-stated (they are abrogated in the Proposals) will almost certainly make a union with the English Section impossible. Nevertheless, I think we should face the second question as to the best way of working towards such a union. I am sure that this is not to think out a theoretical constitution for a new Society, which forces two Societies of very different inner organisation into a common mould, and then bring the whole complicated matter to a General Meeting, before the principles on which its structure is built have been agreed. I believe on the contrary that before any formal union can even be thought of, living human people must find each other through working together. It was to find spheres of common work and discuss mutual problems between us and the Trustees that I first proposed the Committee of Three and Three, of which I was originally a member. This Committee afterwards took upon itself a task which I had not foreseen.

I believe that the right course for 1963 (subject to the agreement of the Trustees) would be to transcend the Committee of Three and Three and have regular meetings between the Council and the Trustees as a whole, out of which might arise some kind of flexible form, under which the two Societies might work together in certain spheres pending an ultimate solution of all differences and difficulties at home and abroad, for which we must not cease to hope and work. I would only like to add that in the working together of any two Societies I think it is axiomatic that the members of each respect scrupulously each other's constitution and principles.

At the same time I am convinced that public or general discussion as to the nature, form, etc., of the Society should not be centred round the Proposals (already generously withdrawn by the proposers) but on Steiner's various indications as to the nature of an Anthroposophical Society. And I would think that the best place for such a discussion is not an Extraordinary General Meeting, which can last only a few hours and which weighs the scale heavily on the side of the Londoners, but the Ripon Conference, more accessible to members from other parts of Britain, at which a daily session could be devoted to the subject. Preparation for such a discussion in smaller groups would be necessary, and the Council is already preparing some important material.

Our Society is on paper more of a democracy than most anthroposophical societies. But our democracy has always—wisely—accepted the principle of leadership, a truly esoteric principle, without which a democracy may easily become the prey of parties and pressure groups. Consequently we have perhaps had fewer disorderly changes and chances than other societies less democratic. I have personally always tried to avoid parties and if I have not sought any signatures to support my point of view it is because I believe that such things, by creating the appearance of a party, tend to create party itself.

I fear however that we can only continue our present method of working if the Council of Officers of the Society substantially agree on certain common principles, which I am democratic enough to believe must be those approved at the General Meetings. Thus, if the next Annual Meeting decides that the Society should be conducted on principles differing from those I have here described, my duty will plainly be to withdraw from the administration of the Society and not hamper the work of those who may be called on to administer it on other principles and towards other ends...

At the AGM that followed on 11, 12 and 13 of January 1963, the Resolution was defeated by an overwhelming majority, and there was a recognition that the focus needed to be on the relation of the AS in GB with General Society in Dornach, especially in view of the continuing split between the Vorstand and the Literary Estate. Harwood accordingly continued as Chairman for a further year.

There then followed an Extraordinary General Meeting in Rudolf Steiner Hall on 30 November 1963, when an important further step was taken, namely, the proposal placed before the meeting by Council 'that this Society should affirm its affiliation to the General Anthroposophical Society at the Goetheanum'. At the meeting Harwood spoke of 'a different temper of mood prevailing in Dornach' over the matter of the relationship in Dornach between the Executive (Vorstand) at the Goetheanum and the Nachlassverein (which is not to imply that the frictions in this relationship had been allayed). He had been 'generously invited' to attend meetings of the Vorstand (now consisting of none of the original members) with leaders of the various national Societies and other larger groups; and at a meeting at Michaelmas he also experienced a 'real determination on the part of everyone concerned not only to solve the Book Question but to establish a General Society which could be a real centre for the activity of all anthroposophists'. The proposed 'affiliation' essentially, therefore, would, if accepted, mean that the Chairman could join as a fully accredited member in the regular meetings of the leaders in the various countries with the Vorstand at the Goetheanum. At the EGM, the members attending in large numbers (about 290) were almost unanimously in favour of Council's proposal. The vote was followed by a short Festival of Reunion. On 2 January 1964 this very important step was followed by a reunion of the Anthroposophical Society in Great Britain with the General Anthroposophical Society on a leadership level and increasingly also on an individual level. This reunion was accompanied and confirmed by the following written words from the Vorstand: 'We extend a most hearty welcome to the Anthroposophical Society in Great Britain which, after long years of separation, is again to be a part of the General Anthroposophical Society. The step thus taken is, we believe, a most important event on the path of development of our General Anthroposophical Society. It is therefore with great satisfaction that we herewith give notice of this event to the members in all countries.'

Meanwhile, joint meetings between the Council of the AS in GB and the Trustees of the English Section as envisaged by Harwood continued, with the first in 1964 taking place on 26 January. A joint committee was to be arranging a Whitsun Conference at Rudolf Steiner House, in which Hermann Poppelbaum and Margarete Kirchner-Bockholt (who were both members of the Vorstand) were to participate. Harwood noted in April that as a result of the reunion with the General Society there were closer relations with the English Section.

Despite these positive steps and fruitful communications, there continued to be difficulties in Dornach which Harwood briefly described at the AGM of the Society on 20–21 March 1965. When the question was raised of a possible union of the Society with the English Section, he 'stated that the Council had held regular meetings with the Trustees of the English Section at which mutual problems had been discussed and arrangements made for common activities. No concrete proposals for a union had been considered and a formidable difficulty in the way of such a union was the fact that there were different organizations for the First Class. This was a matter which had been raised with the Vorstand at the Goetheanum at the time of our re-entry into the General Society, but had been postponed until a general discussion could take place with representatives of all countries concerned in the matter. This discussion had not yet taken place. The question also affected the relation of the Vorstand with the Nachlassverein, in which matter unhappily no progress had been made.' (From Connie Winney's report.) A statement by the Vorstand at the General Meeting of the General Anthroposophical Society did not materially change this situation, except that it openly recognized the existence and the work of the Nachlassverein. By the following year there was still no solution to the problem that books published by the Nachlassverein or by the Anthroposophical Society in Great Britain were not available at the Goetheanum Bookshop and Library; and the matter of responsibility for the First Class also remained intractable.

A letter from Harwood to the Editor of the News Letter of the English Section dated 19 July 1966, which he felt obliged to publish in the September 1966 issue of *Anthroposophical Movement*, is symptomatic of the

continuing problems about the First Class. In view of Harwood's clarity
of expression in these matters, it is important to reproduce this letter here:

Dear Editor,

Will you please allow me to refer to the account of the English Section's
General Meeting in your last issue, in which I am quoted as having said that
I could not unite the Esoteric Class of the Anthroposophical Society in Great
Britain with the School for Spiritual Science at the Goetheanum. I never have
made, nor could I possibly make, such a statement.

I know of no such thing as an Esoteric Class of the Anthroposophical
Society in Great Britain. The Esoteric Class which has been in the use of this
Society continuously since the time of Rudolf Steiner himself *is* the First
Class of the School of Spiritual Science as founded by him. If, of recent years,
the term Esoteric rather First Class has been used, it is solely because the
latter name, perfectly natural when a second and third class were anticipated,
has lost its meaning and in isolation may easily be misinterpreted. As you are
aware, Rudolf Steiner was far from rigid in the matter of names.

This Class is identical with the same Class as practised at the Goetheanum and all other centres where its members meet to hold it. All such
members, showing any card or proof of membership, have always been
admitted to its meetings as a natural right, which it has seemed unnecessary
and even presumptuous to advertise, because it is impossible to conceive of
any other practice in the face of the Leader of the School. The question at
issue is not the unity of the Class within the School—a matter over which
I have no more power than over the rising of the sun—but the form of
expression which that unity should take in view of past history and present
circumstances.

Your issue refers to the effect on this matter of the re-entry of this Society
into the General Society. I naturally raised it, at the time of that re-entry, with
the then Vorstand, and it was *at their request* that this question was postponed
to a future meeting when representatives of other countries also concerned
could be present. That is almost three years ago and the meeting still has not
taken place. I fear that some recent events have made it more difficult to find
a solution than it would have been previously.

Your account reports Miss V. Compton-Burnett as saying that Dr. Steiner
appointed Dr. Wegman Leader of the First Class. I could not go quite as far
as that myself, but I am convinced that it is so far true that any arrangements for the Class deriving from her authority—as does the use of the
Class within this Society—has equal validity with any other organ. I have
always thought it unfortunate that, after the war, the Vorstand of the General Society inaugurated, or re-inaugurated, another use of the Class in this
country without reference to the traditional Class or consultation with the

person then responsible for its conduct [this would presumably have been George Adams].

Yours faithfully, A.C. Harwood.

Things were no clearer by the time of the 43rd AGM of the Society held on 10–11 March 1967. Harwood reported on the Book Question and relations with the English Section, together with the question of the authority for the First Class of the School of Spiritual Science within the AS in GB. It had transpired that the two difficulties were closely interconnected. It was fundamentally due to the fact that the Nachlassverwaltung and the Vorstand took different views as to the existence of, and responsibility for, the School that there was the unhappy situation that the present edition of Steiner's works was still not sold in the Goetheanum or placed in its Library. He added that he saw no prospect of any immediate change in this situation. Moreover, the Vorstand continued not to recognize the authority for the Class within the AS in GB which Harwood had received from George Adams, who had in turn received it from Ita Wegman, the member of the original Vorstand especially concerned with the Class—and the Vorstand's policy in this respect was rigidly adhered to by the English Section.

In February 1968 there was a communication from the Goetheanum to the effect that the Bookshop would henceforth sell the works of Rudolf Steiner published by the Nachlassverwaltung. Herbert Witzenmann, as a Vorstand member, dissented from this view. In the June 1968 issue of *Anthroposophical Movement* there was a report by Harwood of the General Meeting in Dornach, which had taken place in March. There had been many resolutions against the decision promoted by Rudolf Grosse to start selling the books published by the Nachlassverwaltung in the Goetheanum, quite apart from Herr Witzenmann's opposition. These resolutions were principally based on the attitude of the Nachlassverwaltung to the School of Spiritual Science and on the fact that the books were being published outside the School's sphere of influence and activity. Harwood added:

> As far as I could gather, nothing significantly new was said on this vexed subject. What was new was that the Vorstand had separated the question of selling the books from the complex of the School...Thus the strange anomaly that the Centre of Steiner's work was the one place where his writings could not be obtained has been brought to an end—though it must be admitted by force majeure [majority vote] and not by agreement between the parties concerned... It is now possible for the Goetheanum to accept our offer to present our English translations to the Library where Steiner's works certainly ought to be found in all languages. He went on to commend the Vorstand for its 'courageous decision'.

The April 1969 issue of *Anthroposophical Movement* carried a report of the 45th AGM of the Society, when Harwood reported on an important decision concerning the First Class of the School of Spiritual Science. What he said would seem to have represented a crucial step forward and a path towards overcoming what had seemed to be intractable problems:

> Members will perhaps remember that when this Society re-entered the General Society in 1962, one of the questions that was left over for further discussion was that of the responsibility for the First Class of the School of Spiritual Science, which I had taken over from Mr. Adams to whom it had been entrusted by Dr. Ita Wegamn.
>
> This question proved to be much more difficult to resolve than I had anticipated, though not a few efforts were made to find a solution. Early in February, however, after meetings between some of the Leaders of the AS in GB and in the English Section, a meeting was held in Rudolf Steiner House of all the Readers of the Class in the English Section [this would not have included Charlie Gaze, who had previously been the sole Reader but who had died on 22 August 1968] and this Society, with two members of the Vorstand in Dornach, Herr Grosse, the President, and Dr. Hiebel.
>
> The proposal was made [and it is difficult to avoid thinking that this was Harwood's initiative, not least because of his total commitment to the will of the individual founded firmly upon freedom] that there should be established a Circle—to consist in the first place of all the Readers of the Class in this country—to act as an advisory body to the Vorstand on all matters affecting the Class in this country. This 'Readers' Circle' would keep in close touch with the Vorstand and would hope to meet at least one member of that body for consultation every year. The two Vorstand members warmly accepted this proposal.
>
> The solution of this outstanding difficulty will also affect the relations of this Society with the English Section. The Council have therefore informed the Trustees that they would be very glad to enter into new discussions with them on their mutual relations. Mr. Cornish, although he had not yet had an opportunity of discussing the proposals with the other Trustees, had welcomed the idea. This will be a task for the coming year and we will keep members informed of all developments.

There was almost unanimous approval of this statement and a general expression of goodwill and good wishes for the tasks that lie ahead.

It is wholly understandable that the open-minded Grosse and Hiebel welcomed this proposal, since this breakthrough in the context of the Society in Britain had considerable implications for the residual problems in Dornach, which were not of course thereby immediately solved but were presented with a context within which the issues that had led, in turn, to the split in 1935 and the further ruptions associated with the forming of the Nachlassverwaltung in 1942–3 could be viewed in a different, more conscious and individually responsible light. It is for this reason that Harwood's achievement—and of course it was not his alone—needs constantly to be recalled in the context of the world Society so that any residual elements of conflict and discord are likewise penetrated with the fire of individual consciousness. The corresponding efforts of F.W. Zelymans van Emmichoven in Holland, who had died at the age of 68 in Cape Town on 18 November 1961, should also not go unremarked in this respect.

There was next an Extraordinary General Meeting on 10 January 1970 attended by some 200 members, the object of which was to agree to a proposal that the Anthroposophical Society in Great Britain and the English Section should be reunited. Harwood opened the meeting by recapitulating the events that had led up to it and added that discussions had indeed been taking place since the previous March to clarify how the two British Societies could merge, now that the obstacle relating to the School of Spiritual Science had been removed. There was almost unanimous support for this proposal (only one member spoke against); and a comparable meeting of the English Section had a similarly positive result. The union was then agreed at the respective AGMs of the two Societies. In the case of the AS in GB, the AGM (the 46th) was held on 7 March, the necessary alterations to the statutes and bylaws were passed without discussion or dissent; while Owen Barfield formally proposed the re-appointment of Harwood— which was carried with warm applause—and he was himself re-elected as a member of Council for a further three years. A Celebration of the Union of the English Section and the Anthroposophical Society in Great Britain in Rudolf Steiner House and Hall then followed on 23–24 May 1970, in the presence of Rudolf Grosse, Hagen Biesantz (who took the place of Hermann Poppelbaum, who had been invited but was unable to attend owing to illness) and also Marie Savitch and a party of eurythmists from the Goetheanum. Meanwhile, Harwood had attended the General Meeting of the General Anthroposophical Society in Dornach and had himself contributed a report to that meeting from Great Britain. He noted that 'for many years there has also been a Society in Scotland, and I am happy to say that its members will also wish to enter the new united Society'. He indicated that he would have wished that Vera Compton-Burnett[124] would have appeared with him (she was present in the Hall), but she had wished him to speak on behalf of the united Society. 'I would, therefore, say that we have taken this step after many struggles and with great earnestness. We intend to make it a real union in the will and an opportunity for deepening and strengthening our work together.' He added a strong plea for events at the Goetheanum in English (he was speaking in English, the only part of the event that was not in German).

I shall conclude this chapter by referring to an event of a completely different kind occurring at roughly the same time (or at any rate between September 1969 and the early part of 1970). This concerned something that was initially marked in the Summer 1969 issue of the journal *Child and Man,* with an article by Rudi Lissau about the 50th anniversary of the founding of Steiner Education in September 1919 in Stuttgart entitled 'Steiner Education's Jubilee' and then featured by an entire issue of the same journal (Summer 1970, vol. VII no. 1) being devoted to the theme of 'Pioneer Comprehensives', where Hugh Hetherington contributed an article referring to The New School or Michael Hall as being 'Britain's oldest comprehensive'. The event itself, however, was described in the May 1970 issue of *Anthroposophical Monthly* in a contribution by Frank Newell, the Chairman of the journal's editorial board:

> People are coming round to the idea that Steiner (Waldorf) schools have been supplying answers over the last half century in the quest for social and individual comprehensiveness and for unity in knowledge. A sign that this is so was the attendance at the recent Steiner Schools Golden Jubilee luncheon at Brown's Hotel in London of a veritable galaxy of educationalists and education correspondents that included Mr. Edward Short, Secretary of State for Education [referred to in *Child and Man* as a particularly knowledgeable and dedicated holder of that office], Miss Alice Bacon, Professor A.D.C. Peterson of the Oxford Institute of Education, Sir William Alexander, who heads the Association of Education Committees, and a leading representative of the National Union of Teachers. The press conference held a few days before the luncheon was chaired by Professor W.A.C. Stewart, Vice-Chancellor of Keele University.

This is mentioned at the end of a long chapter focussed on the internal affairs of the Anthroposophical Society in order to demonstrate and exemplify the fact that the realm of Steiner Education, which had been Harwood's initial entry-point into the anthroposophical movement and Society and responsibility for which he had had to hand over to others, was in the meantime flourishing as probably never before and was seen by the wider world of education to offer a vital and essential contribution. Some, like the present author, would argue that, despite appearances, the underlying situation has not really changed.

3. Anthroposophia, New Friendships and the Role of Eurythmy

At the reunion celebration in May 1970, John Davy, who had been asked by Francis Edmunds in January 1969 to take a major role at Emerson College, the international college and training centre by now flourishing in its home at Pixton, Forest Row,[125] spoke some deeply pertinent words, indicating that in his view 'young people are perhaps searching for just that impulse which Rudolf Steiner incorporated in the Christmas Foundation. But the difficulties in the Society have meant that it is not yet a true vehicle for Anthroposophia'. Many other meaningful things were said at this event by, among others, Vera Compton-Burnett, Dick Seddon and Cecil Harwood, whose address was on the one hand an expression of gratitude to his predecessors, Harry Collison, Daniel Dunlop and Montague Wheeler and, on the other an expression of a commitment to an act of renewal as a Society which 'has its wellsprings in the Christmas Foundation Meeting'. Everyone then stood while the Foundation Stone Meditation was read in English; it was then performed in eurythmy in German.

The reference by John Davy to Anthroposophia—the heavenly being whom Rudolf Steiner especially associated with the approach of anthroposophy, as a science of the spirit, to earthly humanity and its 'incarnation' through him in the early part of the twentieth century— was most likely not unconnected with the publication in 1965 of a book by Owen Barfield which takes the form of a dialogue with this being (referred to in the book as the 'Meggid').[126] In a letter written in March 1963 to Marguerite Lundgren Barfield writes: 'I have been getting on to a certain extent with the book—perhaps as fast as I could anyway, even if I had more free time, as every bit seems to require an awful lot of shaping down and simmering and sifting, before I can get to the actual writing, and that seems to demand among other things sheer lapse of time. Early mornings are when it mostly happens. I am still far from confident that I am not attempting the impossible.' He goes on to say later in the same letter:

> I have been reading up a lot about [the year] 869 and the surrounding [Church] Councils—also partly with an urge to one bit of the book I am writing... fearfully complicated but rather fascinating stuff. Yesterday, for the first time for nearly a week, I really got going on the book again and wrote about 2,000 words. I wish I knew whether it will really interest anyone, or

whether it's just a clinical example of the way my mind works, the sort of arguments I happen to think worth raising and answering. I suppose I shall finish it now anyway.

In another letter to the same recipient written in August 1964, with the book by now clearly largely in some sort of written form, Barfield adds these further thoughts:

> I sometimes wonder whether, when *Unancestral Voice* comes out, people will think that, beneath the fiction, there is a claim to some sort of direct initiation-knowledge. The truth of the matter... is twofold. The *object* of introducing the Meggid was to have a device that would enable some of the findings of Anthroposophy to be stated without arguing for them. The *incidental* purpose it served, which I felt more and more strongly as the book proceeded, was to give expression to the momentous gulf (not really less than that between one person and another) between: not simply the anthroposophical truths themselves but also my own mental penetration of them, on the one hand and, on the other, anything that could with the remotest approximation to accuracy be called 'me'. I mean it served this purpose in my own feeling (I don't know that it is of much importance to anyone else), the way finding a form relieves you [this would be a reference to eurythmy]—making me feel honester and sincerer.

Those unfamiliar with what is probably Barfield's boldest and most far-reaching attempt to embrace and transmute the prevailing ideas and assumptions of his time by means of anthroposophy may wonder about the relevance of these unique insights into the mental processes accompanying the writing of this book. Suffice it to say that *Unancestral Voice*—together with its not too distant predecessors *Worlds Apart* (1963) and *Saving the Appearances* (1957)—articulated an intellectual legacy that underlay Harwood's last years as Chairman of the Anthroposophical Society in Great Britain following the healings and reunions that he initiated and guided; and in this sense John Davy's words at the reunion celebration may be seen as a symptom of the challenges that still lay ahead for the Society in the early 1970s and beyond. For of course even the 'memorable and inspiring day' of the first AGM of the united Society in Britain (19–21 March 1971) could only be regarded as a new beginning.

The culminating event of the remaining years of Harwood's chairmanship was undoubtedly the Exeter Conference held between 10 and 17 August 1973. This event had been conceived by Harwood as a first conference of the world General Society to be held outside Dornach under the auspices of the Vorstand and bore the title 'The Present Times and Humanity's Path of Initiation', embracing the needs of the soul and the karma of the age. Attended by some 800–900 people, it was considered to have been 'a successful and important event for all who were able to take part, and indeed for the life of the Society in general' (from the report in the September—mid-October 1973 issue of *Anthroposophical Movement*).

Harwood decided not to continue as Chairman after the following AGM held on 1–3 March 1974 (the 50th since its founding in September 1923); and the meeting approved the appointment of 'a small Committee from among its members' to carry the functions of chairmanship (this consisted of John Davy, Gerald Eedle (Treasurer), Rudi Lissau, Dick Seddon and Michael Wilson). On this farewell occasion, Harwood took the opportunity to give an address (on 3 March), every word of which is so discerning, insightful and epitomizing of all that he stood for in his capacity as Chairman of the Society that it will be reproduced here in its entirety.[127]

Fifty years ago at Easter 1924 Rudolf Steiner handed to the Dornach architects the plans for the second Goetheanum. The old Goetheanum was still unfinished when it was burnt down on New Year's Eve 1922–23, and the noise of hammering had been continuously heard on the Dornach hill up to that time. Then came a silence of fifteen months, after which the hammering was resumed on the new building.

That interval of silence had been filled with an almost unbelievable activity on Steiner's part, in the centre of which must be placed the Foundation of the Society anew at Christmas 1923–4. It was a new Society and needed a new content. But in lectures and other ways Steiner continued to complete the work he had done in the old Society. A notable example of such a completion—though it never reached full completion—was his work on the Statue which was to have stood at the eastern end of the old Goetheanum, where alone such a huge wood carving could fittingly have stood. For the old Goetheanum was itself a carving almost as much as a building. As you looked from the west door between the pillars of auditorium and stage you were to have seen in this ultimate creation the modern Representative of Man. We owe it mainly to our member, John Wilkes, that we are able to follow the development of this Masterwork, created in association with the English sculptress, Edith Maryon. For instance, the gesture of the original central figure was a menacing one. It seemed to overthrow Lucifer by its masterful power, and drive Ahriman into the Earth. In the final development it expresses only strength, wisdom and love. Lucifer casts himself downward because he cannot endure that light; for the same reason Ahriman imprisons himself in the Earth in order to escape it.

Steiner was always reluctant to give a name to the Central Figure, but so far as we may think of him as the Christ, gazing at that statue we realise there can be no modern understanding of Christ without an understanding of Lucifer and Ahriman. One might have thought that to bring such an understanding into this modern age could be the crown of a life's work, and would have been magnificently expressed in the placing of the statue in its intended position. Or that when this proved impossible the founding of the Society anew would have been a sufficient task. But Steiner had a further revelation to make to the members even after the Foundation of the Society. It is the revelation of the mission of Michael, beginning with the revelation of karma and reincarnation.

This, of course, was not a new revelation. It had, however, a new emphasis and a new quality. In a lecture at Torquay (August 1924) Steiner said that it was only in the previous few months that he had been able to speak with such complete openness. As a corollary he now expected the members to take earnestly what he said about the new initiation of Michael. The old pre-Christian initiation had been one into wisdom, the new was an initiation of the will. A new fellowship in the Society was to be built not on the knowledge but on the practice of karma. We were to work strenuously to enter into each other's karma. It is here that the Society certainly failed—as its history after Steiner's death only too clearly shows. It is here that we must endeavour—and I believe are endeavouring—to make a fresh attempt.

Perhaps, however, we will only make the attempt at Michael's behest if we grasp the immense significance of the new Michael age and the role which—as Steiner showed us in the last year of his life's work—Michael plays in the destiny of man and universe.

If the members, say in 1912, had heard Dr. Steiner say what he wrote in the fourth Michael Letter, that anthroposophy was intended to be the message of the Michael mission, they would have been very greatly astonished. For in the early years of his teaching he very rarely mentions the name of Michael. It appears with increasing frequency after 1922, and the number reaches a climax in the last year of his lecturing activity and writing in 1924. It is in this year that Steiner places the Michael mystery side by side with the Christ mystery.

One approach to the Michael mystery—naturally it is only one—is particularly appropriate to Steiner's experience in our own country. In the summer of 1923—between the burning of the Goetheanum and the Christmas Foundation—two summer schools were held in England [sic], from which Steiner visited some 'standing stones' near Ilkley and the Druid Circle at Penmaenmawr. He described what a deep experience it was to him to stand where the priest had once stood at the sacrificial stone. A consequence of this visit was that when he gave his lecture course on Mystery Centres in Dornach later in the year it included an account of the Hibernian Mysteries, which of course were to be found everywhere in the Celtic world. He described them as the most difficult of all Mysteries for the seer to approach, surrounded by immense forces of hindrance. The description includes the unique—and difficult—picture of the two statues, male and female, the former associated with a winter landscape, the latter with a summer. Something of a different experience of the will was experienced in the approach to the statues, which, it will be remembered, gave a different kind of resistance to the touch. The summer and winter landscapes, associated with the two statues, were deeply experienced in the initiate's sleep. When he dreamed the winter landscape he felt as though the spirit were dying in it and would utterly perish. But then through his dream of the spring landscape—and he felt it as only possible through his dream—he saw that new life could arise. Man had to dream in order that the world might continue. This was a true dream, says Steiner. Without man the evolution of Saturn, Sun and Moon to Earth could have taken place. The evolution from Earth to Jupiter, Venus and Vulcan can only take place with and through man. Thus the picture of the dependence of the cosmos on man begins in the dream picture of the Hibernian Mysteries.

In the year following his visit to Ilkley and Penmaenmawr, Steiner came to Torquay and made his memorable visit to Tintagel. Before that time he had made only slight—it might almost be said slighting—reference to King Arthur and his Court. Now he describes Tintagel as the greatest centre of the Hibernian Mysteries. Above all he characterises the Arthur stream as a Michael stream, preserving even into Christian times the cosmic quality of the Michael intelligence, and the understanding—indeed the perception—of the Cosmic Christ. In this respect he brought it into sharp contrast with the Grail stream, that of the Christ who had entered through His incarnation into the blood and hearts of men. There is the Grail Castle and there is the Arthur Castle. For Michael the problem posed itself how shall he find his way from the one Castle to the other? In the first place it is when human beings, belonging to different streams, find one another through a living experience of karma. It is noteworthy that the lectures given at this time are full of descriptions of meetings, meetings of individuals, meetings of groups, meetings on Earth, meetings in the spiritual world, meetings leading to light, meetings leading to darkness, starting from all those confrontations centred in the year 869 to the great supersensible School of Michael in the modern age and the promise of the meeting of the Platonic and Aristotelian streams. It is in the study of such things that we begin to appreciate the great diversity of our karma.

But there is something much more than that, a realisation of what had been only a dream in the Hibernian Mysteries, and it is to be found in its fullest expression in the Michael Letters. Michael finds the way he seeks—and finds it alone—through man. It is not only man who has undergone a flight from the divine, nature also has fallen into the state where it is only the finished work, the wrought work of the Gods, no longer the place of their actual working. How is nature to be redeemed? Who is to restore to it the divine light which it has lost? Michael, who is a Master of Time, has preserved in a glorious imagination all the past glory of the ancient God-filled world. It is man alone who can do this. Man alone can work there. To express it in the briefest possible terms, man, spoken himself by the Cosmic Word, must now, in this age of the spiritual [consciousness] soul, himself speak the Cosmic Word into nature. It is man who must kindle anew the divine light in nature. He finds the power to speak that word when within his own being he experiences the Christ. It is the word of love—the love which is wisdom born again in the human heart. But it has to be brought to birth through man's activity. And when man speaks the word of love he raises thinking from its prison in the physical brain into the life of the etheric. Then Michael and his hosts can enter into human thinking and raise it into the sphere where he has gathered the glory of the past divinely inspired world, and man can speak the creative word into the cosmos. For Michael has gathered the glory of the past divine world together not as a memory but as an active force, not as a fruit but as a seed. The right attitude for man today, says Rudolf Steiner, is that when he looks within himself he perceives the Christ, when he looks into the world he perceives Michael. Thus man becomes the bridge between the two Castles.

Even in the early nineteenth century our Romantic poets had an inkling of the fact that man had now something to give to as well as to receive from nature. People are conscious today of the negative task which confronts man on the Earth—to refrain from the pollution and destruction of the Earth. We must develop the consciousness of a far greater task—to share creatively in the future evolution of our planet. It is a staggering responsibility, but ultimately it is what anthroposophy is about.

The Foundation Meditation leads us through the activity of the hierarchies to the Turning Point of Time. After the unparalleled voyage through the ocean being of the spirit, through the rhythmic tides of time, we are allowed to stand in peace with the Kings and Shepherds praying to the Light Divine, to the Sun of Christ. Perhaps we may now be allowed—at least on this occasion—to receive as a prelude to that great meditation the last words given in his own voice to the members by Rudolf Steiner, the Michael verse, 'Springing from Sun's High Powers'. (The address concluded with the reading of this verse and the Foundation Stone Meditation.)

Harwood did not, however, retire either to solitude or inane inactivity; and it is the main purpose of the rest of this concluding chapter to pick up some threads that had by 1974 come to coalesce very firmly in the able hands of Marguerite Lundgren, the leader of the London School of Eurythmy and Harwood's second wife.

The story goes back to Rudolf Steiner's later visits to Britain, which Marie Savitch—who for many years carried responsibility for the Eurythmy School in Dornach and provided the link with the work in Britain—recounted in her address at the celebratory weekend of 23–24 May. I shall quote some of the most relevant parts of this report before drawing upon Melissa Harwood's booklet *Marguerite Lundgren. Recollections of a Life in Eurythmy* (Anastasi, Leominster 2015).

> Rudolf Steiner visited England a number of times during the period between the spring of 1922 and the autumn of 1924. During these visits eurythmy performances were given in Oxford, London, Ilkley, Penmaenmawr and Torquay under the direction of Rudolf Steiner and Marie Steiner. On each occasion Rudolf Steiner brought out some special aspect which should be realised step by step in the further development of eurythmy. In Oxford, the visible picture of the sounds of the English language; in London, the dramatic impulse; in Penmaenmawr, the sensible [sense-perceptible] realisation of the imaginative element; in Torquay, the artistic path towards the future... The dominant impulse in Oxford was the harmony of speech and movement; in London, where scenes from the Mystery Plays were performed publicly in a theatre, it was the task of eurythmy in drama; in Ilkley and Penmaenmawr it was to raise what had been given hitherto into [a] 'visible picture' in accordance with the inner essence of the poems. The whole character of the nature which surrounded Penmaenmawr played its part through the imaginative echoing of past mysteries. In the concluding lectures of the course in Torquay, Rudolf Steiner gave guiding lines for the development of eurythmy, speech and music.
>
> In accordance with the wish of Rudolf Steiner, Vera and Judy Compton-Burnett began the eurythmy in England [in 1922], maintaining in this work a close connection with the original impulse. In London a hall was erected with a big stage which was later extended to 'Rudolf Steiner House', enabling performances of the 'sensible-supersensible' art of eurythmy to find their place in English cultural life. Thus the spiritual impulse which Rudolf Steiner gave at the Goetheanum continued to work on further in England.

Marie Savitch then went on to speak about the post-war situation, when she was asked by Cecil Harwood in 1948 to send a eurythmist to England (Britain) to take over the task of developing eurythmy there. She sent Marguerite Lundgren.

Marguerite Gertrude Lundgren had been born in London on 5 October 1916 to an English mother, Ruby (sister of Gertrude Sargeant and presumably a relation of Miss Beatrice Sargeant, who founded the first Steiner school for children with special needs at Larkfield Hall in 1928) and a Swedish father, Harald, who was a successful hydraulic engineer working for Baring & Co. who designed the turbines for the Kariba Dam on the Zambezi River, Africa. Marguerite grew up in Streatham and attended The New School (this had been her Aunt Gertrude's recommendation to her parents). After completing her education at what had in the meantime become Michael Hall, Marguerite maintained a close connection with it; and when the school moved from Streatham to Minehead in 1939 she cooked for Arthur Sheen's boarding hostel at Little Odell, while studying eurythmy with Liselotte Mann (who taught eurythmy at the school). Shortly after the end of the war she went to Dornach to continue her studies there with Marie Savitch and the Stage Group, returning to England as a result of Harwood's request in 1948.

By 1953 the work developing in London under Marguerite's direction had grown to the point where it was possible formally to found the London School of Eurythmy in that year. Additionally, two special performances of eurythmy were given in Rudolf Steiner Hall on 17 and 24 October together with a group of eurythmists from the Goetheanum under Marie Savitch. In conjunction with this 'new beginning', Owen Barfield—who had always had a great interest in forms of dance, an interest that he shared with his wife Maud—published an article entitled 'The Art of Eurythmy' in the 1954 *Golden Blade*. It would be difficult to imagine how the source of eurythmic gestures in the primal wellsprings of poetic language and song, eurythmy's essential and underlying significance and also the enormous challenges confronting any eurythmist seeking to convey this profound significance to an audience wholly habituated to the cleavage between sound and meaning that is characteristic to some degree of all modern languages, could be more clearly described than they are in this brief article.

Meanwhile, the following letter—one of a series of 14 deriving from the summer and autumn of 1951—had been written to Cecil Harwood from a rock beside a mountain tarn close to Bergen in Norway. Harwood was at this time about to embark on a boat crossing to America, where he was to spend some three months mainly visiting and speaking at anthroposophical gatherings and institutions in New York (including Spring Valley) and California. This is the period covered by this series of 14 letters from Marguerite. The first letter is probably from 27 July.

My dearest Cecil!

Just imagine where I am! Sitting on a rock by a mountain tarn! Somewhere below me, waterfall hidden in the undergrowth; round me on three sides, jagged rather deep walls of rock; sometimes moss covered, sometimes covered with short pines—sturdy, shaggy little trees like moorland ponies. And nowhere a sound, no birds singing, only the waterfall and the sound of the wind and—oh! such a haunting fragrant scent of pine and grass and freshness! There's a straggle of water lilies out on the water, and if I stand up and look round I can see across the fjord to still more water. It's like the glens in Scotland only with water...Why aren't you here too? Why didn't I meet you in Kopenhagn last year? I want to share this north with you, you would love it too—and no one can love things so well as you.

There is a funicular in Bergen which brings you up to this mountain—behind the town—and as I have 4 hours to spare until I catch my sleeper which is taking me to Oslo I have come up here for the afternoon. Bergen is a delightful huddley comfortable old town. Ancient tall wooden buildings line the quay, alleys curve in and out quite sheltered by the overhanging roofs, and nobody seems at all busy—quite unlike the slickness of Gothenburg!

Have you had the information about the ticket? My father promised to get his shipping man on to it at the office—and you ought to have heard today.

You are so kind to me, and I never do anything whatever to deserve it; I can't even make good conversation. And still you are patient, so that I am filled with a desire to say a thousand things which I still find unsayable. It's raining; great big rings on the water—I shall have to find some shelter. If only you were here! Did you feel how much you were with me, yesterday on the ship? Today coming up the coast and entering the fjord? *Please* write to me—here, while I'm in Norway, and love your voyage! With love to you, Marguerite.

Marguerite returned with her eurythmy colleagues to England around the middle of August and, as many another dedicated artist would have done, plunged single-mindedly into the task of inspiring those with whom she was working and creating programmes around their work to present to the members and to other receptive audiences. Cecil, for his part, had a fairly intense schedule of visits, meetings and above all lectures, and, moreover, in a foreign land without the loving companionship of Daphne (who, as previously noted, had died the year before). It is perhaps not wholly surprising that the affection that was growing between Cecil and Marguerite was buffeted during this period by the temperamental and other differences between the two of them. By the time of the writing of letter no. 7 (Harwood's own letters do not seem to have been preserved), something has gone seriously awry (this letter is dated 27 September):

Dear Cecil,

Your letter came today. How I have trampled on your feelings, how unkind I have been. Dare I say a word, now? You say 'if your heart had been with me you would have found time to write a little letter'—but my heart *has* been with you; but it's a distracted heart and doesn't know what to say. And the telegram that seems so empty a thing to you now was sent out of the fullness of my heart, a desire to be present with you, and also out of horror at the discovery that I was so late and had been so long neglectful. It wasn't just an easy throw to keep myself vaguely in touch, it was a warm eager thing even though so slight, and it gave *me* a feeling of nearness so that I forgot that it was after all only two words and that I still hadn't written to you. You know ever since I wrote that first letter to you, up by the mountain tarn, I've not been alone until this week, the beginning of term. Quite literally not—sleeping with at least one other, often with four; and all day involved with people— even on the boat to the north, and even at home with my parents and I slept in a row on mattresses on the floor because our beds were being mended and our guests had to have the only two remaining.

You say that first 'tarn' letter was misleading; had I been alone I would have written others still more misleading perhaps; and because my heart is warm *and* uncertain I have been afraid to write intimately, afraid to write as I feel. So I have let the time slip by in a bewilderment of feeling, uncertain of how to begin to speak to you. Forgetting that unless I indicate something of it to you you can have no inkling of my mind and no idea how much with you I have been. You remember you asked me what I had crossed out in one of the early letters from Norway—I felt shy to answer. I wanted to know what Laura[128] was to you. I have longed to sign myself 'Laura' but didn't in case it would mean too much to both of us. Can you understand that? Oh my dear Cecil you are probably right to write as you have done; only your assumption of no real feeling was wrong—'no abiding affection' you said. It will be a sad home-coming indeed.

You see I felt too much in awe of you. I felt I couldn't possibly explain to you my fumblings about certainty. I felt I ought to try and be formal with you and correct—I remembered your status and was filled with respect. And all the time of course I was liable to write you the most misleading letters out of sheer joy of an affection which is after all of long-standing. The problem was how not to do so before I had come to terms with myself. You guessed at this in one of your letters, but again, I felt too shy to confirm it. My greatest desire now is to see you and talk to you, but I know from past experience, how tongue-tied I become when I am with you, and how often and bitterly I have regretted my lack of words and lack of gentleness when I am with you—so I suppose it would be no good and I would still fail; and yet... I have been steadfast and my love is sure. But perhaps it is not the right kind, and then I shall always fail you. Dear, dear Cecil, forgive me yet again. It is very late now, may I write you the letter I had determined to write today, if your letter had not come? I wanted to tell you about Savitch and the tour. And how to end this? Must it be goodbye? Marguerite.

Marguerite sent this further letter detailing arrangements about the eurythmy tour two days later. However, by the time she wrote the last in this series of 14 letters on 22 October, with Cecil's return by now imminent, things continued to be fairly bleak:

My dearest Cecil, how awful! how horrible! what a nightmarish time we are having!, and all because I couldn't bring myself to open that Washington letter. I'm sure you can never understand that, I hardly can myself. I would never have thought I could let a letter be unopened for even a day... but I *couldn't* open it—I was as sure it was another Los Angeles one and I felt I *must* have time before I found that again—oh! Cecil, *can* you imagine that, and try to forgive it, even when it has caused so much misery again? But now it's my turn to worry about dates—surely you should have got my letter by 19th when you posted yours? I have received your letter in 3 days—how long will my letter take to reach you which I wrote last Monday night? And I've written to you twice in between and all to no avail, of course, all at the wrong time. What mad, distorted ideas one gets and how helpless one is in their grip. Last week, because I was happier myself, I imagined you happy—and I tried to follow you and imagine you, and how wrong it all was—you were miserable and perplexed and found no comfort... and all through my fault again.—If I had only wired! But it was your own remarks about wires which made me desist. How horrible people can be to each other. And you thought I might be offended, and I sent that letter on purpose after I'd read your Washington letter—oh, no! no!—I *did* write immediately I read it. And the letter in answer to your 2nd Los Angeles [letter] was posted so late only because I wanted to write a better letter, and I therefore waited, but I couldn't so it got sent in the end, just as it was because I thought I ought to acknowledge it somehow. What a miserable stupid story, and how cruel it has been in its effect. And those 3 letters on the lecturer's desk—oh! everything—one after another has gone wrong. How dare I assume anything any more? I have had so many wrong ideas—but surely you are not still hurt and angry? Surely you have had my belated answer? But what can I, dare I think?—I hope you've not given as bad lectures as I have given bad lessons. Oh what an awful autumn it has been. It's late again, I have so much to do tomorrow, I must go to bed. Monday is a bad day. Elizabeth [Edmunds] comes to town and we rehearse from 11–1 and from 2–5; at 5 I have a lesson and 6.30–9 two classes—beginners, they are very nice, but it's hard work and no time for a meal and then I'm exhausted after, and too tired to eat, and in no state to write a letter. And *that* is one other thing! It is difficult for you, who can write so easily and well, to understand what an effort it is for people like me who *don't* write well, and can't easily express themselves—it's quite a different thing for stumblers like me.

Which reminds me. I have to prepare an introductory talk for the Glasgow performance—and send it to Miss Currie—I'm probably too late—what *can* I say? Miss Currie has suddenly planted Entertainment Tax Exemption on me—and everyone is ill who knows anything about it—and I had to take over the central figure in Wild West Wind which I hoped Christine [Custer] could do—and I can't even do my own work yet—and what a mad bad dream! Dear Cecil, be comforted now—forgive me... how often, how terribly often I have to beg you that. Love from Marguerite.

Things were not really resolved until Cecil returned at the end of October or the beginning of November. Although it is difficult to date these next letters, I think they still belong to this agonizing time of autumn 1951, when Cecil was making his way back from America:

My very dear, it cut me to the heart to hear you had written me a miserable letter last night. Why? Was it I? Because I give you no answer and say nothing and never write and never tell you how much I love you, nor what content and peace I find with you? Dear heart, you must feel how I need you, too—what solace there is in being with you—and what exciting, scarcely imaginable vistas open up—'terrible and dear'.

I'll write properly tomorrow—I decided on one date for Savitch, Sat. 25th October.

Love Marguerite

My darling, what a wretched, unhappy letter—no wonder such a chill haunted me all after I had spoken to you on the phone. Were it not for the later note I think I would have no heart to write at all. What <u>can</u> I write when everything you say is so unanswerable. All my life I have been a creature of vacillation and doubt, you challenge me at my weakest spot and are surprised and hurt to see me fail. Of course my mind sees difficulties—how can I hope to enter into your life as I should, help you and support you in it, when I am the sort I am, so ungifted in the arts of life? You say you know you would want more of me than I would be willing to give, I wonder if very soon you wouldn't want less— much less—and what makes you think that I wouldn't be demanding? One of the things that frightens me is my own possessiveness. As women go I should say I'm not possessive—except—I'm afraid I might be with you.—It will take me a very long time to get used to the idea that you really want to be with me more than anyone else—I still have moments of absolute stupefaction—can't you understand that? Do you think my work here stands really in the way? You know, I would be nothing, no use to you at all without it—and I could free the weekends more and if only I were with you more I would probably concentrate my work better... it has been such an awful effort during the last months to work properly—I have done the very minimum with the most awful waste of nervous energy, the most frightful effort at concentration; and so little result, of course. Has that been happening to you, too? But my head is not in such opposition to my heart as you think and my heart is heavy with anguish at your letter. You are so oppressed and sad and far away from the you I said goodbye to at Paddington so that I dare not even try to comfort you—I don't know whether you want me to come on Friday—may I—?

This letter has had so many interruptions it's probably not coherent at all—it's taken so long getting written because of the times I stop and think in between—the last interruption has probably made me lose this post, too.

Is it really all as hopeless as you say?

My love, Marguerite.

In the absence of any of Harwood's letters, the poem that he wrote for Marguerite during this time—whose receipt she acknowledged in one of her letters but said she didn't know how to respond to it—may serve as some indication of his feelings for her during this time:

> Standing beneath the stars I knew
> That one among them shone for you,
> Watch'd you with an angel's eye
> To bless each day the work you try;
> A love to clasp you when asleep
> And awake a trust for you to keep,
> Out of its silken treasures weaving
> The rainbow of your joy and grieving.
> It smiles to see your heart is true,
> A brave reflection of its own bright hue,
> As a flower smiles by water clear
> To see her fairness mirrored there.
> And as an instrument of glory
> It frames the trials of your story;
> Breathing one harmony of light
> To make your mind melodious and right,
> With softest airs clearly caught
> In the cadences of your thought.
> Brightly it burns among the many there

> And where you walk scarce fainter here,
> A star whose sphere was once your own
> Through its doors of gold your dance led down.
> Your day of birth it rose on high
> A candle in the Christmas sky,
> And so on wisdom's way you tread
> Its radiance will crown your head.

The relationship between these two very different individuals some 18 years apart in age, but linked by deeply romantic sensibilities and by their shared cultural and spiritual convictions, blossomed over the next couple of years until at some point in the early autumn of 1953 they must have decided to get married. However, between early September and the beginning of October their mutual communication problems resurfaced, eliciting the following pained letter from Marguerite sent from Dornach on 1 October while frantically engaged in eurythmy rehearsals and performances:

> Cecil, my dearest, forgive me. Your second, so unhappy letter came today and caught me, still not having written—I am filled with shame and remorse: when you write so, I realise what I have done—I was longing to write to you on the journey and had no pen—when I got here I got into a bewilderment of situations and didn't realise how soon the days were slipping past...
>
> My parents were very sweet—rather astonished at first but then afterwards not at all...just wished me joy and promised not to breathe a word—and then my father laughed and said 'But he'll have to ask our permission'—such an idea seemed to amuse him greatly—I think they are pleased—they hadn't a word to say against it. I'm terribly sorry about the children[129]—I thought you were going to speak to them any way. Oh! my dear! have I really made it hard for you with them? that you will find it hard to forgive. As for other people I still would greatly prefer it if they didn't know until after—why can't you just say you will be away from England? I have also told Ruth because she is a very dear friend and knows you—and anyway I had to tell someone just for the sake of talking... I was so touched by my parents' reaction I wanted to weep—but oh! if only we were married already—even apart, it would be so much better than this awful interim!
>
> Darling, what are you going to do? Are you feeling very angry and hopeless? How can I make amends?... [There followed some eurythmy performance news.]
>
> Darling, don't be angry and impatient with me—don't cast me from your heart, please write to me at once and if you can find time to visit my parents they would love to see you—you needn't stay long!
>
> All my love, my heart, M.

This was followed by a further letter written the next day, as ever amidst a flurry of rehearsals:

Cecil dearest, I sent you a letter yesterday—if only it would come today—and not have you waiting and wondering even this very moment while I write. I am terribly torn. For the first time since I was here I feel happy today and it's because I've written to you at last—on the other hand I am appalled by what I seem to have done from that poor agonised note...

Last night was the first time the clouds lifted—it was a glorious starry sky and I longed for you to be here. Then we would have walked up to the Dorneck [castle] and home round the Bau and perhaps the lights would still have been shining from the hall and we would have seen the green and blue and rose windows gleaming as though from under the sea... If you think of me and Leith Hill together, I think of you and all starry skies. You are the only person I've ever really seen a falling star with—really seen it together and not just a moment after... And this morning at last, the sun is shining and the sky is blue and cloudless and I'm eating my breakfast watching the people go up the hill to Adam's lecture.

Lunchtime

Another letter from you, much more terrible than the last—now I'm not torn at all, I'm only horrified and helpless. The one thing you can't imagine is what I did. I just let the days slip by before I actually wrote—there it is, to you the worst most unbelievable—and when I see it now through your eyes, I think so too. How could I—after all those horrors of America—how *could* I let it happen? Am I never going to learn? Am I really too irrevocably smothered up in myself? My darling, there is nothing I can, nothing I dare say. You have your bitter proof. Where is love? where faith? where hope? you ask... I suppose it is only in the work we would do together—perhaps I shall always be liable to fail you however hard I try—and you, perhaps, may fail me too... but not in the work we could do... After all, why do I love you, why do I want to marry you? I don't want a child, but I do *long* for the 'something new' that we could surely achieve together. It's your potential 'newness' and creativeness and quite individual spiritual quality that I love, and at last, won't fail.

Oh! I'm expressing myself so lumberingly and I'm probably making you wince, but I can't stay longer to try and put it better, and if I don't rush to the post now, it won't go today because I have rehearsals now up to supper and again after...

Be patient if you can—I don't know where I am, now—you write and tell me.

> That you were depending on me to write before you told your children I had not understood.[129]
>
> Love from Marguerite.

This relatively minor pre-marital discord was fully resolved by the time Marguerite wrote her next letter but one on 10 October 1953:

> My dearest Cecil,
>
> A thousand thanks for that kind, forgiving letter. Yes, I *will* try to answer letters promptly, but please forgive me this time if I write nothing at all. I seem to be having a 'fluey cold and ache all over and can barely summon enough to rehearse. Is it heavenly and sunny in Bristol? I suppose you are there now. The invitations came today. We have a performance tomorrow on the new stage. I hope Bristol isn't too difficult—in great haste to catch the last post. Love, Marguerite.

After Cecil and Marguerite's marriage towards the end of 1953, their correspondence reflected what must have been in general a very happy married life. Melissa Harwood, whose book referred to earlier is a mine of informative reflections from many fellow eurythmists and others about Marguerite as a eurythmist and as a teacher and leader of the London School of Eurythmy, and who had known Marguerite since taking up eurythmy studies with her in 1972 (when, of course, Cecil was still alive), became close friends with her during the five years (1977–1982) that she lived at South Harbour, the house close by Michael Hall that Cecil had largely himself designed for the two of them to live in (they began living there in the mid-1950s). What she writes gives considerable insight into the nature of the Harwoods' relationship as a married couple:

> The death of her dear husband Cecil Harwood hit Marguerite very hard. He had been her inspiration, teacher and rock throughout her eurythmical life. When I had been to visit her before living there myself and Cecil was still alive, I couldn't believe how different she was. Where was the tiger I experienced in the eurythmy room? She was gentle and kind and helpful. It was lovely to see that side of her. I noticed that after several years after his death she began to lose her oomph! in the directing of the Stage Group. She became heavier in herself but still went on directing and teaching in the Eurythmy School.

One has to imagine the busy life that emerged from Cecil's marriage to Marguerite. Rudolf Steiner House must have been the main focus for both of them, and—as Owen Barfield describes in his letters—each of them had a little room adjacent to the practice room of the Eurythmy School at the top of the House for when either of them needed to stay overnight. Additionally, they both travelled a lot, not by any means necessarily together, although Cecil gave Marguerite his unstinting support in the work of the Eurythmy School. But South Harbour in the grounds of Michael Hall was solidly their home; and Cecil continued to contribute in various ways—such as giving addresses on occasion, contributing verses and words for songs, and (perhaps especially memorably) regaling the pupils with his inexhaustible fund of anecdotes and stories such as those he would tell, for example, for Hallowe'en.[130]

★

This book has had a particular purpose, which was outlined in its introductory sections. It has been written in the belief, or more appropriately out of the conviction, that the land of Cecil Harwood's birth has in our present time a particular contribution to make to the unfolding drama of human evolution, the nature of which has been voiced most plainly and explicitly by the insights that Rudolf Steiner has brought to expression through the German culture and language in anthroposophy. Moreover, it has sought to celebrate and exemplify—most especially through his work at Michael Hall and as Chairman of the Anthroposophical Society in Great Britain—the fact that Cecil Harwood not only himself thought as much but showed through his life how such a contribution could indeed be made.

When Harwood retired from the Chairmanship of the AS in GB in 1974, on 2 March of that year three of his erstwhile colleagues in the Society's administration—Owen Barfield, Gerald Eedle and Connie Winnie—typed out for him the messages that had accompanied the contributions to a travel fund for 'Mr. and Mrs. Harwood' to mark his retirement:

> Again and again members wrote:
> 'With best wishes and gratitude.'
> 'I hope the fund will be a great success.'
> 'I am so glad the fund has been organised to give us an opportunity of expressing our appreciation.'
> 'I hope Mr. and Mrs. Harwood will have many happy years.'
> 'I only wish I could send more.'
> Then there were the following more individually expressed messages:
> 'With love' (this from Lois).
> 'We cannot possibly acknowledge fully all that Mr. Harwood has done and given to the movement and the Society.'

'The enclosed has been donated by members of the Group as an expression of all the devoted and dedicated work Mr. Harwood has put into the Society all these years.'

'I am very glad indeed to have the chance to add my name to the list of contributors.'

'It is only a very small gift I am able to send, considering the great delight I have experienced from his talks, his chairmanship and altogether from his presence.'

'My work with Mr. Harwood has been for me a very happy association.'

'The amount enclosed is modest and can only be a token of what one owes—there must be a tremendous number and variety of debts.'

'The enclosed comes as a tribute to the work of Mr. Harwood.'

'What an excellent idea to give Mr. and Mrs. Harwood a well-deserved holiday.'

'Always we look forward to the initials ACH which mean Truth and Quality.'

'I have great pleasure in sending this donation. It comes with my sincere good wishes to Mr. and Mrs. Harwood for the future and for an enjoyable and restful holiday.'

'A very small token of gratitude for all he has done for the Society and for all of us.'

'Thank you for organising this fund, whereby we can show our undoubted gratitude.'

'A small token of the deep gratitude I feel I owe to Mr. Harwood.'

'I should like to send to send my profound thanks to Mr. Harwood for all he has done fur us for so many years.'

'One is dreadfully sorry he is retiring.'

One may truthfully say, it will be very difficult, if not impossible to replace him.'

'We can only be thankful we have had him so long.'

'I know that he has the most fervent wishes of us all for his future happiness.'

'I am so sad about Mr. Harwood's retirement.'

'Often when I have listened to his lectures I have dreaded the day when he would no longer be Chairman.'

'If anyone deserves a well-earned rest, surely it is Mr. Harwood.'

'We join in deep gratitude for all that our Chairman has meant to us and to the Society over all these years.'

'The enclosed is sent with great pleasure that we have been given the opportunity to show our gratitude to Mr. Harwood.'

'I would like to express my appreciation of the years of devoted work for anthroposophy and for the Society.'

'A small appreciation of the deep wisdom Mr. Harwood has always shown in his work.'

'We are so very glad of this opportunity to express our admiration and gratitude for his leadership and wisdom over so many years.'

'It is with a deep sense of gratitude that we join in sending this tribute.'

'We do hope the presentation will be an enormous one.'

'I would have liked to send more, but I have not worked for two years because of illness.'

'I send my own personal thanks to ACH and hope he has a very happy retirement.'

And finally, the dear soul who wrote:

'Mr. Harwood deserves everything he gets.'

As it turned out, Harwood did not live long enough to enjoy more than a brief 'retirement' of one and three quarter years (although he and Marguerite did manage to have a last holiday in Greece in August—September 1974, when—as Peter and Mona Bradley recounted in the Supplement to the News Sheet in February 1976—they visited the Northern Aegean islands of Samothrace and Thassos, 'staying in the small, quiet rest house on the edge of the mystery centre.. and [Harwood] would often remark: 'If only I had come here earlier").[131] That his withdrawal from his formal role as Chairman did not, however, mean any lessening of his other activities is apparent from the number of lectures that he gave from March 1974 onwards. In addition to the transcript of his address at the AGM in March 1974 on 'The Foundation Stone and the Michael Mystery' (published in the autumn 1974 issue of *Anthroposophical Quarterly*), there are records of seven further lectures that he gave, mainly in 1975, at Rudolf Steiner House, Emerson College and Michael Hall.[132] It was during the last of these—probably in July 1975—that he realized, to his immense distress, that his sight was failing. During October 1975 his condition, which ultimately derived from a form of rheumatism that leads to a hardening of the arterial system and can often cause blindness by preventing blood from reaching the retina, became so serious that he consulted different eye specialists, neither of whom was able to arrest the growing severity of these acutely distressing symptoms.[133] Nevertheless, he continued to the end of his life to co-edit the *Anthroposophical Quarterly* with Mildred Kirkaldy (up to and including the Winter 1975 issue, vol. 20 no. 4); and there is among his papers the original hand-written draft of a letter written with very evident visual difficulty to Grange and Mildred Kirkaldy (maybe it was subsequently typed by someone and sent, even though by Harwood's standards it is unusually legible):

Nov. 12, 1975

Dear Grange and Mildred,

Thank you very much for your most kind and sympathetic letter. It was a great blow of Fate but I am trying to treat it as a challenge. And the disaster has brought such a flood of good will to me that I am quite staggered.

If you like to send me any MS, I can have it read to me and send my opinion!

All good wishes and love to you both,

Yours always,
Cecil

It was not long after this that Cecil Harwood died on 22 December. This elicited lengthy tributes from many people published in a special supplement to the members' News Sheet in February 1976 from which quotations have previously been made in this book. I shall conclude by summarizing or, where appropriate, quoting some extracts from this twelve-page document, which has not, of course, seen the light of day in any other context. I shall begin with quoting more or less verbatim Susanne Mainzer's introductory words:

Alfred Cecil Harwood: 5 January 1898–22 December 1975

Introduction

Cecil Harwood died in great serenity at his home in Forest Row on 22 December 1975, and the funeral took place a week later at the Surrey and Sussex Crematorium, near Crawley. The many sides of his life were represented: Marguerite Lundgren, sons and daughters, grandchildren, Dr Georg Unger representing the Vorstand at the Goetheanum, members of the Executive Council of the Anthroposophical Society in Great Britain, old colleagues and old pupils from Michael Hall, past and present eurythmy students and members of the London Stage Group, at least one member of the publications committee of the Rudolf Steiner Press, representatives from St Christopher's School, Bristol, and many, many friends. Adam Bittleston conducted the service: the dignified ritual given by Rudolf Steiner to the Christian Community and put into English by Cecil Harwood, together with Dr Alfred Heidenreich. There was instrumental music from a chamber music group, singing by a small choir (Bruckner's *Locus Iste*) and by a soprano soloist ('I know that my redeemer liveth' from Handel's *Messiah*). Jesse Darrell spoke of a faithful friend. Dr Unger said the following:

Dear Friends of Cecil Harwood,

It is with a feeling of lack of respect that I speak to you in English about a man whose every speech was a piece of art. To meet him meant to meet something of the English spirit and soul! But he will understand as he always did in his disarming way when he patiently listened to my stammering.

I am here in order to thank Cecil Harwood in the name of the Vorstand at the Goetheanum, not only for his work as General Secretary of the Anthroposophical Society in Great Britain, but also for what he did for the work of Rudolf Steiner in all the years of separation and specially for his untiring efforts in bringing about a new and living relation between this Society and the General Anthroposophical Society. He has taught us often enough to see things in proportion, not least by his marvellous sense of humour.

In addition, I have to thank him that he helped a 'Dornach child': eurythmy, in this country. For all of us he was a true Knight of the English Culture with his classical education! And all of it he put to work in such an inspiring and selfless way for the germ of the future that is given in eurythmy.

All this, and the fact that only a few months ago he actually worked at the Goetheanum in that context, is deeply felt in Dornach. I express our heartfelt gratitude also for the wonderful experience so many of us could share in Exeter where one could feel that his physical frailty made him all the more transparent for the Spirit.

Personally, I would say: it was a privilege to know Cecil Harwood and an honour to call him 'friend'.

Later there was a reception at Kidbrooke House, arranged by the Forest Row Group of the AS in GB, and then a Memorial Festival in the school hall. Inside the hall there were great banks of flowers which had been sent in tribute, and candles shining from a tall Christmas Tree and from candle-holders. The stillness and joyousness of the Holy Nights could be experienced but, most appropriately, there was, too, a feeling of freshness, of a new beginning, of spring. We heard chamber music and singing by choirs of children and adults; there were speeches; there was eurythmy. In conclusion, the whole company joined together to sing 'Alleluia for all things', a song with words written by Cecil Harwood for the children of Michael Hall.

Cecil Harwood was a pioneer of anthroposophy and of Steiner education in the English-speaking world. As Chairman, he steered and sustained the Anthroposophical Society in Great Britain for nearly four decades and, for the last twenty-five years of his life, he tended and fostered the art of eurythmy. It seems appropriate, therefore, to have a special News Sheet Supplement in his memory. The contributions illumine his life and work from various aspects but the picture they give of him is remarkably consistent. Nevertheless, what is given here is a sketch rather than a finished portrait. There are some very important aspects of Cecil Harwood's life and work that remain to be written about.

Susanne Mainzer

There followed a lengthy and beautifully written account by Owen Barfield of Cecil Harwood's youth, together with memories of shared school-days and university studies and their sequel. Some of this has been quoted already in the first part of this book, together with the amusing snippet from C.S. Lewis's *Surprised by Joy* and a substantial portion of Jesse Darrell's appreciation of Harwood's manifold contributions to Michael Hall and to Steiner Education. However, the sections relating to Harwood's work for the Anthroposophical Society are too pertinent and insightful to be omitted.

Anthroposophical Society

When I think about Cecil Harwood's life and achievements—now and then, alas, they were not free from pain caused by hostility—and ask myself what I have learnt from them, I find myself answering that in him I have realised something of the creative value of personality, its courage to take difficult decisions, and its power to hold chaotic opinions in check, often enabling harmony to be established. In one's own efforts, to rely on such qualities in others is only too easy; to have courage to act when they are no longer physically available is a very different matter. The loss to the Society and related activities that has been caused by Cecil Harwood's death is very great indeed.

Dorothy Osmond

Cecil Harwood often mentioned the fact that human beings who fully realised in themselves the qualities of their folk soul—a Shakespeare, a Goethe—transcend mere nationality and come to belong, so to speak, to the world. He would have found it immodest to include himself—but I think that now, after his passing, we could and should do so. He lived, in a profound way, the life of an Englishman—not only in his love of the language and the culture of his country, but also as one who lived deeply connected with the spiritual task which had to be pioneered in this island so that it could become the task of the world, the unfolding of the consciousness soul.

To experience Cecil Harwood as Chairman was to glimpse this. There are charismatic chairmen who dazzle or dominate their committees. There are legalistic chairmen, like the Speaker of the House of Commons, who see fair play but do not enter the debate themselves. But there are also chairmen who make it their task to perceive the realities of a situation or a meeting, and to help others to see it too. In this art, which should be the nature of chairmanship for the consciousness soul, Cecil Harwood was a master.

It is not by chance, I think, that he presided over the Anthroposophical Society in Great Britain just during that period when Britain lost its Empire and has had to learn to see realistically a quite new world situation. In anthroposophy lies the impulse which can bear the consciousness soul beyond its initial island awareness, not to a physical empire but to a dawning experience of the spiritual 'empire' in which we all live. Cecil Harwood took anthroposophy most deeply into his heart and into a soul imbued with the consciousness soul experience, and thereby fertilised this experience itself for further development. This, I believe, will have consequences well beyond those which spring from 37 years as Chairman of the AS in GB.

This inner uniting of anthroposophy with a truly and deeply English soul was reflected outwardly in the long road to heal the deep rifts in the Society which he inherited in the 1930s. He took a long time to make up his mind for the decisive steps. He saw, with sober spiritual realism, that the healing must come from within, not without, and must begin with a re-establishment of confidence among those responsible for the First Class of the School of Spiritual Science. Once he saw that this could be done, he guided the path towards unification with unerring and sure-footed skill, leading to the reunification of the Society in Great Britain with the General Anthroposophical Society in 1964, and then the unification with the English Section in 1970.

We now have again a united world Society, whose task in the future must reach quite beyond multiplying nationalisms and power blocks, towards the 'all-human' Society of which Rudolf Steiner spoke at the Christmas Foundation. In this task, the English language, in which Harwood lived with such strength and joy, will have, as a world language, a vital task. Thus Cecil Harwood lived his life in a task for the future, at a time when his country saw the dissolution of its Imperial past. But he was able to take the best of this island's past culture, and transmute and prepare it in his soul, for the new.

John Davy

Although I had been acquainted with Cecil Harwood for many years, it is only in recent years that I got to know him well. When I first entered anthroposophical work he was—for me—the supreme example of English classical scholar turned anthroposophist, whereas for me the impact of anthroposophy came through the German folk soul and its language, and the world of music. Harwood belonged to a world that I could look up to but not attain. I have to admit that I regarded our Anthroposophical Society, represented by its 'Head-quarters' and its Executive Council, in much the same way that some of our younger members seem to regard it today. I had little idea of the task Cecil Harwood was taking upon himself when he succeeded Montague Wheeler as Chairman in 1937.

When, shortly after the end of the Second World War, a handful of those of us who carried responsibilities for some of the 'daughter movements' wanted to change the status of the Society and make it merely a 'group among groups', Harwood was ready to stand down and hand over the chairmanship to someone else if the right person could be found. But when our proposals came before the General Meeting, the members preferred the stability and wise judgment of the Chairman they knew, and so Cecil Harwood remained and the Society was the better for it.

During those painful years when the Anthroposophical Society in Great Britain was separated from Dornach, Harwood kept his loyalty to Dr Ita Wegman and Dr Elisabeth Vreede, the original members of the Vorstand with whom so much of our work in England was linked and who were for us the most direct link with Rudolf Steiner himself. Harwood regarded this as spiritually right and never wavered from it. Only during the 'sixties did it become possible to find a way of uniting the Society once more without compromising the principles for which he stood.

Since 1974 I have been one of the group of five who took over the duties formerly carried by Harwood as Chairman of the AS in GB and I can say that we have found that he carried a much larger load than most members were ever aware of, and this always in a thoroughly unassuming way. For this the Society owes him a great deal. I have also had the privilege of working closely with him in the more esoteric side of the work, and here I want to say that beneath the strictness with which he preserved what is best in the traditional use of English style and English language, there was great sensitiveness for ways in which this could be used to convey the deepest spiritual truths. What has appeared to some friends as a predominance of intellect was really the strict ordering of thought and the accurate use of language. His lectures were a joy to listen to, not only for their profound content but also for the artistry and humour with which this was conveyed. His sense for truth and beauty came out of a very clear awareness of what he was doing, and with all this there was a deep humility. His way of saying 'Thank you' to Herr Grosse at the conclusion of the recent conference for Class members at Leicester was a beautiful example of this, and its deep message was at once understood. I am sure that all this is a true characteristic of the emerging consciousness soul in our time and place.

Michael Wilson

I shall conclude with a moving tribute written by Catherine Grace on behalf of St. Christopher's School, Bristol, with which Harwood had been associated since 1953. I have chosen this particular tribute to end with because it seems to sum up so many of the qualities and attributes that Cecil Harwood displayed in whatever he undertook.

Cecil Harwood first took on his heavy responsibilities for St Christopher's School in 1953 at the request of Irene Groves. He did not wish to bear this extra burden, but finally, thanks to the good spirits guiding the school, agreed to do so. He was for many years Chairman of the Executive Committee, before becoming Deputy Chairman in 1966 and then Chairman of the Council and Finance Committee in 1968.

When Cecil Harwood was convinced of the rightness of a decision, he had the courage, daring and imaginative foresight to see it implemented. Under his guidance, developments at St Christopher's followed one another in swift succession—the Teachers' and Houseparents' Training Courses, the Pupils' Training Course, the building of Groves Hall and a new school house, the sick bay and the complex named after him, linking the school and Groves Hall. Lastly, the two hostels for young adults came into being, the first one while he was still Chairman. The second will open shortly, but might never have reached this stage if it had not been for his few words at the last Council Meeting he attended, which decided the members to take responsibility for it.

He encouraged the cultural side of the work, taking part in school eurythmy festivals run at Christmas by Elizabeth Parker, giving courses of lectures to the staff on world history, the development of consciousness, and the Study of Man, to name those which live most vividly in my remembrance. He sometimes addressed the children at the Opening Assembly if he happened to be at school when term started and one such talk on the New Year Carol 'Here we bring new water from the well so clear' has never been forgotten by staff and children who heard it.

The Senior Girls who cared for the domestic science flat where he always stayed began each day with eurythmy to verses which he himself had written. One child, after carefully making up his bed, decided he should have a book to read on his table and chose her own favourite, *Little Women*. When he arrived, she showed him somewhat diffidently what she had done and he replied, 'Oh, thank you. I've always wanted to read *Little Women*.'

The children loved him without reserve and this called forth a side of his nature which would have surprised many people. I think it awoke an answering affection, so that when he decided to resign in 1967, the parting party and dramatic skit led to him reversing his decision and remaining with the school till his final resignation a few weeks before his death.

The thanks and gratitude of all at St Christopher's flow to him in the new tasks that await him.

Conclusion

The life of any human being is worthy of interest and further study. If I have chosen to write a book about the particular individual who bore the name Alfred Cecil Harwood, it is because what he said, wrote and accomplished in his life epitomizes and is representative of the germinal possibilities for the future of which I wrote in the Introduction to this book. That in his life and work he sought to embody in the context of the English-speaking world and its distinctive mystery-wisdom all that emanated from the work of Rudolf Steiner needs no further comment, since this is germane to the content of the entire book. However, two aspects of the way that he endeavoured to do so should be emphasized here. Firstly—and this is of particular relevance at a time when social life appears to be regarded by some as an expendable or even undesirable commodity—he considered that no constructive, healing progress in human affairs is possible except through the meeting of human individuals with one another (this is especially evident in Part Three, Chapter 2). Secondly, his life was characterized by a quality of sacrificial adaptability: he set out to become a writer and had neither the intention to become a teacher nor the ambition to become effectively the leader of an organization for many years, and yet channelled his considerable literary gifts towards serving these wider practical aims. In respects such as these, Cecil Harwood was, I believe, an exemplary figure not only for the particular circles within which he worked but also for the wider world, both in his own time and on into the present twenty-first century.

Shortly after this book was completed, Laurence Harwood—to whose memory the book is dedicated—died, closely followed on 28 December by the last surviving member of Harwood's immediate family, Lois Olivier. With their passing a chapter is closed; but something is thereby released which can further the development and fructification of some of the twentiety century's dormant or only barely sprouted seeds.

Simon Blaxland-de Lange
February 2021

Notes

1 First published by Michael Joseph, London in 1994

2 I cannot at this point go into a lengthy explanation of what Rudolf Steiner meant when he used the designation 'consciousness soul'; suffice it to say that it represents a kind of 'Hamlet' consciousness, on the one hand the bitter, but also liberating, experience of becoming wholly immersed in one's consciousness in the physical body and bereft of outward inspiration or guidance while, on the other hand, being equipped with the renewed capacity to reappraise the true reality of what this consciousness is able to apprehend..

3 See the compilation of his essays entitled *Romanticism Comes of Age*, third edition, Barfield Press, Oxford 2012, specifically 'Of the Consciousness Soul' and 'Of the Intellectual Soul'.

4 See further in Simon Blaxland-de Lange, *Owen Barfield: Romanticism Come of Age. A Biography*, Temple Lodge, Forest Row, 2006/2021, the chapter entitled 'Vision for a Future Social and Cultural Order'. For Rudolf Steiner's view of this relationship, see his remarkable observations in the lecture of 15 November 1914 (included in GA 158, *Our Connection with the Elemental World*, Rudolf Steiner Press, Forest Row 2016).

5 See the invaluable treatise by Rob Young, *Electric Eden. Unearthing Britain's Visionary Music*, Faber and Faber 2010, p. 63. As this book makes clear, interest in folk songs predated this seminal event; for while Cecil Sharp himself founded the English Folk Dance Society in 1911, the Folk-Song Society had been founded in 1898 (the two Societies amalgamated in 1932) and had arisen out of endeavours going back at least to 1847, when Lucy Broadwood's uncle, John Broadwood, had published a collection of songs from the Sussex Weald.

6 This is not the place to enter into a justification for Rudolf Steiner's insight that the mystery of human languages and cultural identities can really only be penetrated through an awareness that these phenomena are the manifestation of the work of spiritual beings.

7 See 'Owen Barfield: A Biographical Sketch in His Own Words', included in Simon Blaxland-de Lange, *Owen Barfield: Romanticism Come of Age. A Biography*, Temple Lodge, Forest Row 2006 /2021.

8 *Cornish Times*, June 29 1923.

9 See note 7.

10 According to the *Western Morning News* dated June 29 1920, the dances included The Helston Furry, Gathering Peascods, The Black Nag, Brighton Camp and The Butterfly.

11 *English Folk Dance Society News* (Special Festival Number), no. 2, August 1921.

12 Ralph Vaughan Williams's life has been fully chronicled in the biography *R.V.W.* by his widow Ursula (1964, reprinted by Clarendon Press, Oxford in 2002), while the standard guide to his compositions is *The Works of Ralph Vaughan Williams* by Michael Kennedy (1964/1980, likewise reprinted by Clarendon Press in 2002).

13 Included in *Ralph Vaughan Williams in Perspective*, edited by Lewis Foreman, Albion Press 1998.

14 First published by Barrie and Jenkins in 1989, and republished in a revised form in 1997/2008 by Travis and Emery, Cecil Court, London.

15 Op. cit., p. 78.

16 Quoted in Ursula Vaughan Williams's biography of her husband, p. 95. The symphony was dedicated to Butterworth's memory following his death in action at Pozières on 5 August 1916.

17 Mellers, op. cit., p. 90.

18 The Pastoral symphony was first performed in London on 26 January 1922.

19 Op. cit., p. 78.

20 Rob Young includes some fascinating details about Holst's involvement at this point: 'In 1897 Holst was formally invited to conduct the Hammersmith Socialist Choir. His involvement lasted several years, during which time he introduced a mixed repertoire that included Thomas Morley, Purcell, Mozart and Wagner. Seated behind a harmonium installed on a cart, Holst directed the singing during the Society's street demonstrations' (*Electric Eden*, p. 57).

21 Michael Kennedy writes in 'A Personal Note' that concludes his book that 'he was alert to all that was going on in the world; the idea of shutting himself up in an ivory tower was abhorrent' (op. cit., p. 381). While Vaughan Williams himself confirmed this in words from an article entitled 'Who wants the English Composer?': 'The composer must not shut himself up and think about art, he must live with his fellows and make his art an expression of the whole community—if we seek for art we shall not find it' (*R.C.M.* (Royal College of Music) *Magazine*, Christmas 1912).

22 Ursula Vaughan Williams points out that, after having helped to found the Leith Hill Festival, he rapidly became its coach, musical adviser and conductor and continued to be involved almost until his death in 1958 (the only year when he was not present).

23 Mellers, op. cit., p. 123.

24 The information contained in this section derives from Michael Kennedy, op. cit.

25 The book referred to here is *The Riddles of the Soul* (1917). In his autobiography, Rudolf Steiner writes as follows about the immense significance of this discovery in his life's path: 'And in this growing conviction with respect to the supersensible form of the human body that is perceptible by the senses I came to discern—at first in a very incomplete way—a picture of the threefold nature of man's being, and only after I had been pursuing my studies about it in silence for thirty years [from 1887 until 1917] did I begin to speak openly on this theme in my book *The Riddles of the Soul*' (*The Course of My Life,* Chapter 5).

26 This formal, public introduction had been prepared by two previous events, both of which had been initiated—at least in part—by Professor Millicent Mackenzie. The first of these events was a series of lectures that Rudolf Steiner had given in Dornach between 23 December 1921 and 7 January 1922 (*Soul Economy and Waldorf Education*), which had been requested by Professor Mackenzie and was, in Helen Fox's words (the reference is to her article 'Memories of Rudolf Steiner', *Anthroposophical Quarterly*, autumn 1971), 'rather specially intended for English teachers'. The second event was associated with the first through the fact that Miss Margaret Cross, the headmistress of a small boarding school at Kings Langley, had attended this course of lectures at Professor Mackenzie's invitation and was so impressed with what she heard that she had decided to offer her school to Rudolf

Steiner's educational impulse; and so when Rudolf Steiner arrived—for the first time since 1913—in England in April 1922 for a ten-day lecture tour, he visited Miss Cross's school. His subsequent report of this visit is of interest in several ways and is appended here:

'On the Sunday afternoon we were in the environs of London at a school—the Kings Langley boarding-school—run by that lady, Miss Cross, who was also here at the Christmas education course. We could see how a number of children are brought up and educated in a boarding-school of this kind. It is extremely interesting how children in precisely this boarding-school are in a way actually brought into proximity with life out of certain ideals of the present. The roughly forty to forty-five children in the boarding-school have to do everything; there are actually no servants there. The children have to get up early and care for the whole institution themselves, as well as cleaning their own shoes and clothes. They have to make sure there are enough eggs through breeding poultry, which they also do, and various other things you will be able to think of. They clean everything themselves and look after the garden. They have themselves first grown, harvested and cooked the vegetables which come onto the table, and then also eat them. A child is thus led into life in a many-sided way and learns a whole mass of things.

'During the Christmas course Miss Cross formed an intention to organise this boarding-school in the manner of a Waldorf school. This is being considered as a quite serious plan. Mrs. Mackenzie, who was also one of the chief moving forces for my being invited to the Shakespeare festival [this was the main reason for his visit to England in April 1922], is very much in favour of our school movement, supported by anthroposophy, winning a certain terrain in England. There is now an endeavour to form a committee for organising this school from an anthroposophical background, according to our education.

'This will be a very significant and important step forward. If so energetic a will stands behind it as exists in the personalities of Miss Cross and Professor Mackenzie, it can be taken for granted that after various hindrances are overcome, something of the kind will be able to come about.

'We are all hoping that the course I shall be holding at Oxford will contribute towards furthering this plan.

'Eurythmy will then also come to the fore, which this time could not yet be included, at least not in an official way. The hope is that this will all make a good contribution to the anthroposophical school movement in England' (quoted from *Rudolf Steiner in Britain. A Documentation of his Ten Visits*, vol. II, 1922–1925, edited by Crispian Villeneuve, Temple Lodge 2004, pp. 715–6).

27   Ibid., pp. 806–7.

28   Quoted from Villeneuve, op. cit., pp. 790–2.

29   Ibid., p. 807.

30   Rudolf Steiner, *Karmic Relationships, volume 8*, Rudolf Steiner Press, London 1975

31   In the context of this passage from Rudolf Steiner's lecture, it is, I think, not inappropriate to find a connection between the four lines of the refrain of Harwood's poem 'A Song of King Arthur' cited at the beginning of this book (the whole poem appears later on in the book) and man's fourfold bodily organism. Thus the castle wall of the first line relates to

the physical body, the Sun-imbued spray of the second line to the etheric body, the stars in Arthur's Hall to the astral body and the Sun of Day to the human ego and its relationship through Michael to the Christ Being.

[32] Information about Lord Olivier is mainly derived from *Sydney Olivier, Letters and Selected Writings*, edited with a memoir by Margaret Olivier and including an eloquent tribute by George Bernard Shaw (Allen and Unwin, 1948). Some facts are also taken from his obituary in *The Times* and from a memoir entitled *A Socialist in the West Indies: Sydney Olivier in Jamaica, 1907–1912* (May 2010).

[33] For a wealth of further detail about the upbringing of Daphne and her sisters, see the penetrating and well-researched biographical study of the Olivier sisters by Sarah Watling, *Noble Savages. The Olivier Sisters. Four Lives in Seven Fragments*, Jonathan Cape, London 2019.

[34] A further book that is essential reading here is his main study of Jamaican life, *Jamaica: The Blessed Island*, Faber and Faber, London 1936.

[35] The main source of information about Cecil's father's life that has been drawn upon here is the Obituary of Revd. William Hardy Harwood in the Congregational Year Book, 1925, compiled by his son Maurice.

[36] Supplement to Members' News Sheet, February 1976 (Anthroposophical Society in Great Britain).

[37] C.S. Lewis, *Surprised by Joy*, Ch. 13.

[38] *'Cecil Harwood. A Memoir by his Daughter Lois'* (unpublished MS).

[39] See note 7.

[40] Harwood was one of that original 'nucleus of bright young men' who from 1919 began to meet around C.S. Lewis in Oxford and hence formed the original circle of what would later be referred to as the Inklings. See Philip and Carol Zaleski's excellent recent study of this group, *The Fellowship. The Literary Lives of the Inklings: J.R.R. Tolkien, C.S. Lewis, Owen Barfield, Charles Williams*, Farrar, Straus and Giroux, New York 2015, p. 110.

[41] *Rudolf Steiner in Britain*, vol. II, ed. Crispian Villeneuve, pp. 881–2.

[42] Quoted from Joy Mansfield, *A Good School*, Blue Filter 2014, p. 17.

[43] Crispian Villeneuve, op. cit., p. 1039.

[44] See note 36. Both men would by then have become members of the Anthroposophical Society, a step that Barfield took shortly before Harwood.

[45] No doubt Daphne and Cecil would have wished to incorporate even just some of Rudolf Steiner's words into their marriage service. However, quite apart from the fact that the rituals of the Christian Community were not as yet translated (a task that centrally fell to Harwood himself, see below), Daphne's parents—who, according to ordinary custom, would have been hosting the event—would not out of themselves have volunteered this. Not that Lord Olivier was unaware of, or unsympathetic to, Steiner's ideas. One of his last letters, dated 6 October 1942, was written to the anthroposophist Arnold Freeman, founder of the Sheffield Educational Settlement, with whom he had had some correspondence; and it contains the following words: 'My son-in-law is a great propagandist of Rudolf Steiner and I have read his *Threefold Commonwealth*. It has

the same fault as the Webbs' book. The early Fabians about sixty years ago made the same mistake of thinking other people as intelligent as themselves, which they have not proved to be...' (quoted from *Sydney Olivier. Letters and Selected Writings*, ed. Margaret Olivier, p. 183).

46 Daphne does not say which church she is referring to.

47 See note 36.

48 On the day of John's birth, the whole Vorstand (Council) of the Anthroposophical Society came to visit the school (see *A Good School*, p. 27).

49 On the same day, Caroline von Heydebrand spoke about 'Anthroposophical Principles of Education' and Dr. Eugen Kolisko spoke on the theme 'Knowledge of Man, and its Significance in Healing and Education' (they both came from the original Stuttgart Waldorf School).

50 Friedrich Rittelmeyer's theme was 'The Temple at Jerusalem, the Temple of the Holy Grail and Anthroposophy'.

51 Hermann Poppelbaum spoke about 'The Fall and the Overcoming of the Fall, reflected in the Animal World'.

52 This is a reference to the simmering tensions within the Anthroposophical Society following Rudolf Steiner's death on 30 March 1925 which were to lead to a tragic split in 1935.

53 Lili (Lily) Kolisko spoke about 'Cosmic Festivals and their Reflection in Earthly Substances'.

54 Dr. Roman Boos spoke on the (somewhat mysterious) theme of 'The Prose-Word in the Goetheanum' on 5 October.

55 Prof. Hermann Beckh's theme was 'The Picture of the Representative of Humanity, in the Goetheanum, in the Gospel of St. John and in the Stars'.

56 Dr. Maria Röschl's lecture was entitled 'The Power of the Word and the Way of Destiny (a Historical Sketch)'.

57 In English, 'Viaticum', a collection of poems published in 1921.

58 *Memoriae traditum...* A record of discussions by Laurence Harwood with his older brother, John, in Spain in May 2010. Unpublished manuscript, 2017

59 This would seem to be a slightly different version of the same incident recounted by John Harwood, who, in response to his brother Laurence's question as to how the family travelled to Cornwall, replied: 'Father's car. We drove down in the Austin 12 which was bought because we were on our way to Ramsden, in whatever car it was then, which conked out in a thick mist somewhere in Oxfordshire. We somehow got to a garage where the garage man said: 'This car's just packed in, it's finished but we have an Austin 12 here'. Father said: 'Well, I'll give you a cheque for that', but the man said: 'Well, I don't know about that'. Father then said: 'My father-in-law is the Lord Olivier'. The garage actually telephoned him and Lord Olivier said: 'Yes, I think Mr. Harwood is good for the (probably) £ 120'.' (See the previous note.)

60 Then Bucknall, later Marcus. Joan was the sister of Morwenna Bucknall, who would become a prominent member of the Camphill movement.

[61] On 2 September 1939 Harwood sent a telegram to Helen Fox at Leigham Court Road to confirm that the 'evacuation party arrived safely'.

[62] Joy Mansfield, op.cit., p.33.

[63] William Mann (1900–1986) was the wholly German half-brother of George Adams (1894–1963), who took on the surname of his English mother at the time of the Second World War. They shared the same father, Georg von Kaufmann. William Mann joined The New School as a teacher in 1927 and remained associated with the school—as Michael Hall—for 46 years.

[64] These were, or are, the Children's Service, the Youth Service, the Offering Service and the special service that was to be held on the morning of Christmas Day.

[65] See Christian Maclean, *Pioneers of Religious Renewal: A History of The Christian Community in the English-Speaking World*, Floris Books 2016.

[66] 'The Shepherd of New Gifts' was reviewed by Owen Barfield in *Anthroposophical Movement*, 5 July 1931: '…There is indeed a dignity and strength in the verse and prose and a sterling quality of imagination informing the whole myth and structure of the play, for which we look hungrily and in vain in most modern literature, and for which all who read or see it will be most thankful to the author. But there is also something else, much harder to describe, a calm breathing of hope, a sense of reserves of unchecked vigour, such as prove it to have been the outcome of a real *intercourse* between young and adult minds. The freshness and delight with which the children acted and the bold confidence with which they audibly spoke their lines were among the many other symptoms which betrayed this same background of genuine "give and take"—an atmosphere capable, if duly fostered, of bearing untold fruit for the future of our country and our civilisation…'

[67] From *The Voice of Cecil Harwood*, ed. Owen Barfield, Rudolf Steiner Press,, London 1979, p. 308–9.

[68] This was a two-part article entitled 'Greek Gods and Homeric Heroes', which appeared, respectively, in the Easter and Midsummer issues. This was followed at Michaelmas 1932 by his beautiful essay on 'Tobit', which is included in Barfield's miscellany *The Voice of Cecil Harwood*.

[69] This occurred at the same time as the opening of Rudolf Steiner House (35 Park Road), which replaced the original headquarters of the Society at 46 Gloucester Place, the lease of which had just expired. (35 Park Road was subsequently rebuilt and extended, acquiring its present approximate form only in 1938. See *The Building of Rudolf of Steiner House, 1925–2010,* by Terry Goodfellow, 2010.)

[70] In Harwood's imaginative translation from the South German dialect of the original plays, preserved on a remote island in the Danube by a group of German migrants from the Lake Constance region. His translation of all three plays (including the Kings Play) was first published in 1944.

[71] Harwood's themes were 'Man and the Word—the teaching of Grammar' and 'Childhood as the Incarnation of Spirit'.

[72] It should be emphasized that the intention in what follows is to understand how Cecil Harwood and his closest colleagues in the AS in GB experienced these events. Arriving at

an objective judgement as to the rights and wrongs of the actions of those involved would be a different, albeit not unrelated, task.

[73]   This was published as Appendix 2 of a lengthy document dated 24 April 1934 that was sent to members. This included not only the new Declaration but also a full and detailed account of the General Meeting in Dornach where it was considered. Harwood and Barfield were among the signatories of the Declaration, which was signed by all members of the Executive Council of the British Society and by F.W. Zeylmans van Emmichoven on behalf of the Dutch Society. The fact that Harry Collison and the group that he represented supported the decisions made in Dornach underlines the fact that the split in the world Society was reflected at the level of the national Society.

[74]   Barfield also composed a lengthy novel entitled *English People*, which remained unpublished but was reviewed by Eloise Frehn von Ende in the issue of *Anthroposophical Movement* dated 16 August 1931.

[75]   Harwood had a way of opening his books and articles (and probably the same was true of his lectures) with striking first paragraphs, and this article was no exception: 'One of the many fundamental changes which anthroposophy brings into human thinking is to reinstate in the study of human affairs the importance of the final cause, drawing events towards it from the future. Not only in the life of the individual, but of whole nations also, deeds are performed not because the past decrees or the present wills them, but because the future desires them. In the case of nations not less than individuals this final cause working from the future is often seen to work in direct opposition to what is consciously willed out of the present and past by the human beings concerned.'

[76]   Already in 1935 the Anthroposophical Society had been prohibited from functioning in Germany, as is evident from the following notice that appeared in the German press on 16 November: 'The Secret Political Police has now dissolved the Anthroposophical Society... throughout the German Reich, and has forbidden all further activity of this Society. The action is taken on the basis of the order of 28th February 1933 "for the protection of the Nation and the State". The reason for this action on the part of the authorities lies in the fact that the Anthroposophical Society is international in spirit and has maintained to this day close relations with foreign Freemasons, Jews and Pacifists. The teaching methods, based on the educational theories of the founder and applied in the still existing anthroposophical schools, represent an individualistic education—that is, an education directed primarily towards the individual human being and having nothing in common with National Socialist educational principles.' (This notice was printed—in the translation given above—in the News Sheet for members of the AS in GB dated 11 December 1935.)

Furthermore, it was reported in the May 1938 issue of *Anthroposophical Movement* that the original Stuttgart Waldorf School had been closed by the Nazis. And by October the editor of this journal (or was it Harwood himself?) noted: 'As we go to press the peace of the world hangs in the balance, and we do not know how far we shall be able to carry out the programme we have planned. In these days of tense anxiety all our strength is needed to steel our minds and souls against falling into despair or panic, and as anthroposophists we are reminded that this is the time of the Festival of St. Michael and that the guidance of this age rests in the power of this great being of whom Rudolf Steiner has told us in many lectures....'

77 This was held—for the third time—in Bangor.

78 *Anthroposophical Movement*, February 1939 (vol. XVI no. 2).

79 Joy Mansfield, op. cit., p. 114.

80 There are some words in the report on the School's Birthday (January 20ᵗʰ) from the February Monthly Journal (no. 3) which somehow reflect Harwood's position at the school: 'Mr. Harwood, standing mid-way up the staircase [there was no room big enough to hold the whole school community, and children were gathered in the entrance hall below and on the landing above], then addressed the children, top and bottom deck. As he spoke, we could feel, once more, how thankful we may be, in a time like ours, to have been given a great and positive task, bearing as our ideal, love for the free individuality of man.'

81 This is included in *The Voice of Cecil Harwood*, Rudolf Steiner Press 1979, p. 315.

82 In his book *Shakespeare's Prophetic Mind*, published in 1964, Harwood includes a lengthy synopsis of the play *Pericles,* which he refers to as a bridge between the worlds of Shakespeare's second and third periods.

83 Published in two parts in the Monthly Journals dated October and November 1940 (nos. 11 and 12).

84 Printed in the Monthly Journal for December 1940/January 1941, nos. 13 and 14.

85 Included in *The Voice of Cecil Harwood*, p. 304.

86 Harwood had previously cited the fact that Owen was an uncompromising atheist.

87 From the Monthly Journal for October 1941 (no. 23).

88 It should be a simple matter to ascertain what the approximate figure would be today.

89 Monthly Journal nos. 29 and 30 (April–May 1942).

90 The questions on which he discoursed in a wholly down-to-earth way were: 'Is my child too old to go to a Rudolf Steiner School?' and 'Is a Rudolf Steiner School suitable for all children?'

91 From the Editorial for the August 1945 issue of the Monthly Journal (no. 69).

92 Op. cit., p. 46–47.

93 At the time there were four such schools in the country, including Michael Hall, with two more in the early stages of being founded.

94 The Zarathustra Group met at Heywood-Smith's Kensington home, 47 Redcliffe Square, which was where, for example, Rudolf Steiner's remarkable lecture of 2 May 1913 entitled 'Christ at the Time of the Mystery of Golgotha and Christ in the Twentieth Century' had been given to a small group of members of the recently formed Anthroposophical Society. See Crisipian Villeneuve (ed.), *Rudolf Steiner in Britain. A Documentation of his Ten Visits,* Temple Lodge 2004, pp. 419–421.

95 The Canteen and Rest Room continued to serve the needs of many hundreds of members of H.M. Forces and Civil Defence workers until it was closed on 29 April 1944.

96 *Anthroposophical Movement* vol. XXII nos. 1 and 2 (January – February 1945).

97 Even Hazel Straker, who at the time of writing is in her 99ᵗʰ year, joined the Society only in the latter part of 1946.

[98] Friedrich Rittelmeyer, a founding member and, for many years, Leader of the Christian Community, had died on 23 March 1938.

[99] König was writing on 29 November 1939, which also happened to be the day when Eugen Kolisko, an Austrian medical doctor who frequently visited England, where he was dearly loved, died at the youthful age of 46.

[100] For further details about this, see Hans Müller-Wiedemann, *Karl König: A Central-European Biography of the Twentieth Century*, English translation published by Camphill Books, 1996, pp. 165–7.

[101] This appeared in the November 1940 issue (vol. XVII, no. 11).

[102] It is worth mentioning here that both Francis Edmunds and Karl König were of orthodox Jewish descent, with Edmunds's family deriving from Eastern Europe and König's from Central Europe. Both men, moreover, were born in 1902. We have already traced in the previous chapter the fruitful colleagueship between Cecil Harwood and Francis Edmunds at Michael Hall; and something similar, albeit on a less tangible level, can be discerned in the interaction between König and Barfield, especially in view of the fact that Harwood and Barfield were both born in London in the same year of 1898.

[103] Hans Müller-Wiedemann, op. cit., p. 176.

[104] This information and other details have been kindly made available to the author by Richard Steel on behalf of the Karl König Archive.

[105] Although he does not refer to it, Arnold Freeman would doubtless have been aware that it was President Woodrow Wilson's particular impulse in the closing stages of World War One to raise the nation-state to the position that it came to occupy in the war's aftermath. This was, moreover, the main reason why Rudolf Steiner so strongly opposed everything that the American President stood for.

[106] I am indebted to Richard Steel and the Karl König Archive for this information.

[107] It would be fitting to note here that the introductory articles for the last two issues of the Society's journal for that year (the AGM was reported on in the October issue, vol. XXII, no. 10) were both concerned with the destructive effects of the war, and especially of its closing stages. The November issue featured a translation of an article by Dr. Ernst Müller entitled 'The Problem of the Newest Weapon' which concluded with the words: 'As to the atom bomb itself, we are responsible for it in face of all mankind and every one of us has a share in this responsibility'; and the December issue was almost wholly devoted to a report by Dorothy Lenn on 'Hungry Europe', which graphically described the horrific suffering and devastation most especially in Germany in the immediate aftermath of the war.

[108] He relinquished this responsibility after the first three issues 'through pressure of other work', and Hugh Hetherington became the editor from November 1948.

[109] Harwood's short book on Shakespeare is deserving of more than a brief comment. However, it is essential to emphasize, firstly, the immense importance to him of the great poet and dramatist's legacy and, secondly, his insights into Shakespeare's prophetic character: 'I do not mean that he prophesies actual events...; I mean he is prophetic in the sphere of consciousness. He lives intensely in those powers of feeling and apprehension which he has inherited from the past, he carries them into new forms which influence and even

create the experience of his day, and… he leaves a seed dropping from the ripeness of his powers which, like the fabled wheat in the pyramids, may only germinate after long centuries' (p. 7). In this way Harwood, through his book, shows how Shakespeare's unfolding journey of consciousness speaks no less directly to us today than to his own time.

[110] It is interesting that among his lecture-notes Harwood retained a newspaper cutting of an article by John Davy praising a recommendation from the Dainton Report that urgent steps be taken to ensure that technological innovations be balanced by greater emphasis on the Humanities and on an enhanced understanding of the human context that they need to serve. (Every word of this article, moreover, applies even more to today's situation than to the time when this article was published.)

[111] *The Faithful Thinker, Centenary Essays on the Work and Thought of Rudolf Steiner, 1861–1925*, Hodder and Stoughton, London 1961. Harwood's essay was entitled 'The Historical Process and the Individual'.

[112] E.G. West, *Education and the State*, 1965, p. 134. (This and subsequent references in the article are Harwood's annotations.)

[113] The former has been advocated by Sir Robert Birley, the latter by Sir Cyril Norwood.

[114] In 1940 I took up the idea of grants to parents using (approved) independent schools of a value equivalent to the cost of public education. Mr. R.A. (now Lord) Butler wrote that he would consider introducing it into his education act. Sir Percy Harris (then leader of the Liberal Party) said he considered it an excellent idea, but his party would not touch it because it would certainly lose them votes. It now appears again in California and at the recent Liberal Conference (1972).

[115] See, for example, the remarkable manifesto of the Scott Bader Company in *The Times*, of 1 January 1973.

[116] Now called the World Energy Conference.

[117] Fourteen lectures given in Dornach, July–August 1922.

[118] These words are being written in late December 2019.

[119] From a public lecture given in Toronto and Missouri in May 1968 through the kind offices of the Anthroposophical Society in Canada; and in May 1969 at the University of Missouri (Columbia) under the auspices of the Department of English. (Barfield's footnote)

[120] This was a Public Conference in Dornach running from 25 July until 3 August, including a performance of one of Steiner's Mystery Plays and part one of Goethe's *Faust*.

[121] Among these books were Owen Barfield's *This Ever Diverse Pair* (Gollancz, 1950) and *Saving the Appearances* (Faber, 1957, together with two further books in the 1960s), Canon Alan Shepherd's *A Scientist of the Invisible* (Hodder and Stoughton, 1954), Ernst Lehrs's *Man or Matter* (Faber, 1951), and Charles Davy's *Towards a Third Culture* (Faber, 1961—Faber had already published his *The Three Spheres of Society* in 1946). Harwood himself would publish his second book on Waldorf/Rudolf Steiner Education, *The Recovery of Man in Childhood*, through Hodder and Stoughton in 1958, and the same firm published the important miscellany of articles marking Steiner's centenary in 1961, *The Faithful Thinker* (of which more later). Additionally, an edition of the lectures given by Rudolf Steiner about Thomas Aquinas in May 1920 (GA 74) was published in 1956 by Hodder and Stoughton.

[122] I went to visit Dick Seddon, who had attained the age of 100 the previous December, at his home in Ross-on-Wye on 20 and 21 February 2019. This was with the aim of trying to achieve a more balanced understanding of the relationship between the two British Societies as it was at this time. Dick had joined the English Section simply because the people by whom he had been introduced to anthroposophy during the war, Brian Stockwell—who worked during the war as a journalist for Reuters in Singapore—and Thomas Gordon Jones, who was a Group Leader when Dick met him in Aldershot, happened to be members of it. Dick became a trustee of the English Section after he had moved to London in 1954 and after Gordon Jones had retired; and he joined the First Class of the School of Spiritual Science in 1958 through Charlie Gaze, who was the sole Reader for the English Section. Thereafter his main function in connection with the English Section was to represent the Goetheanum in England and to invite speakers, the main contact being Hermann Poppelbaum, although Rudolf Grosse, Friedrich Hiebel and Albert Steffen would also come over. He characterized the English Section as being more inward and intimate in scale, in contrast to the more outward, public gesture of Park Road. He never went near Rudolf Steiner House (until, presumably, Christmas 1961) and never met—for example—Owen Barfield or Francis Edmunds. In his mind the English Section represented the Grail stream and saw itself as the true representative of anthroposophy in Great Britain (a conviction which can be understood in terms of the inter-Society wrangling after Rudolf Steiner's death, even though the group that subsequently became the nucleus of the English Section had, in point of fact, split off in the late 1920s from the Anthroposophical Society in Great Britain founded in Rudolf Steiner's presence in 1923). Thus, for example, he pointed out that the statutes of the English Section were fully based on those of the General Anthroposophical Society, whereas the Anthroposophical Society in Great Britain had its own statutes (and, of course, had no option to do otherwise in view of what happened in 1935). Nevertheless, he agreed that what had happened in 1935 was terrible. The coming together of the two groups, a process that is still to be described and took some ten years, he described as a sacrificial deed, a sacrifice of the English Section's identity.

[123] Harwood refers here to a long letter in the October 1962 issue which broadly recapitulates the history already presented in the present book (and it is helpful to read his excellent summary). However, he makes two explicit points which have not hitherto been made. Firstly, when Marie Steiner established the Nachlassverwaltung in the early 1940s (as noted above) she had restored to the Anthroposophical Society in Great Britain publishing rights which she and her Vorstand colleagues had previously denied it. The second point is that the English Section still refused to recognize the Nachlassverwaltung (even after the court case resolved in 1952) and accordingly would neither sell nor in any way promote books published through the agency of the Anthroposophical Society in Great Britain.

[124] According to Dick Seddon, Vera Compton-Burnett was an important figure in the English Section.

[125] See Michael Spence, *The Story of Emerson College*, Temple Lodge, Forest Row 2013, p. 53. Emerson College had been initially founded by Francis Edmunds in Clent, near Stourbridge in 1962. It then officially opened at the Training Centre in the St. Anthony's Huts

in the grounds of Michael Hall on 23 September 1965 and had by September 1967 moved to Pixton Hall, where it continues to this day.

[126] It was ably and lucidly reviewed by Jeffrey Gibian in the Winter 1965 issue of *Anthroposophical Quarterly*. 'Above all,' he concludes, 'this book testifies to the ever living voice of Anthroposophia who seeks to renew mankind.'

[127] From the *Anthroposophical Quarterly*, vo. 19 no. 3, autumn 1975.

[128] 'Laura' was a name with which Harwood had long associated feelings relating to loving relationships and perhaps also to the 'eternal feminine'. See *The Voice of Cecil Harwood*, p. 78.

[129] This cannot have been an easy situation for anyone, least of all the children. There is a typically humane and gracious observation by Laurence, the middle of Cecil and Daphne's five children, in Melissa Harwood's monograph about Marguerite Lundgren: 'When, in 1953, we children learned that father planned to remarry I believe each of our reactions was different according to our ages and other factors. For Marguerite it must have seemed a formidable and daunting prospect to take on five step-children all at one go! For us there was naturally apprehension and worry about the inevitable change of regime three years after my mother's passing; but I, for my part, soon began to realise that my father both needed and would cherish the support of a new wife and that Marguerite's arrival in our household would give him a new lease of life and a sympathetic and like-minded companion for the rest of his days' (op. cit., p. 66–7).

[130] 'Drama at Bockley Manor' is a particularly fine example of this genre in which he so excelled. See *The Voice of Cecil Harwood. A Miscellany*, Rudolf Steiner Press, London 1979.

[131] According to Stephen and Libby Sheen, who had been invited to live at South Harbour in the early 1960s when Stephen's father, Arthur, suddenly died, Cecil and Marguerite took groups of Michael Hall pupils elsewhere in Greece. Cecil, incidentally, loved Libby's singing (she was the daughter of Cecil Cope, who took up the position of Music Teacher at Michael Hall in 1961); and it must surely have been she who sang 'I know that my Redeemer liveth' at his funeral.

[132] The Rudolf Steiner House lecture, entitled 'Rudolf Steiner: Interpreter of a New Age', was a public lecture given on Easter Sunday.

[133] I am indebted to the curative eurythmist Christine Hebert, who frequently—as also in this instance—recorded Harwood's accounts of events from his dictation, for this information.

Index

A

Aberdeen, educational lectures in, 165

Abolition of Man (Lewis), 181

absolute regularity, 104

academic-cum-social life, 23

Achilles, 126

active military service in 1916, 23

Adams, George, 13, 14, 25, 26, 72, 222

adult
    consciousness, 74
    human being, 74
    social life, 23

Alexander, 125, 128
    and Ephesus, 128
    time knowledge and power, 126

Allon, Henry, 20

American group, 47

ancient civilisations, 126
    inaugurated, 126

ancient Eastern clairvoyance, 128

ancient initiation, 128

ancient myths, 124

Angles Road, family's life at, 48–50

Anglo-American democratic world, 171

Anthroposophical Association Ltd., 156

'Anthroposophical Education', 81

Anthroposophical Monthly, 244

Anthroposophical Movement, 15, 45, 83, 90, 92,
    95, 99, 155, 158, 163, 165, 166, 173,
    181, 234
    April 1969 issue of, 242
    December issue of, 230, 236
    on 'Evil and the Devil', 172
    Harwood, Cecil, 224
    January issue of, 223, 228, 229
    March-April issue of, 226
    May issue of, 224, 226
    November issue of, 229
    October 1950 issue of, 226
    September issue of, 225, 239

anthroposophical path of knowledge, 53

Anthroposophical Quarterly, 263

Anthroposophical Society in Great Britain
    (AS in GB), 12, 27, 99, 154, 266–270
    amalgamation of, 235
    Annual General Meetings of, 81–83, 91,
        92, 94, 156, 163, 172, 173, 221, 263
    Anthroposophical Movement, 83, 90, 92, 95.
        See Anthroposophical Movement
    Autumn Programme, 155
    Barfield, Owen, 181
    Council of, 187
    Dunlop, Daniel, 84
    English Section and, 243
    Esoteric Class, 240
    Executive Council of, 82, 84, 87, 88
    Extraordinary General Meeting, 83,
        90–91, 222
    Forest Row Group of, 265
    General Anthroposophical Society,
        238, 239
    gradual consolidation of, 229
    Harwood, Cecil, 51, 79, 80, 93
    and healing of divisions, 221–241
    leading members of, 226
    members of, 87, 156
    'memorable and inspiring day', 246
    Memorandum, 85
    Michael Hall and, 179
    open letter, 84–87
    opportunity to work, 156
    Resolutions, 83, 90, 91
    by Steiner, Rudolf, 85, 89
    during war-time years, 157

Anthroposophic News Sheet, 82

anthroposophy, 12, 38, 39, 245, 267
    approach, 245
    and Christian festivals, 104
    Davy, John, 245
    German culture and language in, 261
    power of, 88
    Society's activities used for, 156

Steiner, Rudolf, 53
and Waldorf education, 44
Anti-Combination Act of 1800, 202
anti-cultural materialism, 9
Apocalypse, 47
Aristotle, 127
art, 33
Arthur, King, 15–16
artistic experience, 106
Art of Thought, The (Wallas), 38
Arts Council, 222
'Athens, Rome, London', 162
Atli (King), 122
Autumn Programme, 155
avowed Socialist aim, 202

B
Bahr, Hermann, 40
Bailey, Edward, 156
Baker, Leo, 181
Barfield, Marguerite Lundgren, 245, 246, 251
Barfield, Owen, 7, 12, 22, 24, 27, 52, 82,
    83, 91, 155, 158, 160, 162, 178,
    180, 187, 188, 196, 209, 227, 260,
    261, 266
  academic-cum-social life, 23
  challenging questions of, 23
  and Daphne Olivier, 29
  early compositions, 54
  education and social life, 25
  English Folk Dance Society, 24
  handwriting as quizzical record, 53
  and Harwood, Cecil, 27
  The Disappearing Trick, 209-220
  This Ever Diverse Pair (Barfield), 180
  universal approach, 187
  in Whetstone, 22
Baum, John, 94
Beckett, Eric, 30, 94, 180
Bee Cottage, 23, 24
'behavioural' sociology, 209
Belgian Baron, 99
Bennell, Margaret, 181
Biesantz, Hagen, 243
biological theory of evolution, 215
Bittleston, Adam, 166, 167, 221, 225
Blake, William, 114–115

Book of Revelation, 11
Brave New World (Huxley), 210
breathing exercises, 146, 149
Bridport, proposed holiday in, 41
Bristol Channel, 175
Britain
  social and political life, 13
  Steiner, Rudolf in, 15
British Empire, 9
British Government, 133
British Honduras, 18
British regular army, 161
'British Way of Life', 198
Broadwood, John, 8
Broadwood, Lucy, 8
Browne, Roma, 230
Bunyan, John, 11
Butler Education Act, 202
Butterworth, George, 9
Byron, Lord, 110

C
Camphill movement, 165
caterpillar, 69
Cecil, William, 20
Celtic strain, 9
'Chairman of the Executive Council', 172
'Chairman of the Society', 172
Chamberlain, Neville, 160
'The Champions', 18
Charles II, 194
Charles Potiphar, 8
Chaucer, Geoffrey, 110
Child and Man, 52, 66, 67, 76, 187, 244
childhood, education in, 113
childrens
  Birthday Song, 115–117
  development, articles on, 104
  Wordsworth's experience as, 135
'children's questions', 67–71
  answering, 71
  fundamental questions, 68
  intellectual understanding, 71
  to investigate scientific theories, 69
  true explanation, 70
Chriemhild, 122
Christ, 73

Christ Church College, 23
Christian agnostic, 9
Christian Christ stream, 17
Christian Community, 66, 163, 166
Christianity, philosophy of life, 25
Christmas Conference Society, 221
Christmas Day 1892, 18
Christmas Foundation, 248
civilisation, 128
    distinct forms of, 167
    modern, 170
    technological, 219
    trend of, 126
    Western, 168
classical scholarship, 23
Coleridge, Samuel Taylor, 135, 150
Collingwood, J.R., 214
Collison, Harry, 245
Colonial Service, 18
comprehensiveness, aspect of, 112
Compulsory Purchase Order, 139
Congregationalist Minister at Islington
        (1892–1914), 20
consciousness, 106, 108, 217, 250
    deathlike, 114
    evolution of, 215
    imaginative, 112
    intellectual, 153
    modern, 215
    of puberty, 114
    self-consciousness, 216
    spiritual, 136
    states of, 126
    tribal, 216
    type of, 111
consciousness soul, 131, 132, 191, 192,
        208, 267
conscious thinking, 128
Conservative aim, 202
'constitutional questions', 79
Contemporary Review, 234
contrasting moods, 148
Cornish festival
    of English folk song and dance, 7
    folk dancing (1921), 7
Cornwall Folk Dance Society, 7
Cotterell, Mabel, 228

Coué Method, 20
Cox, Margaret, 18
creative power, 72
    of mind, 151
crime against humanity, 171
Criminal Law, 210
Crusade of defence, 112
cultural centres, 18
cultural educational sphere, 206
cultural knowledge, 106
Cymbeline, 109

D
Darrell, Jesse, 35, 226
Darwin, Charles, 159
Darwinian theory, of evolution, 215
Davy, Charles, 180, 221
Davy, John, 245
deathlike consciousness, 114
Declaration of Will, 83, 86
democracy, 118, 237
    programme of, 172
Denkschrift, 226
Department of Psychology, 209
Department of Sociology, 209
destructive experience, 115
'Dispensing with Responsibility', 210
Disraeli, Benjamin, 112, 118
'Dives and Lazarus', 8
Divine Powers, 168
Doctor's Dilemma, The (Shaw), 179
Doomsday Book, 55
Dunlop, Daniel, 26, 45, 82, 84, 88, 205, 245
    death events in Dornach, 84
dying money, 206
Dylan, Bob, 11

E
early writings
    Jordan water, 57–65
    Mr. Garnsea, 54–57
East End of London, 156
Easter Conference, 163
economic life, 107
    independent cultural and, 107
economic sphere, 204–206
economic system, 197

Edmunds, Francis, 67, 99, 104, 110, 144, 164, 225, 244
education, 107
    in childhood, 113
    of children, 76
    of children costs, 118
    efficiency view of, 119
    experience, 198
    Harwood, Cecil, 36
    life, 12
    proposed unification of, 119
    recent movements in, 117–120
    socialisation of, 117
    and social life, 25
    state control of, 140
    Steiner, Rudolf, 143, 145
    Steiner's lecture courses, 37
    theory or system of, 145
    Waldorf, 13
Educational Conference, 26, 224
educational lectures, in Aberdeen, 165
Education Bill, 132, 140
'The Education of Children and the Education of Humanity', 81
Edward VII (King), 161
Eedle, Gerald, 261
egoism, 46
ego principle, 75
eighteenth-century individualism, 197
Electric Eden (Young), 10
Elementary School, 119
Eliot, T.S., 234
Elizabeth, Ann, 18
Elizabethan World Picture, The (Tillyard), 134
England, 107–111
    Darwin, Charles, 159
    English character, 108
    and Englishmen, 109
    of mid-nineteenth century, 201
    pursuing, 200
English Civil Wars, 193
English Common Law, 84
English County Songs, 8
English Culture, 265
English equality, principle of, 118
English Folk Dance Society, 7, 24
    by Cecil Sharp in 1911, 7

English folk song and dance, 7
    festival (1920-21), 7
English Folk Songs, 12
English History, 108
English Hymnal, The, 10
English Law, 223
English Nation, ideal consciousness of, 108
English sculptress, 247
English social history, 200–201
English-speaking peoples, 170–174, 265
English Spirit, The (Faulkner Jones), 84
Ephesus, 128
Esoteric Class of Anthroposophical Society in Great Britain, 240
Esoteric Studies: The Flaming Word (Steiner), 226
Essay on Man (Pope), 135
Etzel (Atli), 122
European Common Market, 204
European Law, 223
European nations, 105
eurythmy, 47, 258
evocative words, 225
evolution
    biological theory of, 215
    of consciousness, 215
    Darwinian theory of, 215
    modern consciousness, 215
Evolution of Consciousness as revealed through Initiation Knowledge, The, 26
Executive Council, 79, 81, 82, 84, 87, 88, 155, 222, 229, 230, 268
Exeter Conference, 246
Existentialism, 219
ex parte statement, 85
Extraordinary General Meeting, 79, 83, 90–91, 243

F

Fabian movement, 18
Fabian Society (1884), 18
Faithful Thinker, The, 234
Fantasia on a Theme of Thomas Tallis, 9, 10
Faroe Islands, 121
Faulkner Jones, D.E., 84
Field, W. O. Capt. (1893-1957), 23
First Cause in Nature, 135

First Class of the School of Spiritual
Science, 241, 242, 267
First Revolutionary Assembly, 136
First World War, 9
Five Variants of Dives and Lazarus, 8
Flos Campi, 12
folk dance festivals
in 1921, 7
in Cornwall, 7
Folk Soul of Britain, 8, 161
formative power making, 113
Forster Act of 1870, 201
Foundation Meditation, 250
Foundation Statutes of our Society, 86
Foundation Stone Meditation, 245
Fox, Helen, 25, 28, 42, 43
freedom in cultural sphere, 201–202
'Freedom in Education', 144
Freeman, Arnold, 166, 170, 190
free trade, 197
French Revolution, 136, 195, 200
Freud, Darwinian, 214
Freud, Sigmund, 214
Fry, Christopher, 227
Fuller Maitland, J.A., 8

G
Garden of Eden, 72
Garnett, Constance, 19
Garnett, Edward, 19
General Anthroposophical Society, 82, 222,
230, 238, 239
English Section of, 230
General Meeting of, 239
membership of, 235
General Election (2019), 208
General Meeting in Dornach, 83
General Strike, 37
George, Albert, 57
Germanic culture, 221
German music, 107, 160
Germanophile, 160
Germany
culture and language, 261
Haldane, Richard, 161, 162
human souls, 162
karma works, 161, 162

national egotism of, 167
people, 161
and Russia, 169
Goetheanum
and Christmas Foundation, 248
fellow-members at, 86
Goetheanum Terrace, 45
Golden Blade, The, 166, 190, 209, 252
Golding, William, 234
Good School, A (Mansfield), 33, 48, 99, 139
Great Year, 147
Greek intelligence, 127
Green Party, 208
Grosse, Rudolf, 231, 241, 242, 243
Gudrun, 122

H
Hahn, Herbert, 66
Haldane, Richard, 161, 162
half-mythological war, 127
Hamlet, 109
Hardy, Emma, 20
Harold Fairhair, 121
harvest mood, 44
Harwood, Alfred Cecil, 7, 8, 12, 17, 22, 25,
27, 30, 34, 37, 66, 91–92, 110, 127,
154, 155, 163, 165, 178, 182, 189,
220, 245, 251, 252, 255, 256, 258,
264–270
academic-cum-social life, 23
during academic year, 110, 119, 125,
131, 133
active military service in 1916, 23
Anthroposophical Movement, 224
Anthroposophical Society in Great
Britain, 51, 79
autumn of 1928, 45
Barfield, Owen and, 27, 29
with Beckett, Eric, 94
change of personal destiny on, 28
contribution lay, 52
contributions to Monthly Journals, 125
and Daphne Olivier, 28, 42, 44, 45
death (1976), 187
distinctive stamp, 100
early family life, 33
education, 36

'Essays in English Literature', 115
and Executive Council, 155
family, 99
first article, 81
imaginative thinking, 110
in Islington, 22
leadership, 221
life, 51
marriage, 260
mother's home in Mill Hill, 48
New School's founding group, 35
personal journey, 187
phrase, 229
public lecture, 166
Recovery of Man in Childhood: A Study of the Educational Work of Rudolf Steiner, The, 188
role as stand-in Treasurer, 163
school-career, 23
sense of empathy, 54
on Shakespeare, 107
Shakespeare's Prophetic Mind, 188
Summer School, 93
in *Surprised by Joy* (Lewis), 22
Way of a Child, The, 67, 76, 180, 188
words, 128
writings, 52
Harwood, Daphne, 177, 178
Harwood, Jabez, 20, 21
Harwood, John, 178
Harwood, Melissa, 251, 260
Harwood, William Henry, 20
Haughton, Emily, 165
Heidenreich, Alfred, 66, 163
Helen of Troy, 121
Henry IV, 108
Henry V, 108
Heywood-Smith, Herbert, 79, 155
Hibbert Journal, 234
Hibernian Mysteries, 249, 250
High Church movement, 58
Hill, Octavia, 19
Hitler, Adolf, 160–161, 192
   broadcast speeches, 160
   crime against humanity, 171
   and German people, 161

Hjordis, 122, 123
Hoare, Samuel, 94
Hobbs, Henry, 65
Howard, Alan, 235
Hubback, Eva, 176
Hugh the Drover, 10–12
Huizinga, Johan, 211
human consciousness, 106
   national and, 110
human evolution, 67, 73, 114, 120
human psychosomatic organism, 217
human speech, 72
Huxley, Julian, 215

I

Iliad, 126
Ilkley and Penmaenmawr Conferences, 26
Ilkley Conference (1923), 33
Imagination, 111
imaginative thinking, 110, 113
imaginative thoughts, 111–113
imperialism, 9
in-breathing, 148
independent cultural, 107
individual consciousness, 113
individual freedom, in England, 84
individualism, 168
   eighteenth-century, 197
industrialism, 184
Industrial Revolution, 201
'inevitable conclusion', 112
'inherited memory', 214
   concept of, 215
Inklings, 24
innocence, 114
intellectual consciousness, 153
intellectual thinking, 111
intellectual thought, 107
international relations, 169
International Summer School in Penmaenmawr, 15, 26, 27
International Whitsun Conference at Odense, 229
interpenetrating processes, 107
Isle of Man at Whitsun (1940), 159

J

James II, 194

Jewish people, 73

Joan of Arc, 40, 108

John, Don, 112

Jones, Kenneth, 235

Jordan Water, 57–65

K

Karma of Vocation, The (Steiner), 167

karma works, 161, 162

Kaufmann, George, 25, 45, 164

Kaufmann, Mary, 83, 88, 89

Kendall, Tony, 8

King of Ireland's Son, 69

'King's Forest', 66

Kirchner-Bockholt, Margarete, 239

Kirkaldy, Mildred, 190

Kirkton House, 165

knowledge

    of anatomy and physiology, 159

    limited, 115

Kobbé, Gustav, 164

König, Karl, 93–94, 158–160, 162, 163, 165,

    172, 182, 183

L

Lady Mary Trefusis, 7

laissez-faire, 196, 203, 223

Langland, William, 110

languages, 33, 213

    origin, 71

    written or printed, 213

Lark Ascending, The, 9, 11

Law of Force, 224

leadership quality, 92

League of Nations, 107

Lear, 109

legal community, 193

Lehrs, Ernst, 165, 174, 181–183

Leicester Conferences, 234

Leith Hill Musical Festival, 10

L'état c'est moi, 207

letter writting, 42

Lewis, C.S., 22, 23, 49, 181, 266

Life-spirit of Christ, 17

limited knowledge, 115

'literally the labour of a life-time'

    (Mellers), 11

'Little John', 40

Liverpool Street Station, 26

Locke, John, 115, 150

London

    symphony, 9

    World Conference on Spiritual Science

        in, 94

London Conference of 1952, 228

London County Council, 50

London School of Eurythmy, 251, 252, 260

Lucas, Caroline, 208

Lundgren, Marguerite Gertrude, 252–253,

    255, 257, 258, 260

Lyrical Ballads, 135

M

Macdonald, George, 71

MacDonald, Ramsey, 19

Mahabharata, 126

Mainzer, Susanne, 264

Mann, William, 45, 66, 139, 176, 188

Mansfield, Joy, 33, 66, 99, 139

Marguerite Lundgren. Recollections of a Life in

    Eurythmy (Harwood), 251

Marriage of Figaro, The, 178

Martin, Dorothy, 33

Maryon, Edith, 247

mass egotism, of Russia, 167

Mass in G Minor, 12

McLuhan, Marshall, 210

Medieval and Modern Languages in 1913, 20

Melland, Frances, 165

Mellers, Wilfrid, 8, 11

Members' Conference, of Mid-September,

    166–167

Members' Weekend Conference on Social

    Questions, 223

Memorandum, 85, 88

Michael Hall, 33, 50, 51, 76, 110, 116, 145,

    179, 187, 221, 261

    to Minehead, 99, 139, 163

    teachers, 163

Michael mission, 248

Midsummer Festival, 129–134

Midsummer Night's Dream, A, 66, 164

Mill Hill, 21, 22, 30, 44
    Cecil's mother's home in, 48
Mill Hill Church, 21
Mill, John Stuart, 144, 198, 201, 223
Minehead
    Edmunds, Francis, 99
    first academic year in, 104
    Michael Hall to, 99, 139, 163
    Monthly Journals, 157
    school building at, 101–105
    Summer Conference at, 163–165
minor pre-marital discord, 260
modern atomic theories, 70
modern civilisation, 170
modern consciousness, 215
modern speech, 72
Moi, je suis l'état, 207
Monthly Journals, 107
    Harwood during this academic year,
        110, 119, 125, 131, 133
    issue of, 120, 128, 133
    of Midsummer Festival, 129
    Minehead, 157
    on 'Recent Movements in Education', 116
    teachers in Bristol, 125
mood, of music, 9–10
Morris, William, 10, 18, 121
Mr. Garnsea, 54–57
'the Museum', 44
music, 33
musical imagination, 10
musical quality, 130
Mystery of Golgotha, 16, 17, 218
Mystery Plays, 162
'mystical philosophy', 38

N

Nachlassverwaltung, 233, 241
Napoleonic Wars, 195
national and human consciousness, 110
national egotism, of Germany, 167
National Gallery, 179
Nationalism, 159
nationality, 106
National Trust, 19
Nation, The, 13
nature, 136–138

Nazi leadership, 168
neo-liberalism, 208
New Age, The, 54
New Democratic World, 171–172
new Education Act, 145
New Education Bill, 140–145
    affect, 144
    implications of, 143
Newell, Frank, 244
The New School, 33, 35, 38, 44, 45, 47,
        79–82 187, 244, 252
Newtonian planetary system, 70
Newton, Isaac, 134–135
Niebelungenlied, 121, 122
    splendid myth of Gods, 123
Nonconformity in London, 20
Northern myths, 120

O

Occult History (Steiner), 173
Ode on the Intimations of Immortality, 149
Odyssey, 126
OFSTED, 140
old Catholic Church, 112
Old Hall, 39
Olivier, Brynhild, 18
Olivier, Daphne, 12, 14, 17, 18, 20, 24, 33, 187
    Barfield, Owen and, 29
    conference at Oxford, 13
    'dark and dreamy', 24
    educational conference, 26
    extant letter, 27
    Harwood, Cecil and, 28, 42, 44, 45
    letter, 34, 42–44
    Mill Hill Church, 21, 44
    Waldorf School project, 27
Olivier, Lois, 24, 33, 37, 48, 50, 175, 177
Olivier, Margaret, 18-19
Olivier, Sydney, 18
    autumn of 1921, 19
    Colonial Office in 1882, 18
    Colonial Secretary of Jamaica
        (1899-1904), 19
    death in 1943, 19
    Fabian interests, 18
    last diplomatic tenure, 19
    public life, 19

'O Mensch, erkenne dich', 46
On Liberty (Mill), 144
On the Origin of Species by means of Natural Selection (Darwin), 159
opening ceremony, 101
    for taking possession, 101–104
Opening Conference of the (Second) Goetheanum, 45, 66
organism/organisation, 199–200
origin of language, 71
Osmond, Dorothy, 84
Othello, 109
Ottershaw College, 176
out-breathing, 148
Owen, Robert, 110, 116, 203, 223
Oxford Book of Carols, The (Shaw), 10
Oxonian tradition, 15

P
Parish Church of Stratford-on-Avon, 107
Parker, John, 59
Party Political Broadcast for Green Party, 208
Pastoral symphony, 10, 12
Penwilly, Albert George, 59, 64
    domestic arrangements, 61
    exceptional interest, 65
    furniture-dealer, 59, 60
    holiday in Black Forest, 59
    and Vicar, 59–65
personality, 217
Pfeiffer, Ehrenfried, 184
Philosophic-Anthroposophic Press, 233
Philosophy of Spiritual Activity (Steiner), 138
physical body, 68
physical identity, 113
physical world, 74, 191
physiology, 218
Pilgrim's Progress, The (Bunyan), 11, 12
Planetary System, 135
Platonic Year, 147
Plutarch records, 128
pneuma, 148
Poetic Diction, 25
poetic language theory, 135
polarity, of intellect and senses, 150–154
political allegiances, 128
political life, 12

political Nationalism, 159
Pope, Alexander, 135
Poppelbaum, Hermann, 231, 239
positive force, 169
post-graduate studies, 23
pre-existence, 149
Prelude, 136–138
press campaign, 160
Press Conferences, 234
Princess and Curdie, The (MacDonald), 71
printed language, 213
professionally-taken family photograph, 20
Protestant Europe, 112
psyche, 217
psychedelic movement, 215
psychiatrists, 210
psycho-analysis, 214
psychology, 218
'psychosomatic', 217
psychosomatic organism, 212, 214
puberty, 111
    consciousness of, 114
public awareness, 11
public educational authorities, 141
Public International Conference, 228
Public Schools, 198
publish translations, 82

R
Radford, Evelyn, 31
Radford, Maisie, 31, 32, 179
Radford, Marion, 30, 31
Raine, Kathleen, 234
realm of education, 13
'Recent Movements in Education', 116, 125
Recovery of Man in Childhood: A Study of the Educational Work of Rudolf Steiner, The (Harwood), 188
'Red Sails in the Sunset', 49
refraction process, 75
reincarnation, 218
'The Religious and Moral Basis of Education', 81
religious, Protestant, 112
religious sensibilities, 128
Renaissance, 191, 192
Resolutions, 83, 90, 91, 235

Rights State, 204

Ripon Conference, 237

Robinson, J.H., 146

Roger de Coverley, 145

Roman Law, 84

Romantic Movement, 193

Rope their Pulley, A, 176

Röschl-Lehrs, Maria, 47, 182

Round Table (Arthur), 16, 17

Royal College of Music in 1922, 12

Rudolf Steiner Fellowship, 79

Rudolf Steiner Hall, 45, 80, 81, 83, 91, 156, 163, 173, 222, 234

Rudolf Steiner House, 91, 99, 155, 156, 159, 162, 165, 173, 178, 222, 260, 263

Russell, George William, 84

Russia

    Germany and, 169

    mass egotism of, 167

    political life, 169

Russian Communism, 169

S

sacred waters, 58

Salt, Henry, 19

Sancta Civitas, 11, 12

Saving the Appearances (1957), 246

Savitch, Marie, 251

Schindler, Maria, 91

science, 159

scientific knowledge, 106

scientific theory, 69

sculpture, 213–214

'A Sea Symphony' (1909), 11

Secondary School, 119

Second World War, 117–120, 128

secret, 114

Seddon, Dick, 245

selection theory, 159

self-consciousness, 216

self-determination, 199

self-development, 142

self-education, 107, 142

self-knowledge, 36

self-renewal, 36

senses

impressions, 150

    intellect and, 150

    part of, 151

    theory, 150

Shakespeare, 134, 200

    and England, 107–111

    Harwood, Cecil on, 107

Shakespeare's Prophetic Mind (Harwood), 188

Sharp, Cecil (1911), 7

Shaw, George Bernard, 14, 18, 19, 40, 205

Shaw, Martin, 10

Sheen, Arthur, 50, 67, 82

'The Shepherds of the Delectable Mountains', 12

Shockhead, 121

Siegfried, 121, 123

Siegmund, 122, 123

Siggeir (King), 121, 122

Signy, 122, 123

Sigurd, 120–124

Silesius, Angelus, 131

Skinner, B. F., 210

Sleep of Prisoners, A (Fry), 227

socialisation, of education, 117

socialism, 118

Socialist solution, 118

social life, 12

    adult, 23

    education and, 25

social organism, 13

Society's Legal Statutes, 83

sole function, 156

soma, 217, 218

'somatopsychic', 217

Songs of Experience, 114

Songs of Innocence, 114

Soviet Russian, 167

Special Committee's Report (1928), 79

speech and religion, liberty of, 195

Spence, Basil, 234

sphere of rights, 202–204

Spirit of Michael, 110

Spirit of the Age, 46

'spiritual activity', 166

spiritual consciousness, 136

spiritual educational impulse, 14

'spiritual giraffe', 168

spiritual knowledge, 100
spiritual life, 117, 184
spiritual powers, 109
spiritual science, 12, 100
spiritual world, 73, 148
spiritus, 148
St. Anthony in Roseland, 31
State or public authority, 118
State religious rites, 124
St. Christopher's School, 269–270
Steffen, Albert, 47, 226, 231, 232–233
Steiner, Marie, 226, 232
Steiner, Rudolf, 12, 25–28, 45, 66, 75, 125,
    158, 189, 250
  advocacy, 128
  advocacy of crucial importance, 76
  anniversary of, 105–107
  Anthroposophical Society, 12
  anthroposophy, 53, 85
  approach in, 133
  Barfield, Owen and, 12
  birth of thinking, 111–115
  Body, Soul and Spirit, 74
  in Britain, 15
  Child and Man, 66, 187
  childhood described by, 73
  conviction, 220
  in Cornish festival. *See* Cornish festival
  course, 26
  cultural and social ideas, 105
  cultural life, 107
  death in 1925, 12
  economic affairs, 128
  economic life, 107
  education, 12–13, 33, 143, 145
  educational ideas of, 25, 45
  essential element in, 150
  Foundation of the AS in GB, 85
  ideas, 25
  Ilkley and Penmaenmawr
    Conferences, 26
  imaginative thoughts, 111
  individual freedom in England, 84
  Karma of Vocation, The, 167
  lectures, 82
  lectures in Oxford (1922), 20
  life of rights, 117
  life-work, 87
  in London lecturing, 28
  Members' Conference, of Mid-
    September, 166–167
  methods, 141
  Mystery Plays, 226
  'mystical philosophy', 38
  New Education Bill, 140–145
  nine public lectures, 80
  Occult History, 173
  Philosophy of Spiritual Activity, 138
  political life, 12
  psychology and physiology of threefold
    man, 218
  publish translations, 82
  Resolution, 82, 83
  rights to, 233
  school movement, 13
  schools lacking, 124
  scientific subjects recommended by, 76
  social and cultural malaise, 14
  socialism and democracy, 118
  social life, 12
  Society founded by, 88
  Society's life in 1941, 163
  soul-development, 131
  speech indicated by, 72
  'spiritual giraffe', 168
  'Spiritual Values in Education and Social
    Life', 12
  teaching, inspiration in, 141
  threefold social order, 191, 199–209
  in Torquay (1924), 52
  *True and False Paths in Spiritual
    Investigation,* 27
  Waldorf School, 119
  world citizenship, 106
  World Economy, 206
Stein, Walter Johannes, 180
St. George's Day, 109
St. John Passion, 11
St. John's Wood, 19, 35
St. John the Baptist, 163
St. John the Evangelist, 163
St. Matthew Passion, 11

Streatham, 49, 50
  pre-war incarnation in, 77
  Shakespeare Group of the Society in, 79
  'The Shepherd of New Gifts' performed
    in, 66
sugar cane industry, 19
Summer Conferences, 156, 163–165, 206
Summer School, 93
Surprised by Joy (Lewis), 22, 266
Sussex Songs (1889), 8

T
Tambourine Man, 11
technological civilisation, 219
telegram, 28
Tempest, The, 109
Thirty Years War, 128, 131, 193, 200
  liberty of speech and religion, 195
This Ever Diverse Pair (Barfield), 180, 227
Threefold Social Conception, 172
threefold social order, 190–198
  economic sphere, 204–206
  in English history, 200–201
  freedom in the cultural sphere, 201–202
  interplay and interpenetration, 206–209
  organism/organisation, 199–200
  sphere of rights, 202–204
  Steiner, Rudolf, 199–209
  trade unions, 202–204
Three Spheres of Society, The (Waterman),
    190, 221
Tillyard, E. M. W., 134, 147
time knowledge and power, 126
'Toward the Unknown Region' (1906), 11
trade unions, 202–204
traditional Class, 240
Training Course, 110
transmutation, of law, 168
Treasury and Colonial Office, 18
'tree-climbing' theory, 215
Tree of Knowledge of Good and Evil, 114
tribal consciousness, 216
True and False Paths in Spiritual Investigation
    (Steiner), 27
Twelfth Night, 130

U
Unancestral Voice, 246
Unconscious, 216
unconscious processes, 68
Understanding Media (McLuhan), 211
Union Chapel, 20
unitary systems, 171
Universities, 198
unreality hung, 51

V
Vaughan Williams, Adelyne, 30, 49
Vaughan Williams and the Vision of Albion
    (Mellers), 8
Vaughan Williams, Ralph
  biography of, 8
  Celtic strain, 9
  compositional activity and public
    awareness, 11
  in Cornish festival. *See*
    Cornish festival
  'Dives and Lazarus', 8
  'double nature', 10
  English Hymnal, The, 10
  favourite image, 11
  Five Variants of Dives and Lazarus, 8
  Hugh the Drover, 11
  Lark Ascending, The, 9
  life and musical sensibility, 9
  life's work, 9
  'literally the labour of a life-time'
    (Mellers), 11
  London symphony, 9
  love of English folk songs, 8
  Mass in G Minor, 12
  Pastoral symphony, 12
  religious, 11
  Sancta Civitas, 11, 12
Vicar, 59–65
Villeneuve, Crispian, 27, 28, 226, 233
The Vision of Piers Plowman, 115
Voice of Cecil Harwood, The, 52, 54
Volsung Saga, 121, 123, 124
Vorstand Members, 85, 86
Vreede, Elisabeth, 172, 224

W

Wachsmuth, Guenther, 231–233
Walden Two (Skinner), 210
Waldorf education, 13, 104, 119, 142, 146, 190
    anthroposophy and, 44
    principles of, 25
Waldorf School project, 27
Wallas, Graham, 18, 38
Waterman, Charles, 190
Way of a Child, The (Harwood), 67, 76,
      180, 188
Webb, Sidney, 18
Wegzehrung, 47
Wells, H.G., 44
Wells, Mary Elizabeth née, 20
Western civilisation, 168
Western Morning News, 7
Wheeler, Montague, 245
Whitman, Walt, 11
Wilkes, John, 247
Wilson, Effie, 33
Wilson, Michael, 164, 199
Wilson, Sir Steuart, 9
Winnie, Connie, 261
Winter's Tale, The, 109
Witzenmann, Herbert, 241
woodcutter, 130
words, 72–78, 212
    child's experience of, 72
    evocative, 225
    Harwood, Cecil, 128

    human speech, 72
    modern speech, 72
    of opening ceremony, 101
    primeval power of, 73
    'psychosomatic', 212
Wordsworth, Dorothy, 136, 137
Wordsworth, William, 134–140
    and Coleridge, Samuel Taylor, 135–136
    experience as child, 135
    faith broke, 136
    French Revolution, 136
    moral impulses and spiritual
      impressions, 134
    poetic language theory, 135
    teach and reform, 134
World Conference on Spiritual Science in
      London, 45, 79, 94, 158, 228
world economic order, 128
World Economy (Steiner), 206
World Power Conference, 205
written language, 213
Wynstones School, 50

Y

Young, Rob, 9, 10
Yuille-Smith, C.R., 164

Z

Zarathustra Group of Society, 79, 155
Zelymans van Emmichoven, F.W., 243

A note from the publisher

For more than a quarter of a century, **Temple Lodge Publishing** has made available new thought, ideas and research in the field of spiritual science.

Anthroposophy, as founded by Rudolf Steiner (1861-1925), is commonly known today through its practical applications, principally in education (Steiner-Waldorf schools) and agriculture (biodynamic food and wine). But behind this outer activity stands the core discipline of spiritual science, which continues to be developed and updated. True science can never be static and anthroposophy is living knowledge.

Our list features some of the best contemporary spiritual-scientific work available today, as well as introductory titles. So, visit us online at **www.templelodge.com** and join our emailing list for news on new titles.

If you feel like supporting our work, you can do so by buying our books or making a direct donation (we are a non-profit/charitable organisation).

office@templelodge.com

TEMPLE LODGE

For the finest books of Science and Spirit